"THE TEMPEST" AND ITS TRAVELS

"The Tempest" and Its Travels

Edited by
PETER HULME and WILLIAM H. SHERMAN

PENN

UNIVERSITY OF PENNSYLVANIA PRESS
Philadelphia

Originally published in Great Britain by Reaktion Books, London

10 9 8 7 6 5 4 3 2 1

First published in the United States of America and Canada in 2000 by
University of Pennsylvania Press
Philadelphia, Pennsylvania 19104–4011

Series design by Philip Lewis

Printed and bound in Great Britain by Biddles Ltd, Guildford and King's Lynn

U.S. Library of Congress Cataloging- in-Publication information
is available from the Library of Congress

We gratefully acknowledge the permission of Merle Collins and David Dabydeen
to print or reprint their poems on pp. 267–8, 263 and 252–6.
By Avon River, by H.D.: Copyright 1949 by Hilda Aldington.
Used by permission of New Directions Publishing Corporation,
agent for Perdita Schaffner.

Cloth ISBN: 0-8122-3582-7
Paperback ISBN: 0-8122-1753-5

Contents

Notes on the Editors and Contributors

RIC ALLSOPP is a joint editor of the international journal *Performance Research* and founding partner of Writing Research Associates. He is currently Research Fellow at Dartington College of Arts, UK.

CHRISTY ANDERSON is Assistant Professor of Art History at Yale University and the author of two forthcoming books, *Inigo Jones: Books and Buildings in the English Renaissance* and *European Architecture 1400–1600* (for the *Oxford History of Art*).

CRYSTAL BARTOLOVICH is Assistant Professor of English and Textual Studies at Syracuse University. She is currently completing *Boundary Disputes: The Culture of Capital and Early Modern England*.

GORDON BROTHERSTON is Professor of Spanish and Portuguese at Indiana University. His many books on Latin American and Native American literatures include *The Book of the Fourth World*.

JERRY BROTTON is a lecturer in the Department of English, Royal Holloway, University of London. He is the author of *Trading Territories: Mapping the Early Modern World* and co-author (with Lisa Jardine) of *Global Interests: Renaissance Art between East and West*, both published by Reaktion Books.

RAQUEL CARRIÓ is the Cuban author (with Flora Lauten) of *Otra Tempestad*. She has also written a collection of essays about the theatre and modernity: *Teatro y Modernidad: Siete Ensayos de Ficción*.

MERLE COLLINS is Professor of English and Comparative Literature at the University of Maryland. She is the author of two novels and two books of poems, *Because the Dawn Breaks!* and *Rotten Pomerack*.

PHILIP CRISPIN, a doctoral student at Royal Holloway, University of London, was formerly the Literary Manager at the Gate Theatre, Notting Hill. His translation of Aimé Césaire's *Une tempête* is published by Oberon Books.

DAVID DABYDEEN is Professor in the Centre for British and Comparative Cultural Studies at the University of Warwick. He has published three books of poems and four novels (the most recent of which, *A Harlot's Progress*, reinvents Hogarth's famous prints of that name).

ELIZABETH FOWLER is Associate Professor of English at the University of Virginia. She writes mainly on medieval and early modern poetry and political thought, and her work on the category of person and its importance for literary character is forthcoming as *The Human Figure in Words*.

JOHN GILLIES is an Australian Research Council Fellow in the Department of Theatre and Drama at La Trobe University in Australia. He is the author of *Shakespeare and the Geography of Difference*.

ROLAND GREENE is Director of the Comparative Literature Program at the University of Oregon. He is the author of *Post-Petrarchism: Origins and Innovations of the Western Lyric Sequence, Unrequited Conquests: Love and Empire in the Colonial Americas* and many articles on literature and exploration.

DONNA B. HAMILTON is Professor of English at the University of Maryland. Her books include *Virgil and 'The Tempest'* and *Shakespeare and the Politics of Protestant England*. She is writing *The History of English Renaissance Literature* for Blackwell.

ANDREW C. HESS is Director of the Program in Southwest Asia and Islamic Civilization at The Fletcher School of Law and Diplomacy, Tufts University, Massachusetts, and the author of *The Forgotten Frontier: A History of the Sixteenth-Century Ibero-African Frontier*.

PETER HULME is Professor of Literature at the University of Essex. He is the author of *Colonial Encounters: Europe and the Native Caribbean, 1492–1797* and of *Remnants of Conquest: The Island Caribs and Their Visitors, 1877–1998*. His edited volumes include *Cannibalism and the Colonial World*.

ROBIN KIRKPATRICK is a critic and poet who teaches English and Italian at Cambridge University. He is the author of *English and Italian Literature from Dante to Shakespeare* and three books on Dante.

BARBARA A. MOWAT is Director of Academic Programs at The Folger Shakespeare Library, Washington, D.C. She is the editor of the New Folger Library Shakespeare editions, senior editor of *Shakespeare Quarterly*, Chair of the Folger Institute and the author of *The Dramaturgy of Shakespeare's Romances* and of several articles on *The Tempest*.

LUCY RIX studied at Cambridge and Essex. She currently works in London for two NGOs – Kalayaan: Justice for Migrant Domestic Workers, and RETAS: Refugee Education and Training Advisory Service.

JOSEPH ROACH, Professor of English and Theatre at Yale University, has chaired the Interdisciplinary PhD in Theater at Northwestern University, Illinois, and the Department of Performance Studies at New York University. He is the author of

The Player's Passion: Studies in the Science of Acting and *Cities of the Dead: Circum-Atlantic Performance*.

PATRICIA SEED is Professor of History at Rice University, Texas. Her most recent books are *Ceremonies of Possession in Europe's Conquest of the New World, 1492–1640* and *American Pentimento*.

WILLIAM H. SHERMAN is Associate Professor of English at the University of Maryland. He is the author of *John Dee: The Politics of Reading and Writing in the English Renaissance* and of essays on Elizabethan exploration, Renaissance drama, and the history of reading.

MARTHA NELL SMITH is Director of the Maryland Institute for Technology in the Humanities (MITH) and Professor of English at the University of Maryland. She is the author of many articles on American poetry and popular culture and of three books on Emily Dickinson, most recently *Open Me Carefully: Emily Dickinson's Intimate Letters to Susan Huntington Dickinson*.

ALDEN T. VAUGHAN recently retired as Professor of History at Columbia University. He is the author of many books on American colonial history, co-author of *Shakespeare's Caliban: A Cultural History*, and co-editor of the new Arden *Tempest*.

MARINA WARNER is the author of several novels, including *Indigo*, and of many works on myth, symbolism and fairy tale (most recently, *No Go the Bogeyman: Scaring, Lulling, and Making Mock*). In 1994 she gave the Reith Lectures on BBC Radio, *Managing Monsters: Six Myths of our Time*.

Preface

PETER HULME AND WILLIAM H. SHERMAN

Shakespeare's *The Tempest* has been re-read and re-written more radically, perhaps, than any other play. Long a source of inspiration and provocation for writers and artists, it has also emerged as one of the most contested texts in the critical sphere. It has been classified as every genre and no genre, located in every place and no place, and enlisted in support of colonial, anti-colonial and apolitical views. While Shakespeare has been re-invented by every generation and while his plays have been re-staged all over the globe, the stakes involved in *The Tempest*'s travels have been unusually high. The power and mobility of its language and its themes have made it a renewable resource like few other texts; a touchstone for critical, political and creative work throughout the modern world – and especially in countries formerly under British rule.

The three main sections of this book follow *The Tempest* on a journey which proceeds steadily outwards. The first part, 'Local Knowledge', is mostly concerned with the historical circumstances within which *The Tempest* was written and performed in seventeenth-century England. 'European and Mediterranean Crossroads' then places the play in the larger context demanded by its explicit geography – 'Naples', 'Milan', 'Tunis', 'Carthage', 'Algiers' – regions marked by complex negotiations between European and North African cultures and between classical texts and Renaissance politics. Finally, 'Transatlantic Routes' moves across the oceans, mostly in the direction of the Americas, where the play has often been seen as having particular relevance and where it has certainly received some of its most powerful readings.

To capture the vitality of the travels both in and of *The Tempest* it is necessary to cross the conventional boundaries of Shakespearean criticism, and indeed to be (like the play itself) in many places at once. This book sheds new light on the play's engagement with the world of its time, extending our knowledge of Elizabethan England's local contexts and global horizons; and it also charts the play's own movement through time and space, pointing to some of the ways in which it has been inherited and used by very different cultures. The Tempest's movements invite the collaboration of experts from diverse geographical and disciplinary backgrounds, and across the critical–creative divide – bringing together voices that are too rarely heard in dialogue. The productions described in 'On the World Stage' provide some vivid glimpses of the strategies being devised to reinvent the play, and re-enact (for audiences in the Caribbean, in Latin America, and even in Europe itself) its living lesson on the politics of location and dislocation. And the poems we include offer compelling evidence of the play's power to elicit artistic responses that reflect on the ends of art.

While this collection is wide-ranging, however, we are all too aware of what it excludes. It has not been possible to accommodate, within our structure and our available space, The Tempest's travels in Asia and the Pacific, its appearances in science fiction and on film, or in the work of W. H. Auden, Peter Greenaway, Derek Jarman and many others. All maps are partial, and this one is no exception – though we hope, of course, that this collection will open up some new routes of its own.

What accounts for The Tempest's extraordinary ability (even by Shakespearean standards) to translate and be translated?[1] In the second half of the twentieth century, much of the credit has shifted from Prospero – and, through him, from Shakespeare – to Caliban. As Russell Hoban put it in the introduction to his libretto 'Some Episodes in the History of Miranda and Caliban',

> The way I see it Shakespeare didn't invent Caliban; Caliban invented Shakespeare (and Sigmund Freud and one or two others). Caliban is one of the hungry ideas, he's always looking for someone to word him into being so he can have another go and maybe win Miranda this time or next time. Caliban is a necessary idea.[2]

Recent critics have tended to agree. Harold Bloom has noted that, when it comes to readings of The Tempest, we live in 'the Age of Caliban', although this is not a development he views with much satisfaction.[3] Since the publication in 1954 of Frank Kermode's Arden edition of the play (which casts Prospero as a benign magician who embodied an 'Art' in opposition to Caliban's 'Nature'), readers have gradually given less credence to Prospero's account of the past and more sympathy to Caliban and his claims. Critics and artists alike have been haunted by the 'puppy-headed monster' who has some of the most beautiful and witty lines in the play, and some have actually identified with him (in this sense, he has peopled various islands with

Calibans). A handful of literary characters seem to break free of their original text and become culturally available across a wide spectrum. Hamlet is probably the best-known Shakespearean example; Don Quixote and Robinson Crusoe also come to mind. But Caliban is perhaps the only literary character to achieve this status from the starting-point of being a *minor* character, with considerably lower status, fewer lines, and shorter stage presence than the main figure in the text.

If the 'hunger' of Caliban has been crucial to the play's renewed power, so has the concept – and practice – of 'appropriation'.[4] Appropriation may be associated with abduction, theft and usurpation, but in both critical and artistic response the process is unavoidable: 'every act of interpretation can be seen as an act of appropriation – making sense of a literary artefact by fitting it into our own parameters. The literary work thus becomes ours; we possess it by reinventing it as surely as if we had secured its physical presence by force.'[5] This language is especially pertinent to *The Tempest* in that it is itself about usurpation and force – and, in Caliban's case, the seizure of books.

Such appropriations, which have sometimes been dismissed as modern impositions on the play, have in fact marked its entire history. Before the political allegories of Aimé Césaire (*Une tempête*, 1969) and Ernest Renan (*Caliban: Suite de 'La Tempête'*, 1878) there were the parodies of Robert Barnabas Brough and William Brough (*The Enchanted Isle*, 1848) and Thomas Duffet (*Mock-Tempest*, 1674), and the sequel 'discovered' by F. G. Waldron (*The Virgin Queen*, 1796). Indeed, the text of Shakespeare's *Tempest* as we now know it has only been used on stage for just over half of its existence: William Davenant and John Dryden's 1667 adaptation (itself revised into an opera by Thomas Shadwell in 1674) displaced Shakespeare's original, and well after William Macready's production in 1838 of 'the genuine text of the poet', the play continued to be performed in an astonishing array of altered forms – even playing a part in the birth of modern pantomime. As a text to be staged and not just studied, *The Tempest* 'remains endlessly malleable'.[6]

These factors help us begin to get some purchase on *The Tempest*'s will to travel and on the 'openness' that has characterized the play for so many critics and editors. *The Tempest* seems to be so full of 'blanks' that it 'tempts us to fill in',[7] that it has struck some readers as unfinished (intentionally or unintentionally).[8] It is, after *The Comedy of Errors*, Shakespeare's shortest play, and his most elliptical. What it offers its audience, from the opening shipwreck to the Epilogue's plea for applause, is a set of questions on which we must deliberate: How are we supposed to feel toward Caliban? What are we to make of the play's absent women? What happens to the balance of power at the end of the play, after Prospero renounces his magic and prepares to return to Milan? And – the question at the heart of our project – where, or what, is the island on which the play is set?

The question is crucial, yet unanswerable. While this book explores the play's geographical and historical contexts in the New World, the Old World and the Classical World, it does not attempt to fix the play's coordinates, to pin it down to any one time or place. Our aim, rather, is to chart *The Tempest*'s implicit cartographies in order to provide resources for understanding the world of the play, and the play's own journeys through the early modern and modern worlds.

The essays that follow have all been commissioned for this project. At the editors' request, they range in length and directness of approach to *The Tempest*. Interspersed among them are free-standing pages of supplementary material supplied by the editors. Throughout this book we cite Stephen Orgel's Oxford edition of *The Tempest* (1987). We have tried to avoid duplicating information available in Orgel's edition: for essential background readers will want to turn to his Introduction, to the Introduction to the new Arden *Tempest* by Alden T. and Virginia Mason Vaughan and to the other texts described in our essay on 'Further Reading'.

Prologue

'After Prospero'
ROBIN KIRKPATRICK

ENTER, *as wearing no apparent mask*
and so (where in Venice at Carnival
carmine raptors plashing out, raddle-eyed,
from deep arcades of shadow, never were)
free to smile, a figure who nervously –
being unknown here – does smile, and carrying
no staff, sceptre, whip or biro, prepares
to say there is no world but persons. This one
is neither naked nor clothed but changes
(not with any frisson of transformation
from girl to spider or lozenge-bright snake)
nearer to us, as every glancing step
raises out of the coughing boards a gauze
of elm-dust in human shape, and calls
upwards like fallen grapes the glimmering
of brazen nails in hands that move towards
our own, where we imagined in the dark
no need to answer, alter or be happy.

Here (were this allegorical) we might
suppose we saw the figure of Gentle Death
in triumph over Dreams and Cruelty
or else the Perfect Teacher, who – likewise
affirming nothing – reveals around us
the space that each of us has now to fill and then
make way. But that's not it. The moment is,
when presence rings a risk in mind and sense.

THEREFORE *throughout – coming, in time, to know*
who this transparency might be – we hear
a certain, though intermittent, music.
(Also – it's true – the turgid clocking-on
of rivers, and whealing squeals where compliant
elements – pulp, ore, steam – play together
at deltas with industrial reason.)
Rhythms and modulation here will not
even be the sound of wind or bird-song,

rather our own – our own being an ending
and echoing within and between us –
so that we follow, to hear again how
bone sings, in Joplin, to mock march-time,
or how, in nuances that Schubert frees
from frozen hurdy-gurdies, loss and fear,
a blush fans all through being, recognized.

Be realistic: old harlequinades
of fog, of course, will sneer and writhe around
the present action. Schubert and Joplin
both knew that, each dying of the same disease –
the symptoms were baroque incrustations
of stupid power around the arches of their
native cities, and filigree windows
of subtle enslavement. Yet still they steal
their pickings home: ivories and glistening
string, reed and hollowed horn. So, nights like this,
we're fed, light-hearted, on melismata.

THE LIGHTS GO UP. It should, by now, be clear:
this could be paradise. Simply enough,
there is, nearly, no distance between us,
or none – as though, incandescent in air,
viewless, impassable, there were a brook –
we ever might cross by main-force. Movement
is over and even (as the actor
ought already have made us realize)
the appetite for staple themes: life, death,
the obvious screaming 'better be unborn'.
As for events, a single tree is seen.
Cool and colour-plumed, all its scented bells
erect, this may still rise and, drawing up
fine milky roots like limbs so long caressed
by mosses and dark, trail out the vivid
fungi, desires and danger, then, folding
inward on itself, leave only a space
for perfect attention. Or else may not.

Looking, for a last time, around this room,
you'll see, now scattered in free lights – fallen
from the stage-arc – the few there are who choose
to remain and ask neither for happenings
nor snarling traffic in fixed ideas
but hope in contingencies to see once more
our makings – feathered breath and lash; a touch
sounding in creases of death or down: a tone –
as if this were all. And thus we begin.

THE
TEMPEST.

(Preceding page) This printer's ornament marks the beginning of *The Tempest*, the first play in Shakespeare's First Folio (1623). The central figure – who might be called a feathered fowler – wears only a scanty drape knotted on his shoulders and a crest of feathers on his head, brandishes two fanciful long-tailed birds and is flanked by two foliate herms with bows and arrows and hunting dogs.

Introduction

Where do *The Tempest*'s travels begin? Prospero's plot unfolds on what the First Folio describes only as 'an uninhabited island', and the play's origins in the *terra incognita* of Shakespeare's mind are no more clearly defined. Scholarship on *The Tempest*'s early texts, intertexts and contexts has, however, filled out the circumstances in which the play was written and performed – on the island inhabited by Shakespeare and his contemporaries in the second decade of the seventeenth century.

[1]

It is possible to fix with some certainty the play's earliest appearances, first on stage and then in print.[1] According to the *Revels Accounts* for 1611, *The Tempest* 'was presented at Whitehall before the kinges Maiestie' on 'Hallowmas nyght' (1 November). A year and a half later, on 20 May 1613, the play was performed again for James I at Whitehall, during the festivities leading up to the marriage of his daughter, Princess Elizabeth, to Frederick, the Elector Palatine. The play was probably staged at the Blackfriars and possibly also at the Globe; but no other performance during Shakespeare's life is known, and the text was not published until seven years after his death, as the opening play in the 1623 First Folio. The significance of these various dates has long been the subject of debate, with critics using the meaning of Halloween or the royal wedding as ways of locating the play's concern for seasonal ritual and dynastic marriage in the particular circumstances of its composition.[2]

If these readings appear to give less than full weight to the play's wide-ranging geographical references, to its apparent setting in the Mediterranean, and to the presence of a cast of Italian courtiers, then it has always been possible to argue that Shakespeare's various geographies were indicative less of his interest in other worlds than of the perceived need for artistic conventions that enabled the staging of issues too close to home for the comfort of the playwright and his company. Douglas Bruster has recently suggested, in fact, that we need look no further than the early modern playhouse itself to make sense of *The Tempest*'s characters and power struggles. Prospero is the 'playwright/director'; Miranda 'a figure of an idealized spectatorship'; Ariel a 'boy actor'; and Caliban a coded jab at Will Kemp ('a celebrated Elizabethan clown known for his physical, even priapic comedy, his independent spirit, folk ethos, and intrusive ad libs'). As for the ship that opens and closes the play, and would seem to gesture toward distant horizons, 'By 1611 the trope of theater as ship had become commonplace.'[3]

If a precise local reading of this kind had ever proved conclusive, there would be no need for our book – and probably little critical interest in the play. But in recent years, alongside the consolidation of the 'colonial reading' of the play (discussed below, pp. 170–75) – and often as a backlash against it – scholars have begun again to bring a wide range of domestic discourses to bear on *The Tempest*, recovering the shared vocabularies of Shakespeare's England and arguing for their presence in the play's language and themes.

For example, one important cluster of local readings has concerned the rebellions that drive the action of the play. Glynne Wickham proposed that Caliban's failed attempt on Prospero's life replayed the Gunpowder Plot which threatened King James in 1605, and that the 1611 performance at court celebrated James's survival and his efforts both to reconcile Protestants and Catholics and to unite Britain with continental Europe.[4] More recently, Curt Breight found the play 'a politically radical intervention' in the 'vast discourse of treason that became an increasingly central response to different social problems in late Elizabethan and early Jacobean London'.[5] For Breight the most pressing of these social problems was the growing population of 'masterless' men and women around 1600, and Paul Brown had earlier argued that 'masterlessness' – 'the unfixed and unsupervised elements located at the internal margins of civil society' – provided a 'discursive matrix' for *The Tempest*'s colonial concerns.[6]

The 'local' materials that lie behind *The Tempest* need not, of course, belong only to court politics or metropolitan anxieties. As Terence Hawkes has consistently reminded us, English colonization does not begin with voyages to the New World. Even those who never travelled further west than Stratford itself would be familiar with the discourse of landlord and tenant; and there was a domestic colonization by the English state that was far from complete in Shakespeare's time.[7] This refers not just to the 'celtic fringe',[8] but to parts of the country such as the Fens, which have echoes in Caliban's curses ('wicked dew . . . / from unwholesome fen / Drop on you both'; I.ii.321–3) and in the play's almost obsessive concern with dirty and stagnant water. The massive draining of the Fens in the mid-seventeenth century was the culmination of many decades of discussion, at the national as well as local level, which had come to a head right at the turn of the century.

The technical knowledge on which Shakespeare drew also points across the seas. The nautical vocabulary of the play (especially its opening scene) has sent editors running to Renaissance treatises on navigation for definitions of 'boatswain', 'beak', 'waist', 'bowsprit', 'main-course', 'hatches', 'yare', and so on. While Shakespeare elsewhere displayed a command of the terminology related to seafaring, in *The Tempest* he outdoes the specificity of his other plays and, in fact, of most contemporary voyage literature. In 1910 W. B. Whall ('Master Mariner') published a glossary entitled *Shakespeare's Sea Terms Explained*, and devoted an entire chapter to the first scene of *The Tempest*, which, he suggested, 'might have been written by an experienced seaman'.[9] But, Shakespeare's technical precision notwithstanding, these terms had larger implications: as Elizabeth Fowler here suggests, the language of navigation and the image of the ship were available for more general rhetorical purposes and were commonly used, by early modern authors (as well as their classical sources), to handle the sensitive questions of governance and authority.[10] Julie Robin Solomon has pointed out that both of the rulers who are on the move in *The Tempest*, Prospero and Alonso, refer to the navigational 'plummet', one of the most traditional of instruments for measuring depth and location at sea:

> Both rulers envision the essence of their powers, both sovereign book and body, as beyond the measuring capacity of the 'plummet'; Prospero's promise to bury his magic books 'deeper than did ever plummet sound' (5.1.56) thus significantly echoes Alonso's desire to plunge his royal self 'deeper than e'er plummet sounded' (3.3.101) in the bowels of the muddy earth.[11]

The Tempest is not alone, of course, in its emphasis on travel and its invocation of distant places: maps appear throughout the work of Shakespeare and his contemporaries. As John Gillies has explained, 'What these references suggest is that the reference to a "new map" in *Twelfth Night* was not plucked from a discursive vacuum . . . Shakespeare is demonstrably conversant with quite a variety of geographic discourses and . . . cartographic genres.'[12] In the late sixteenth century the tools available for measuring and representing the world were undergoing far-reaching transformations; and as Elizabethans became more 'mapminded', the globe itself became more and more locally known.[13]

A

Regiment

for the Sea.

Containing very necessarie matters
for all sorts of men and trauailers:

Whereunto is added an Hydrographicall
discourse touching the fiue seuerall
passages into Cattay:

Written by *William Borne.*

Corrected and amended by *Thomas Hood, D.*
in Phisicke, who hath added a new Regiment
and a Table of declination vvith the Mariners
guide, and a perfect Sea Card there-
unto belonging.

AT LONDON:
Printed by *Thomas Snodham,* for
Edmund Weauer.
1611.

Mariners using the 'cross-staff' and 'plummet': Title page of William Bourne, *A Regiment for the Sea*, expanded edn (London, 1611). British Library, 51.c.3.

As the essays in this book demonstrate over and again, any easy separation of the supposedly local from larger concerns, whether European or Mediterranean or transatlantic, can never hold. Crystal Bartolovich here argues that the local had become so 'globalized' that it was already difficult to isolate in Shakespeare's London. What signalled London's status as a 'world city' by the time *The Tempest* was written was not only its increasingly important position as a hub for international trade, but the extent to which its theatre was staging problems of location and identity (of the sort that tend to be associated with much later stages of capitalism and colonialism). Equally, however, the wider references in the play are only there because they found their way in some form to London. Publishers played an essential rôle in disseminating words and images from other places – and of course other times. As Barbara Mowat explains here in her guide to *The Tempest*'s intertextual relations, the play has close and complex ties to a wide range of texts; and, for all its originality, it is unusually full of borrowings from earlier authors (including Virgil, Ovid, and Montaigne, to name only those about whom there is most consensus). Prospero's power comes from his books; and part of the play's power as what Mowat calls 'an evocative instrument' depends on its network of textual echoes.

While the play does not have a single controlling source, its key intertext is often seen as William Strachey's letter from Virginia, which has inspired much work on the play's American connections and has also been used to set a limit on the date of the play's composition. In the summer of 1609, the *Sea-Venture*, the ship carrying the new colony's governor, was driven off course and wrecked on Bermuda. But the company survived, built two small ships, and eventually reached Virginia. Their seemingly miraculous survival was greeted as the work of Providence in a group of texts that have come to be known as 'the Bermuda pamphlets'. William Strachey's account, dated 15 July 1610 and entitled 'A true repertory of the wreck and redemption of Sir Thomas Gates, Knight, upon and from the islands of the Bermudas . . .' (usually called simply 'the Strachey letter'), found its way to Shakespeare, possibly through his association with members of the Virginia Company.[14]

The verbal parallels in the Strachey letter thus provide the most immediate evidence for connecting the play with the activities of the Virginia Company, and (more generally) with London's incipient overseas ventures. Although the echoes from the Strachey letter in *The Tempest* are usually limited to the storm scene, Strachey does go on to discuss the state of the

Virginia settlement and to describe in some detail the settlers' relations with the local Indians. Trinculo's quip that the English 'will not give a doit to relieve a lame beggar' but 'will lay out ten to see a dead Indian' (II.ii.31–2) has led to speculations about Caliban's possible affiliations with Native Americans, and to a search for evidence about the exhibition of Indians in Elizabethan and Jacobean England. Alden Vaughan here revisits the question,[15] and provides the fullest survey to date of the considerable Indian and Inuit presence in Shakespeare's London. While the question of what exactly Caliban owed to London's visiting Americans is unanswerable, Indians (both dead and alive) turn out to have been more visible and topical than we might expect.

The range of possible models for Prospero also shows just how much of 'the world' travelled in one way or another to Elizabethan England. There were, first, various figures available in Shakespeare's own country for the literary representation of a 'magus' whose learning has given him command over the forces of nature and the power of books. The name most commonly associated with such mastery and most commonly proposed as the inspiration for Prospero is John Dee. Dee was one of the preeminent scholars at Queen Elizabeth's court and the owner of the period's largest library: with nearly 4,000 books, a large collection of scientific instruments, maps and globes, and an accompanying alchemical laboratory, his library was England's most famous repository of scientific and occult learning.[16] Dee travelled extensively on the Continent, however, and very few of his books or instruments were English. He even owned artefacts from the New World, including an obsidian mirror of Mexican origin. Like many of the period's museums, Dee's book-lined cell was a place where the whole world could be studied and displayed.

Another scientist–magician who offered an archetype or analogue for Prospero was the Dutch inventor Cornelis Drebbel.[17] By 1610 Drebbel was among the group of European scientists, engineers, and artists drawn to the Jacobean court and the patronage of James's son, Prince Henry. One of his most famous inventions, which was on display at the royal palace at Eltham during 1610, was his 'Perpetuum Mobile', or continual motion machine: according to the historian and cartographer John Speed, who had seen it some years earlier, it featured a hovering 'ball or round globe', a 'diall . . . shewing the courses of the heavens', and a crystal container filled with water that appeared to 'ebb and flow with the Seas in every part of the world'.[18] Drebbel's career ran parallel to that of Salomon de Caus, another itinerant inventor who impressed the English nobility with his fantastic gardens and fountains. In her essay on the hydraulic engineering of de Caus and others,

Figure studying the heavens with cross-staff and sphere: 'Studia Inoportuna'
(Untimely Studies), from Henry Peacham's emblem book based on King
James I's *Basilicon Doron*. British Library, MS Harley 6855, art. 13, fol. 27.

Stephen Orgel's Oxford edition of The Tempest *first brought Peacham's
emblem of 'untimely studies' to light. He reproduced an image from a manuscript
at the British Library (dedicated to Prince Henry), with its depiction of what he
described as 'a royal magician', and its quotation from King James's advice that
'as for the study of the other liberal arts and sciences, I would have you reason-
ably versed in them, but not pressing to be a pass-master in any of them: for
that cannot but distract you from the points of your calling' (pp. 21–2).*

*Peacham prepared another copy of this manuscript for King James himself: in
this version it is clearer that the figure is neither royal nor magical but one of the
great scientists of antiquity, Archimedes of Syracuse, who pressed on with his
cosmographical studies (represented here by the navigational instruments of the
sixteenth century) even as the Romans conquered his city. The emblem warned
Prince Henry, who took a strong interest in the arts and sciences, against
becoming an Archimedes – or, indeed, a Prospero.*

Christy Anderson suggests that Prospero was not the only one in England *circa* 1600 who inspired amazement by domesticating and aestheticizing the forces of nature.

Scholars have also turned up several past Prosperos, characters real or imagined from whom Shakespeare could have taken the name. Since 1868 it has been known that William Thomas's *History of Italy* (1549) contained an account of Prosper Adorno, Duke of Genoa, who was deposed by his rivals and went on to serve as deputy for the Duke of Milan.[19] In 1985 William Slights proposed Remigio Nannini's *Ciuill considerations upon many and sundrie histories* (translated into English in 1601) as a source for both the names and the concerns of *The Tempest*. The third chapter of that book tells the story of Alfonso, King of Naples, his son Ferdinand, and a pair of noblemen named Prospero and Fabritio Colonna.[20] And in 1990 E. H. Gombrich offered yet another candidate in Prospero Visconti, a great scholar and book collector who was deprived of his ducal rights in Milan.[21] None of this necessarily inconclusive evidence establishes what, or whom, Shakespeare knew; and the search for definitive sources has now given way to a much broader exploration of relevant 'discourses', 'congeners' and 'contexts'. After all, as Henry James suggested a century ago (facing the futility of any *direct* attempt to pin down the *The Tempest*'s sources and meanings), 'We stake our hopes thus on indirectness, which may contain possibilities . . .'[22]

[3]

The Tempest has had a long, if discontinuous, connection with its local origins through the tradition of Shakespearean performance on the London (and more broadly British) stage. As Joseph Roach reminds us, however, the *Tempests* mounted from the mid-seventeenth century to the mid-nineteenth looked very different from the one encountered by readers and spectators at the beginning of the twenty-first. These adaptations were themselves open to the most local of readings, but for Roach the 'enchanted island' of the Restoration playhouse can properly be read as offering a 'vicarious tourism', which he defines as 'the commodified experience of a local event substitut[ing] for the direct experience of a remote destination'. When the spectators are 'tourists' who never leave home, and the theatre is a place for the staging of secrets by actors who are 'natives of the island' both in and out of rôle, the local and the exotic have become truly inextricable – at least for the duration of the theatrical experience, which for both the tour-guide Tom Brown and the tourist Samuel Pepys extended beyond the performance of the play.

The first of the Restoration versions – *The Tempest, or the Enchanted Island* – has been read, in Roach's words, as 'a complicated allegory of legitimacy, dislocation, and return', with Prospero standing in for one or more of the Stuart monarchs. By the late eighteenth century, as questions of political legitimacy reappeared across the Channel, Caliban's insistent claim to the island was beginning to get a more sympathetic hearing in a climate marked by a Romantic interest in 'natural man', revolutionary sympathy for the downtrodden, and a burgeoning aversion to the slave trade.[23] Local readers were, of course, not all sympathetic to these ideas: Coleridge tartly associated Caliban with the dangers of Jacobinism, though Hazlitt responded that since Caliban was in fact the legitimate ruler of the island, any analogy should properly associate Caliban with Louis XVI and Prospero with the usurping Jacobin.[24]

As this book's structure suggests, readings and productions of *The Tempest* have increasingly moved onto the 'world stage'. It is therefore worth noting that the play keeps washing up on local shores, refusing to allow British readers and viewers to remain vicarious tourists in front of some exotic spectacle. Jonathan Miller's two productions of the play, in 1970 and 1988, placed it firmly within the context of the British loss of Empire;[25] and two of the finest novels based on *The Tempest*, George Lamming's *Water with Berries* (1971) and Marina Warner's *Indigo* (1992), both conclude in contemporary London. In an obvious way, the play has a global presence at the beginning of the twenty-first century. But in a host of less obvious ways, it keeps coming home from its travels.

Terrestrial globe by Emery Molyneux (London, 1592, revised 1603), 62 cm.

Prospero's 'great globe' contains an obvious theatrical reference to one of Elizabethan London's most important playhouses. However, the technology for the construction of globes had been mastered during the sixteenth century, providing resonant images of a singular and interconnected world. This terrestrial globe and its celestial counterpart were the first made by an Englishman and the first printed in England. Molyneux, a mathematician from Lambeth, was assisted in the construction of the globes by Edward Wright and the engraver Jodocus Hondius, an emigré from the Netherlands. The globes were financed by the merchant-adventurer William Sanderson – at a cost of more than £1000. Richard Hakluyt heralded their publication in his Principall Navigations *(1589), Thomas Blundeville described them in an appendix to* A plaine description of Mercator his two Globes *(1594), and Shakespeare referred to them in* The Comedy of Errors *(III.ii).[1]* The Globe Theatre itself played on the current conceit linking theatres and contemporary atlases – which offered a theatrum mundi, or theatre of the world.[2]*

1 'Baseless Fabric': London as a 'World City'

CRYSTAL BARTOLOVICH

In a 1999 cover story for *The New York Times Magazine*, the expatriate British writer Andrew Sullivan took up the issue of 'the end of Britain' after a visit to the town in which he grew up following a long absence abroad.[1] The story is familiar: devolution, globalization, the European Union, and immigration from the former colonies as well as continental Europe have combined to produce a 'loss of national identity'.[2] London, in particular, shows the signs of this 'transformation': 'London is Europe's cultural and financial capital, as well as one of the world's truly international hubs'.[3] Having become a 'global city', London is no longer, apparently, a wholly 'British' one. Closer to home the same discourse thrives. A 1999 issue of the London entertainment weekly *Time Out* (itself a successful franchise export to New York) featured a cover in which the familiar London Underground symbol was filled-in with a representation of the globe, and the inscription along the bar in which stations are usually designated read 'The World'. Inside, two articles detailed how a Londoner might make a 'world tour' without ever leaving the capital. Common to all such articles are observations about the different languages one hears while walking down the streets these days, as well as descriptions of unfamiliar commodities, corporations, food and so on – experiences which give rise to the impression, as Roland Robertson has put it, that the world is becoming 'compressed into a single place'.[4] The novelty of this situation is emphasized.

But when we jump onto the down escalator of time, we discover that in certain important respects, these seemingly novel experiences are not so new.[5] As David Harvey has argued, 'certainly from 1492 onwards, and even before, the globalization process of capitalism was well underway . . . Without the possibilities inherent in geographical expansion, spatial reorganisation and uneven geographical development, capitalism would long ago have ceased to function as a political-economic system.'[6] Thus we should not find it surprising that the process of 'globalization' that preoccupies current journalism and scholarship alike so profoundly was well-enough advanced by the early eighteenth century for a much earlier journalist, Joseph Addison, to take his own world tour while walking through the Royal Exchange in London:

> There is no place in the town which I so much love to frequent as the *Royal Exchange*. It gives me a secret Satisfaction, and, in some measure, gratifies my Vanity, as I am an *Englishman*, to see so rich an Assembly of Country-men and Foreigners consulting together upon the private Business of Mankind, and making this Metropolis a kind of *Emporium* for the whole Earth . . . I have often been pleased to hear Disputes adjusted between an inhabitant of *Japan* and an Alderman of *London*, or to see a Subject to the *Great Mogul* entering into a League with one of the *Czar of Muscovy*. I am infinitely delighted in mixing with these several Ministers of Commerce, as they are distinguished by their different Walks [areas of the Exchange] and different Languages: Sometimes I am justled among a body of *Armenians*: sometimes I am lost in a crowd of *Jews*; and sometimes make one in a group of *Dutch-men*. I am a *Dane, Swede, or French-Man* at different times, or rather fancy my self like the old Philosopher, who upon being asked what Countryman he was, replied, that he was a Citizen of the World.[7]

This is not an early modern experience restricted to the Exchange, or to Addison; and it can be traced back even earlier than the eighteenth century. Indeed, the view of London as an 'emporium for the whole earth' was increasingly widespread from the late medieval period with the growth and centralization of the cloth trade there, and was boosted considerably in the sixteenth and seventeenth centuries by the proliferation of joint-stock companies, a substantial influx of Protestant refugees from the Continent, expanding exploration, trade and colonization, as well as the official opening of the Royal Exchange in 1570.[8]

These conditions and forces combined to produce a world quite different from that of Diogenes (Addison's 'old philosopher') in the third century BC. Although one can find many observations about the inter-mixture that has characterized ports and large cities throughout recorded history, the emergence of capitalism gave this intermixture a new form.[9] This new form is well-captured by Thomas Dekker's observation in 1630 that not only was the world *in* the Royal Exchange, as Addison contended, but that the whole world had *become* an Exchange:

> This World is a Royall Exchange, where all sorts of Men are Merchants: Kings hold Commerce with Kings, and their Voyages are upon high

Negotiations: As, the deare buying of anothers Country, with their owne Subiects Blood: The Purchasing of new Crownes, and new Scepters, not satisfied with the old. And, as Kings, so Princes, Dukes, Earles, Lords, Clergymen, Iudges, Souldiers, have their Trading in particular Marchandizes, and walke every day for that purpose upon this old Royall Exchange. They talke in severall Languages . . . insomuch that the place seemes a Babell (a confusion of tongues).[10]

A variation on the commonplace of 'all the world's a stage' (on which Dekker also draws extensively in his pamphlet), the world-as-Exchange conjures up an image of *generalized* market relations inconceivable before there was a critical mass of market participation, from princes to 'Penny Stinkards', such that the metaphor would seem plausible; a generalized market in Dekker's terms would also be less imaginable in a world in which England's trade was almost entirely subordinated to one or two Continental entrepots: 'at Henry VIII's accession in 1509, London was still playing a subaltern role within the trading system of the low countries and the Mediterranean. By the Restoration in 1660 its population had increased tenfold and it presided over an economic empire of its own.'[11] Such an empire was not built in a day, but emerged slowly over the course of the late sixteenth century and early seventeenth, as London became a true 'world city' by loosening its dependence on Antwerp and diversifying its trade relations, geographically and in content.[12]

Hence, though it was often seen as dangerous rather than desirable, or as a sign of ridiculousness rather than sophistication, 'globalization' references turn up frequently in early modern England. Henry Fitzgeffrey, for example satirizes the walking internationalism of a Blackfriars playgoer's attire in 1620:

In Turkie colours carved to the skin.
Mounted Pelonianly untill hee reeles,
That scorns (so much) plaine dealing at his heeles,
His Boote speakes Spanish to his Scottish Spurres,
His Sute cut Frenchly, round bestucke with Burres.
Pure Holland is his shirt, which proudly faire,
Seems to out-face his doublet every where:
His Haire like to your Moor's or Irish Lockes,
His chiefest Dyet Indian minced Dockes.[13]

Critics worried not only about the language of fashion, which so often had an 'alien' accent in early modern England, but were troubled too by the (supposed) deleterious effect of other languages on English itself. Edmund

Spenser, for example, mourned through 'E.K.', the 'editor' of *The Shepherd's Calendar* (1579), that his 'mother tongue' had been unhappily 'patched . . . with pieces and rags of other languages, borrow[ed] here of the French, there of the Italian, everywhere of the Latin . . . so now they have made our English tongue a gallimaufry, or hodgepodge of all other speeches.'[14] A Londoner did not have to travel far to hear these various languages: Paul's Walk (the area in and around St Paul's Cathedral) was a major meeting-place for merchants prior to the opening of the Royal Exchange, and retained its significance as a place for such meetings into the seventeenth century, when it was described by John Earle as 'the whole world's map . . . with a vast confusion of languages . . . nothing liker Babel'.[15] Indeed, even 40 years earlier John Lyly had observed more generally that 'traffike and travell hath woven the nature of all Nations into ours'.[16] Ambivalently underscoring the effects of such 'trafficke', Donald Lupton described merchants in 1632 as 'strange politicians for they bring Turkey and Spaine into London, and carry London thither'.[17] Apparently, many Londoners were sensitive to the 'globalization' of their city long before the onset of late capitalism's more recent version of it.

Visitors noted globalization as well. Witnessing the effects of a massive inflow of commodities and 'curiosities' into the city in 1599, the Swiss medical student Thomas Platter described the ritual of smoking tobacco, 'imported from the Indies in great quantities', and paid particular attention to the collections of travellers.[18] Directly after detailing William Cope's curiosity cabinet, he likens the city as a whole to such a collection, remarking that it 'is not only brimful of curiosities, but so populous also that one simply cannot walk along the streets for the crowd'.[19] Unsurprisingly, moralists worried about the effects of the introduction of 'foreign' elements into this populace:

> . . . we have derived to ourselves, with our commerce with foreign Nations, with their wares and commodities, their vices and eveill conditions; as our drunkenness and rudeness from the Germans; our fashions and factions from the French; our insolence from the Spaniards; our Machiavelianism from the Italians; our levity and inconstancie from the Greekes; our usury and extortion from the Jew; our atheism and impiety from the Turks and Moors; and our voluptuousness and luxury from the Persians and Indians.[20]

In their apparent anxiety, passages such as this indicate an awareness not only of the expansion of trade and trans-national interchange, but that such exchanges tended to transform their participants. That the material effects of such a process are displaced onto an allegory of moral corruption here should not lead us to ignore the actual intimate entanglements of so-called independent states. England imported knowledge of fine clothworking from Italy as well as political theory; religious doctrine came from Germany, with or without 'rudeness'. We need to explore these experiences of so-called 'contaminations' for what they might tell us about the disavowed hybrid formation of the European cultures that later imposed their supposedly pure selves on the rest of the world.[21]

The theatre is a compelling site for such an exploration since it provides many of the references to, and metaphors of, intermixture and exchange that have come down to us, as the examples above from Fitzgeffrey and Lyly have already hinted. Indeed, in The Gull's Hornbook (1609), Thomas Dekker – who, as we have already seen, equated the world with the Exchange – observes, more specifically, that 'The Theater is your poets Royal Exchange, upon which their Muses (that are now turnd to Merchants) meeting, barter away that light commodity of words for a lighter ware than words, Plaudities . . . Which . . . vanish into aire.'[22] This image draws the theatre into an *international* economy, since the Exchange – unlike, say, a local shop – was *explicitly* a site for trans-national commerce to be conducted. Likewise, source material for plays certainly participated in this international circulation, from translations of foreign plays to plots lifted from Continental novellas or histories and settings inspired by 'exotic' locales and even atlases. As Dryden would put it in 1689, 'plays you will have; and to supply your store, / Our poets trade to every foreign shore.'[23] So extravagant was the geographical variety offered by the playhouses that Thomas Platter considered one useful service performed by the theatres for Londoners was that of 'learning at the play what is happening abroad; indeed men and womenfolk visit such places without scruple, since the English for the most part do not travel much, but prefer to learn foreign matters . . . at home.'[24] What is perhaps most interesting about Platter's remark is that he seemed to think that people *could* learn about what was 'happening abroad' without leaving London. Plays not only conjured up many elsewheres, but, at times, even directly depicted London's links to them, as in Thomas Heywood's play (1632) about the founding of the Royal Exchange, in which Thomas Gresham in London dispatches his factors to their tasks: 'I mean to send you into Barbary, / you unto Venice, / you to Portingall' and so on.[25] Even as this play was being performed, 'English' factors were actually being dispatched to such places, and returning with, or sending back, bits and pieces of elsewhere.

For many historians and literary critics, however, direct representations of trade are not the most important link between the market and the theatre in the early modern period. With the expansion of capitalism, the English understanding of 'market' itself began to shift, as Jean-Christophe Agnew has argued, so that it designated not only a specific *place* but an abstracted and generalized *process* of exchange, just as Dekker's world-as-Exchange metaphor suggests. As more and more people were forced off the land and into the cash nexus, the market became not an extraordinary site to visit, but a condition of existence. Agnew, among others, links this transformation of the market to the transformation of the form and function of drama in England.[26] The public theatres, he argues, like the market(s) for commodities, facilitated exchange of identities, and a sense of destabilization and fluidity (a position well-supported by the Addison passage cited above: 'I am a *Dane, Swede, or French-Man* at different times'). Furthermore, the theatre became one of the principal sites in which market ideology was worked out and disseminated. Drama, according to Agnew, was not only caught up in this transformation of the market itself, but it also put aspects of the disorienting change on display.

This is a particularly helpful optic through which to read *The Tempest*, especially given the notorious difficulty with locating its island. *Why* is this island so hard to locate on a map? Such a question takes on added interest because of all Shakespeare's plays, *The Tempest* is singular in its insistent spatial ambiguity: the others spread themselves out on a more or less familiar Old World map, even if the details are a bit hazy or fanciful. Conversely, critics (and directors) have made strong cases for setting *The Tempest* in the Caribbean, Virginia, Bermuda, the Mediterranean or Ireland (and these are only the most favoured locations), yet incertitude remains.[27] While for Roberto Fernández Retamar, for example, 'there is no doubt . . . that *The Tempest* alludes to America, that its island is the mythification of one of our [Caribbean] islands', Stephen Greenblatt – though also interested in the relation of the play to early modern colonialism – avers matter-of-factly that 'the island is not in America but in the Mediterranean.'[28] Such uncertainties have dogged twentieth-century criticism of *The Tempest*, which simply describes itself to be set on 'an uninhabited island' (of unspecified location). Perhaps, then, as Jeffrey Knapp indicates, it is most accurate simply to emphasise that the play, like Spenser's *Faerie Queene* and More's *Utopia*, unfolds 'Nowhere'. Spatial ambiguity is significant in these works, he argues, because 'the purpose of Nowhere . . . is to turn the English into imperialists by . . . help[ing] the English reader see the limitations of material investment in little England alone.'[29] 'Nowhere', in other words, encourages the imagining of *anywhere* as one's own proper place.

However, it is also possible to see *The Tempest*'s island as Nowhere in a rather different sense than Knapp suggests. For in one crucial respect even *The Tempest* can be located alongside other early modern plays produced in England: as a *performed* text, it 'takes place' in London in the early seventeenth century. Scholars may dispute the location of *The Tempest*'s diegetic island, but no one has disputed that it was performed in the capital city of a wholly locatable island in its moment of emergence. My contention here, however, is that there should be far more uncertainty than there is about the locatability of that latter island, and particularly of that capital city. Indeed, it is a certain *parallel* between the undecidable space of *The Tempest* and the space in which it was performed that most interests me. The Nowhere that I have in mind, then, is actually closer to the space of the 'boundless market' Agnew describes in *Worlds Apart* which I discussed above. Capitalizing markets produced a novel space, a Nowhere of generalizing exchange, and this Nowhere inaugurates what might be called a 'world city' in the *modern* sense – a necessarily dis-located space, or, to borrow (and transcode) one of Prospero's phrases, a 'baseless fabric' (IV.i.151).

Indeed, Anthony Giddens has argued that dis-location is one of the most important hallmarks and attributes of modernity:

> in pre-modern societies, space and place largely coincide, since the spatial dimensions of social life are, for most of the population, and in most respects, dominated by 'presence' – by localised activities. The advent of modernity increasingly tears space away from place by fostering relations between absent others, locationally distant from any given situation of face-to-face interaction.[30]

While Giddens concedes that there were, of course, movements of travellers, merchants and migration of populations prior to 'modernity' as he defines it, he sees a shift 'from about the seventeenth century onwards' toward an increasingly *general* experience of modernity (as dis-location) in Europe.[31] From a decidedly Marxist position, Fredric Jameson has come to a strikingly similar conclusion about the space of a specifically capitalist modernity in which 'the truth of . . . experience no longer coincides with the place in which it takes place.'[32] Capitalism encourages delocalization in several ways: first, in vastly increasing the specialization, fragmentation and combination of labour, it increases dependencies among peoples, whether separated by a few feet or thousands of miles; second, in the drive to accumulate, the capitalist is forced to seek expanded markets, supplies of raw materials, and even labour, beyond his immediate location; finally, competition among capitals is by no means restricted to a 'home market' – events and decisions in one place have material effects on numerous 'local' economies. For all these reasons, even at the moment of the emergence of capital, the world was 'in' London and London in the world in novel ways in the seventeenth century as labour and trade practices transformed, rendering it 'baseless', in the sense of dislocated. The selection of citations I have collected above indicates vestigial awareness of this process at work in the early modern period.

Thus, the Nowhere Knapp describes – if understood in terms of this radical dis-location – is not so much, or only, *anticipatory* of colonial expansion as he suggests, but rather *descriptive* of London itself. Understanding London as a 'world city' in this way has important implications for the new 'domestic' interpretations of *The Tempest* as well as 'colonial' ones.[33] In a probably inevitable reaction to the New Historicists' colonial readings, several critics have undertaken to emphasise the ostensibly 'closer to home' (as Meredith Skura puts it) preoccupations of *The Tempest*. Skura questions the colonial reading, suggesting that it may be the new *historicist* dominant interpretation, but it is not *historical*:

> the recent criticism not only flattens the text into the mold of colonialist discourse and eliminates what is characteristically 'Shakespearean' in order to foreground what is 'colonialist', but it is also – paradoxically – in danger of taking the play further from the particular historical situation in England in 1611 even as it brings it closer to what we mean by 'colonialism' today.[34]

She claims it would be more true to the text – and history – to underscore what she describes as 'most local' about it: Shakespeare and 'what was on his mind' in relation to the 'political' discourses that preoccupy new historicist 'revisionist' readings; the 'mind' of Shakespeare is available, according to Skura, through the plays, among which she situates *The Tempest* in terms of what she sees as an abiding concern with a 'crisis of selfhood'.[35] A series of other 'local' readings followed in the wake of this essay. Fran Dolan, for example, explores *The Tempest*'s figuration of fraught household relations in England, especially in relation to the laws against 'petty treason', or insubordination directed toward a head of household.[36] Douglas Bruster has argued that the play allegorizes English playhouse politics and asserts the 'essential homeliness of *The Tempest*', which he finds evidenced in the lack of any period commentary on the 'new world' aspects of the play that preoccupy many current critics, along with perceived parallels between the plot and Shakespeare's likely experience of the Globe and Blackfriars.[37] Hence, for Bruster, Thomas Duffett's *Mock-Tempest* of 1674 was especially insightful in its transfer of the plot to London.

Duffett's decision about setting was inspired to be sure, but not because there is anything 'homely' about *The Tempest*, as the domestic readings suggest – or at least not in the way they suggest – but rather because associating *The Tempest* with London, understood as a 'world city', indicates how *unheimlich* it had become. In other words, what is 'most local' about the play is that 'the local' in which it is performed has been irreducibly undermined, such that its location is in certain respects as indeterminate as Caliban's island. Freud argued that the *unheimlich* (literally 'unhomely' or, in English, 'uncanny'), a specific type of fearful or anxious feelings that had been associated by earlier theorists with a response to the 'new and unfamiliar', was actually a response to 'something which is familiar and old-established in the mind and which has become alienated from it'.[38] He gives several examples of such alienated familiarities, including omnipotence of thoughts, animism, magic and other 'infantile' beliefs that are later rejected by the 'rational' adult. The uncanny emerges as an effect of an experience that seems to *confirm* one of these rejected beliefs (for example, wishing a person dead, and then being discomfited if the person actually dies shortly after), which arouses the trace of the previously rejected belief in the adult. The uncanny experiences that most interest me here are those that call boundaries into question. Freud traces these to an 'infantile source' (the infant's undifferentiated body and ego, alienated when the sense of 'unified' self develops), but we need not restrict them to an 'individualist' and evolutionary interpretation as he – and Skura – do.

Instead, following the logic of what might be called the *socially unheimlich*, we might ask what has been 'alienated' (in the sense Freud uses it here – rejected or repressed – not the technical Marxist sense) by peoples with the emergence of capitalism. Marx suggests that it is the interconnection among peoples – which capitalism *encourages materially* (in a debased form) but *disavows ideologically* by diverting our attention from human relations to relations among things: 'the definite social relation between men themselves . . . assumes . . ., for them, the fantastic form of a relation between things.'[39] Along these lines, Duffett not only brings the plot of *The Tempest* into London, but does so via one of the most explicit transformations of the 'human' into a 'thing': prostitution.[40] The *Mock-Tempest* explicitly concerns itself throughout with the 'wenching trade' (II.ii.73); its tempest is the storming of a brothel by a rabble set on by the keeper of Bridewell workhouse, Prospero, and his servant Ariel. Its reification of the human is extremely direct. Here, for example, is how the Bawd character describes the blunt come-on of a 'thriving Tradesman': 'I want a Wench, give me *good sound ware*, here's your money, ready money . . .' (III.i.82–3, emphasis mine). Though the plot of *The Tempest* is framed by a trans-national exchange of women (first Claribel and then Miranda), references to specifically financial circuits of world trade – which either a Mediterranean or Atlantic location for *The Tempest's* island would call to mind for a period audience – and even 'local' references to commerce, are virtually absent.[41] Duffett, however, not only subsumes *The Tempest's* exchange of women to the cash nexus, and foregrounds it, but situates this trade in a site that both is – and is not only – 'London': the 'straights' of Mediterranean shipping are given a London analogue at various points in the play, rendering the two not only interconnected, but superimposed. For example, when the 'rabble' propose their terms of truce in the *Mock-Tempest*, they insist (referring to the brothel and its inhabitants) on being given 'Dominion of the Straights mouth, and all the Mediterranean Sea – That every Frigot, Fireship, you have, shall strike, furle up their sail, and lye by to the least of their Cock-boats, where-ever they meet, and receive a man aboard to search for prohibited Goods, and permit him to romage fore and aft without resistance' (I.i.141–6). By transferring the 'exotic' action of *The Tempest* to one of London's red-light districts, Duffett engages in a typical strategy of satire and burlesque, the clash of 'high' and 'low' elements, and the 'exotic' and 'familiar', while, in the process, drawing attention to how the 'familiar' might be other than it superficially appears. In other words, through the metaphorization of London-as-Mediterranean, Duffett's play not only alludes to the 'Mediterranean' setting and imagery of *The Tempest*, but also hints that 'London's' seemingly stable and intact self-identity might literally be at sea. By situating the dislocated *Tempest* in London, Duffett unsettles boundaries of emergent nationalism in ways that might be expected to arouse anxiety at a *social* level, but he diffuses the 'uncanny' effect by way of broad humour, as Freud notes literature, unlike life, is capable of doing.[42]

That the significance of *The Tempest's* indeterminate location for early seventeenth-century London viewers might not have been so different can be inferred from a brief detour through another play performed around the same time, and often linked with it – *Bartholomew Fair*, which, at first glance at any rate, appears to be quite emphatically located in London.[43] However, as Duffett would do much later, Jonson suggests that London was already permeated by the global, calling into question any simple binarization of local and global.[44] Specifically, Jonson's Fair is emphatically not restricted to 'English' elements. Indeed, for all its seeming locality, his play contains more clear and direct references to the New World than does *The Tempest*. The Stage-keeper, who pronounces doubtfully on Jonson's representation of the Fair, observes, for example: 'When't comes to the Fair once, you were e'en as good to go to Virginia for anything there is of Smithfield' (Induction.10–12). Usually 'Virginia' is read here as simply referring to a generic faraway place to which Smithfield bears no resemblance.[45] The joke is on the Stage-keeper, however, since the play indicates in some subtle and not-so-subtle ways, that to go to Bartholomew Fair is, in a way, like going to Virginia.

Jonson's Smithfield is, after all, a site in which tobacco, 'whose complexion is like the Indian's that vents it' (II.vi.24), offers itself at every turn, an aspect of London much remarked on by contemporary observers. In addition, the very items that were often offered in trade with 'Indians' were for sale at the Fair as well, as is emphasised by one character's observation that his master should buy a collection of them 'for all [his] tenants, [since] they are a kind o' civil savages that will part with their children for rattles, pipes, and knives' (III.iv.37–9). The Fair is also a space in which the Justice of the Peace, Adam Overdo, sees himself as a 'discoverer' in the same league with 'Columbus; Magellan; or our countryman Drake of later times' (V.vi.40–41). And what he discovers is the 'enormity' that 'The Straits' and 'the Bermudas', local slang for red-light districts (which we have already seen put to later use by Duffett), are right in London (II.vi.80–81). Linking parts of London to the Mediterranean and to the New World in this way draws attention not only to the quite prevalent equation of 'low' members of European cultures with supposed New World 'wildness' and Southern luxuriance, but also to the various elements of the New World and elsewhere that were becoming parts of (and fracturing) 'Britain's' own identity, such as tobacco and sugar. Indeed, regular references in *Bartholomew Fair* to travellers and other displaced persons and items, including Coryat, Jews, Huguenots, ships, parrots, monkeys and 'the black boy in Bucklersbury' intensify the sense that, as the fanatical puritan Zeal-of-the-Land puts it in itemizing its dangers: 'the world [is] in the Fair' (III.vi.37). Although Jonson's play is seemingly elaborately 'located' (in Bartholomew Fair, in London, and in Britain) it is ultimately, I would suggest, as unlocatable as *The Tempest* because the Fair is depicted as an effect of flows from elsewhere and in flux. As a market, it is being swept into the market.

Hence it is not extravagant to claim that *The Tempest* is set – or, more properly, un-set-tled – in London, a London that Henry Peachum would describe in 1642 as 'like a vast sea, full of gusts, fearful-dangerous shelves and rocks, ready at every storm to sink and cast away the weak and inexperienced bark'.[46] Peachum goes on to describe himself – like Jonson's Overdo before him – as a 'skifull pilot . . . like another Columbus or Drake, acquainted with [London's] rough entertainment and storms'. This is not a quirky or extravagant image for a port city through which population, labour, commodities, ideas, money and news from 'elsewhere' circulated constantly.

In such a milieu, might not *The Tempest* resonate with a 'local' condition – that, as in the play itself, the space of London is uncertain? Lest some unsympathetic critic perversely assume that I mean by this that people woke up one day around 1611 suddenly unable to find their way around city streets, or lost their way between their fields and their houses in the countryside, or became confused when asked where they lived, I hasten to add that I do not refer to an immediately manifest condition of spatial confusion at that level, but rather a vestigial recognition, in the complex ideological matrix of a cultural form, that perhaps – in Jameson's words – the 'truth of experience no longer [fully] coincide[d] with the place in which it t[ook] place.' Such a recognition need not be 'conscious' on the part of Shakespeare or his audience. Cultural forms and ideologies can perform work of crisis management beyond any authorial plan, or immediately perceived audience need. Indeed, their unconsciousness often adds to their strength. Even now most people take the stability of the place in which they live to be self evident, and yet globalization has long undermined any such stability. As Christopher Pye has noted, 'it has been the [fiction of a national] economy more than anything else that has preserved the idea of society as a totalized field even among those analysts apparently most willing to embrace the discursive open-ended nature of social forms.'[47] Theorizing London as a 'world city' might help us think more adequately about its actual 'open-ended[ness]'.

The Tempest captures this 'open-endedness' well in its indeterminate location, its familiar–unfamiliarity. Although the play in many respects concerns itself with *distance*, its island is also a place where distance is *collapsed*. Claribel might have been deposited 'ten leagues beyond man's life', a distance remarked not only by Antonio, but also by Alonso and others (II.i.245), but the island is simultaneously a place where displaced persons converge, where conspiracies that once unfolded in Italy are again set in motion, and where the long-time residents already speak the language of newcomers. And while the mythical marvels of distant places are alluded to – the unicorn, the phoenix, the 'mountaineers dewlapped like bulls' (III.iii.43–4) – and credited, because apparently too far off to be disconfirmed, and even the island on which the shipwrecked parties land is described as 'almost inaccessible' (II.i.39), what appears to be a distinct new world to Miranda does not look so new to Prospero: "Tis new to thee' (V.i.184). Gonzalo is thus able to produce an accounting of the events in which everything that is 'lost' is 'found' – for the most part, *on the island*:

> In one voyage
> Did Claribel her husband find at Tunis,

And Ferdinand, her brother, found a wife
Where he himself was lost, Prospero his dukedom
In a poor isle, and all of us ourselves
When no man was his own. (V.i.208–13)

That 'magic' accounts for much of this sea-change in the play should not blind us to its applicability to actual experience in early modern London, itself a site of numerous flows and convergences, which bourgeois economics would later attribute to an (equally magical) 'invisible hand'.

Shakespeare's play turns to a familiar and soon-to-be-anachronistic discourse – magic – to work through a novel crisis in the social order, as is typical at moments of radical disruption.[48] Through magical auspices, the play attempts to re-establish precisely the sort of 'order' that markets were breaking down, as complaint literatures of various kinds attest in their outrage and dismay that older 'personal' relations – and status distinctions – were becoming muddled.[49] Spatial decentering and social disruption, however, were necessary to the establishment of the market and colonial hegemony London elites so fervently desired to wrest from Continental competitors. As was the case with many of his actually existing contemporaries, Prospero turns his thoughts to the vanity of human aspiration when confronted with the disruption of settled order, and declares the world a 'baseless fabric': a 'product of skilled workmanship' that is shown to be 'without . . . foundation'.[50] He flees from magic into renunciation of the worldly. Poststructuralism has taught us, however, to understand that human constructs can be 'without . . . foundation' and yet not 'insubstantial', as Prospero would have it.[51] Marxism, more importantly, has taught us that capitalism is a material and not a magical force, with human, not supernatural, origins and ends, which can be addressed in the here and now. The Tempest offers a powerful fantasy of control for an unsettled London in the throes of massive change. Like Jonson's Bartholomew Fair and Duffett's Mock-Tempest, Shakespeare's play dramatizes the conditions of a city that was becoming 'the countryman's labyrinth' – a site in which he 'could find many things . . . but many times lose himself.'[52] Like the reporters for Time Out and The New York Times I cited at the beginning of this essay, early modern subjects, too, were struggling to come to terms with a rapidly growing and bewilderingly dispersing city. We need to keep in mind in such moments – past and present – that the very forces which to Time Out indicate that London is 'The World', or in the early modern period were seen as 'contaminating' influences, can also be read as evidence of disavowed debt accrued by London to the world as an effect of a bid for ascendancy literally built by stones and sweat from everywhere.[53] Not only on seemingly remote islands, but at 'home', the 'West' could not exist without the Calibans who 'serve[d] in offices that profit[ed]' it (I.ii.312–13). While the island in *The Tempest* seems to be a site that Europe permeates, the play ends before the other part of the story can be shown: the island permeating Europe. Nevertheless, *The Tempest* gives us a glimpse of that world in the making, not least, in London.

2 'Knowing I loved my books': Reading *The Tempest* Intertextually

BARBARA A. MOWAT

Peter Greenaway's *Prospero's Books* directs our attention, in its title and in image after striking visual image, to a central feature of Shakespeare's *Tempest* – namely, its dependence on and foregrounding of the book.[1] Greenaway's focus is on those books referred to repeatedly in the dialogue of the play, the books that, as Greenaway puts it, 'Gonzalo hastily threw into Prospero's boat as he was pushed out into the sea to begin his exile'.[2] These are the books that, according to both Prospero and Caliban, give Prospero his considerable power; these the books that, twelve years into his exile, Prospero still prizes above his lost dukedom; and these the books (or one of these books in particular) that Prospero will drown when he abjures that power.

But there is another set of books implicated in *The Tempest*, books that the text brings to our awareness in what Ralph Williams calls 'intertextual moments', moments, that is, 'when, as we read one text, another so obtrudes on our awareness that it is importantly and simultaneously present to our consciousness.'[3] Once summoned, whether through actual quotations within the dialogue or through less obtrusive echoes, the books in *The Tempest* leave traces that weave themselves in our minds into an intricate intertextual melange. This essay will argue that, among the several contexts in which *The Tempest* exists, one of the most significant is this rich intertextual system that extends the play's geographical and temporal boundaries far beyond its apparent limits.

The model that will be used here to explore *The Tempest* and its books is the intertextual model set out by Claes Schaar, which he describes as a vertical context system.[4] Schaar begins with the fact that many literary works are composed in part of semantic echoes of earlier works. These echoes serve as signals, calling into our minds the works that are echoed; these memories in turn affect our response to the work we are reading or hearing, either annotating, enriching or commenting on it. The process happens in two stages:

first is the recognition, the moment when 'the surface context, operating as a signal, triggers a memory of the infracontext. Then, as recognition turns to understanding, the signal is transformed into a sign as surface and infra-context coalesce.' At that moment, when surface context and infracontext 'merge in the reader's mind', the literary work being directly experienced may be invested with 'associative and emotive richness' or may be 'expressly elucidated or explained'.

Schaar's system is a useful intertextual model in that, first, instead of focusing on authorial intentions, it looks instead at literary effect. As Schaar puts it, his methodology replaces the question 'Is this passage an allusion?' with 'two questions: "Does this passage suggest some other passage?" and, if so, "How does this other evoked passage affect it?"' It is useful, second, in that it moves us helpfully away from the 'tracing of origins' that is the busi-ness of the source-hunter: 'The student of infracontexts', writes Schaar, 'deals with the expansion and stratification of meaning. His aim is thus ... to utilize infracontexts in an intensified appreciation of literary texts, not to store away parallel passages in a collection of notes'.

The Tempest, like the works discussed by Schaar, is a work that 'depends for its full effect' on our recognition of its intertextual signals. While the full implications of the play's infracontexts have not been explored, many of the books that it signals intertextually have long been recognized. Scholars agree in finding echoes in the play from the *Aeneid*, from Ovid's *Meta-morphoses*, from Florio's translation of Montaigne's 'Of the Caniballes', and from Strachey's report on the voyage and shipwreck of the *Sea-Venture*. While others would add to this list such works as for example William Thomas's *History of Italye* (1549), Chaucer's 'The Franklin's Tale'[5] and the Acts of the Apostles, they would not challenge the scholarly consensus that the most important books that the play echoes were written by Virgil, Ovid, Montaigne and Strachey.[6]

The Tempest is thus, famously, different from such plays as *Richard III*, *Romeo and Juliet* and *The Winter's Tale*, plays in which a single literary or historical work provides an obvious controlling infracontext;[7] but it has much in common with, for example, *A Midsummer Night's Dream*, a play whose surface context rests on a disparate and complex infracontextual system. Like *Dream*, *The Tempest*'s infracontexts are various (classical, medieval, Biblical, contemporary), and some of its infracontexts are (or may be seen to be) rhetorically oppositional: that is, just as the image of Theseus in *A Midsummer Night's Dream* is constructed from infracontexts that present con-flicting ideologies,[8] so the image of Prospero supported by Virgilian and Ovidean infracontexts may be perceived as ideologically at odds with those

'Aeneae Troiani Navigatio', from Abraham Ortelius, *The Theatre of the whole vvorld*
(London, 1606/8?), plate between fols xxxiij and xxxiiij.

infracontexts that bring to the surface the colonialist implications of the
play. Such rhetorically oppositional infracontexts are characteristic of
Shakespeare's technique.

But *The Tempest* as a Shakespearean vertical context system stands effectively alone in two respects. First, its infracontextual citations are strangely
obtrusive. Ferdinand's speech on first seeing Miranda – 'Most sure, the
goddess . . .' (I.ii.422) – is, to quote Donna Hamilton, a 'verbatim translation'
of a 'famous phrase' from the *Aeneid* – 'O dea certa' – set by Shakespeare
'in a context . . . that prompts reader or audience recognition'.[9] Gonzalo's
'commonwealth' speech (II.i.145–54, 156–62) follows Florio's translation of
Montaigne so precisely that, where Shakespeare adds a word – Montaigne's
'no use of wine, corne, or mettle' becoming Shakespeare's 'no use of metal,
corn, or wine, *or oil*' – scholars find this slight change so startling that they
use it as evidence in determining which Biblical passage the word 'oil' alludes
to.[10] And Prospero's speech abjuring his magic (V.i.33–57) is at many points
little more than a restatement of one of Ovid's most famous, most easily
recognizable passages.[11]

Peter Hulme has noted that 'the difficulties attendant on' the claim that 'behind *The Tempest* stood . . . the great Mediterranean epic of Virgil's *Aeneid* have never revolved around the question of the *presence* of such Virgilian echoes in the play: on the contrary such echoes are, if anything, rather *too* present.' His example is the infamous 'widow Dido' passage (II.i.71–99), where, as he notes, 'Rather than appearing as shadowy outlines beneath the words of the text, satisfactory reminders of generic and ideological continuity, the very question of classical parallels to the dramatic narrative breaks through the surface of the play to become a subject for discussion by the characters.'[12] This excessive Virgilian presence, this example of 'classical parallels' breaking through 'the surface of the play', goes beyond what Hulme notes as 'an intrinsic characteristic of *The Tempest* . . . [namely,] its confident use of classical allusions and analogues.' It signals as well *The Tempest's* characteristic – and, for Shakespeare, anomalous – use of obtrusive citation through lengthy quotation and through allusion to famous literary (bookish) moments.

A second oddity of *The Tempest* as a vertical context system – an oddity that stands in some ways in opposition to obtrusive citation – is the infracontextual multiplicity so often triggered by the surface text's allusions. Many of the play's citations, in other words, point obtrusively but complexly. The storm, for example – featured in the play's title, represented in its opening scene, and described in detail in the second scene – cites an intricate, and intricately linked, set of infracontexts. As Donna Hamilton notes, the storm is at first glance an explicit reference to the *Aeneid*. But Hamilton recognizes a complicating factor: 'Virgil's tempest had, over the centuries, been reused by writer after writer until it had passed into the literary language as topos, convention, even as cliché.' Thus 'no literate audience experiencing this first scene and inclined to relate it to earlier works would think only of the *Aeneid* as a precedent.'[13] While Hamilton is surely right that the literary storm had become 'topos, convention, even . . . cliché', it is somewhat misleading to call the topos 'Virgil's tempest'. The tradition of the literary storm predates Virgil – there are three such storms in the *Odyssey*, for example, which together spawn an intertextually dependent storm in Apollonius of Rhodes's third-century BCE *Argonautika*[14] – and the storm as a literary topos entered Renaissance rhetoric not only from Virgil but also from Ovid and Achilles Tatius, among others.[15]

The important point, though, is that the literary storm (or, as Harold Francis Watson calls it, 'the formula storm')[16] was in itself a recognized intertextual topos that pointed almost inevitably to the world of fiction (as J. H. Mozley put it, 'no Latin Epic is without one')[17] or, minimally, to the world of the literary and rhetorical.[18] In the formula storm, sea and sky contend, darkness obliterates the light, crew and passengers on the storm-besieged ship cry aloud and fight with despair, and, often, important characters escape by floating to safety on a piece of the wrecked ship. These details are so familiar to today's readers of Renaissance literature as to seem normal descriptors of sea storms, but, as Watson points out, they rarely appear in travel narratives, where tempests and even shipwrecks are described briefly and with little rhetorical elaboration.[19] The following account in Richard Hakluyt's *Principal Voyages of the English Nation* is typical in reporting a tempest thus laconically:

> . . . the wind being northerly, and increasing continually more and more, it grew to be a storm and a great fret of wind: which continued with us some 24 hours, with such extremity, as it carried not only our sails away being furled, but also made much water in our ship, so that we had six foot of water in hold, and having freed our ship thereof with baling, the wind shifted to the Northwest and became dullard: but presently upon it the extremity of the storm was such that with the laboring of the ship we lost our foremast, and our ship grew as full of water as before. The storm once ceased, and the wind contrary to go our course, we fell to consultation which might be our best way to save our lives . . .[20]

Missing here is any description of the terror, the days and nights of darkness, the contention between sea and sky, or the sense of miracle in the storm's cessation.

Watson, noting the difference between such accounts of storms in travel narratives and William Strachey's account of the tempest off Bermuda, proposes intriguingly that Strachey's version of the tempest that tossed the *Sea-Venture* itself belongs among the formula storms. He points out that most of the details of Strachey's account that do not appear in other reports of the voyage – the details that persuade us that *The Tempest* echoes Strachey's manuscript – are also to be found in Virgil, in Achilles Tatius' *Clitophon and Leucippe*, and in Sidney's *Arcadia*. 'The implication', writes Watson, 'is fairly obvious. "William Strachey, Esq.," a gentleman of education, after what was probably one of the great events of his life, sat him down to do justice to what Purchas [in a marginal note to his 1625 printing of Strachey's letter] calls "a pathetical and retorical description".' That Strachey was writing with 'attention to literary effect', notes Watson, 'is indicated by his long philosophical commentary' on the threat of death by drowning; 'that he had the classics in mind is shown' by his lengthy Latin quotations from Horace. Watson's proposal becomes even more persuasive when we notice that Strachey's meditation on death by drowning seems itself to have been modelled on a passage in *Clitophon and Leucippe*.[21]

Shakespeare's storm, then, calls up a complicated set of infracontexts. The surface context triggers memories of the *Aeneid* and of Strachey's 'True Reportory'. But Strachey's report itself recalls the *Aeneid* and *Clitophon and Leucippe*, and perhaps the *Metamorphoses* and the *Arcadia* as well. This does not mean, though, that Strachey's report does not belong among the play's probable infracontexts: Ariel's description of his 'flaming amazement' as St Elmo's fire echoes only Strachey among the recognized infracontexts.[22] Nor does the set of intertextually related texts from Homer to Strachey exhaust the list of probable infracontexts. Ariel's 'not a hair perished', for example, almost certainly echoes the formula storm found in chapter 27 of the Acts of the Apostles – the tempest that after fourteen days of darkness and despair wrecks St Paul on the island of Malta.[23] (In Acts 27, as in Strachey, we have an eyewitness account that reads like epic because composed by a highly literate author with an eye to rhetorical effect.)[24]

We find a comparable complex of infracontexts in the scene of the Harpy confrontation in *The Tempest* (III.iii). The encounter of the Harpy with King Alonso is shaped as a sequence of verbal and visual events that re-enact and thus recall ancient confrontations between harpies and sea voyagers. In each of the familiar harpy encounters – from the third-century BCE *Argonautika* (of Apollonius of Rhodes) through the first-century BCE *Aeneid* to *The Tempest* itself – harpies are ministers of the gods sent to punish those who have angered the gods; they punish by devouring or despoiling food; and they are associated with dire prophecies. The most familiar infracontext here would again be the *Aeneid*. But the *Aeneid* presents Aeneas' meeting with the harpies as itself a sequel to the earlier harpy encounter in the *Argonautika* – and it is the Argo story that is recalled in *The Tempest* in such details as the bringing in of food by 'islanders' (in the *Argonautika*, 'countless dishes', all of them inevitably defiled by the harpies, are brought to Phineus by 'neighbours'; II.185), by Shakespeare's describing the Harpy and her 'fellows' as 'ministers of Fate' (in the *Argonautika* the harpies are 'great Zeus's hounds'; II.289), and by his connecting the Harpy with an exiled duke-magician and a ship-wrecked king (in the Argo epics, the harpies are linked to a blinded and exiled king-prophet). To complicate matters further, Shakespeare has his Harpy descend into a dialogue-context that recalls not so much ancient travel narratives as sixteenth-century reports of real-world creatures of 'monstrous shape'.[25] In the Harpy scene, as in the scenes around the play's tempest, infracontexts of classical and mythological voyages intersect with those of contemporary travel tales.[26]

These moments of infracontextual multiplicity in *The Tempest*, as I noted at the outset, stand in some ways in opposition to the play's other intertextual peculiarity, its obtrusive citation of quite specific infracontexts. But the two kinds of citational oddity also share common features. The most obvious is that they both direct our attention to the same set of infracontexts, namely, stories of sea voyages. The obtrusive quotations, as we remarked earlier, lead us to the *Aeneid*, to Montaigne's long meditation on New World discoveries ('Of the Caniballes'), and to Ovid's reprise (in the *Metamorphoses*) of Jason's travels on the Argo; among the play's sets of complex infracontexts, as we have seen, those echoed in the Harpy scene and in the play's tempest are largely composed of familiar books about epic journeys.

Given the anomalous nature of *The Tempest*'s infracontextual structure, it is hard to believe that only by accident is the play so strongly linked to stories of epic voyages. Joseph Farrell, examining the *Aeneid*'s intertexts, has suggested that 'the poetics of intertextuality is one of Virgil's most powerfully evocative tools for communicating ideas . . . and for eliciting the reader's active collaboration in making meaning.'[27] I would here argue that *The Tempest*'s intertextuality is a comparably evocative instrument that (again quoting Farrell) makes the text 'part of something greater than itself, as if it were merely an episode within a greater, continuous text of almost unimaginable scope.'[28]

The most immediate sense of *The Tempest* as an episode in a 'greater, continuous text' is created by the play's harpy encounter, which, as suggested earlier, repeats and extends its specific precedents: to free the tormented Phineus, Jason's men chase the harpies from the Bosphorus to the Strophades (*Argonautika*, II.269-90); Aeneas and his men, sailing through 'the great Ionian sea', land in the Strophades, 'where dwelled dread Celaeno and the other Harpies, since Phineus' house was closed on them, and in fear they left their former tables'(*Aeneid*, III.209 ff.). After his fearful encounter with Celaeno, Aeneas flees the island; Celaeno herself flies back into the forest (l.258) – and next appears (unnamed, but once again uttering frightening prophecies) on Prospero's island, confronting Alonso and his courtiers.[29]

But *The Tempest*'s storm, too, replicating as it does a familiar sequence of words and images, also makes of the play 'an episode within a greater, continuous text'. The storm that Poseidon unleashes capsizes Odysseus off the coast of Drepano (i.e., Corfu), where he meets Nausicaa; the storm created by Zeus at the northernmost reach of the *Argonautika*'s Black Sea wrecks a ship near the offshore island of Ares where Jason and his men have camped, an incident that serves as a prelude to Jason's finding Medea in Aia. The storm that Juno (through Aeolus) sends to destroy Aeneas drives him through 'the Libyan gulf' to Carthage, where he meets Dido.[30] In *The Tempest* the storm raised by Prospero sends Ferdinand onto the island where he meets Miranda (with words, as we noted, that quote the *Aeneid* – but since the sequence in Aeneas' story carries Homeric and Apollonian episodes intertextually, Ferdinand's shipwreck replicates a series rather than a single incident).

Seeing *The Tempest* as one in a sequence of familiar voyage stories affects our response to the play in at least two ways. First, it colours our view of Prospero by making us aware that the rôle of voyager, first played by Prospero (in the play's prehistory), is then taken by Ferdinand (in the Miranda–Dido–Medea–Nausicaa sequences), and later by Alonso (in the Harpy encounter). When Ferdinand and Alonso take on, in turn, the voyager rôle, Prospero assumes a pseudo-godlike function: he raises the storm, he sends the Harpy. Awareness of Prospero's replication of the function served by Zeus, Poseidon or Aeolus in previous versions of this story makes Prospero seem, by comparison, all-too-human in his relative frailty. He shares with his Olympian forebears a desire for revenge and a wish to crush his enemies; but Prospero's is inevitably a human version of Olympian wrath, and both his storm and his Harpy are mere illusions – even if effective ones – performed by Ariel. While it is possible to claim (as does Donna Hamilton)[31] that Shakespeare bestows great dignity on Prospero by 'shifting the godlike powers in this play to a mortal' and by 'arranging that Prospero's magic be articulated through patterns that Virgil used for his gods', it is also possible to see (as I would argue) that the play shows us the unbridgeable gulf between even a petty god like Aeolus and an unhappy mortal like the play's exiled duke.[32]

Reading *The Tempest* as part of this larger intertextual continuum also affects the way we respond to the play's colonial implications. Jerry Brotton has recently suggested that 'in dismissing the significance of the Mediterranean, or Old World references in *The Tempest*, colonial readings have offered an historically anachronistic and geographically restrictive view of the play, which have overemphasized the scale and significance of English involvement in the colonization of the Americas in the early decades of the seventeenth century.'[33] Brotton seeks 'to redress the marginalization of the Mediterranean contexts' of the play by examining the ways the play is 'inflected with English involvement in the trade and diplomacy of the Mediterranean world.' As helpful as Brotton's work is in redirecting our attention to the Mediterranean, *The Tempest*'s voyage infracontexts suggest that such redirection need not do away with the play's colonial implications. They suggest, rather, that what is needed is a broadening of these implications, a placing of the play and indeed of sixteenth-century New World exploration, expansion and plantation within the old, old story of finding, conquering and dominating New Worlds.

The *Aeneid* is considered the ur-story of the founding of empire. It begins with Carthage ('Tyrii tenuere coloni' – 'colonists from Tyre dwelt there')[34] and goes on to Jove's promise to Venus about 'great-souled Aeneas': 'he shall crush wild peoples and set up laws for men and build walls' (I.63–4). And the poem as a whole is grounded in empire-building ideology – as one sees in such casual remarks as Ilioneus' address to Dido: 'O queen, to whom Jupiter has given the right to found a new city and to curb proud tribes with laws . . .'(I.522–23).

But Aeneas' story is not alone among *The Tempest*'s voyage infracontexts in being linked to exploration and empire. The Argo story, for example, was from the time of Strabo explained 'as a colonizer's quest for gold', and in the *Argonautika*, as Peter Green notes, 'the quest for the Fleece is seen as a Hellenic venture to the world's end, a confrontation between Greek civilization and barbarian savagery'.[35] Green adds that 'There may . . . be a political element at work here: Ptolemy II not only nursed expansionist dreams, but liked to think of himself, *qua* Alexander's successor, as a protector of Greeks and Greek interests.' Green adds that Alexander's conquests and the concomitant expansion of geographical boundaries had 'merely sharpened the Hellenic appetite for conquest and empire'.[36]

It is within this larger world context that the expansionists of Shakespeare's day placed their own yearning for an English empire as they looked into the past and to distant lands for examples of proper national expansion. Richard Hakluyt, for example, begins the dedicatory letter for his 1582 *Divers Voyages Touching the Discoverie of America* to 'master Phillip Sydney Esquire' by citing, as proper models for English colonizing, 'examples of the Grecians and Carthaginians of olde time'[37] and prints first among this small collection of documents an exhortation addressed to 'king Henrie the eight' urging the king to 'amplifie and inriche this your saide Realme', citing 'experience', which shows 'that naturally all Princes bee desirous to extend and enlarge their dominions and kingdomes'.[38]

We close our eyes and ears to much of the meaning of *The Tempest* when we restrict the geographical and temporal bounds of colonization to New World colonizing in the early modern period. Colonizing began in prehistory and, as *The Tempest*'s infracontexts show, stretched from Carthage and beyond on the Western end of the Mediterranean to the Black Sea and beyond in the East. More significantly, the larger context of colonization presents a narrative that strongly affects the tone of *The Tempest*, a narrative that is not yet, in Shakespeare's day, a part of the story of New World empire building. Carthage, settled by the Phoenicians, in turn became itself the center of a vibrant and growing empire, only to become, in turn, mere ruins; Rome, the dream city of Aeneas, having founded the empire promised Aeneas by Jove, fell into ruins in its turn, these 'crumbling stones of past glory' revealing, in Thomas Greene's words, 'the hollowness of . . . cultural hope' contained in Jove's promise.[39] As Greene notes, Du Bellay's *Les Antiquitez de Rome* makes clear that, for sixteenth-century Europeans, confronted as they were with the ruins of Rome, Palmyra, Persepolis and Carthage, such ruins made suspect the very monuments that 'stand synecdochically for all the arrogance required to create an empire'. Du Bellay and his fellows knew that 'Empires rise and fall with the steady rhythm of natural growth'.[40] When empire building is put in its ancient and Old World setting, it reveals itself to be as transitory as 'the great globe itself, yea, all which it inherit', at which point the voyage infracontexts merge with the seemingly unconnected Biblical infracontexts recently noted by Peter Donaldson: 'Then I saw a new heaven and a new earth, for the first heaven and the first earth had vanished . . . Every island vanished, and there was not a mountain to be seen . . . Earth and heaven vanished away, and no place was left for them.'[41] In this larger setting, Caliban becomes every 'barbarian' that 'civilized' man has tried to subdue (from the 'Barbarian Other' of the Argonauts to the famously wild Britons civilized by the Romans);[42] and 'This Tunis, sir, was Carthage' and ''Tis new to thee' become reminders that empires 'are such stuff as dreams are made on'.

Peter Greenaway, as I noted at the outset, focused his script – and his camera – on the books that *Prospero* loves. But Greenaway seems at least to have skimmed the books whose echoes reverberate through the language of the play. More than one camera shot in *Prospero's Books* emphasises the play's elegiac tone, and in one sequence Greenaway shows Prospero sitting in his study: 'As well as having his scattered books around him, their loose pages flapping in a draught, he is surrounded by his antique collection.' The camera moves in to show him in close-up opening 'a book from his library – *Love of Ruins*'. The book is 'a checklist of the ancient world for the Renaissance humanist interested in antiquity': 'Full of maps and plans and diagrams of the archeological sites of the world . . . temples, castles, towns and ports, graveyards and ancient roads . . . descriptions of every discovered obelisk and pedestal of the Mediterranean . . . street directions in Thebes, Ostia and Atlantis . . . the tablets of Heraclitus, the signatures of Pythagoras.' As Greenaway writes, this is 'An indispensable volume for the melancholic historian who knows that nothing endures'.[43]

3 The Ship Adrift

ELIZABETH FOWLER

In the fiction of *The Tempest*, the instruction to imagine is an invitation to deliberate. The two scenes of Act One shape the audience's apprehension of the whole play by repeating a central image, the ship, once staged and once described. They do so in a way well explained by pre-modern rhetorical theory: the opening scene presents a *topos*, a commonplace or location familiar in cultural memory, which functions for Shakespeare not so much as an allusion, but as a *pictura* or *Bildeinsatz*, an inaugurating image that serves to introduce, order and memorialize the matter of the play.[1]

The Tempest opens with a ship out of control, overmastered by a storm. As the mariners attempt to govern her, the courtiers harangue them. The boatswain complains of interference – that the courtiers 'assist the storm', howling 'louder than the weather' (I.i.15, 36). He taunts Gonzalo:

> You are a
> councillor; if you can command these elements to silence,
> and work the peace of the present, we will not hand a rope
> more – use your authority. (I.i.20–23)

The topos is that of the ship of state, and when it founders the cries are of the severing of social bonds:

> *A confused noise within.*
>   'Mercy on us!' – 'We split, we split!' – 'Farewell,
>   my wife and children!' – 'Farewell, brother!'
>   – 'We split! we split! we split!'
> ANTONIO   Let's all sink wi' th' King.
> SEBASTIAN   Let's take leave of him. (I.i.60–64)

The image calls up an ancient tradition. For example, a pitiful ship without rigging or oars is tossed by an African gale in Horace's famous Ode 1.14, 'O navis'. Quintillian and most later commentators consider the poem allegorical; thus its title is conventionally rendered 'To the Ship of State' by English translators.[2]

But the image is not confined to poetry. The Latin verb for steering a ship (*gubernare*) also designates political governance, and so, perhaps by paronomasia, the image became a useful memorial location for propositions about statecraft. Engravings of ships are familiar political symbols on coins in many cultures, and medieval English towns often chose ships to represent them when they inaugurated their town seals.[3] From ancient to early modern times, the convention appears across media and genres. One *locus classicus* for the ship of state can be found at the very beginning of the philosophical treatise on kingship attributed to Thomas Aquinas, *De regimine principum*, which uses the topos for its own opening *Bildeinsatz*:

> We must first explain what is meant by the term, king. When a thing is directed towards an end, and it is possible to go one way or another, someone must indicate the best way to proceed toward the end. For example, a ship that moves in different directions with the shifting winds would never reach its destination if it were not guided into port by the skill of its helmsman.[4]

That Shakespeare shares his opening gambit with Thomas Aquinas links *The Tempest* to jurisprudence and political philosophy, where the power of rhetorical topoi to move audiences was not neglected.

Shakespeare's *pictura* is used by Prospero to stir up strong passions in his daughter Miranda. In the second scene of Act One, she cries, 'O, I have suffered / With those I saw suffer' (I.ii.5–6); Prospero quickly glosses the shipwreck and explains Miranda's response to it, categorizing her emotions as amazement and pity (I.ii.14), noble passions that, Stephen Orgel reminds us, comprise 'the full Aristotelian response to tragedy'.[5] In causing her (and us) to associate such strong passions with the image of the ship of state, Prospero follows the pedagogical practice of the art of rhetoric, which makes use of the propensity of shocking and violent events to make a lasting impression upon the memory. By describing her suffering as pity and amazement, he begins to train her feelings; he continues this ethical shaping of Miranda by attempting to transfer those passions to another object – himself – and then, of course, by the conclusion of the scene, to transfer the same passions to her future husband. The term 'amazement', which can include fear, wonder, and, in the diction of the sonneteers, sexual captivation, is ideally suited to allow Miranda to move from tragedy to comedy and from hatred of Caliban to love of Ferdinand in a process of education (or at least habituation) that instills in her a princely condition.

In addition to his shaping description of Miranda's passionate response, Prospero provides an explanatory historical gloss for the *pictura*. The ungovernable ship just lost is revealed to be a reparative echo of the long lost 'rotten carcase of a butt, not rigged, / Nor tackle, sail, nor mast' (I.ii.46–7) in which Prospero and Miranda were set adrift by the treachery of Prospero's usurping brother. Explaining the spectacle to Miranda, Prospero aims to explain her to herself. The butt is another version of the topos of the ship of state, one known to scholars as the rudderless boat: it appears as a juridical trial or punishment described in legal codes, chronicles and saints' lives, and as a central, organizing image in the romance adventures of Chaucer's and Gower's Constance and her sources and analogues so beloved by English readers from the thirteenth century to Shakespeare's time.[6] The scene that we, with Miranda, are instructed to imagine (it is not staged), casts Prospero in a rôle held by saints, exiled criminals and innocent virgins. We must consider which best diagnoses him.

Like the ungovernable boat of *The Tempest*'s opening scene, this drifting butt invites us to deliberate on the limits, duties and sources of authority. What has caused this suffering and what are its remedies? What is the proper rôle of art – the technical skill of the mariners, the statesmanship of the courtiers, the learned magic of Prospero – in one's relations to other people? The audience is led to cogitate on the meanings and proper responses to the *pictura*; so too the players (including Prospero) are led, though they give various degrees of consent or resistance to the ethical activity of that cogitation. Thus the doubled image of the distressed ship in the first two scenes introduces us to a frame, a means for thinking about governance. The rest of Act One introduces various kinds of social relations, all of which may be used to measure the actions of authority: mastery (both that of skill and that of knowledge), office, kingship, counsel, paternity, fraternity, servitude, signory, homage, pedagogy, marriage, slavery. All these forms of social relation are tested by the play, and all suffer a sea-change within it: not in order to describe ideal relations to us (far from it, as all are vexed), but rather in order to turn these forms before us like jewels in the light, to invite us to search out their flaws and facets.

In the final act, after some redistribution of authority and affiliation, the ship is magically restored by Ariel, 'tight and yare and bravely rigged as when / We first put out to sea' (V.ii.224–5). Yet it remains to be seen how well it will sail. Though Prospero has regained his dukedom and all the men have found themselves, at least according to Gonzalo, nevertheless in the final speech it is the auditor who must provide the motive power that will waft the restored ship back to its European polity. Prospero petitions his audience to release its fictional spell upon him:

> Gentle breath of yours my sails
> Must fill, or else my project fails,
> Which was to please. (V.i.329–31)

Should Prospero be faulted or indulged? In accordance with good rhetorical practice, the topos of the ship requires an active response from its audience – a response that engages them in deliberation and ethical habituation, whether they profit from it by learning to curse or by accepting some 'print of goodness' (I.ii.351, 361–3).

I think the analysis of the rhetorical function of the ungoverned ship produces a more precise description for that prized quality of the play that Stephen Orgel calls its 'openness'.[7] We should not consider such openness a matter of undecidability (nor decidability, as he warns), but an openness of collocation designed to draw the audience into an activity, a habit of cognition and affection – not a *what* to think and feel, but a *how*. The *what* – the mass of propositions about authority generated in the plot – is copious, wonderfully contradictory, and so it is open. Yet it is merely a motive power that fills the sails of the *how*, an ethical and political activity set in motion by the play.

4 Wild Waters: Hydraulics and the Forces of Nature

CHRISTY ANDERSON

The winds blow through *The Tempest*, carrying travellers off their course into worlds of exotic and strange nature. 'Blow till thou burst thy wind', cries the Boatswain during the storm that starts the play (I.i.7), and drives the events to follow. Wind and water are the mobile and fluid forces of nature, and appear in various guises throughout the play: the sea that surrounds the island, the winds controlled by Prospero and Ariel. By the second scene, however, we learn that this is not a natural storm, but one created by the hand of Prospero and his mastery over natural forces. The winds and water that surround the island have been moulded and formed by Prospero, who, acting in the guise of gardener, has also transformed the wilderness and tamed the raw material of nature into pleasurable matter.[1] Like the storm itself, the entire island is a creation caught in a miraculous moment of feigned primitiveness. Miranda, an embodiment of an inviolate nature, proclaims her own amazement at what she sees: 'O, Wonder! / How many goodly creatures are there here!' (V.1. 181–2).[2]

Prospero directs the storm that begins the play, which is the prelude to Miranda's understanding of her past, and to the action that determines her future. She begins to understand that everything she sees is controlled by her father and that nature can be an effect of artifice: 'If by your art, my dearest father, you have / Put the wild waters in this roar, allay them' (I.ii.1–2). Miranda loses her innocence by learning about her father's powers and the source of his art. She begins to understand the mechanics and the machinery of the storm.

The artificiality of nature as portrayed in *The Tempest* had a parallel in designs of contemporary English gardens, especially those made for the court. Like the landscape in the play, these gardens were also self-conscious places of display where the forces of nature were harnessed for marvellous effects. Often based on Continental examples, English gardens were organized into sequences of regular geometries that demonstrated the control of the landowner over his estate and established the boundaries of his property.³ Each of these rooms or areas had a particular character: wilderness, orchard, covered walk, labyrinth, and so on.

Renaissance gardens were as much a product of technology as husbandry, and the science of hydraulics provided the technology for their artificial storms and elaborate fountains. By the late Tudor period gardens were increasingly places of pleasure, wholly distinct from the agricultural world of fields and farms. Especially in the gardens for major houses or the court there was a new emphasis on invention and artifice. Often this shift of meaning meant finding a new use for the permanent elements already there. For example, moats that were no longer needed for defence were newly valued as the relics of a chivalric past. And where water had once had a primarily practical rôle in the garden as fishponds that provided food or as streams for agricultural irrigation, by the end of the sixteenth century gardens exploited the fantastic effects of water through the invention of fountains, grottoes and automata. Garden design controlled the landscape through planting and earthworks, while fountains harnessed the force of water through engines and pumps.

Since antiquity hydraulics had been an important part of the science of architecture and agricultural building.⁴ Architectural skill included the knowledge of engineering and the control of the forces of nature (wind, water, raw materials) into the stable stuff of buildings. The Roman architect Vitruvius devoted the eighth book of his treatise on building (*De architectura*) to the architecture of water, the mechanics of irrigation and the benefit of interior plumbing. Renaissance translations of works by Hero of Alexandria, Archimedes and Pliny all fed a revival of interest in the machinery and technology of hydraulics.⁵

As a science hydraulics encompassed the eminently practical as well as the purely pleasurable. In 1590 Cyprian Lucar showed in his practical handbook, *A Treatise Named Lucarsolace*, how a pump could be used to put out fires: in an accompanying illustration, a man cranks the handle and activates the pump to power a water jet and save a building from the flames.

But this practical side of hydraulics coexisted with another more magical dimension of its use. In 1635 John Bate wrote a small book on 'the mysteries of nature and art' that included chapters on hydraulics, fireworks, drawing and painting and 'sundry experiments'. He was a popularizer of arcane information, and sought to show how technology (and art) could exploit the innate qualities present in the natural world. This was practical science based on natural philosophy:

It hath beene an old saying amongst Philosophers, and experience doth prove it to bee true, Non datur vacuum, that is to say, Nature will not admit of any vacuity or emptinesse. For some or other of the elements, but especially Ayre, and Water doe insert themselves into all manner of concavities, or hollownesses, in, or upon the earth, whether they are such as are formed either by Art or Nature.[6]

Wind was like water; both shared the same physical properties and powers. Authors like Cyprian Lucar had also urged that houses should be planned in accordance with the winds, and even the most practical manuals paid special attention to healthy and evil winds:

Insomuch as aire doth both enclose vs about, but also enter into our bodies, especially the most noble member which is the hart, and that we can not be separated one houre from it for the necessitie of breathing, we ought to have therof a speciall regard, and make our habitation

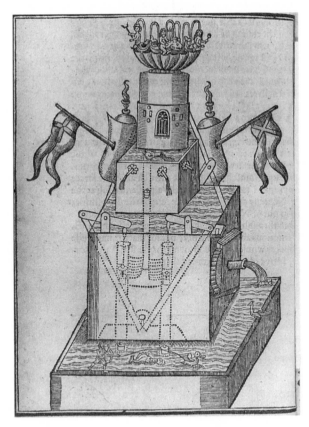

John Bate, *The Mysteries of Nature and Art. In Foure severall parts* (London, 1635), p. 52.

in an wholsome aire which is alwayes faire and cleere without vapors and mists, lightsome, and open, not darke, troublous, or close, nor stinking, infected or corrupted.[7]

These characteristics of the natural world inspired authors to go beyond the purely practical in order to garner the forces of wind and water for their effect alone. The basic scientific principles were also applicable to much more elaborate machines and inventions. John Bate's book demonstrates the mysteries of nature and art, and much of the first book on hydraulics shows how to make fountains, water-organs, and automata that move and make sound. Bate's multi-storeyed and fantastic fountain uses the dynamics of water and pressure 'having at the top, Neptune riding on a Whale, out of whose nosthrils as also out of Neptunes Trident, the water may be made to spin through small pin holes.'[8] These were complete dramatic presentations, often like this one with complex mythological references that were known to the audience or explained through accompanying texts.

The control of these natural forces allowed figures to move and turn as if they were alive or controlled by magical means. The uses of automata were comparable to the theatrical effects developed for the court masque by Inigo Jones and others. The Tempest reveals a similar world, the island inhabited by strange sights and sounds and controlled through the power of a wizard who orders nature and its forces to perform for the spectator's delight or edification.

The courtly taste for marvels and wonders provided opportunities for professionals with an advanced knowledge of the art and science of hydraulics. The Huguenot engineer, Salomon de Caus (1576–1626), found an eager market for his expertise in the creation of gardens for the early Stuart court. He appears on the register of aliens in England in 1598, and his first known work there was for Anne of Denmark.[9] He most likely designed a fountain for her in London at Somerset House (1609) with an island and the figures of Apollo and the Muses, a version of one in Italy at Pratolino that he had recorded in his book Les Raisons des forces mouvantes (1615–24). From other descriptions of the fountain at Somerset House it is known that within the mountain was a grotto, on top of which sat four river gods representing the rivers of Great Britain, headed by the Thames.[10] On the side shown in a print in Les Raisons, are the nine muses with Apollo. The water that sprouts from the other side of the artificial island comes from urns held by the river gods. And the whole sits within a moat or pond, like the sea around the island of Great Britain or the island within The Tempest.

De Caus's designs had more complex machinery and elaborate mytho-

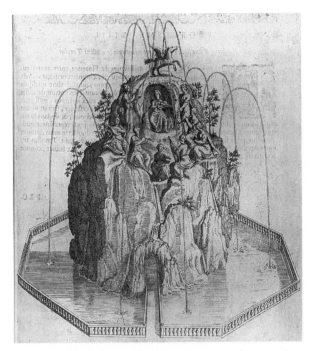

Salomon de Caus, 'Desseing d'un Mont Parnasse, ou l'on pourra
faire quelques grotes dedans', from his *Les Raisons de forces mouvantes
avec diverses machines* (Frankfurt, 1615—24), Livre II, Problesme XIII.

Salomon de Caus, 'Machine par laquelle l'on representera une Galatee qui sera trainee sur leau
par deux daufins, allant en ligne droite, & se retournant d'elle mesme, cependant qu'un ciclope
ioüe deffus un flaiolet', from his *Les Raisons de forces mouvantes . . .*, Livre I, Problesme XXIIII.

logical themes than those popularized by Bate. And *Les Raisons* itself was aimed at a more noble and courtly reader: this collection of De Caus's ideas was dedicated to the royal children – Prince Henry and Princess Elizabeth. The Parnassus, for example, 'est fort à propos pour orner vn Iardin Royal, ou il y auroit abondance d'eau' (is especially appropriate to ornament a Royal Garden, where there would be an abundance of water).[11] And the book itself was in a larger and more expensive format, with detailed engravings, and a text in French.

De Caus was not only interested in the effect and story line of his creations; the first book of the treatise demonstrates the mechanics and principles of hydraulics. These engravings are elaborate and detailed, rich images that fully convey – even to a non-technical reader – a view of the internal workings of the machinery. De Caus often splits the image, pulling the curtain aside to show the viewer how something operates and what is the result. In the book the reader is shown more than would ever be possible; the illustrations are Escher-like in their manipulated angles and exaggerated scale. Throughout there is a fascination with the anatomical workings of these pumps and systems: the images bear a striking resemblance to the dissections used by Andreas Vesalius and other anatomists. Within its elegant presentation and courtly demeanour, De Caus's treatise is self-conscious about the mechanics that drives the new taste in garden design, and the continuum between science and art. The hydraulic machinery is as much a cause for wonder as the fountain itself.

In *The Tempest* Prospero too reveals his art in the mechanics of the storm that start the play. And like de Caus, there is never a sense that revealing the method will diminish the art and artifice of language or visual effect. We know that the storms and transformations are all fabricated in order to astound us, but that does not detract from the pleasure in watching it unfold. Yet it is a delicate balance of power between knowledge of wonder's machinery and the enjoyment of its effect. If Prospero takes the rôle of the gardener, magician and artist who sets the pageant in motion, it is Alonso who serves as the innocent eye, the spectator astounded at all he sees and fails to understand. 'I cannot too much muse / Such shapes, such gesture, and such sound expressing, / Although they want the use of tongue, a kind / Of excellent dumb discourse' (III.iii.36–9).

At the end of the play Alonso presses for more information and insights into this strange world:

> This is as strange a maze as e'er men trod,
> And there is in this business more than nature

Was ever conduct of. Some oracle
Must rectify our knowledge. (V.i.242–5)

Yet Prospero stalls and promises an explanation later: 'Do not infest your mind with beating on / The strangeness of this business' (V.i.246–7). The play ends with Alonso's desire to have this world and its curious characters explained (pointing to Caliban: 'This is a strange thing as e'er I looked on', V.i.289) and he wants to know the mechanisms of Prospero's art and life ('I long / To hear the story of your life, which must / Take the ear strangely', V.i.312–14).

Are we more amazed and astounded when we know how something is done than when we look childlike at the spectacle? Only Caliban is disillusioned: 'What a thrice-double ass / Was I to take this drunkard for a god, / And worship this dull fool!' (V.i.295–7). The machinery of artifice can hold us spellbound, even as we wander in the garden of delights.

These four Indians, carved in low relief, form part of a monument constructed in
1569 in the north aisle of the parish church of St John the Baptist at Burford in
the Oxfordshire Cotswolds. The monument was set up by Edmund Harman
(1509–77), a Privy Councillor and Royal Barber to Henry VIII who had been
given land in Burford in the 1540s.

This seems to have been the very first depiction of American Indians in Britain,
and may be the first three-dimensional representation in the whole of Europe.
The figures are copied from a cartouche drawn by Cornelis Bos in the
Netherlands in the 1550s. Bos may himself have copied them from Cornelis
Floris. The ultimate models were probably the figures depicted on what is usually
called the 'Treasure of Montezuma', displayed in Brussels in 1520, where it was
famously seen and described by Albrecht Dürer.

Mystery surrounds Harman's choice of Indians for his tomb, since surviving
documents give no indication of any links with the Americas. The best guess is
perhaps that the (unknown) sculptor provided Harman with various prints or
drawings as possible models, and that he was – as Royal Barber – attracted or
intrigued by the hairstyles and headgear of the Indians.

Burford is only some 30 miles from Stratford-upon-Avon, but there is no evidence
that Shakespeare ever went there.[1]

5 Trinculo's Indian: American Natives in Shakespeare's England

ALDEN T. VAUGHAN

Epenow reached London in 1611, one of the five Indians kidnapped that year on coastal New England by Captain Edward Harlow.[1] Epenow was uncommonly tall, sturdy and renowned for courage; during three years' captivity he was 'shewed up and downe London for money as a wonder', and may have been Shakespeare and John Fletcher's inspiration for the 'strange Indian' in *Henry VIII* who fascinated the ladies with his 'great tool'.[2] But unlike many American natives who participated in the small, usually involuntary, eastward migration across the Atlantic in the sixteenth and early seventeenth centuries, Epenow survived his European tour. In 1614, en route back to Martha's Vineyard, where he had promised to show his hosts a gold mine, Epenow leapt overboard and swam ashore through a hail of bullets.[3]

A more typical fate for American natives who lived briefly in England befell two or more 'Virginians' from the Chesapeake Bay area who were 'taken awaie . . . by force' in the summer of 1603. Early that September, Sir Walter Cope paid the Indians five shillings to paddle their canoe on the Thames near Sir Robert Cecil's house on the Strand – no doubt to a curious audience. Although Cecil himself seems to have been away from London during that autumn of lethal plague, the Indians probably lodged in his house for several days and strolled the city's streets. Yet Cope's Virginians do not appear again in accounts of Indians in England, nor did they return to Chesapeake Bay as interpreters with the Jamestown expedition of 1606–7, which would have been the logical conclusion to their English sojourn.[4] If they succumbed to the plague or another disease in 1603 or soon afterward, the record leaves no trace.

Whether Shakespeare drew, consciously or not, on American Indians such as Epenow and Cope's Virginians when crafting Caliban is unknowable; yet a familiar argument holds that *The Tempest*'s brief allusions to New World natives signify Caliban's geographic origins. Although neither Trinculo's quip that the English 'will not give a doit to relieve a lame beggar,

[but] . . . will lay out ten to see a dead Indian' (II.ii.32–3), nor Stephano's suspicion that he's been tricked by 'savages and men of Ind' (II.ii.57) identifies Caliban as an Indian *per se*, they may imply an affinity between Shakespeare's 'savage and deformed slave' and a prevalent, pejorative view of American natives. At the very least, they reflect the Indians' topicality in Elizabethan and Jacobean England,[5] where nearly two score American Indians and Eskimos dwelled for varying periods, mostly in London, during Shakespeare's lifetime.

A few Americans trickled into England before Shakespeare's birth. An unidentified expedition to northern North America probably initiated the eastward traffic *circa* 1501, when three men wearing animal skins, behaving 'like to bruite beastes' and speaking 'such speach that no man could understand them', were presented to Henry VII.[6] Several decades later William Hawkins brought a Brazilian king (voluntarily) to Henry VIII's court. At Whitehall Palace the newly arrived Brazilian met the English monarch, whose court 'did not a litle marvaile, and not without cause: for in his cheekes were holes . . . and therein small bones were planted . . . He had also another hole in his nether lip, wherein was set a precious stone about the bignes of a pease: All his apparel, behaviour, and gesture, were very strange to the beholders.' A year later, the Brazilian king, en route to his homeland, died at sea.[7]

No other American natives are known to have reached England before the 1570s,[8] which helps to explain England's enthralment with four Eskimos from northeastern Canada brought home by Martin Frobisher in 1576 and 1577. On his initial search for a northwest passage to China, Frobisher seized an adult male who was soon 'such a wonder vnto th[e] whole City [of London], & to the rest of the Realm that heard of yt, as seemed neuer to have happened the like great matter to any mans knowledge'.[9] Of more than a dozen portraits known to have been made of this anonymous Eskimo, eight were by the prominent Flemish painter Cornelis Ketel, then living in London, from which many copies and engravings were rendered; and a wax cast was apparently taken of the Eskimo's head.[10] But England's fascination with the 'strange man of Cathay' was tragically brief, for he died a few weeks after his arrival. Although he must have suffered severely from a self-inflicted wound – 'when he founde himself in captivitie, for 1 very choller & disdain he bit his tong in twayne within his mouth' – he probably succumbed instead to pneumonia. The Eskimo's body was embalmed but not, apparently, returned to his homeland as initially intended, nor does the evidence suggest that it was buried in the London churchyard for which it was then prepared.[11] That the corpse was instead displayed for ten doits per customer is speculative but not implausible.

The attention lavished on Frobisher's first captive encouraged a larger human haul on the second voyage (1577). On Baffin Island the English captured a native man at one location, a woman and her infant child at another. The three captives – Kalicho, Arnaq and Nutaaq respectively[12] – arrived at Bristol in early October and were instant celebrities, especially Kalicho, who dazzled onlookers with manœuvers on the River Avon in 'a little boat made of skin' and with his ability to shoot ducks with darts 'a good distance off and not miss'.[13] But scarcely a month after his arrival, Kalicho died, apparently of complications from a wound he had received in Canada when his attempt to avoid capture was thwarted by one Nicholas Conger, who 'being a Cornishman, and a good wrastler, shewed hys companion suche a Cornishe tricke, that he made his sides ake . . . for a moneth after.' Dr Edward Dodding, who examined the ailing Eskimo in Bristol, noted headaches, deafness and shortness of breath, as well as excess weight from an 'unhealthy voraciousness' encouraged by his well-meaning hosts. Dodding's autopsy of Kalicho in early November 1577 revealed two badly broken ribs and an infected lung, both almost certain results of Conger's 'Cornishe tricke', and a head injury of unspecified origin.[14] Two days after Kalicho's death, Arnaq 'was troubled . . . with boils (which broke out very densely on her skin . . .)'; she died a few days later. Both were buried at St Stephen's, Bristol, but with notations in the parish register that they were heathens.[15] Only Nutaaq, in care of a nurse hired by Frobisher, reached London, where he died about a week later. The Cathay Company paid to have Nutaaq, like the Eskimo of 1576, buried in St Olave's Church on Hart Street, yet the parish records show no such interment.[16]

Of longer life and greater visibility were Indians from southern Virginia (later Carolina) who arrived in the 1580s as Walter Ralegh tried repeatedly to establish a permanent English plantation. On a scouting expedition in 1584, Captain Philip Amadas persuaded Manteo and Wanchese from the Roanoke area to accompany him back to England, where they would provide practical information for the forthcoming settlement and serve as liaisons between the natives and English colonists. Manteo, a captain or *werowance* of some prominence, was apparently adept in linguistics and diplomacy. He spent most of 1585 with Thomas Hariot, the polymath soon to be the colonists' interpreter, ethnographer, astronomer, biologist and publicist; along with the less cooperative Wanchese, Manteo accompanied Sir Richard Grenville's colonizing expedition of 1585.[17]

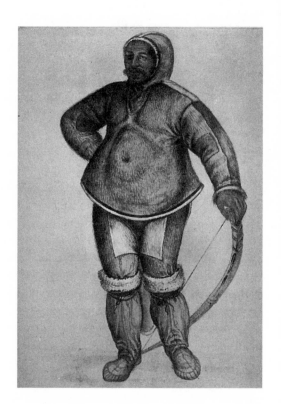

John White's portrait of Kalicho, the Eskimo (Inuit) man captured on Baffin Island by Frobisher's 1577 expedition.

The following year, Manteo hazarded a second European tour. With another coastal native, Towaye, Manteo sailed to England with most of the Roanoke colonists on Sir Francis Drake's passing fleet. In London, Manteo apparently worked closely with Hariot again, as well as with Ralegh and governor-designate John White, to plan the second major colonial enterprise on the southern Virginia coast; and in 1587 Manteo and Towaye returned with Hariot and White to Roanoke, where both Indians apparently lived out their lives.[18] A fourth adult male from Roanoke, whose Indian name is unrecorded, reached England shortly before Manteo and Towaye sailed west. He had been captured by Grenville and would subsequently live in one of Grenville's homes, probably in Bideford, Devonshire, where he appears to have profoundly, if briefly, adopted English culture. Bideford's parish records note the baptism in March 1588 of 'Raleigh, A Wynganditoian'; the following April 'Rawly A man of Wynganditioa' was buried in the parish cemetery.[19]

Seven years after the death of the Virginian who bore his name, Sir Walter brought home one or more natives from his first expedition to Guiana.

According to Ralegh, a chieftain named 'Topiawari . . . freely gaue me his onlie sonne to take with me into England'; a Spanish document adds that the Indian, eighteen to twenty years old, was accompanied by three other Indians; and en route to Guiana, the Spaniard reported, the English 'put ashore two Indians . . . whom they had brought with them from England' – a statement that is partly confirmed by Ralegh's mention of 'my Indian interpreter, which I caried out of England'. This anonymous native had probably been brought home by Jacob Whiddon's scouting expedition for Ralegh in 1594.[20]

These and other Guianan visitors to England diverge from the customary profiles by the apparent voluntarism and often the longevity of their visits, the high incidence of return to their homelands and the preponderance of recorded Christian names and even a few surnames, which may indicate religious conversions. The repatriated Guianans seem also – unlike Epenow of Martha's Vineyard – to have welcomed English explorers. When, for example, Captain Charles Leigh in 1604 attempted a settlement in Guiana, he encountered two Indians 'which had beene before in England, and could speake some English', and employed one of them, named William, as his interpreter. A few months later Leigh sent four Guianan volunteers to his brother in England and claimed that 'if I would, I might have twentie'.[21] Five years later, Robert Harcourt encountered in Guiana an Indian named John (probably 'John Provost', Lawrence Keymis's interpreter in 1596) who 'could speake our language well, and . . . that sometime had been in England, and served Sr. *John Gilbert* many yeeres.' Harcourt's hosts were pleased that he brought with him two natives: '*Martyn* their countryman . . . being aboue foure yeares since hee departed from them', probably one of Leigh's Indians, and '*Anthony Canabre*, who . . . had liued in *England* fourteen yeers', which identifies him as one of Ralegh's recruits in 1595. Harcourt's explorations were greatly aided too by an Indian chief named Leonard Ragapo, who 'hath been heretofore in England with Sr. *Walter Raleigh*, to whom hee beareth great affection . . . and loueth our Nation with all his heart.'[22] When Ralegh finally returned to Guiana in 1617, he sought 'my old sarvant Leonard the Indien who [had] bine with me in Ingland 3 or 4 yeers'; at another place, 'the Cassique was also my sarvant and had lived with mee in the tower 2 yeers'; elsewhere he encountered 'my [Indian] sarvant Harry . . . who had almost forgotten his Inglish'.[23] These tantalizing snippets comprise most of what we know about the nine or more Guianan visitors to England between 1594 and 1617.

Meanwhile, Manteo's usefulness to English colonists at Roanoke encouraged further kidnappings along the North Atlantic coast, especially in the region soon to be named New England. In 1605 Captain George Weymouth seized five Abenakis in Maine. Two of them, Maneddo and Skicowaros, lived for a time in Plymouth with Sir Ferdinando Gorges, captain of the fort. Weymouth's other captives, Tahanedo, Amoret, and Sassacomoit (aka Assacomoit), resided in London – one or more in Cornhill with John Slany, treasurer of the Newfoundland Company, the others in the household of Lord Chief Justice John Popham. Gorges later claimed that Weymouth's captives were 'the meanes under God of putting on foote, and giving life to all our Plantations.'[24] A year after their arrival in England, the Spanish ambassador complained to Philip III that Englishmen were 'teaching and training [the Indians] to say how good that country is for people to go there and inhabit it.'[25]

Most of these Abenakis returned to native soil. Amoret's fate is unknown, but he very likely sailed to Pemaquid with an expedition of 1606 that took Tahanedo; Skicowaros returned in 1607 with a party of colonists under Raleigh Gilbert and George Popham. In 1606 Maneddo and Sassacomoit headed for Maine as scouts and interpreters with Captain Henry Challons[26] but were intercepted by a Spanish fleet in the West Indies; Sassacomoit was wounded in the ensuing battle. English authorities sought to recover 'the two Salvages Manedo and Sasacomett, for that the adventures do hold them of great prize, & to be used to ther great availe for many purposes.' Although Maneddo probably died in captivity, Sassacomoit was soon ransomed and lodged once more with Gorges in Plymouth. In 1614 Sassacomoit accompanied an expedition to Maine, where he disappears from the historical record.[27]

A third American native – after Manteo of Roanoke and Sassacomoit of Sagadahoc – known to have lived in Shakespeare's England on two occasions was Squanto (also known as Tisquantum and perhaps Tantum), who may have endured three translatlantic round trips. If Ferdinando Gorges's questionable recollection can be believed, Squanto first journeyed to England as one of Weymouth's captives and subsequently returned to New England. More certain is Squanto's capture in 1614 by Captain Thomas Hunt, who sold him and about twenty other New England Algonquians in Spain. Squanto somehow reached England a year or so later and lived in London for a time with John Slany. In 1617 Squanto went to Newfoundland, perhaps as an interpreter, but later that year returned to England with Captain Thomas Dermer, who in 1619 took him back to New England once more. Two years later, Squanto befriended the infant Plymouth Colony and lived the remaining eighteen months of his life among the 'pilgrims', who considered him 'a spetiall instrument sent of God for their good.'[28]

Several natives from the Chesapeake Bay area had overlapping sojourns with the northern Indians taken by Weymouth in 1605 or Harlow in 1611. In April 1608 one of Powhatan's men, Namontack – 'his trusty servant, and one of a shrewd subtill capacity', observed Captain John Smith – crossed the Atlantic of his own accord with Captain Christopher Newport. The purpose of the trip, Smith believed, was to discover 'our strength and countries condition'. Namontack seems to have received a shipboard promotion, for in England he was presented as 'the son of an emperor', according to the Spanish ambassador, who was 'amused by the way they honour him, for I hold it for surer that he must be a very ordinary person'. In any event, the visit was brief, for Newport took Namontack back to Powhatan that autumn. Namontack perhaps made a second and longer trip to England, but the evidence is ambiguous.[29]

William Strachey attested to other Virginia Algonquians in England. His 'True Reportory' of the Sea-Venture's wreck on Bermuda and the survivors' subsequent arrival at Jamestown relates Chief Powhatan's displeasure with the Virginia colonists for not giving him a coach and horses, 'for hee had understood by the Indians which were in England, how such was the state of great Werowances, and Lords in England, to ride and visit other great men'. The 'True Reportory' also mentions Kainta, son of a local chieftain, who had recently been captured and was 'sent now [c. July 1610] into England, untill the ships arrive here againe the next Spring'. In a slightly later manuscript (1612), Strachey attributed much of his information about Virginia to 'the Indian Machumps, who was sometyme in England'.[30] Powhatan's informant on English equestrian customs was probably Namontack, but it could have been Machumps or others from the area, their travels unrecorded, who visited England before 1610.

At least one Virginia Indian's life ended in England. Nanawack, recalled in a pamphlet of 1630 as 'a youth sent over by the Lo. De Laware, when hee was Governour there', which dates the native's arrival at 1610–11, lived for 'a yeare or two in houses where hee heard not much of Religion, but saw and heard many times examples of drinking, swearing, and like evills' and so 'remained as hee was a meere Pagan; but after [he] removed into a godly family, hee was strangely altered, grew to understand the principles of Religion, learned to reade, [and] delighted in the Scriptures, Sermons, Prayers, and other Christian duites.' When nearly ready for baptism, Nanawack died.[31] Nothing is known of his burial, nor the fate of two other Virginians whose English sojourns may have overlapped with Nanawack's. Engravings of Eiakintomino and Matahan appeared in early 1615 on a London Company broadside for a 'great standing Lottery'; the Indians need not have posed in person, but the possibility that their images were drawn in London is

The Dutch captions to this painting of Eiakintomino (as translated by Charles T. Gehring) read (above) 'A young man from the Virginias' and (below) 'These Indian birds and animals, together with the young man, were to be seen in 1615, 1616 in St James's Park or zoo which is [illegible] near Westminster before the city of London.' From the autograph album of Michael van Meer. Edinburgh University Library, La.III.283, fol. 254v.

enhanced by a contemporaneous watercolour of Eiakintomino in St James's Park. Because both pictures of this American native probably derive from an earlier original that does not survive,[32] Eiakintomino and Matahan may have been in England for a year or more before 1615.

Scarcely a month after Shakespeare's death in 1616, Rebecca Rolfe, alias Pocahontas, accompanied by her brother-in-law Uttamatomakkin (aka Tomocomo) and several attendants, arrived in London. The Powhatans' year-long visit climaxed the many journeys of American Indians to England in the sixteenth and early seventeenth centuries: it was the largest group of American natives thus far, numbering a dozen or so; it included several women (the first, almost surely, since Arnaq in 1577); and the Powhatan 'princess' was the most prominent North American native to cross the Atlantic since the Brazilian 'king' of the 1530s. Her visit was also, not surprisingly, the most thoroughly recorded. From lodgings in the Bell Savage Inn, we are told, Pocahontas attended the Queen at Whitehall, a dinner at Lambeth Palace, and (perhaps) a private interview with the Earl of Northumberland in the Tower of London; witnessed a Twelfth Night masque; sat for an engraved portrait that was subsequently copied and widely distributed; conversed with an eclectic assortment of English dignitaries, including Ben Jonson, Samuel Purchas, the Bishop of London (John King), and (possibly) Sir Walter Ralegh; and in January 1617, John Chamberlain reported, '[t]he Virginian woman . . . hath ben with the King and graciously used'.[33] Pocahontas's death at Gravesend in March 1617 of pneumonia or tuberculosis brought to a tragic close the era's most triumphant American expedition to England. Shakespeare, one imagines, would have loved the spectacle and lamented the loss.

England's visiting Americans aroused widespread curiosity, partly by their perceived strangeness in clothing, bodily ornaments and behaviour, and partly by their rapid if superficial adoption of English ways and appearance. In 1501 the court of Henry VII marvelled at the Newfoundlanders' animal-skin garments and decorated faces, yet two years later the chronicler Robert Fabian encountered a pair in Westminster Palace dressed in English garb and 'could not discerne [them] from Englishmen, til I was learned what they were'. In the 1580s Manteo's and Wanchese's native costumes seemed out-landish, but they quickly adopted their hosts' sartorial standards, according to a German visitor to London: 'Their usual habit was a mantle of rudely tanned skins of wild animals, no shirts, and a pelt before their privy parts. Now, however, they were clad in brown taffeta.' Early in the seventeenth cen-tury, New England Indians were reported to 'paint their bodies with blacke, their faces, some with red, some with blacke, and some with blew'; others 'weare an ornament of white bone [beads] vpon their head; and Chaines, and Bracelets, and Girdles, and haue their skinne garments laced with them',[34] yet the several Algonquians from the same region who came to England in 1605 soon shed their exterior exoticism. In an era of extravagant English garments, clothes – up to a point – fashioned the man, native or newcomer.

Much harder for the English public to assess or appreciate was the new-comers' linguistic adjustment – a crucial matter for European notions of civility. Fabian noted of the first Americans in England: 'as for speach, I heard none of them utter one word',[35] and Lupold von Wedel, who observed Manteo and Wanchese, complained that 'no one was able to understand them'; the German thought 'they [with an implicit 'therefore'?] made a most childish and silly figure'.[36] Given the paucity of fellow natives from the same language group to converse with, and the English colonizers' determination to create competent interpreters, some Indians in England – Machumps, Squanto, and Anthony Canabre, for example – soon became conversant in English. Others, apparently, did not. Although Manteo soon spoke effective English, which helps to account for the high favour in which he was held by

Hariot and Ralegh, Wanchese resisted his hosts' theology and probably their language as well. He withdrew among his people as soon as he and Manteo returned to Roanoke in 1585 and thereafter shunned the colonists.[37] Pocahontas, in extreme contrast, early acquired the veneer and accompanying approbation of virtual Englishness. By the time she arrived in London, the Indian princess was fluent in English, had converted to the Anglican Church, adopted a Christian name, accepted English clothing and accoutrements, and acceded to English social norms. She also had an English husband; their son Thomas Rolfe would spend his adult life as an English colonist rather than a colonized Virginian. Unlike most of the early American travellers, Pocahontas was a showpiece in England because of her acculturation rather than her 'savage' exoticism.

Since most Americans lived in England for only a few years and had little of Pocahontas's preliminary exposure to English ways and language, they retained for a time their exotic appeal. The prevailing public response to native Americans in England seems to have been widespread fascination on their arrival, a gradual diminution of interest if they remained in towns like Plymouth or Bristol and acquired the outward trappings of Englishmen, with renewed attention when they appeared in native costume or moved to a new locale, especially to London. But most American visitors soon returned to America with an English expedition or succumbed to a premature death in England, where their lack of immunity to European diseases often ensured a short life.

Those who survived rapidly lost some of their physical as well as their cultural distinctiveness. Decorative painting faded without reapplication, and wearing full English clothing and observing English propensities to lighten rather than darken the body's natural colour obliterated much of the 'olive' or 'tawny' hue that came almost entirely from vegetable stains and persistent exposure to sun and wind.[38] The profit-minded owner of a dead Indian might have clad it in skins and wampum and restored its darker shade. There could be a double meaning to Trinculo's urge to have 'this fish painted'.[39]

An Indian corpse may have had substantial appeal, for Jacobean popular culture extended far beyond the theatres that staged the works of Shakespeare and his fellow dramatists. Blackfriars, the Globe and other playhouses were relatively exclusive, with limited engagements, limited seating and standing space, and with entrance fees – however modestly priced for the groundlings. Far more accessible to far more people were England's parades, fairs, masques, wonder cabinets, travelling shows, cock fights and bear-baitings, and, on a smaller scale, local displays of exotica – material, animal, or human (dead or alive) – in busy streets or taverns.[40]

Local and county fairs often lured unsophisticated and sometimes gullible customers like Ben Jonson's Bartholomew Cokes to gawk at real and ersatz wonders. How often those wonders included American Indians is impossible to know. Epenow, for one, was surely on commercial display, as were, perhaps, Cope's Virginians and Frobisher's Eskimos. But the determination of their guardians to groom Indians like Manteo, Sassacomoit and Squanto as guides and interpreters in the colonial enterprise assured that live American natives would seldom be available for exhibition.

The body of a dead Indian, properly preserved, may have been a more plausible showpiece. Of the 35 or more American natives who arrived in Shakespeare's lifetime, the records are usually silent about the final resting place. Some American visitors – Manteo, Namontack, and Leonard Ragapo, for example – unquestionably returned to America; others – Kalicho, Arnaq, Rawly – were buried in English churchyards and presumably remained there. But no records attest to the departure or burial of more than a dozen Americans whose presence in England during Shakespeare's lifetime is certain.[41] With their 'heathen' corpses exempt from customary civil and religious safeguards, some American visitors may have had post-mortem careers as Trinculo's 'dead Indian' or, during their brief lives in London or its environs, contributed – along with one or more Indians who regained their homelands – to Shakespeare's eclectic Caliban. Perhaps *The Tempest*'s 'savage and deformed slave' shared more than an anagrammatic tie to Frobisher's reputedly cannibalistic captive of 1576, who seemed to English eyes a 'strange Infidel, whose like was never seen, red, nor harde of before, and whose language was neyther knowne nor understoode.'[42]

6   The Enchanted Island: Vicarious Tourism in Restoration Adaptations of *The Tempest*

JOSEPH ROACH

Increasingly, pure experience, which leaves no material trace, is manufactured and sold like a commodity.[1]

In the imagination of one popular commentator at least, the beguiling subtitle of late-seventeenth-century adaptations of *The Tempest* seems to have given the Restoration theatre its name. The insinuating tour-guide Tom Brown, gossiping in *Amusements Serious and Comical* (1700), begins his promotion of the London stage with this come-on: 'The Play-House is an Inchanted Island, where nothing appears in Reality what it is, nor what it should be.'[2] Puffing the exotic allure and deceptive magic of the playhouse itself, Brown refers to one of the most successful theatrical productions of the previous quarter-century, *The Tempest, or The Enchanted Island*. The genesis of this popular Shakespearean adaptation was complex. By terms of the royal regulation of theatres of December 1660, *The Tempest* was assigned to Sir William Davenant's company. Davenant secured the assistance of John Dryden in 'improving' the text. Then Thomas Shadwell took credit for converting it into a semi-opera under the same title. To this collaboration, a number of musical additions and revisions, fitted to changing tastes and conditions, subsequently adhered, including at least one song by Henry Purcell, 'Dear pretty youth'. Tom Brown's reiterated description of the London stage itself thus conforms to the mutating textual and theatrical history of the Restoration *Tempest*, as well as to the conditions of Prospero's magical (and consummately theatrical) isle: 'I have told you already, that the Play-House was the Land of Enchantment, the Country of Metamorphosis, and perform'd it with the greatest speed imaginable.'[3]

Each revision of *The Tempest* discovered a brave new world, with such creations in it. The Davenant and Dryden version, which premiered in 1667, introduced innovative couplings: Ariel finds a lover in Milcha; Caliban finds a sister monster named Sycorax; and Miranda and Ferdinand find their romance doubled and inverted by another couple – Dorinda is Miranda's sister, added to provide a love interest for Hippolito, a displaced prince raised separately by Prospero to sexual maturity without having seen a woman. In 1674 Shadwell, changing very little of the 1667 dialogue, lent his name to a production in which various composers and the machinists associated with the Duke's Company, newly ensconced in the technically well-equipped Dorset Garden theatre, intensified Davenant and Dryden's already highly successful incorporation of music and scenery.[4] Calling for an onstage orchestra of 24 violins, 'with the Harpsicals and Theorbo's', the stage directions for the opening scene describe

> a thick Cloudy Sky, a very Rocky Coast, and a Tempestuous Sea in perpetual Agitation. This Tempest (suppos'd to be rais'd by Magick) has many dreadful Objects in it, as several Spirits in horrid Shapes, flying down amongst the Sailers, then rising and crossing in the Air. And when the Ship is sinking, the whole House is darken'd, and a Shower of Fire falls upon 'em. This is accompanied with Lightning and several Claps of Thunder to the End of the Storm.[5]

The collaborators made available to the English public the glories of baroque stagecraft, sights and sounds otherwise and elsewhere fit for kings. With their flying machines and pyrotechnics, the producers of *The Enchanted Island* quite possibly could have been quoting the extraordinary *fête* staged for Louis XIV in the gardens of Versailles called *Les Plaisirs de l'île enchantée* (1664). In so doing, they expanded the franchise of a privileged spectatorial position – the right to see everything, even mysteries, clearly. In the fullness of time, bourgeois audiences repaid their efforts with continued patronage. Long after the age of absolute monarchs had passed, the operatic version of *The Tempest* (or variations of it) retained a place in the repertory, its courtly erotic symmetries forestalling numerous efforts to bring back an unadulterated version of Shakespeare's text. The rôles of Dorinda and Hippolito held the stage until 1838, when *The Tempest* finally reclaimed the last bits of *The Enchanted Island* as they slipped beneath the waves of the rising tide of Bardolatry. Already in the waning years of sacral monarchy, however, Shakespeare had become an object of veneration, a cultural surrogate for the royal sovereign: in the Prologue to *The Tempest, or the Enchanted Island*, the improvers wrote, 'Shakespear's Pow'r is sacred as a King's', but they invoked that authority only to manufacture and market a very different kind of theatrical experience.

Whereas Shakespeare's title dramatizes a sensational event, the Restoration adapters' subtitle popularizes a destination. This combination of event and destination points toward the growing theatrical phenomenon of vicarious tourism in the late seventeenth and eighteenth centuries. In the history of popular performance, tourism emerged as vicarious experience long before the safety and affordability of travel made actual tours possible for large numbers of people. Vicarious tourism is the elaboration of the stage into a medium that is both a means of imaginary conveyance to exotic locales and an exotic locale in itself. Vicarious tourism occurs when the commodified experience of a local event substitutes for the direct experience of a remote destination. Such a convergence of practices may be traced through a complicated genealogy that includes the proliferation of public ethnographic exhibitions of many kinds, from Dorset Garden to Disney World,[6] but for the purpose of the present argument the most pertinent are theatrical events that explicitly offer up the actors as surrogates for 'Natives'.

Islands have often been imagined as particularly promising backdrops for such transformative performances. In an essay on *Les Plaisirs de l'île enchantée*, Orest Ranum notes that received geographic opinion regarded islands, especially 'volcanic southern islands', as encounter zones where ungovernable copulation between different species produced natural mutations but also natural attractions.[7] Paradoxically, islands also enter into the popular imaginary as scenes of sexual innocence and 'unspoiled' cultural authenticity, the attraction of which is an historic mainstay of vicarious (and actual) tourism.[8] Anticipating the now familiar structure of modern tourist performance (as explored by Dean MacCannell in the sociological language of Erving Goffman), vicarious tourism on the early modern stage makes the spectator acutely aware of the dichotomy between the 'front region' and the 'back region' of the playhouse. Touristic performance offers its consumers 'staged authenticity' in the form of 'front-region behavior', which provokes their desire to know about the 'real' behind-the-scenes truths belonging to the local culture. Everyone despises tourists, MacCannell observes, especially other tourists; and their self-loathing and consequent disavowals take the form of a need to learn the secrets of the Natives, who (somehow, somewhere) possess the only authenticity that is *not* staged.[9] This relationship of tourist and native puts a premium on the layered disclosure of secrets, and the resulting agon of information and mystery necessarily offers itself as a performance. 'In the theatre of secrets', notes Barbara Kirshenblatt-Gimblett, 'hiding and showing are mutually constitutive':

One is necessary for the other, even though they may not be equally elaborated. This peekaboo writ large creates critical discontinuities in the field of awareness, thereby giving shape not only to social life but also to knowing and to aesthetic experience. Little dramas of hiding and showing structure our perception and attention. They create channels and pathways for transmission. They regulate the rhythm, pace, range, and distribution of value.[10]

Tourism, vicarious or otherwise, divides the world into two kinds of people: the tourist, who, however despicable, is the one who is entitled to know; and the native, who, however circumspect, is the one who is known. The first may ask questions about the secrets; the other must somehow answer or evade them. In the modern evolution of spectatorial positions, the tourist is a proxy king. The goal that beckons the sovereign tourist, whose point of departure is a fallen world, thus typically takes the form of 'innocence'; but innocence, once visited, must perforce recede further still, retreating into more remote 'back regions', which succeed one another as the ultimate, yet ever more fugitive destination of the quest for the Grail of authenticity. This recession appears to the spectator as a series of transformations – metamorphoses – as discoveries accumulate and secrets mutate into commonplaces. It is often said that the only true paradise is the one that has been lost. For purposes of understanding *The Tempest* in the context provided by Tom Brown's 'Inchanted Island', that truism should be amended to reflect the fact that the only true paradise is the one that the tourists, accidental or otherwise, have (so far) left unspoiled.

The full title of Brown's *Amusements Serious and Comical, Calculated for the Meridian of London* is significant in the history of vicarious tourism as performance. The word *meridian* means a representation of a great circle or half circle of the celestial sphere, numbered for longitude (as on a map or globe), passing through the poles at its zenith. A meridian can mark the longitudinal coordinate of a place, and it can show one aspect of the relationship of that place to an entire world. The imagery of navigation indicates that Brown's text is a travel narrative. It fixes the coordinates of a voyage across town, as if that town were the globe, charting a course through 'The Court', 'The Walks', 'Bedlam' and 'Westminster-Hall', bound for the archipelago of the theatre district and its insular playhouse. The professed purpose of the entire voyage is touristic and ethnographic:

London is a World by it self. We daily discover in it more New Countries, and surprising Singularities, than in all the Universe besides. There are among the *Londoners* so many Nations differing in Manners, Customs, and Religions, that the Inhabitants themselves don't know a quarter of them.

But on this grand multicultural tour, Brown finds his definitive ethnograph-ical object in his encounter with the actors, as he describes the performance of their bizarre and simple-minded rituals of staged authenticity:

> Let us now speak a Word or so, of the Natives of this Country [the play-house], and the Stock of Wit and Manners by which they Maintain themselves, and Ridicule the whole World besides. The people are all somewhat Whimsical and Giddy-Brained: When they Speak, they Sing, when they Walk, they Dance, and very often do both when they have no mind to it.[11]

Reflexivity about such second-order encounters makes the familiarity of the experience of theatre-going seem strange, even as it makes the strangeness of the scenes they represent seem more familiar. On this 'Inchanted Island' the natives (actors and actresses) will change themselves into anything in order to ensure that the spectators will be induced to return:

> The Play-House was the Land of Enchantment, the Country of Metamorphosis, and perform'd it with the greatest speed imaginable. Here, in the twinkling of an Eye, you shall see Men transform'd into Demi-gods, and Goddesses made as true Flesh and Blood as our Common Women. Here Fools by slight of hand are converted into Wits, Honest Women into errand Whores, and which is most miraculous, Cowards into valiant Heroes, and rank Cocquets and Jilts into as Chast and Vertuous Mistresses as a Man would desire to put his Knife into.[12]

The emphasis of Brown's final image suggests that a major draw of this mag-ical destination is what late-twentieth-century readers might recognize as sexual tourism. It also suggests that the power of the tourist's gaze is felt at a distance, setting changes in motion by the celerity of desire across space, something like the communication that links Prospero's will to Ariel's per-formance of it. What Brown describes, therefore, is an early modern version of the commodification of experience itself. This includes the experience of innocence and the experience of losing it, a metamorphosis that the 'Inchanted Island' of the playhouse was especially good at marketing and that The Enchanted Island was created especially to exploit. 'Modern man', MacCannell concludes, 'has been condemned to look elsewhere, every-where, for his authenticity, to see if he can catch a glimpse of it reflected in the simplicity, poverty, chastity or purity of others.'[13] The result of the suc-cessful commodification of this experience by the Duke's Company was a runaway hit.

Restoration production records are spotty, especially before the introduction of daily newspapers in 1702–3, but the available evidence suggests that *The Enchanted Island* was one of the most lucrative properties as well as the most popular play in the repertory. Samuel Pepys had trouble finding a good seat on the opening night, and he couldn't stay away from repeated showings, during the intermissions of which he undertook to memorize samples of the tunes and dances.[14] Many years later the old prompter of the Duke's company remembered the production for its scenery, its magical effects, and its box-office:

> *The Tempest*, or the Inchanted Island, made into an Opera by Mr Shadwell, having all New in it; as Scenes, Machines; particularly, one Scene Painted with *Myriads* of *Ariel* Spirits; and another flying away, with a Table furnished out with Fruits, Sweet meats, and all sorts of Viands; just when Duke *Trinculo* and his Companions, were going to Dinner; all things perform'd in it so Admirably well, that not any succeeding Opera got more Money.[15]

Summoned from beneath the stage by Caliban and Sycorax in Act IV. ii (p. 59), this phantom feast might be supposed to presage the guilty pleasures of so much escapist spectacle that has followed it: rich in sensuous appeal but short on nourishment. The scale of *The Enchanted Island*'s success was sufficient to prompt the rival company at the Theatre Royal to mount a burlesque version called *The Mock-Tempest; or, the Enchanted Castle* by the erstwhile milliner Thomas Duffett. The 'Enchanted Castle' of the title is a particularly ill-run brothel, which alternates by rapid scene changes with Bridewell prison. The mock-Prospero sends Ariel flying off with the warning that the rival Duke's Theatre will steal all his magical effects: 'Then do as I commanded, but make hast [sic] least the Conjurers of to'other House steal the Invention – thou knowest they snatch all Ingenious tricks.'[16] In his account of Duffett's literary career in the context of the early modern competition to commodify experience, Gerard Langbaine candidly assesses the motives of the producers: 'The Design of this Play was to draw the Town from the Duke's Theatre, who for a considerable time had frequented the admirable revis'd Comedy called *The Tempest*.'[17] Langbaine alludes to the glamour of the original audience, whom he supposes to have been inhabitants of the fashionable 'Town', a point made by Pepys in connection with his hard won vantage-point on opening night: 'close by my Lady Dorsett and a great many great ones: the house mighty full, the King and Court there'. Trailing the stardust of proximate celebrity, Pepys's summary remark reveals a good deal about the vicariousness of the experience he had purchased: 'the most innocent play that I ever saw'.[18]

There has been provocative speculation on the political double meanings of 'innocence' in *The Tempest, or the Enchanted Island* – whether Prospero stands in for one or more of the Stuarts in a complicated allegory of legitimacy, dislocation and return.[19] Some or all of these suggestions may be well-founded, but for purposes of the argument about vicarious tourism, the commodification of 'Shakespeare' makes each audience member a sovereign in his or her transactions with the event: innocence is what they are buying as well as losing; authenticity is what they are taking away with them as well as bestowing on the performance. Like Miranda and Hippolito, what they want is what they have never seen before but also what they know they are fully entitled to. In a parallel scene of enduring Prospero's tutelage (a book-end lecture to the one, retained from Shakespeare, in which Miranda's attention deficit so amusingly manifests itself), Dryden and Davenant stage Hippolito's prelapsarian authenticity as a front-region extravaganza:

> HIPPOLITO Sir, I have heard you say, no Creature liv'd
> Within this Isle, but those which Man was Lord of,
> Why should then I fear?
> PROSPERO But here are Creatures which I nam'd not to thee,
> Who share Man's Sovereignty by Nature's Laws,
> And oft depose him from it.
> HIPPOLITO What are those Creatures, Sir?
> PROSPERO Those dangerous Enemies of Men call'd Women.
> HIPPOLITO Women! I never heard of them before. (p. 21)

Generally speaking, Eden serves as an unbeatably popular destination for the vicarious tourist. With that certainty in mind, Dryden, as the house playwright for the rival company, tried to counter the Dorset Garden *Tempest* of 1674 with his own operatic adaptation of Milton's *Paradise Lost*, which he called *The State of Innocence*, but the scenic demands scared off the managers.[20] So *The Enchanted Island*, staged by the Natives of 'The Inchanted Island', monopolized the spectators with its tantalizing secrets and revealing disclosures, staging their authenticity both in the scenes and behind them.

In at least one notorious instance connected with *The Tempest*, the manipulation of front-region and back-region experience was quite literal: the gendered dramaturgical economy of the Restoration stage assigned the part of Hippolito to a woman as a 'breeches' role. Such a leg show defamiliarizes every word the character speaks, especially when he emphasises his physical ignorance of women. A number of historians have speculated that the Duke's Company entrusted the role to Mary 'Moll' Davis, whose singing of the ballad 'My Lodging it is on the Cold Ground' in Davenant's *The Rivals* in the same season as *The Tempest* brought her to the attention of Charles II: 'She perform'd that so Charmingly, that not long after, it Rais'd her from her Bed on the Cold Ground, to a Bed Royal.'[21] The authoritative *Biographical Dictionary* assigns Davis the rôle of Ariel,[22] which would have created a different, but not wholly different, impact: the King's magical power to effect action at a distance might still take on an erotic as well as a political meaning. The Prologue to *The Enchanted Island*, in announcing that the actress magically transforming herself into a boy who has never seen a woman can only be found out for what she truly is 'abed' (that is, by means of a backstage liaison), brings off a very complicated dirty joke that turns on the audience's prurient knowledge of the front region and the back region of the playhouse, in which the dressing rooms were, notoriously, open and available for tours:

> But, if for Shakespeare we your grace implore,
> We for our theatre shall want it more:
> Who by dearth of Youths are forc'd t'employ
> One of our Women to present a Boy,
> And that's a transformation, you will say,
> Exceeding all the Magick in the Play.

In the place that Brown called 'the Country of Metamorphosis', the recession of secrets invites the privileged spectator into the back region for a vicarious tour in the footsteps of a king:

> Or if your fancy will be farther led
> To find her Woman, it must be abed.

That such a 'fancy' could be realized as an actual tour is attested by Pepys. On one of his forays to *The Tempest*, he arranged to go backstage to get the actor Henry Harris to help with his transcription of the 'Echo' song, 'and in going thither, had the pleasure to see the Actors in their several dresses, especially the seamen and monster, which were very droll.'[23] The 'monster' is assumed to have been Caliban.[24] Pepys's encounter with Brown's 'Natives' on a backstage tour enacts the classic moment of estrangement in tourist performance, when the artifice of the front region is penetrated as the secrets of the back region are brought forward to become the performance itself. The last entry in Pepys's *Diary* concerning *The Tempest* records only disappointment: the performance was 'ill done' in the absence of Moll Davis, for she had left the Duke's Theatre for the King's bed, and apparently Pepys's 'innocence' went with her.[25]

Tom Brown left a substantial footnote to his account of the staged

Anne Bracegirdle as 'The Indian Queen' in either the title rôle in the operatic version of Dryden and Howard's heroic drama or as 'Semernia' in Behn's *The Widow Ranter.* Bernard Lens II's mezzotint of *c.* 1695.

authenticity of 'The Inchanted Island' by its 'Natives'. His memoir of the actress Anne Bracegirdle offers an occasion for summing up vicarious tourism on the Restoration stage, even though it has no direct bearing on performances of *The Tempest per se*. Known as the 'Romantick Virgin' because she kept her love-life discreetly but tantalizingly veiled,[26] Bracegirdle was widely considered the model of English beauty, her dark brown hair and famous blush, an 'involuntary Flushing in her Breast', setting off the transparent whiteness of her skin.[27] The most famous visual depiction of Bracegirdle, significantly, is of her exotic appearance in the rôle of 'the Indian Queen'. This image exists in several mezzotints, including one that shows her, fabulously overdressed, attended by parasol and train-bearing children of colour and another solo portrait of her in the same rôle. She wears the plumes and ornaments that popular imagination accepted as authentic Native American dress, and indeed some pieces of which may have been among those that the narrator of Aphra Behn's *Oroonoko* claims to have brought back from Surinam for use in the original production of Dryden and Howard's *The Indian Queen* (1664).

In her befeathered glory Bracegirdle looks as if she has been recruited from the population of an enchanted island, and in fact she was adopted as a child and raised within earshot of the theatre by the actor–manager Thomas Betterton and his wife. The elaboration and intensity of the fantasies she inspired are best studied in the extraordinary rôles that William Congreve, who loved her passionately but frustratedly, wrote for her, including Mrs Millamant in *The Way of the World* (1700). In his sardonic account of what contemporary gossips regarded as the unconsummated sexual liaison between Bracegirdle and Congreve, Tom Brown discloses his own touristic fantasy about the teasingly available and yet ultimately elusive beauty. Pornographically, he places himself (and implicitly his readers and Bracegirdle's audiences in the theatre as well) in the rôle of the bewitched but physically unrequited playwright. Performing what Barbara Kirshenblatt-Gimblett calls a 'peekaboo writ large', he follows the actress backstage to her dressing room, pointing out the highlights of her lingerie on his guided tour:

> But 'tis the way of the World, to have an Esteem for the fair Sex, and She looks to a Miracle when she is acting a part in one of his own Plays ... Look upon him once more I say, if She goes to her Shift, 'tis Ten to One but he follows her, not that I would say for never so much to take up her Smock; he Dines with her almost ev'ry day, yet She's a Maid, he rides out with her, and visits her in Publick and Private, yet She's a Maid; if I had not particular respect for her, I should go near to say he lies with her, yet She's a Maid.[28]

This recession reiterates the process of mimetic desire out of which the intimate fantasy world of 'The Inchanted Island' perpetuated itself in the public imagination: the vicarious tourists, whose spokesperson and guide is Tom Brown, learn to want what Congreve wants: that which he cannot have himself as a man, but which he alone as a playwright can give them: the 'Romantick Virgin' with his words on her lips.

Such an action at a distance or 'Metamorphosis' characterizes the performance of vicarious tourism in Restoration theatre, a performance to which *The Tempest, or The Enchanted Island* gave both a name and an exemplary instance. Brown illuminates this process as he seeks knowledge of the back regions of the performance, worrying the imagined disjunction between staged authenticity and true innocence, the final destination towards which he is directed, at which he will never arrive, but in the name of which he books the popular tour. The contribution of Shakespeare's *Tempest* to this conception was to provide both an imagined locus – the enchanted island; and an action – the transformation of a state of innocence. Its success hastened the veneration of the author as the eventual touristic centrepiece of the 'heritage industry'. Prospero's famous speech at the end of the masque in Act IV, scene i of Shakespeare's play might therefore be read as a valediction to the magical powers of art prior to the systematic commercialization of leisure and the rise of the scenic stage: they are 'melted into air, into thin air.' Bringing down the costs of pure vicarious experience from Louis XIV's internationally famous *fête*, but now aggressively marketing 'the baseless fabric of this vision' (*The Tempest*, IV.i.150–51), Davenant, Dryden, Shadwell and Duffett could organize and launch tour packages toward the scenic vanishing-point of the world's authentic secrets.

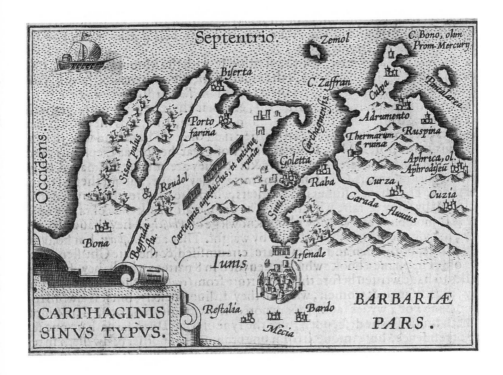

Introduction

The explicit geography of *The Tempest* points primarily to Italy and North Africa. The place names mentioned in the text include Milan, Naples, Tunis, Carthage and Algiers. And the ship that is wrecked in the opening scene is making the return journey to Naples after Claribel's wedding to the King of Tunis, which places Prospero's island, if we are being literal-minded, somewhere in the Sicilian archipelago. Most of the sources and analogues that have been proposed for *The Tempest*, moreover, derive from European and Mediterranean rather than English or American texts.[1] The region explored in this section was once seen as the ground for the unified, traditional readings that New World materials would challenge and complicate. In the last decade, however, Europe and the Mediterranean have begun to generate readings and appropriations of surprising currency and complexity.

[1]

When Shakespeare and his contemporaries wanted to represent other European powers (or to represent English power through indirect means), they most often turned to Italy for the settings of their plays. While *The Tempest* is not, strictly speaking, set in Italy, Jan Kott was not alone in considering it 'the most Italian of all Shakespeare's plays',[2] and Robin Kirkpatrick's essay suggests that it offers what may be the period's most sophisticated engagement with the legacies of Renaissance Italy. Kirkpatrick here elaborates on the poem that opened our collection of essays, and extends his earlier work on what used to be called (in yet another nautical metaphor) the 'crosscurrents' between English and Italian culture.[3]

In his account, the guiding spirits of *The Tempest* are Guarini and Machiavelli. The former's generic innovations (especially with pastoral tragicomedy) made a strong impact in England toward the end of Shakespeare's career;[4] and the latter's ruthless political theories were both imitated and parodied on the Renaissance stage. These two authors seem to preside over the island – like the personified figure of Revenge who controls the action in Thomas Kyd's *The Spanish Tragedy*, remaining on stage for the whole of the play – accounting for its unusually disorienting and violent version of the pastoral romance.[5] While the pastoral was usually political in the Renaissance, few arcadias are as full of sufferings, curses, drownings and coups as this one.

From this perspective, the play belongs less with the love stories in the comedies it appeared alongside in the First Folio than the turbulent dynastic dramas represented in the history plays (and played out, as *The Tempest* was written, at other European courts).[6] The play famously begins with a series of challenges to the political order, and virtually every character is involved (directly or indirectly, tragically or comically) in a plot to increase their power. In a careful reading of *The Tempest*'s political contexts, David Norbrook suggested that 'The later Shakespeare, and Jacobeans in general, were tending to give more and more sociological specificity to Italian settings by drawing on the discourses by which Italians represented their own history. Particularly influential were Machiavelli and Guicciardini, who offered a radically sceptical analysis of political power which undercut any claim by monarchy to be natural.'[7] In *The Tempest*, Prospero's usurping brother Antonio has furnished the most obvious example of Machiavellian cynicism in action. However, Kirkpatrick also finds echoes in Prospero's own language and behaviour of Machiavelli's philosophy – and specifically his theory of the *arcana imperii* or 'mysteries of state'.[8]

For Machiavelli, these *arcana* were the secret arts employed by rulers in order to establish and maintain their power. Like Prospero's 'art' they were often severe, and part of their force was their very secrecy. (In *The Tempest*, Prospero may promise to drown his book and bury his staff, but he never reveals the mysteries of his art to his bewildered guests.) They appeared, as Peter Donaldson put it, 'like an artificial or fictive miracle, secret, sudden, extraordinary, apparently supernatural'.[9] Which is exactly what Prospero effects at the climax of the reconciliation scene when he pulls the curtain back to reveal Ferdinand and Miranda playing chess. At the sight of his nephew, resurrected from a watery death, Sebastian cries out, 'A most high miracle!' (V.i.177); and as the ship itself resurfaces a few lines later, Alonso concludes, 'These are not natural events, they strengthen / From strange to stranger' (V.i.227–8).

As this episode implies, the tradition of the *arcana imperii* was linked with both magic and theatrical illusion. And with this *The Tempest* once again proves uncanny in its ability to anticipate later texts and events. In the 1620s and '30s, the leading theorist of the mysteries of state was the Parisian diplomat and librarian Gabriel Naudé.[10] Naudé was a great debunker of the occult tradition and wrote an early work that explained away all purported acts of magic from the past as illusions generated by a superior knowledge of nature, by those who wanted to bring about political or religious change. He warns that with ancient magicians like Orpheus and Zoroaster (as with Prospero) it is difficult to distinguish between magic as knowledge, magic as metaphor, and magic as political ruse.[11] In his later book on the *arcana imperii* (first published in 1639 and eventually translated into English in 1711) he associates the *coup d'état* with the *coup de théâtre*, emphasizing the rôle of dramatic illusion in the mysteries of state. Although he never mentions *The Tempest*, Naudé's description of the politician's theatrical control over nature could have been written with Shakespeare's play in front of him. 'As if he were plac'd upon some high Tower', the magus–prince

> looks down upon the whole World, which appears to him as a Theatre, ill regulated, and full of Confusion, where some act Comedies, and others Tragedies, and where he may intervene; *Tanquam Deus aliquis ex machina*, like some Divinity from a Machine, as often as he pleases, or the variety of Occasions shall persuade him to do it.[12]

As with Shakespeare's use of Montaigne or More, the magic and theatricality of the *coup d'état* lead to a fundamentally sceptical argument about the nature of power – which, for Naudé, amounts to no more than political violence masked by the illusions of magic. Shakespeare was, of course, the 'King's playwright',[13] and *The Tempest* can be seen on several levels as a tribute to King James. But in drawing on these political themes, Shakespeare made Prospero's island a place not of inherent, absolute rule but of competing political alternatives.

This may, as Roland Greene explains, be a function of its very island-ness. As Shakespeare's 'island play', *The Tempest* participates in the imaginative logic that characterized representations of islands in European atlases, novels and travellers' tales. Since the epics of Homer and Virgil, and especially during the Renaissance and Enlightenment, islands were sites *par excellence* of encounters and transformations. What seemed natural on the mainland gave way, on the island, to alternative stories and new perspectives.

[2]

It is easy to fall back on the phrase, 'Prospero's island', and to overlook not only Caliban's claims but the figure on whom those claims depend – the

Algerian witch Sycorax, who was exiled to the island, gave birth to Caliban, imprisoned Ariel, and died, all well before the beginning of the play's action. We are told most of what we know about her by Prospero and (like Claribel and Prospero's wife, the play's other missing women) she does not even appear in the cast of characters.[14] Yet, as Marina Warner argues in her essay, Sycorax remains an important presence in *The Tempest*. What she brings to the island is not so much a 'black' magic against which Prospero's 'white' magic can be set (and over which it can triumph), but a competing discourse of magical transformation. Diabolical, unstable and grotesque, Sycorax's power still haunts Prospero's island after she is gone.

Sycorax invokes the memory of two witches from the classical Mediterranean: Circe and Medea. But she also points to an emerging repertory of images and issues from the New World. In this respect, Warner's essay looks back to our first section and ahead to our last, suggesting that Sycorax can serve as an unlikely emblem for the play's multiple locations. As Diane Purkiss has observed,

> for early modern Europeans ... the category of witch and the category of native were elastic enough to contain one another. Like early modern genre categories, the categories of otherness available were not as distinct to Shakespeare as they might have seemed to us ... *The Tempest* represents the last moment of innocence in which a New World native woman, an Old World witch, and a classical world witch might be the same thing ...[15]

Another figure who not only has a ghostly presence in *The Tempest* but has been translated between the New World, the Old World, and the classical world is Virgil.[16] Editors of *The Tempest* have long acknowledged its allusions to the *Aeneid*; and some accounts (including Donna Hamilton's earlier forays on the subject) have found in Shakespeare's play a deep engagement with Virgil's great Mediterranean epic. Recent work has emphasized the ways in which Virgil was appropriated in Renaissance Europe to authorize its educational and imperial programmes. Hamilton here takes a different approach to the topic, returning to the editions of the *Aeneid* that were available in Shakespeare's England. By tracing the timing of their publication and the communities responsible for their production, she reveals the extent to which the *Aeneid* was (by the time Shakespeare came to it) already implicated in the politics of post-Reformation England.[17]

[3]

To Shakespeare and his contemporaries, the Mediterranean represented more than just the source of the *Aeneid* and other classical texts, and the last few years have seen some forceful attempts to recover *The Tempest's* contemporary Mediterranean contexts and its representation of the international relations in what Andrew Hess has labelled the 'forgotten frontier' between Europe and North Africa. In the fifteenth and sixteenth centuries this frontier was the site of active contact between European and Ottoman rulers, involving both cultural exchange and military confrontation.[18] While England's rôle in these transactions was relatively marginal (compared to that of the Habsburg Empire), by the time *The Tempest* was written – as Hess here explains – the English sense of and relationship to the Mediterranean was particularly charged. During Queen Elizabeth's reign there was considerable traffic – both mercantile and diplomatic – between the English and the Ottomans;[19] and they contributed both personnel and technology to the violent and intensely multicultural pirate community that would have a major impact on the balance of power in the region – and a considerable presence in plays and popular literature back in England. By 1604, English and North Africans were working together in the crews of pirate ships; and after 1610 Mediterranean piracy could be described as 'systematic plunder transcending religious barriers'.[20]

Richard Wilson has boldly argued that this environment of rampant piracy (with its accompanying discourses of adventure, slavery, and nautical mastery) is more resonant for *The Tempest* than the Virginia literature.[21] Building on a similar argument, Jerry Brotton's essay explores the play's Mediterranean contexts by turning to an unexpected source – tapestries.[22] These lavish displays of European artistry and ambition were (like the Restoration *Tempest* in Roach's account) a form of vicarious travel and (like Hamilton's account of the English *Aeneid*) a vehicle for shuttling between the past and the present. Like *The Tempest* itself, they offer a complex picture of the border politics of sixteenth-century Europe.

7 The Italy of *The Tempest*

ROBIN KIRKPATRICK

Shakespeare himself almost certainly never travelled to Italy. Nor is there any evidence that he could read Italian. To presume, however, that he could not over-estimates the difficulty which his contemporaries generally experienced in acquiring a reading knowledge of the language and suggests, furthermore, an unlikely limitation in Shakespeare's own linguistic and intellectual curiosity. Knowledge of the Italian world would have been available through the information disseminated by merchants, cultural travellers, political propagandists, spies and exiles. Equally, the achievements of Italian literature had for generations been an open book to scholarly and passionate readers. Information and opinion may often have been distorted, either by Italophilia or else by patriotic animus against an older and Catholic culture. But misrepresentation itself ensured that, alongside scholarly enthusiasm and political or economic report, the English mind had developed by Shakespeare's time a potently self-generating and chimeric myth of Italy.

Whether as myth, literary influence or talking-point, Italy undoubtedly occupied a central position in Shakespeare's imagination. No less than half of his plays are set in Italy or draw on Italian sources. Nor (in the account I shall offer) is Shakespeare's rôle in this relationship merely that of passive recipient. For if Shakespeare – like many of his contemporaries – recognized in Italy a culture that was simultaneously foundational and foreign to English thinking, he also demonstrates a remarkable capacity to analyse the implications of this legacy. *The Tempest* is the last and most original in a life-long series of experiments, responding to both the political thinking and artistic models that Renaissance Italy had fostered.

Of the many Italians with whom Shakespeare engages in his work (including Petrarch, Boccaccio, Ariosto, Cinthio and possibly Bruno) two in particular will dominate the following pages: Machiavelli, who wrote at the beginning of the High Renaissance, and Guarini, who emerged at its conclusion. From these originals – the one a hard-headed philosopher, the other the author of a play concerning nymphs and shepherds – Shakespeare in *The Tempest* derives his own unlikely compound in which two closely related questions are at issue: the first concerns the conception of space (or, more specifically, the way in which human persons envisage other persons in the spaces we mutually occupy), and the second concerns the view we take of the human person *per se*. These questions are ultimately ethical in character, and bear on the connections that may be established between ethical and artistic practice. Renaissance humanism characteristically affirms the validity of such connections; but in doing so, humanists often attempted (as Prospero may once have done) to isolate the ethical and artistic sphere from the working world of history. Shakespeare himself does not. We may, then, begin with a brief account of the currents – political and cultural – that *The Tempest*, knowingly or otherwise, negotiates.

[1]

In the last decade of the fifteenth century, France invaded the Italian peninsula in pursuit of ancient dynastic claims and thus aroused a response from the Habsburg Empire (shortly to be joined by marriage to the Kingdom of Spain), resonating in a series of vicious wars that only concluded in 1559. In the course of these wars, the political culture of the Italian city-states disintegrated; and it was this culture that, in the fourteenth century, had generated the civic humanism and educational programmes on which originally the Renaissance movement had thrived.

It is significant (when our theme is *The Tempest*) that the two main targets of the Franco-Spanish wars were Naples and Milan. Naples – an Angevin Kingdom until the succession of Alfonso I in 1443 – seems to have stirred a taste for chivalric adventure in the French monarch Charles VIII; though Naples was ostensibly the first step in a renewed Crusade to the Holy Land, it had also a reputation for its high Gothic culture and festive elegance. But Imperial Spain, asserting its own rights, realized that Milan was the true political target. Milan was a modern, almost industrial city, the product of centuries of absolutist rule, sitting now on the road that joined the Germanic and Iberian territories of the Holy Roman Empire.

By 1559 Milan and Naples both lay under the dominion of the Habsburgs; and most of the rest of Italy was drawn into the same sphere of influence. One-time city-states became increasingly the clients of foreign powers, degenerating into a constellation of small courts often rent by intrigue and instability. Rome, it is true, came to assume new importance as a centre of international activity. But with the Counter-Reformation, allegiances against the Protestant cause ensured a fierce association of Rome and Spain. Milan itself, in Shakespeare's time, reflected these allegiances, being ruled in effect by Cardinal Carlo Borromeo (1538–84), a saintly but rigorous disciplinarian in his dealings with both clergy and laity. To the Elizabethan Englishman, Milan would have seemed as dark, dangerous, and impenetrable as any country in the Eastern Block at the height of the Cold War.[1]

In the sixteenth century, then, Italy came to experience (in sophisticated, even collaborationist form) something akin to the colonial oppression that Spain contemporaneously was visiting on its American empire. Understandably if unsympathetically, English writers responded to Italy's calamities with a mixture of patriotic *schadenfreude*, imaginative prurience and polemical certitude, scavenging in the ruins of Italy for stories of treachery and lunacy.[2] Milan itself may not have been a favoured site for this hunt, and Ben Jonson suggests a reason when setting *The Case is Altered* (1609) in Milan against the background of the Franco-Spanish invasions: 'You know how far our Milan laws extend / For punishment of liars' (V.xii.85–6); authority in Milan seems ever likely to inhibit displays of interesting deceit. Yet England had heard of Milan. Bolingbroke – Shakespeare's Henry IV – spent part of his exile there; and Chaucer viewed the regime of the city with suspicion as dangerously authoritarian (in contrast to the broadly Republican Florence, which resisted Milanese expansionism in the second half of the fourteenth century). Notably, this suspicion incriminates Petrarch, one of the earliest of the Florentine humanists, who willingly accepted the favour of the Visconti despotism. In an attempt – remotely anticipating Prospero's own – to blink at worldly cares in pursuit of 'secret studies', Petrarch's complaisance foreshadows a union, very familiar in the Renaissance, between scholars and absolutist patrons.[3]

Of all English responses to Italian politics in this period none is more familiar than that which gleefully represents the archetypal Italian as a 'Machiavillain' – demonic, unscrupulous and fiendishly resourceful. Yet such a view grossly under-estimates the complexity of the political and the intellectual issues that the invasions of Italy had aroused. Effectively, this period marked the beginning of a new European order, dominated by ambitious nation states and commercial imperialism; and Machiavelli (in *propria* rather than *dramatis persona*) was driven by his vision of this dire alteration to an analysis all too acute in its realism for most of his successors to tolerate.

It is worth recalling (with *The Tempest* in mind) that Machiavelli was a humanist, scholar and author of brilliant comedies who would ritually wash his hands (as one imagines Prospero doing) and change his clothes before entering his study to commune with the classics. In Machiavelli's case, the result of this communion was no abdication but a passionate attempt to address the practicalities of the new political order. Machiavelli's works – some of which by 1600 had been published surreptitiously in England in Italian versions by John Wolfe[4] – taught, not immorality, but a realization that in politics we should, in Bacon's admiring words, consider the actions of men 'and write what they do not what they ought to do'.[5] On such a view, the only way to preserve any semblance of freedom, glory and honour was to summon up a *virtù* (a *vir-tus*, a manliness, an energetic and pragmatic response to circumstances as they are) so as to defend a higher principle. *The Prince*, consequently, is deeply interested in the moment at which 'new' states are formed either by vigorous acts of political courage or by dereliction of 'virtuous' government. Speaking of Milan, Machiavelli sees a state where a new absolutism had been established by the guile and energy of the onetime mercenary, Francesco Sforza (1401–66). But the Sforza lineage declined into 'infamy' when Francesco's heirs proved unwilling to think assiduously enough of military exercises – which should be pursued 'more vigorously in peace than in war'.[6]

It is not perhaps surprising that Machiavelli's *realpolitik* should have become, in the hands of subsequent political thinkers, a programme for the absolutist regimes of monarchs such as James I and Louis XIV.[7] In particular, Machiavelli's undoubted interest in the necessities of political deception and illusionism led to practices in which the *coup d'état* was understood to be not merely a military event but any propaganda stroke – or act of political theatre – that displayed in public the reserves of political energy and knowledge (the *arcana imperii*) that an absolutist monarch had the power to summon up.

There can be no doubt that Machiavellian double-think lends itself to misrepresentation. Yet the ambiguity – even pathos – of Machiavelli's position is itself a reflection of the extremely volatile sensibility that was engendered by the upheavals of the sixteenth century. *The Tempest* itself will display – in Prospero and in its overall conception – Shakespeare's own correspondingly complex response to these disturbances.

[2]

So far, the drama we have been tracing is a drama – both divisive and generative – of violent political change and vigorous intellectual response. Yet such an account ignores, as Machiavelli himself was inclined to, the particular vigour and (in the circumstances) almost miraculous continuity displayed by sixteenth-century artists, poets and musicians. (Michelangelo outlived Machiavelli.) It is indeed an example of such cultural *virtù* that a country such as England should have remained in energetic and competitive, but always fruitful and frequently admiring, contact with Italy.

Since the time of Sir Thomas Wyatt and the authors represented in Tottel's *Miscellany* (compiled 1557–87), lyric poets had recognized the importance of the Petrarchan lyric tradition. But as the English literary language developed, so too did its own characteristic resistance to this tradition, not least in Shakespeare's *Sonnets*. In a similar spirit of imitation and eventual out-doing, English authors recognized in Italian literature of the sixteenth century the most sophisticated example of what might be accomplished in a vernacular tongue. Theories concerning the epic and tragic genres – and also the mixing of genres to produce 'epic romance' and 'tragi-comedy' – flooded out of Italy, as did the primary texts of Ariosto and Tasso, stirring Sidney and Spenser to acts of authorial usurpation. Tragic dramatists had learned from Trissino the value of blank verse, while Gascoigne and Whetstone knew how much could be derived from Italian stage comedy. The *novella* too – going back to Boccaccio's originals, which were available in translations by Painter and others – had produced, in the hands of Bandello and Cinthio, a revelation of the imaginative possibilities that might be discovered in the sophisticated corruption of the Italian court; and Webster, as well as Shakespeare himself, diverted these resources to spectacular use.

Unlikely as it now may seem, the most *avant-garde* influence to flow from Italy in the early seventeenth century emanated from the writings of the Farrarese dramatist Battista Guarini (1538–1612), who accompanied his pastoral tragi-comedy *Il Pastor Fido*[8] with an ambitious theory of mixed dramatic genres whereby tragi-comedy was represented as superior alike to simple comedy and simple tragedy. In *Volpone* Ben Jonson declared that 'All our English writers . . . Will deign to steal out of this author. . . He has so modern and facile a vein . . . catching the court ear' (III.iv.87–92).

Writing for a courtly audience, Guarini sought to reveal a space – simultaneously moral and theatrical – in which an alternative to Machiavellian *realpolitik* might be cultivated. Shepherds in *Il Pastor Fido* display no Tamburlanian tendency to ruthless *virtù*; Guarini is rather interested (with Oedipus to the forefront of his mind) in the vulnerability of human beings and correspondingly (in his own version of Sophocles's Tiresias) in the wise passiveness that reveals our dependency on the actions of Divine Providence. This suits a mood, widespread in the Counter-Reformation, that favours submission to Divine authority. At the same time, the author, in a series of dramatic *entrelacements* and *denouements* (which he duly points out in a commentary on his own work), is himself the real providence who delivers this golden world, revealing not least the aesthetic appeal that quasi-religious or ritualistic theatre may exert. Connoisseurs among English authors were impressed; and John Fletcher attempted, in close chronological proximity to *Cymbeline*, his own *The Faithful Shepherdess*. Indeed in *Measure for Measure* Shakespeare had already responded in his own way to a principal tenet of Guarinian theory, which is that in tragi-comedy there may be a full consideration of all the issues raised by death without the violence of death itself – a contention which is supported, in Guarini's thinking, by the explicitly Christian view that all our lives are seen to be in the hands of a Higher Good.[9]

[3]

Turning to Shakespeare's own contribution, it appears at times that, in his sustained reference to Italian motifs, he was determined to review the whole foregoing history of association between English and Italian literature. For instance, humanist education and the associated practices of philological scholarship – fundamental factors in the development of the Italian Renaissance – are central in the early comedies, *Two Gentlemen of Verona* and *Love's Labour's Lost*. Philology may in the latter be mocked; nonetheless, Shakespeare continued to avail himself of the rhetoric which such scholarship inculcated and especially of the 'theatre-grams' (to use Louise Clubb's phrase)[10] that were generated by Italian humanists in the *commedia erudita*. *The Comedy of Errors* is (relatively) true to this type; *The Taming of the Shrew* takes Ariosto's *I Suppositi* (in Gascoigne's faithful translation) as its play-within-a-play; *Twelfth Night* and *Much Ado About Nothing* display vertiginous variations on themes of twinning and disguise that had recently been explored by Ariosto. Notably, Shakespeare is at his most characteristic and furthest from the constraints of the original when he introduces elements of meta-theatre or reflects upon the insufficiencies and beguilements of language. (It is sometimes argued that the most Italianate of all Shakespeare's plays is *The Merry Wives of Windsor*, which largely eschews meta-theatre in favour of observational precision.) Yet even Shakespeare's reflection upon the processes of theatrical illusion may have arisen from an encounter with the Italian.[11]

Alongside such formal and thematic developments, Shakespeare displays an interest as searching as Machiavelli's own in the practice, psychology and play of political power. *Richard III* may thus represent Shakespeare's own version of the stereotypical Machiavillain. But it seems likely, according to Ann Barton, that in writing *Coriolanus* Shakespeare consulted a copy of

Machiavelli's *Discorsi* (in an Italian version),[12] sharing with Machiavelli (as he had since *Titus Andronicus*) a grim fascination with those critical moments at which cultural codes shift, decay or struggle to revive themselves. Indeed as a student of such moments, Shakespeare in one respect outdoes Machiavelli. For Machiavelli is no economic historian. Yet the codes and practices Shakespeare investigates in *Coriolanus* (and in *The Merchant of Venice*) are revealed (with all the perspicacity of a new historicist) to be intertwined with questions of food, body and cash.

There is, however, another respect in which Shakespeare transcends Machiavelli; and this derives from his concern with the deeply problematical question of how one human perceives another – and also with how the experience of art may bear on that perception. For while it is always important to emphasize that Shakespeare is as interested in cultures as he is in 'character', he is also, as a dramatist, profoundly concerned with the problematics of our encounters with others. This will prove to be a central issue in *The Tempest*. But already in the *Sonnets* and in *Othello* the issue is one that brings Shakespeare into dispute with the Italian tradition: 'My mistress' eyes are nothing like the sun' (Sonnet 130) asks us to bend language against the very conventions that constitute language itself, as if to catch in some epiphanic miracle beyond 'black ink' (Sonnet 65) the particularity that lies in the presence of the other. In *Othello* (an Italian play by virtue of source as well as setting) a comparable interest in the wonder – or miracle – of particularity becomes the central factor defining Shakespeare's tragic consideration of individuals in relation to their cultural group. Here, a mentality of courtliness (exemplified by the Florentine Cassio) and mentalities of apparently honest pragmatism (exemplified by the Venetian Iago) conflict and confuse Othello's perception of the uniquely honest Desdemona – and equally challenge the audience's own perception of the uniquely complex Othello. Italy, in pursuit of true courtliness, invites us to celebrate the human person; Italy, in characteristically sophisticated cynicism, denies that the human person can ever be worthy of celebration. The English eye is at its most acute in tolerating the painful ambiguity.

In all these respects – in regard to learning, language, illusion, prowess, power and personhood – Shakespeare's most comprehensive engagement with Italy prior to *The Tempest* is *Cymbeline*. For in this play Shakespeare not only synthesizes and reformulates many of his earlier preoccupations with Italy but also consciously sets Italy against itself, testing the implications of Machiavellian polity against those that flow from the theatrical experimentation of Guarini's *Pastor Fido*.

In polemical terms, *Cymbeline* may be seen as Shakespeare's own version of the Italianate sleaze-play. Of course, the play is set chronologically in the era of the Roman Empire. But the Rome Shakespeare depicts is unmistakably a Renaissance city, sophisticated, international and decadent. And it is this anachronism that allows him to develop, patriotically, the moral alliance between Ancient Rome and Ancient Britain that ultimately defeats the corrupting influences propagated by Iachimo in his attempts to make his 'Italian brain' 'in your duller Britain operate most vilely' (V.v.196–7). Posthumus recovers his own moral virtue by putting on 'English weeds'; and finally – in a phrase that wonderfully combines perspectival effect and political significance – the Roman eagle 'lessen'd herself' in the West to allow 'the crooked smokes' from domestic altars to rise in a newly-liberated sky (V.v.470, 474).

At a stroke Shakespeare offers here a political vision that is consistent with, but transcends, the best of Machiavelli (who had himself looked to the example of Ancient Rome as a way of resuscitating a thirst for civic freedom in the contemporary world); such a view – of the global in harmony with the local – would have been the envy of any Italian caught beneath the heel of Spanish Imperialism. Yet in formal terms this utopian *finale* draws on and develops considerations that are themselves to be found in the Italian world.

The sources that Shakespeare turns to here (as also in *All's Well That Ends Well*) are located in the Boccaccian *novella* tradition. The wager on Imogen's virtue – though explicitly parallel to the story of the Rape of Lucrece – can be traced (through William Painter) to a *novella* in the second Day of the *Decameron*, where a merchant (not a member of the Roman Royal House) allows the commercial ethos of risk-taking and exchange to eclipse his understanding of his wife's intrinsic virtue, only to be countered by a wife who – enterprising in her own way – has the know-how and determination to repair the damage that her husband has done. This story reflects much of Boccaccio's interest in the pragmatic cut-and-thrust that characterizes the *Decameron* and has led it to be described as a 'mercantile epic'. Yet Shakespeare rises above the mercantile interests of the original story, favouring a myth of imperial proportions. And in doing so, he fashions a play that draws directly on the refined dramaturgy which Guarini suggests we should prefer to tragedy and comedy alike.[13]

The conclusion of *Cymbeline* triumphantly shows how a dramatist – subtly 'knotting and unknotting' – can avoid the histrionic vulgarity of violent death-scenes. Cloten of course does die, only to be transfigured by the funeral rites that he shares with Imogen, and by Imogen's initial misapprehension of him. All of which takes place against a pastoral background, which also proves to be the newly consecrated realm of a liberated Britain.

Yet if this much outdoes Guarini at his own art, the conclusion of *Cymbeline* goes further still and reveals the divergence between a central concern of the Renaissance itself and Shakespeare's own profound preoccupation. The point at issue is our perception of ourselves as persons in the spaces which we as human beings construct. Yet in *Cymbeline* the space which finally its protagonists occupy is not, after all, a geographical or political space but one that (as in the *Sonnets* and *Othello*) is designated by the looks which persons bestow on each other. Famously *Cymbeline* concludes with more than a score of mutual recognitions. It is this 'counterchange' (V.v.396) that truly resolves the action in *Cymbeline*. At the core of the play is a telling contrast in modes of perception. On the one hand, there is the possessively commercial and essentially Renaissance gaze which Iachimo projects on the sleeping Imogen as he attempts to write down an 'inventory' of her person (II.ii.30). On the other, there is the yearning, all but inarticulate desire to envisage a space beyond linguistic definition which Imogen expresses when she declares, on hearing of Posthumus's departure by sea:

> I would have broke mine eye-strings, crack'd them but
> To look upon him, till the diminution
> Of space had pointed him sharp as my needle:
> Nay, followed him till he had melted from
> The smallness of a gnat to air. (I.iii.17–21)

Such a view, directed upon the feckless Posthumus, plainly goes beyond all reason. But it also goes beyond the mercantile script that the over-intelligent Iachimo attempts to engrave. The aim of Imogen's attention is to reveal, in wonder, a place that only human glances inhabit.

The Tempest, in its recurrent concern with effects of wonder, will begin at the point where *Cymbeline* ends; and in doing so it will consolidate an implicit attack on that central tenet of Renaissance art which assumes that linear perspective allows us to command the realities of the world we inhabit, even to the extent of placing our fellow human beings definitively in our field of vision. Familiarly, the Italian Renaissance begins with, in John White's phrase, the 're-birth of pictorial space';[14] and this supposed advance is still measured by the extent to which Renaissance painters transcend the hieratic idiom of the Greek manner and locate the human figure, volumetrically, in a grid of perspectival orthogonals. In retrospect, however, it is hard to forget that optical illusions of this sort are akin to the devices that allowed artillery to be trained on those who fell within its sights. Leonardo and Michelangelo knew how to build and celebrate the civilized life; they could also conceive

Model theatre set, from Sebastiano Serlio, *The first Booke of Architecture* (London, 1611), bk 2, chap. 3 (fol. 25).

of engines of destruction and aim them at the city walls within which learning and scholarship flourished.

The perspectives which Imogen seeks to open up in searching out the 'gnat' of Posthumus's presence denies that we can ever make mere lines – visual or written – the guide to our human actions. Yet there is still in *Cymbeline* a vestigial concern (both romantic and patriotic) with the parameters of Arcadian space. *The Tempest* – in its dealings with Italy, the human person and the perspectives of wonder – will prove more ambiguous and more harshly realistic.

[4]

Unlike *Cymbeline* (or for that matter *The Winter's Tale*) *The Tempest* never makes landfall in Italy. None the less, it has become a topos of *Tempest*-criticism, particularly in interpreting the figure of Prospero, to invoke Italianate archetypes.

On one view, Prospero is the descendent of thinkers such as Pico della Mirandola, who famously saw a magical power in human nature to marry the elements of the universe and 'bring forth into the open the miracles concealed in the recesses of the world, in the depths of nature, and in the storehouses and mysteries of God'.[15] On this understanding, Prospero is the seer or mage; and his proper orbit is the Book, the sacred homeland of the Renaissance, from which derives the power to rule all lesser territories. Such a reading is supported – and also qualified – by the moment at which Prospero proposes to 'drown' his book (though we never see him doing this). He owns here an affinity to the magician Faustus who means to 'burn his books' but distances himself from suspicions of mere sorcery by resort to the regenerative medium of water. The same qualification may also recall the wise passivity of Guarinian priests and heroes, whose virtue lies not in over-reaching but in the Oedipal acknowledgement of vulnerability and an ultimate submission to Providence.

On the other hand, asking whether Providence has any place at all in *The Tempest*, we may look askance at Prospero's providential or benevolently magical actions. Recent criticism has encouraged such suspicion and there are again good Italianate – and Machiavellian – reasons for doing so. After all, *The Tempest* is undoubtedly concerned with the Machiavellian topics of usurpation and the forming of new principalities. Antonio and Sebastian are plainly Machiavillains observed by an eye as searching as Machiavelli's own; and so perhaps is Prospero, the scion of tyrannical Milan. Is he not himself the cause of all subsequent disasters? Does it not all stem from Prospero's original unwillingness as ruler of Milan to cultivate that *virtù* that, for Machiavelli, is the (albeit shady) ground in which liberty and honour must always be rooted? Pursuing such suggestions, Prospero bears an uncanny resemblance to the Machiavellian absolutists who (on Donaldson's account) are virtuosi of the *arcana imperii* and the *coup d'état*. In this case, Prospero's magic would lie in a knowledge of political needs and in the exercise of appropriately impressive illusionism. His repeated *coups de théâtre* might in this case be read as recurrent *coups d'état* (as indeed might Shakespeare's own if *The Tempest* is meant to celebrate a dynastic marriage).

Prospero, then, may be regarded as the product, simultaneously, of Renaissance learning and of Milanese power-politics; and to this extent he articulates a continuing interest on Shakespeare's part in that synthesis of concerns – involving education, rhetoric, art and control – which the Renaissance clearly bequeathed to him. Yet in *The Tempest*, no less than in

Love's Labour's Lost, Othello or *Cymbeline*, Shakespeare also calls that synthesis into question.

So, as will appear in the final section of this essay, the action of *The Tempest* is one that invites its audience constantly to expect yet constantly to interrogate the principles of coherence on which the play itself depends. Here as elsewhere (though not in *Cymbeline*) the source of Shakespeare's questioning and also of his originality is a certain meta-theatrical consciousness that leads him, notably in the Epilogue, to disclose and reflect on those features of his own practice – a command, for instance, of dramatic space and spectacle – which are fundamental to the order which the play itself has instituted. It should not, however, be supposed that Shakespearean meta-theatre points merely to a deconstructive scepticism. For the point of convergence in all the questions that *The Tempest* raises – concerning particularly space and language – will be decidedly ethical in character. This of course is an issue which the Renaissance itself, with its famous (or infamous) enthusiasms for the Dignity of Man may be thought to have settled long since. Yet how far from settled the issue is in Shakespeare's mind is already apparent from his representation of Prospero. Here, as the centre of our attention, we are offered no confident self-fashioner, no clean-cut Vitruvian man, inhabiting the geometry of his own perfect performance. Prospero, rather, is a figure stretched ambiguously across a gamut of extreme and unresolved possibilities, ranging from magus (or Guarinian seer) to despotic illusionist or even (on a Machiavellian interpretation) contemptible dropout.

How then is the audience of *The Tempest* to view this supposed hero? With admiration? With scepticism? Or else in some unthinkable combination of wonder and contempt? This is a question that other Shakespearean heroes have stimulated – notably Hamlet, himself uncomfortably a Renaissance man; and the Duke in *Measure for Measure*, whom Shakespeare wilfully allows to complicate any facile optimism in his first attempt at Guarinian tragicomedy. But in *The Tempest* the questions that such figures raise (without ever answering) become the very action – or *agon* – that the play as a whole delineates; and, meta-theatrically, these same questions dislocate the satisfactions that Prospero might be thought to project in the orderly conclusions of his plot.

But then – in a further turn of the meta-theatrical and ethical spiral – we discover as we examine the details of *The Tempest* not only that Prospero and Shakespeare himself are in question but that we as audience are likewise under inspection. In the Epilogue we are called on to respond to a figure who is still 'Prospero' yet does not wish to be – a man more than an actor yet a man who seeks our appreciation of the rôle that he, as player, has just performed. More radically than Imogen ever did, the audience will strain to realize anew what it means to locate another human being in its own field of vision.

[5]

In the Epilogue to *The Tempest*, as Stephen Orgel has written, 'Prospero puts himself in the position of Ariel, Caliban and Ferdinand, and the other shipwreck victims throughout the play, threatened with confinement, pleading for release from bondage'. And the freedom he seeks is the 'freedom to continue his history beyond the limits of the stage and text.'[16]

Or else one might say (in terms derived from Guarinian theory) that *The Tempest* is finally concerned with 'unknotting' rather than with knotting, and with freedoms altogether different from those that are expressed in the formal control of art, ethics or political life. While *Cymbeline* had displayed a magisterial disregard for the unities of time and place, *The Tempest* by contrast seems to emphasize its own commitment to the unities (as at V.i.136); and the dramaturgical unities, in common with visual perspective, had been intended, since the time of the *commedia erudita* – acted on a perspectivally chequered floor – to provide a learned defence of mimetic realism.

For all that, the concluding act of *The Tempest* encourages us to contemplate, at the very point where unity seems to be achieved, a disintegration not only of space and time but also of action. Witnessing the centrifugal flight from the island, attention is drawn to stories yet to be told, on events and consequences which the audience itself has only partial knowledge. Alonso badgers Prospero for 'particulars' (V.i.135). But any attention to such particulars is deflected: 'For 'tis a chronicle of day by day / Not a relation for a breakfast' (162–3). Later, 'some oracle must rectify our knowledge' (244). Yet there is no suggestion here (as there was in *Cymbeline*) of temples off-stage in which oracular understanding can be brought to utterance. Whatever punctuation there is will be offered at 'every third thought' by the unfathomable spaces – or vanishing-point – of the grave (311).

It should not, however, be supposed that in this perspective (which is no perspective at all) the play invites merely a meditation on Yorick-like concavities. For while the Epilogue looks out into darkness, this darkness is one that is inhabited by shadowy human persons – ourselves – who will demonstrate how alive they are by their reaction to the pleading protagonist. From the first, indeed, wonder is represented as a necessary if not sufficient condition of any ethical response. (Compare the *Sonnets* with their emphasis upon the 'miracle' of art.) Miranda's rôle is precisely to insist on this. She is

herself both the object and instigator of wonder, of an attention which identifies and illuminates the particularities of human value; and it is she who,
before Prospero has uttered any word, peers out (as Imogen did) across the
ocean and demands – as a check on the power alike of magic and of the all-
consuming elements – a humane attention for the persons who have fallen
into the grip of her father's providential pretensions.

As the play opens, the world of Renaissance space is broken apart. The
storm famously inverts the social hierarchy and reveals the ship (which is an
emblem both of commercial enterprise and of the imperial ambitions that
flow from such enterprise) to be a fragile object of confusion, its lines and
angles pointed up by the calligraphic highlights that Ariel 'flames' upon it.
Volumetric space itself here implodes, so that the final moments of this
voyage are registered not by sight at all but rather by sound, and not by
harmonious sound (or any articulate utterance) but 'by a confused noise
within'. It is this cry that 'knocks against' Miranda's heart and stirs in her the
particular mode of vision which, distinguishing humans alone from the darkness into which they are absorbed, is henceforth to be her distinguishing
characteristic. Sight here is suffering ('I have suffered/ With those that I saw
suffer'); but it is also liberation – as it is for the suffering Ferdinand, who
would willingly abandon mere liberty of movement for the freedom of won-
dering at Miranda herself ('space enough/ Have I in such a prison'; I.ii.492–4).
Miranda likewise can create a universe out of admiration ('O brave new
world / That has such people in't!'; V.i.183–4).

Wonder, as an ethical and dramaturgical principle, remains throughout
an important feature of The Tempest, whether in its masque-like components,
in its tracing of the maze through which the displaced nobles wander, or
else, most testingly, in the demand that the audience should display (as
Miranda herself cannot) a wonder even at the opaque alterity of Caliban. Yet
it is not only Caliban but the figure of Prospero which tends to complicate
and darken that concentration of view which Miranda's herself insists on. 'O
brave new world', says Miranda; to which Prospero replies with a less-than-
gracious, 'Tis new to thee' (V.i.184). This subdued phrase need not be read as
cynical. It does, however, express an aching weariness. And the source of
that weariness is that Prospero has still a plot to maintain, a sequence to pursue, a command to exert over the consequences of past, present and future
which disallows any instantaneous expense of energy or any response to the
epiphanic moment.

At the heart of Renaissance humanism, there is an urgent desire to recover
the past and – by reading successfully in the present – deliver to the future
monuments of unageing intellect. Now Prospero seeks, for Miranda's sake, to

recover his own past history. Yet his words reveal only the skeletal sounds that are discernible under the bloom of all sequential discourse. In his long expository speech, Prospero proves incapable of sustained narrative perspective and is wracked continually on sudden marks and spurts of sound, the gaps and silences that shape and punctuate articulate utterance. At moments, Miranda reacts with wonder at Prospero's tale and claims to possess a unifying memory of her earliest days. Yet Prospero tetchily assumes that any such remembrance must be wholly beyond her. For him the past is measured from no originary point of innocence but moves ever onward as a splintering tale of crimes and laxities to which Miranda – 'a cherubin' – can contribute nothing. So on he goes (like a nameless Beckettian half-life): and the very syntax of coherent utterance, along with all aspiration to learned rhetoric, dissolves – especially when speaking of his brother Antonio – into unrhythmic agitation:

> . . . new created
> The creatures that were mine, I say: or changed 'em
> Or else new formed 'em; having both the key
> Of officer and office, set all the hearts i'th' state
> To what tune pleased his ear, that now he was
> The ivy which had hid my princely trunk,
> And sucked my verdure out on't – thou attend'st not! (I.ii.81–7)

Moving between the secluded spaces of the study, on to the corridors of Antonio's power, and thence to the leaking confines of a boat adrift on the open sea, Prospero's opening speech is addressed as much in anger to the absent Antonio as it is to the present Miranda; and this points to a further feature that Prospero's discourse displays throughout *The Tempest*, which is that he finds it easier to speak to (or about) non-human beings than he does in response to human persons. Notably, in the opening scene his own words even take colour from those of his non-human interlocutors. With Ariel, Prospero shares a chilly but vivid intellectual glee at the efficient operation of his strategem; with Caliban, he speaks a language of sensation, so that where Caliban's cthonic poetry speaks of molehills, raven feathers and footfalls, Prospero will turn this to perverse punitive effect: 'Thou shalt be pinched / As thick as honeycomb' (I.ii.328–9). All of which is to suggest that where clarity and control are at issue language pursues its destined function; and the Renaissance cult of the magisterial book would have led us to expect no less. Yet this same cult encourages one to gloss over the disturbing fact that human voices can themselves answer back to the human voice. This realization is borne in on us as Prospero battles in his solitary mind with the voices of those whom he dare not let speak.

It need, however, be no criticism to reveal the wounds in Prospero's discourse. Guarini, after all, has shown how fertile the vulnerability of a hero might be; and we have only to turn to Antonio to see what discourse can become when it successfully disguises its own intrinsic deficiencies.

For at the dark heart of *The Tempest* we hear the voices of Sebastian and Antonio, speaking as a vigorously commonsensical, Machiavellian but also derisive chorus to Prospero's plot, wittily self-possessed, always presuming to gauge their interlocutor's drift and equally determined to establish their command over the places and persons around them. So, as they plan their own *coup d'état*, the first move that the two conspirators make – though themselves watched over by Ariel and ourselves – is to summon up the malign intensity and self-control of Machiavellian *virtù*: 'My spirits are nimble / They fell together all, as by consent' (II.i.201). It is Antonio's intention to turn Sebastian into a torrent (again with a Machiavellian preference for impetuousness over lethargy and apathy): 'I'll teach thee to flow' (II.i.219). Antonio and Sebastian, keeping watch over an indeterminate arena – marked out by still-breathing and enchanted human bodies – attempt to translate this intimate and confusing space into a perspective of military and political geography, viewing inheritance and temporal lineage purely as the coordinates of opportunity. (One recalls how Machiavelli's Prince is urged constantly to survey a landscape in terms of military advantage and danger).

Yet their plot (in common with the plot of *The Tempest* at large) is a failure; and the resistance it meets is, significantly enough, expressed not simply as some countervailing stratagem of power but rather as an indeterminate vibration, a buzzing in the ear, an aural and ambiguous epiphany. From the outset, music in *The Tempest* has offered an alternative to the control exerted by the tongue in discursive speech; and music as harmony could also stand in the Renaissance as an acoustic alternative to visual organization.[17] Even so, song in *The Tempest* is as likely to be raucous, inebriated and aleatory as it is harmonious; and beneath even the acoustic patterning which the play is sometimes supposed to favour, there are rhythms more primal than speech, sight, or even melody might eventually be. Caliban knows that the isle is full of noises. Ariel too can create a music that is so close to the cerebellum as to be *smelled*: Caliban and Trinculo and Stephano 'lifted up their noses / As they smelt music' (IV.i.177–8). To Antonio, any such music is transmuted into a strident and bellicose occasion for treacherous heroics. But to Gonzalo – so often confused and so far from ever seeking heroic delineation – the sound that saves him from a sleeping death comes as 'a humming / And that a strange one too' (II.i.315–16).

As *The Tempest* draws towards its own shadowy conclusion, Prospero (at some indeterminate point in his renunciation speech) describes a circle on the ground, invoking solemn – or 'heavenly' – music to lead his victims into his sphere. There will, however, be no such theophany here as in *Pericles* and *Cymbeline*. The marriage-masque is enacted by spirits, not by the Gods themselves, and ends prematurely in 'hollow and confused noise'. At which point a process begins, pointing to Prospero's Epilogue speech, in which the fictional harmonies of space and sound dissolve and leave only a growing awareness of that shifting theatrical frame in which the final knottings of marriage, the foiled plots of Caliban and Trinculo, and the offer of redemption are all to be observed. Simultaneously, the play sets itself to create an audience – including Prospero himself – that will be able to tolerate the descent into a human world where magic and power have both been abandoned. Many acts of identification will be witnessed – and of grudging acknowledgement – but no ultimate or consoling moment of recognition of the kind that *Cymbeline* offered.

It is thus a part of Prospero's renunciation speech to locate himself increasingly as a spectator on the margins of the drama he has created. From the circumference of the circle, the figures which Prospero – and Prospero's own audience – observes are 'spell-stopped' and frozen (V.i.61). Then, as these figures return to waking life, frame within frame is revealed, descending (in hierarchical order) from the discovery of Miranda and Ferdinand, then to the entry of the crew-men, and finally to the appearance of Caliban, Stephano and Trinculo. Miranda and Ferdinand, poised above their chessboard, playfully rehearse on this (significantly) chequered surface the familiar sleights of the world they will shortly return to.

Has order, then, been restored? Caliban, speaking with renewed wonder at the sight of his master, seems to think that it has been. Yet the human audience – faced by so many viewpoints and frames of attention – is hardly likely to agree or be more than momentarily impressed by Prospero's thaumaturgical invocation, beginning 'Ye elves of hills, brooks, standing lakes and groves' (V.i.33). Though apparently more sustained than the expository speeches of Act I, this piece of (Ovidian) rhetorical display lacks a main verb, as if coherent and directed action lay far beyond the speaker's control; and much that Prospero refers to seems in excess of – or irrelevant to – the action that the audience has witnessed. There is a *coup* here but not so much a *coup* of theatre or state, rather a wave of word and gesture.

It is an indication of the sphere to which Prospero is now returning that reason itself should be seen as a rush of tide, a flow, a ripple (as in applause). As the frozen spirits return to consciousness:

Their understanding
Begins to swell, and the approaching tide
Will shortly fill the reasonable shore. (V.i 80–81)

Reason, on such a view, offers neither design nor control; it is not a geodesic instrument. Rather it is analogous to those very oceanic rhythms which once it seemed to oppose or control. Likewise, addressing himself to his audience, Prospero asks that a space should be opened for him which only human attention can designate. Consigning mere magic to Ariel and territorial possession to Caliban, Prospero's last words to his variegated fellows are: 'Please you draw *near*'.

[6]

And, like this insubstantial pageant faded,
Leave not a rack behind. (IV.i.155–6)

Were this the concluding speech of the The Tempest, we should be left with a sober understanding of how illusory human pretensions are; and certainly The Tempest sets itself (as Guarini did) against any Marlovian confidence in the constructions and ambitions of the human intellect. At the same time we recall (as Machiavellians and historicists) that Renaissance monarchs (including Henry VIII) would sumptuously erect an auditorium only to dismantle it the following day in a final stroke of both state and theatre.

Yet this is not the conclusion of The Tempest. Rather, we must ask once again how we, as persons in Shakespeare's audience, are to view the person of Shakespeare's fictional creature; and to this question no answer which designates Prospero as a Machiavellian or a Guarinian is ever likely to be adequate. For finally the appeal of the Epilogue is to an audience that – now part of the action – is revealed by the mirror of Prospero's address to be itself an oceanic force of renewal. We are brought to life by these lines. Yet we are denied any judicial frame or secure ground for the judgements we are called upon to make.

For all such frames and securities have been questioned in the course of the play. Persons, certainly, have been presented in terms of their territorial claims and possessions, of their crying need for homes and also, perhaps, for libraries. Yet the space that the play itself invites us to enter is neither the geo-political arena which a merchant or Machiavellian might survey, or fight over or profit from. Nor is it an aesthetic safe haven of the sort that Guarini's thinking suggests we might construct for ourselves. It is not even the patriotic homeland that *Cymbeline* imaginatively offers. In *The Tempest* foreign noblemen wander, displaced, in a world that hints at Arcadia yet can equally prove a place of terror, another Milan. Nor is anyone except Caliban to remain on the island. Human beings here are all temporary residents; and when they leave for Italy, they do so almost as nomads pursuing those dynastic marriages and political machinations which – since the Renaissance – have become the song-lines of the European tribe. And then, when the houselights go up, the space in which we, as an audience, find ourselves confirms this dream: we are in a theatre, part Everyman's castle, part No-man's land. How are we to think of Prospero? The question is identical to the question of how we are to orient ourselves in such a space.

The spaces revealed by *The Tempest* and the ethical and intellectual optics the play requires us to exercise must then be seen not as any intellectual chart through troubled waters but rather as a thought-experiment. Pico may define the human being as potentially either beast or angel; philosophers may now debate whether computers or animals are to be regarded as persons. Similarly, Shakespeare's portrayal of Caliban and Ariel invites us to test our own tolerance of life-forms other than our own. The final test, however, is to countenance not the non-human but the human itself. In the closing moments of *The Tempest* Prospero is revealed to be as strangely two-fold as the amphibious Caliban, a character in search not of an author but rather of freedom from all authority, even his own. In its familiar lineaments of power and control, this figure is one which we immediately recognize as human. Yet its abdication demands that we see it – and ourselves – as no less different and other than Caliban in his indefinable materiality.

At the end of *King Lear*, human beings go on, usurping life and submitting to it, casting shadows in the very act of seeking to remove them. So do they also at the end of *The Tempest*. In the utter paradox of this there is much to wonder at. But wonder in the face of such a transforming mirror will not be that dangerous curiosity which led, in the minds of many a Renaissance explorer, to possession and self-affirmation.[18] Against that, *The Tempest* reveals, in the vanishing Prospero, a reflective darkness which gathers its intensity from those who stand before it. Theatre has here become a kinetic – and secular – form of those great mosaics which, pre-dating the dangerous invention of Renaissance space, designated the human person as an object of veneration, always (somehow) other than its own well-fashioned self.

8 'The foul witch' and Her 'freckled whelp': Circean Mutations in the New World

MARINA WARNER

Among the noises of the isle, the voice of Sycorax is silenced. Her story is evoked in a few scant lines that do not flesh out a full character or even tell a coherent tale; in fragments, like the siftings of an archaeological dig, her past is glimpsed, only to fade again: she, 'this damned witch Sycorax', was exiled from Algiers, where, 'for one thing she did / They would not take her life' (I.ii.266–8). What was that one thing? When she arrived on the island she was pregnant with Caliban, whom she had conceived, we are told, by the devil (I.ii.319);[1] she has since died in circumstances that remain unspecified.

In its ellipses, *The Tempest* has the feel of a legend or fairy tale so well-known to its audience that the plot does not have to be filled in. The chronology of Sycorax's life warps against the chronology of the play: she was carrying Caliban when she arrived, and 'through age and envy / Was grown into a hoop' (I.ii.560–61). Her ageing is somehow accelerated, moving faster than the pace of other characters' stories; the suddenly raging, bent old hag then dies during Ariel's twelve years' captivity in the pine. From swollen-bellied mother, she turns into a crone; all within 26 years at the most, since Prospero and Miranda arrived fourteen years before the action of the play. Yet her mysterious, indeterminate story and character suffuses *The Tempest*; the 'foul witch Sycorax' occupies the drama like a prompter who accompanies the action throughout, hidden and unheard, beneath the stage. As Ted Hughes puts it, 'Sycorax, the ultimate Queen of Hell, is still everywhere, like the natural pressure of the island's atmosphere. Prospero's statement that she died is little more than a figure of speech: the island . . . is hers.'[2]

The island is bewitched. It exhibits many of the special features of diabolical enchantment, according to both classical tradition and current Elizabethan and Jacobean beliefs, yet Sycorax is the only witch who is named as such in the play. Prospero's 'secret studies', his 'so potent art', perform the magic metamorphoses of witchcraft, but he embodies the presiding consciousness of the drama, and his perspective provides the moral viewpoint and the emotional colour. So his magic does not figure as malign – except to Caliban, of course, who rains down curses on his head. (Peter Greenaway's film *Prospero's Books*, in which he gives the entire play to John Gielgud as Prospero to intone, catches accurately this unusually condensed first-person angle on the unfolding drama.) But Prospero performs his feats of magic – the storm, the enchanted sleep of the victims, the torments of Caliban, the phantasmic banquet – through Ariel his airy messenger, and Ariel provides a historical as well as emotional link between Prospero and Sycorax. More particularly, Ariel hyphenates the magic of Sycorax who bound him in a cloven pine and the 'charms' of Prospero, who allows Ariel spectacular mobility in his service, but nevertheless keeps him enslaved to his will.

The contrast between the two magi of the play – the living male duke and the dead female hag – does not lie so much in polarities of white and black magic, or theurgy and goety, as Frank Kermode developed so suggestively in his edition of *The Tempest*. It lies rather in the difference between metamorphosis and stasis, between a condition of continuing somatic, elemental and unruly mutation and a steady-state identity. The one is subject to the random strike of the magician's wand, or other spells (the fickleness of pagan charms), the other is achieved by the flash of epiphanic conversion (the vision of divine truth). In other words, pagan notions of physical identity as multiple and shapeshifting clash on the isle with a Christian idea of fixed, stable and seemly bodily identity. The wonder of human appearance at which Miranda exclaims consists in body–soul integrity: these humans are so like themselves, so unchanged by Prospero's kind of magic that even their clothes have remained untouched by the storm. Prospero's magical helper sings of 'Nothing of him that doth fade, / But doth suffer a sea-change / Into something rich and strange' (I.ii.400–3). By contrast, the survivors of the shipwreck shadow forth, after their near-death experience, the antithesis of pagan magic: the promise of Christian beatitude, the glorious mien of the resurrected who have been reunited with their unchanged bodies. In distinction from these incoming exemplars of humankind, the island's denizens surrounding Miranda are monstrous and deformed, ghosts and spectres, diabolically enthralled to hell's processes of disfigurement and bestial transformation.

As we are told at the start, the isle was 'not honour'd with / A human shape' (I.ii.284) except Caliban's, and Caliban's deficiencies in appearance are insistently reiterated, from the 'savage and deformed slave' of the list of *dramatis personae* to the 'misshapen knave' Prospero calls him, to the contradictory zoology by which others evoke his looks and his smell: he is above all redolent of fishiness, but he is also described as 'a freckled whelp'

(I.ii.284), a 'tortoise' (I.ii.316), and, no less than five times, a 'mooncalf' (II.ii.102, 105, 129; III.ii.20, 21). The word monster recurs in Trinculo and Stephano's drunken banter as its key signature, and they explicitly evoke some form of grotesque hybridity when they call Caliban 'a puppy-headed monster' (II.ii.148–9). Since it is the devil who shape-shifts, and is bestial, pied, assymetrical and otherwise jumbled and jangled, these conflicting attempts to evoke Caliban point to his fiendish paternal origin, and more specifically to his mother's god Setebos, who was reportedly worshipped by the 'giants' who inhabited Patagonia.[3]

These shuffling, overlapping pictures have made Caliban notoriously difficult to cast and dress. The fantastic poetic invective of his descriptions defeats visualization, or indeed historical or geographical context. But in this very disparity, it adheres to the character of all phenomena on the island, whose chief characteristic is uncertainty. As Prospero says:

> For more assurance that a living prince
> Does now speak to thee, I embrace thy body . . . (V.i.109)

> You do yet taste
> Some subtleties o'th' isle, that will not let you
> Believe things certain. (V.i.124–5)

The pageants and scenes, the noises and sweet airs are insubstantial, 'cloud-capped towers', subtle in the sense of vapours, gases, spirits, that 'are melted into air, into thin air', and 'leave not a rack behind' (IV.i.150–56). In this cumulus of phantasms and miasma, only some of the bodies honoured with a human shape turn out to be solid and enduring and capable of withstanding the threat of metamorphosis. Caliban fears that

> We shall lose our time,
> And all be turned to barnacles, or to apes
> With foreheads villainous low. (IV.i.248–50)

But at the end, when Prospero takes ambiguous responsibility for Caliban, declaring 'This thing of darkness I / Acknowledge mine' (V.i.275–6), Caliban later responds equally cryptically, saying that he will 'seek for grace' (V.i.295), a phrase that has been interpreted, on the evidence of the words, as contrition, but determined beyond its immediate contents to a desire for redemption in the form of Christian shriving, or baptism. In this aspect, Caliban takes on the rôle of the missionary's target: the heathen who has come to virtue through putting his own gods (Setebos) behind him, and recognized where grace lies. In this way, Caliban is shown to step over the divide between the Pythagorean (and bewitched) realm of shapeshifters into the zone of conversion, which changes inner natures but not outer shape, and this will perhaps save him.

The play does not state that Prospero has inherited some of Sycorax's powers along with the island kingdom he has seized from her 'whelp' ('This island's mine, by Sycorax my mother, / Which thou tak'st from me,' accuses Caliban; I.ii.232), but Prospero's lines imply it when, at the conclusion, he describes Caliban's lineage:

> His mother was a witch, and one so strong
> That could control the moon, make flows and ebbs ... (V.i.269–70)

And, when Prospero makes his fervent speech of renunciation, he describes his conjuring of the tempest in terms that reveal his similar mastery over the elements: 'I have bedimmed / The noontide sun, called forth the mutinous winds . . .' etc. He thus acknowledges that his art too exercised power over the elements with the same 'rough magic' he abjures (V.i.41–50).

As is well known, Prospero does not speak his own words here, but borrows from the incantation that Ovid gives the sorceress Medea in the *Metamorphoses*, a poem that Shakespeare drew on so richly and deeply in manifold ways, beyond this homage in *The Tempest*. Proper indeed to an isle of mysterious music that comes from spirits and voices that float, unanchored to bodies, this score which gives Prospero Sycorax's part and accords their duet the backing support of past figures of female magic.

The usurped Caliban enters, invoking his mother when he calls down a curse on his enemies. He thus sets up, from the beginning, the ventriloquizing of Sycorax that recurs throughout, played out between the antagonists, with Prospero turning his cruel witchcraft against Caliban – 'thou shalt have cramps, / Side-stitches . . . Urchins / Shall . . . / All exercise on thee . . .' (I.ii.325–8) – and Caliban railing in apparently hapless protest, 'All the charms / Of Sycorax, toads, beetles, bats, light on you!' (I.ii.339–40). Though Sycorax's furious enchantments are often described with horror, the drama reveals that her *ancien régime* has been drained of force by the new ruler of the island, since Caliban's invocations of her magic, however vehement, cannot protect him from Prospero's plagues.

Behind Sycorax lie two of the most notorious witches of antiquity: Circe and Medea. These two, aunt and niece in divine genealogy, seem to be standing in the wings of the play and the lights behind them cast their interlaced shadows across the stage, forming the phantom, Sycorax, whispering to Prospero how to command the insubstantial pageant of the action. Editors of the *The Tempest* have proposed that the name of Shakespeare's witch recalls Latin *corax* (raven), which was an oracular bird in Greek divination, a familiar of witches, including Medea, and often a portent of death. Caliban even alludes to this cluster of associations in his first, imprecating, lines:

As wicked dew as e'er my mother brushed
With raven's feather from unwholesome fen
Drop on you both!' (I.ii.321–5)

Corax may be compounded in her name with Greek *sus*, for pig or hog: she is a 'swine-raven'. However, even without this etymological pointer to swine, several references to pigs and piggishness scattered in the play stir resonances with the other notorious witch of Greek and Latin myth, the Homeric enchantress Circe, whose English name Sycorax echoes phonetically. In several further respects, the figure of antiquity's most famous and most alluring enchantress flits behind the dimmed and muted persona of Shakespeare's 'foul witch Sycorax.'

Circe also figures prominently in Ovid's *Metamorphoses*, where she is bathed in a malignant, characteristically Roman and misogynist light. An insider's knowledge of female monstrosity characterizes Circe – and her avatars – throughout the tradition, but in Homer the enchantress puts her cunning arts to use on the hero's behalf and saves him from the lures of the sirens and the predatory attacks of Scylla and Charybdis.[4] In Ovid, she is more sinister, perverse and vengeful. Out of mere jealousy, for example, she blights the sea-nymph Scylla, turning her into a hideous cannibalistic, octopus-like monster. Circe's black magic, her goety, often includes carnal knowledge. Witchlike, she holds sway over the risky and polluting effluvia of the body, and, like Medea, she can restore youth by her art and perform other erotic spells. Minos turns to Circe, for example, when he has been cursed by a jealous Pasiphae to the effect that he will ejaculate nothing but scorpions and other insects. Circe gives him a brew to reverse the curse.[5] When Ovid makes Circe responsible for Scylla's monstrous transmogrification, he is simply stitching the associations more tightly together: Circe commands monsters because in some sense she is herself monstrous, as witches are.

Circe's powers of enchantment in the *Odyssey* are transformative, above all. She is a mistress of magical changes of shape, and famously turns the companions of the hero Odysseus into swine, while mountain wolves and lions also roam her grounds, victims of her enchantments. In later mythographers' and poets' interpretations, her zoomorphic range extends even beyond mammals: Apollonius of Rhodes, in the *Argonautika*, written in the third century BC, describes Circe on her island surrounded by 'a number of creatures whose ill-assorted limbs declared them to be neither man nor beast . . .' He draws on a pastoral metaphor for Circe's relation to her menagerie: she presides, he says, 'like a shepherd over a great flock of sheep'. The fawning which in Homer conveys the emasculation of her victims' bewitched condition returns here as contemptible domesticity, tameness, loss of individuality, sheepishness. Ovid imagines a whole bewitched menagerie rampant in Circe's palace gardens: 'a horde of wild animals, a thousand strong, wolves and bears and lionesses . . .' But they too, like the sheepish, emasculated men of the *Odyssey*, 'even wagged their tails affectionately and fawned upon us'.[6]

Nearer Shakespeare's day, Machiavelli included a giraffe among the witch's victims in his poem about Circe, 'L'Asino' (The Ass), while the Italian cobbler and savant Giambattista Gelli even included, in his *Circe* of 1548 a hare, a snake, an ostrich and an oyster in her enchanted realm. This was a highly successful work, quickly translated into French and English and Spanish, and Shakespeare could therefore have known it.[7] In Renaissance poets, the stress falls less on the animal shape *per se* than on deformity: Machiavelli described her brutes as 'disfatti' (undone) – missing ears and tails, jumbled like a game of consequences. The Dutch engraver who illustrated a seventeenth-century emblem book by Joost van den Vondel, inverted the noble classical prototype of the upright animal-headed hybrid, and gave one or two of Circe's victims – a pig, a bear – ungainly animal posteriors and crawling, creeping or rampant motion, beneath men's faces.[8] In Circe's zoo, systems break down and labels are mixed up and mismatched; hybrids and monsters result from this mingling of species; she brings generic disorder to natural phenomena, assembling around her an anti-ark, a freak show, a variant on the cabinets of curiosities and medical museums of biological monstrosities from the discovered world that were becoming popular among the learned in the seventeenth century.

An assemblage of parts not proper to the form – natural bricolage, combinatory synecdoche – epitomizes the condition of the monster in the Aristotelian tradition that was disseminated through Aquinas's teaching. If the transformed men had been wholly lion or hog or boar, they would not have transgressed the propriety of natural things; their singularity makes them, not individual but spare and strange, irregular and therefore accursed.

The island of *The Tempest*, like the classical and Renaissance Aeaea of Circe, also teems with animals, assorted as in a circus show or a cabinet of curiosities rather than a natural habitat: as well as all the names Caliban is called, there are mentions of urchins (hedgehogs in one editor's gloss, but maybe sea-urchins?), marmosets, crabs and the unidentified 'scamels'. The interplay of echoes carries into the sound texture of this most musical of plays as well.

Ariel's groans, before Prospero freed him, 'Did make wolves howl, and penetrate the breasts / Of ever-angry bears' (I.ii.288–9). When Ariel sings to Ferdinand, 'Come unto these yellow sands', the chorus summons dogs and cocks until Ferdinand cries out in bewilderment at the source of the sounds (I.ii. 375–87). Later, Sebastian imagines – or says he imagines – 'a hollow burst of bellowing, / Like bulls, or rather lions' (II.i.309–10), and Caliban is beset by Prospero's evil apparitions, 'like apes that mow and chatter at me . . . sometime am I / All wound with adders, who with cloven tongues / Do hiss me into madness' (II.ii.9–14). The play's fascination with monsters and their sounds draws, famously, on medieval teratology and travellers' tales (men with their heads in their chests, giants barking, and so forth) as well as on more ancient mythological prodigies: Ariel can turn himself into a nymph and a harpy, revealing that ungodly metamorphosis flouts the order of sex as well as breaking down the borders between human and beast, natural and unnatural.

But of all the beasts that haunt *The Tempest*, it is the pig that links the play to its Homeric shadow self. Caliban sees himself cast as this animal when he complains, 'and here you sty me / In this hard rock . . .' (I.ii.342–3). In spite of making a strong bid in contemporary culture to oust fluffy kittens from birthday cards, pigs have retained their long history of negative symbolism. Swine, hog, porker, pig are words of abuse in English, and the related adjectives – in English – figuratively denote beastliness more strongly than words associated with other animals: hoggish, swinish, piggish. Verbs describing the activities of pigs pass as metaphors of baseness, instincts and low status: to grunt, to wallow, to swill. The suitors in the *Odyssey* are referred to as swine, consuming the goods of Odysseus in his absence. Horace works up the metaphor with mordant moral vehemence:

> You know about Circe's drink, and the siren voices;
> Had Ulysses let himself go and drunk what he wanted,
> He'd have lost his true shape and from then on lived like a nitwit
> At the mercy of a sleazy mistress, lived like a hog
> Settling down cosily in the mud, lived like a dog.
> In comparison with him, the rest of us look rather weak:
> As they put it in Greek, we simply don't COUNT. We CONSUME . . .[9]

The hog and the dog, taken at their most negative, the one gluttonous, the other ravenous, become emblematic of the monster and of insatiable hunger. In medieval symbolic schemes of morality, pigs often accompany the Vices of *Luxuria*, Lust, and *Gula*, Gluttony: Lust looks at herself in the mirror of Venus in the background of Sassetta's *Ecstasy of St Francis*, painted in

1437; and Gluttony, mounted on a hog, guzzles a meat pie in a sixteenth-century sculpture in the cloisters of Chartres cathedral. Alimentary metaphors for the passions, the virtues and the vices, drawing on both the proverbial greed of the pig, the cruelty of the sow, and the species' closeness to human nature, circulate in Ben Jonson's dark comic fantasies.[10] Shakespeare's stied savage reflects this feared carnality – in his frustrated designs upon Miranda and his revengeful boast about peopling 'this isle with Calibans' (I.ii.349). Is there a connection, too, between his confined, savage and hog-like state and the blunt non-sequitur of his reply to Prospero's bitter imprecations: 'I must eat my dinner' (I.ii.330)? Even Caliban's celebrated lyric apostrophes focus on food, from the first reproaches to Prospero – 'Thou . . . woulds't give me / Water with berries in't' (I.ii.332–3) – to his blandishments to Trinculo and Stephano – 'I with my long nails will dig thee pig-nuts / . . . I'll bring thee / To clust'ring filberts . . .' (II.ii.162–4).

Homer tells us that Circe drove Odysseus's companions into pens and sties like swine, and describes how the 22 companions were transformed in head, shape, voice and skin (he specifically mentions bristles sprouting from their flesh). But he goes on to say, 'their minds were as human as they had been before the change'. Her victims are not inhuman, but are experiencing being trapped as humans in not-human form, unable to express themselves, only, sometimes, to weep. In Caliban's disillusion with Prospero's changed behaviour towards him, in his rage and grief, as well as his prone obse-quiousness towards the drunkards, there reverberates this mythological abhorrence of a humanity perverted from its true nature and degraded to the condition of a brute.

Prospero's island magic borrows less familiar features from the Circean repertoire of spells. The enchantress's retreat is characterized in Homer as above all a place of music. Circe does not at first appear before us as an *image* of a beautiful woman. We do not *see* her, as we see, when Eurylochus describes it to Odysseus, her house of polished stone with its beckoning smoke, standing on open ground after the dense screen of oak scrub and forest with the drugged victims. She does not make a visible entrance into this mind picture: she is conjured up, before us and before Eurylochus and the men, as a *sound* – she is first heard, from inside the house, as she weaves some airy delicate cloth at her loom, 'singing sweetly', Polites, dearest of Odysseus' men, exclaims, so that (in Chapman's version) 'the pavement rings / With imitation of the tunes she sings.'

After the potent charm of her voice, the men succumb to her wand, her *rhabdos*, the *maga*'s recurrent, identifying attribute, just as Prospero's staff is imbued with his 'art' in *The Tempest*. Furthermore, when Ferdinand draws his sword on Prospero, 'and is charmed from moving', the scene inverts the encounter of Circe and Odysseus, who also draws his sword against her magic (I.ii.467). But when she waves her wand over the hero to prevent his assault she finds, to her surprise that her magic avails her nothing, as he is protected by the magic plant moly, which Hermes has given him.

Beyond these charmed chords that play between Shakespeare, Homer and Ovid, two larger themes expand the double motif of Circe–Sycorax. First, the enchanted island is a liminal place, a staging-post, a ritual zone where things pass from one form to another, where the victims of the shipwreck undergo an ordeal and emerge repentant (with the exception of Antonio), where Miranda the maid is wed and Caliban is 'converted' and Prospero restored, and all turn for home. *Nostos*, the desire for home, drives the *Odyssey*, and Circe both ensnares the hero and his men and then gives them the means to overcome the terrors that lie in the path of their homecoming. Paradoxically, her magic proves benign, and equips Odysseus to descend into the Underworld and to return, to pass the sirens' shore, to escape the clutches of Scylla and the vortex of Charybdis. The symmetries are not identical, but the island setting and its native witchcraft, in the classical epic and the romance play, serve chiming redemptive conclusions. However there is no duchess of Milan to whom Prospero returns: I shall come back to this veiling of the female face, analogous to the muting of the female voices, and to the occlusion of Sycorax.

The second shared motif emerges more perplexingly and perhaps stirs at a greater depth. In the First Folio, *The Tempest* leads the first category of the plays in the Catalogue, under the heading 'Comedies'. Apart from the 'happy ending' of the story, *The Tempest* can be taken as comic because its supporting cast of spirits, monsters and apparitions, its noises (its babble and tunes and charms), its magical mutations and phantasms belong in a faery realm, with its close ties to the grotesque, that brand of mordant and capricious humour that mocks truthful representation with hybrids, with impossible newfanglings, and flouts nature's order with contrivance and fabrication. (The name Sycorax, if it does join a pig to a raven, exemplifies this tendency of the grotesque to jumble and shuffle species.) In the mythological tradition, Circe can be read as comic in this perverse sense: she occupies the seductive, erotic area where humour overlaps with entertainment, not jokes, with fantasy, not common sense. It may not seem so on the face of her story, because the moralizing tendency has glamorized her vice and dalliance, turning her into a terrifying witch, a serious *femme fatale*. Her mythical island embodies the grotesque, when she mocks human littleness and vanity with her transmutations of men into beasts. Milton was not sympathetic to Circe, but he caught this central trait of her literary function, when he invented a son for her and gave him the name Comus, personification of revelry and enchantment. In Milton's masque, Comus has inherited his mother's magic and, from Bacchus, his father, his wicked ways with wine, women and song.

The grotesque affiliations of *The Tempest* interestingly reach out to connect the play's imagery with perceptions of the New World circulating in the time of its writing. A growing fashion for grotesque ornament, visual and verbal, of an arbitrary, whimsical and outlandish character coincides with circulating reports of wonders and horrors. The developing taste for this in-itself hybridized connoisseurship, poised between seriousness and frivolity, can throw light on the zoomorphic phantasmagorias of the play, on its magical performances, musical passages, its inclusion of masque and pageant.

As has been much remarked on, Sycorax comes from Algiers, and Alonso *et alii* are returning from Claribel's wedding in Tunis, the neighbouring country on the same African shore of the Mediterranean, so that the geographic location of the island in *The Tempest* is likely to be closer to the position of the Monte Circeo, Circe's homeland south of Rome in Hesiod and in Ovid, or to the imprecise, but Mediterranean, coordinates of Aeaea in the *Odyssey*. However, the many references to New World themes and even places (Ariel once famously flew in a trice to 'the still-vexed Bermudas') complicates – or rather condenses – this geography: the play's imaginary locus super-imposes, it could be argued, two sea roads most notorious in Shakespeare's lifetime for storms, shipwrecks, maroonings, usurpings, mutinies, pirates, buccaneers and other adventures – the Barbary Coast of North Africa and the Spanish Main in the Caribbean. Captain John Ward, for example, died in Tunis in 1623 where he had 'turned Turk' after a fabulously successful career as a pirate; he received the Scots traveller William Lithgow in 1616 in his 'fair palace, beautified with rich marble and alabaster stones', and gave him a safe conduct to 'Algier'.[11] It is not impossible that 'blue-ey'd Sycorax' may refer, correctly, to the colouring of the Berbers with whom successful renegades traded and did their business. Trinculo and Stephano refer in their conversations twice to the pirate flag – not the Jolly Roger in this instance, but 'the Man I' the moon' (II.ii.131–2). But it is the fantastic iconography of the Spanish Main, not of the Barbary Coast, that colours the fauna – and the flora, too – of the island in the play. Botanical and zoological drawings of marvels from the 'Indies' – East, West and South – as illustrated in compendia appearing in the sixteenth century, inform Shakespeare's hybrid imagery. Conrad Gesner's truly marvellous *Historia animalium*, the first part of which appeared in 1551, with subsequently illustrated volumes following in 1554-60, includes various fantastical creatures, monsters and serpents.[12]

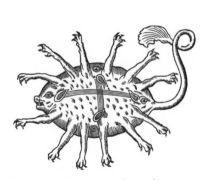

Sea creature between Antibes and Nice, from *Conradi Gesneri Medici Tigurini Historiae Animalium Liber IV. Qui est de Piscium & Aquatilium animantium natura . . .*, 2nd ed. (Frankfurt, 1604), Paralipomena, p. 31.

Sea monster seen near Rome in 1523, from *Nomenclator Aquatilium Animantium. Icones Animalium Aquatilium in mari & dulcibus aquis degentium . . . per Conradum Gesnerum Tigurinum* (Zurich, 1560), p. 175.

In 1607–8, Edward Topsell edited Gesner's magnum opus into two volumes on mammals and serpents, where he described the human-headed manticore with 'a treble row of teeth beneath and above': 'and although India be full of divers ravening Beasts, yet none of them are stiled with the title of *Anthropophagi*, that is to say, *Men-eaters*, except only this *Mantichora*.'[13] The Lamia figures specifically as ' a compounded monster of a Beast and a Fish . . .',[14] while the Tatus or Guinean Beast which 'is brought for the most part out of the new-found world . . . is naturally covered with a hard shell, divided and interlined like the fins of fishes, outwardly seeming buckled to the back like coat-armour; within which the beast draweth up its body, as Hedgehog doth within his prickled skin; and therefore I take it to be a

'The Tatus, or Guinean Beast', from Edward Topsell, *The Historie of Foure-footed Beastes* (London, 1607), p. 705.

Brazilian Hedge-hog'.[15] These beasts were borrowed to evoke the strange wonders of the New World in seventeenth-century prints.[16]

Shakespeare does not quote from Gesner's text, so the fishiness, the scaliness and the hedgehogs may either be fortuitous echoes, struck by the appetite for wonders, or Gesner's zoology may have reached the playwright, as has been persuasively argued, through a French study that specifically focusses on monsters: Ambroise Paré's *Des Monstres et prodiges* which appeared in 1573. Nevertheless Gesner's armadillo offers a highly suggestive insight into Shakespeare's imaginative world on the island: for this creature often provides the New World, 'America' herself, with her throne, her seat, her mount, in allegorical representations. The tatus is one of the several outlandish beasts that distinguish her from other quarters of the globe, as does another frequent attribute: cannibal remains. Commonly in late sixteenth- and early seventeenth-century prints, printed in Holland and in Italy, 'America' appears as a female nude, often in a feathered skirt and a feathered headdress to match, sometimes riding side-saddle on a giant armadillo or Komodo dragon-like monster, or surrounded by a menagerie of animals, fantastical and other (leopards, parrots, winged and crested snakes, bizarre ostrich-like birds), frequently holding a trophy severed head in one hand, while behind her the lopped limbs of victims seethe in cooking-pots.[17] Sometimes, this fantastic scenery of the New World includes zoological hybrids and ill-assorted beasts with human physiognomies that pick up the concurrent representations of Circe's realm. Following in the tradition of Ovid and Pliny and other mythographers who had located monsters like Scylla and Chimaera in the landscape of the ancient world, Lamiae and harpies are shown as if they were discovered species in its new, surpassingly fabulous manifestation. Seventeenth-century printers/engravers sometimes even provided extended captions with eye-witness accounts of the harpy's depredations and capture.

Boundaries between legal documents, zoological anthologies and dramatic fantasies were wide-meshed. In a royal grant of 1625, Charles I invested the first English governor with authority over the 'lately discovered' islands of St Christopher's, Nevis, Barbados and Montserrat. The document's illuminated border recapitulates in the ornamental grotesque style this kind of fantastic ornament.[18] A portrait of the King in full regalia appears within the initial C of his name in the top left hand corner; in the right, on the opposite side of the document, a black female figure in the conventional costume of feathers (in this case red) carries a bow, quiver and a club, and rides side-saddle on a giant armour-plated beast; below her in the right hand margin, a highly elaborate arch, such as might be erected for a royal entrée, frames a

Royal grant from Charles I, investing the first English governor with authority over
St Christopher's, Nevis, Barbados and Montserrat, 1625. Royal Commonwealth Society
Warner/Grant Ms 7.

marine scene where another figure – white and sprite-like – rides a white
sea-serpent. Below them, a double-tailed mermaid spreads her limbs, and
above them, on the top of the architrave, three archers are standing, two of
them painted a ruddy brown and wearing the feathered headdresses and
skirts of the female allegory. In the bottom corners of the charter, tusked and
corkscrew-snouted sea-monsters break the surface of the waves while
caravels in full sail ply the sea beyond them. The whole miniature sequence
opens windows onto the worlds evoked in the Charter's rhetorical flourishes,
and does not merely ornament but illustrates and even expands on the
proud claims of this founding document of the British seaborne empire.

The prevalent taste for such wonders as mermaids and monsters also
leads the selection of ornaments on the First Folio. A comparable example
of light-heartedly grotesque decoration appears in three places: above
the Catalogue of the Plays, over the title of *Henry V* and over the title of
the Folio's first play, *The Tempest* (reproduced on p. 1 of this volume). It
would be pressing the argument too far to propose that the book's
designers intended the ornament to supplement the text, or even draw out

Details of Charles I's royal grant showing
sea monsters.

Detail of Charles I's royal grant showing America seated
on an armadillo-like creature.

Detail of Charles I's royal grant showing feathered
Indians with bows and arrows, a sea monster and,
below, a mermaid spreading her two tails.

Detail of the border of Charles I's royal grant showing ornamental grotesques with Moorish heads.

implications of the plays (its position over *Henry V* would preclude this), but it is nevertheless interesting that the ornament should have been selected at all. It looks like the work of a Dutch engraver, in the school of Frans Floris or Maarten de Vos: in a graceful interlacing of leafy rinceaux, two foliate herms, one young and beardless, the other older, larger and bushy-bearded, are taking aim with bows and arrows at a central cross-legged naked figure, who holds up long-tailed, crested birds in both hands and wears a crest of feathers on his own brow. On each end of the ornament hares with exaggeratedly long ears are sitting up, alertly, and fantastic dogs are intertwined with the greenery in such a way that their tails and ears/horns turn into fronds while from between their back legs long shoots appear, half-penis, half-stem.

The same artist appears to have provided the grotesque endpiece that fills the blank space, when it occurs at the close of a play: this 'Satyr ornament', as it is called, appears 24 times in the First Folio.[19] This decoration comes from a printer's repertory, and here too, the grotesque's conventional mixture of fantastic beasts, exotic, savage mythical figures, and animated foliage creates a playful, frothy, comic combination that makes a virtue of invention for its own sake. Such unnatural and artificial concoctions, such make-believe, revels in the disassociation of representation from truth to appearances – an intrinsic aspect of the grotesque that related it to unnatural magic and to the devil's pleasure in traducing and perverting God's handiwork. It earned the genre of the grotesque much criticism, and deepened its capacity to disturb and disorientate viewers. Both documents' imagery – in the painted illumination of the charter and the ornament on the First Folio – reveal the currency of the iconography in the decade following the first performances of *The Tempest*. They provide a possible way of hearing – and envisaging – the play's scene-setting in contemporary terms. It is worth noting

The 'Satyr Ornament', decorative tail-piece, from Shakespeare's First Folio (London, 1623), p. 303.

that, as William Sherman has pointed out, the 'featherd fowler' ornament on *The Tempest*'s title page appears in other printed tales of imaginary travel or voyages to the New World, including Hakluyt's *The Principall Navigations* (1589), where one of Shakespeare's sources, Antonio Pigafetta, was published.[20]

The Tempest revisits a Circean realm of grotesque transformation, but whereas in Homer and in Ovid, the enchantress's world belongs in the divine perspective of eternity, the play closes with the renunciation of magic by Prospero, and of the metamorphoses and mutations consequent to its processes. But Ariel does not change into a sea-nymph or a harpy simply for the purposes of entertainment; the island domain of Sycorax is also a feminine space, and its aberrations – its rough magic – are implicitly effected by the suppressed witchcraft that is Caliban's inheritance.[21] Ariel has often been played by a woman, and dramatised as female, since the stage directions in the First Folio, which are unusually specific for Shakespeare, indicate: 'Enter Ariel like a water Nymph' and 'Enter Ariel, like a harpy' (III.iii.51).[22] As other commentators on the play have pointed out, *The Tempest* sees a multiple restoration of due patriarchal order according to Salic principles. Not only does Prospero regain his dukedom, but two daughters are given in marriage to become consorts of rulers, not rulers in their own right: Claribel to the King of Tunis and Miranda to Ferdinand, future King of Naples. The repeated pattern of male lineage sets to right again the disruption that Caliban threatens when he claims the island through his mother, while the union of Ferdinand and Miranda, blessed by the goddesses of marriage and plenty, is explicitly absolved from the turmoil of that unruly and independent deity, Venus, and inaugurated as a solemn, holy, official alliance in the interests of society and law.

The apt language for the pervasive menace, for metamorphic magic and erotic disequilibrium is the grotesque; it erupts in order to characterise passions and conduct and values that are assigned to the unruly feminine, witchy, Circean category of experience. The ultimate defeat of Sycorax, that incubus of disorder, and reformation of Caliban, entails an ending to the grotesque pageants as well.

This theme is taken up in a purported sequel to *The Tempest* 'by Shakespeare's hand', which introduces the foul witch herself, *ex machina*: 'The Spirit of his Dam, Sycorax, descends, amid thunder, lightning, etc.' She has a confederate in witchcraft, one Hyrca, whose spells hold in thrall Claribel and her husband, here called Abdallah, and prevent them consummating their love. Hence the title of the play, *The Virgin Queen*. This is not a reference to Elizabeth I, but to Claribel, the author F. G. Waldron explains, and goes on to write, 'a woman of her masculine mind would not have endured to see herself pageanted in a Stage-play, or Interlude'.[23]   For Waldron, the lack of substance in pageants was conspicuously associated with feminine lightness, frivolity and lack of 'masculine mind'. Even more suggestively, when he communicates his tongue-in-cheek deliberations over the authenticity of this sequel to *The Tempest*, he writes 'Unskilled as I am, the only doubt that struck me, on hearing the papers read, was of the word *whymsycalle*; which I then observed, I did not remember to have met with at so early a period: this objection was soon overruled by the supposition that, as the word must have been produced at some period, Shakespeare might have then coined it'.[24]   Waldron is making fun of whimsy, not only in the spoof drama *The Virgin Queen*, but, by extension in *The Tempest* itself, when he ascribes the very invention of the epithet 'whimsical' to Shakespeare.

The grotesque is the aesthetic genre that obeys no principles, only whims, just as witchcraft is the practice of power that disobeys nature's laws of propriety. Circe was the most famous mistress of such mutations; through the grotesque figure of the foul witch Sycorax, Shakespeare simultaneously condemned these Circean powers and annexed them for his own art. Grotesque offered a means to express contemporary inventions; it combined the newly discovered with the newfangled to produce hybrids and monsters; it could be used to communicate the splendours, the savagery, the sheer whimsical novelty of the brave new world.

9 Re-Engineering Virgil: *The Tempest* and the Printed English *Aeneid*

DONNA B. HAMILTON

Empire and colonization, royal absolutism in competition with constitutionalism, and marriage negotiations for the children of King James have dominated discussion of the historical contexts relevant to *The Tempest*, even as interest has grown generally in early modern studies in the European contexts of early English texts. This turning toward Europe requires of us also a returning to the *Aeneid*, the play's primary precursor text. If frequently the *Aeneid*'s status as a literary text has diluted attention to its potency as a 'political vocabulary',[1] the *Aeneid*'s status as the pre-eminent text of empire has continued to foreclose discussion of the implications of that status in relation to Shakespeare's play; for some critics, the *Aeneid* has remained the inviolable monument that the monumental Shakespeare appropriated as royal apologist. Rather than pursuing again the matter of how the *Aeneid* resides in the play,[2] in this essay I return to the subject of how the *Aeneid* resided materially in England prior to 1611.

One way to speculate about the *Aeneid*'s potential valency has been to refer to Tudor and Stuart reliance on Trojan mythology as a means of authorizing royal power and national identity at home and in relation to Europe.[3] A different strategy has been to turn to the place of Virgil in the English educational system; the authorizing language of Virgil in grammar schools and among the learned can help gauge the shifting ideology and intentionality represented in the wide range of Virgilian moments in the works of Ben Jonson and Shakespeare.[4] A survey of dedication practices and the accompanying print history of the English translations of the *Aeneid* confirms and also qualifies these perspectives, while producing an array of information more specific than one might have anticipated about how the *Aeneid* as a printed book was situated in English culture. This history documents the practice in England of appropriating the cultural authority of the *Aeneid* for moments when England's relation to European powers, and especially to the Habsburg empire, was most at issue, as indeed was the case in 1611. This history provides evidence for the conclusion that new editions of the *Aeneid* were themselves participants in political and religious controversy, and clarifies some of the points at which *The Tempest* confronts those issues while also departing from the imperialism and absolutism associated with the *Aeneid*.

The relevance of the *Aeneid* to England and the unexpected nature of its European connections is powerfully demonstrated in the fact that the first three English translations of the *Aeneid*, originally prepared decades apart from each other – by Gavin Douglas (*d.* 1522), Henry Howard, Earl of Surrey (*d.* 1547), and Thomas Phaer (*d.* 1560) – appeared in print for the first time during the reign of Mary Tudor. Because the *Aeneid* is the story of the founding of Rome and because Rome and the Catholic church were, on the Continent, virtually inseparable concepts, the appearance of these editions during Mary's reign speaks first of all to her Catholic identity and European connections, including her close relationship with the Holy Roman Emperor Charles V,[5] and, in 1554, her marriage to Philip II of Spain.

As Anthony Kemp has written, prior to the Reformation and thus to 'the rejection of the *translatio imperii*, the doctrine that the Holy Roman Empire was identical with its classical model', 'Roman cultural identification' had been a 'cement' to Christian unity.[6] Inheriting from his grandfather Maximilian I the symbolic practices of tracing his genealogy to Troy, Charles V had promoted this mode of self-representation as consistent with his domination of a vast empire, 'a united Spain; the newly discovered continent of the Americas; the two Sicilies; the Burgundian Low Countries; Austria; and the Hapsburg lands within Germany.'[7] Charles's defeat of the Turks at Tunis in 1535 would come to epitomize Habsburg glory, which, celebrated first in Charles's entry to Rome in 1536, was to be continuously re-enacted by way of the portable tapestries depicting Charles at Tunis, which, from 1554, first Charles and later Philip used for state occasions in Spain and throughout Europe.[8] When Philip II had acquired sovereignty over Portugal through his marriage to his first wife, Mary of Portugal, he acquired the Portuguese territories in the New World. His self-representation utilized all heroic aspects of the Trojan legend, including the stories of Jason and the argonauts retrieving the Golden Fleece, of Hector defending Troy, and of the adventures of both Aeneas and the heir Ascanius,[9] as though all generations of imperial dignity resided in him.

In returning England to the values that preceded Henry VIII's break with Rome, Mary re-established papal supremacy and reconstituted England's investment in the Habsburg empire and its symbolism. A London printer who had access to the right books at the right time was William Copland, who produced in 1553 the first printed editions of two works by Gavin Douglas, the *Palice of Honour* and the *Aeneid*. Douglas's translation of the *Aeneid* retained the dedication to Henry, third Lord Sinclair, but the title-page now identified Douglas as both 'Bishop of Dunkel [Dunkeld] & unkil to the Erle of Angus', the latter of whom had married Margaret Tudor following the death of James IV.[10] Printing these books by the former Bishop of Dunkeld honoured the continuance of the Tudor line and also England's return to the Catholicism that Scotland had not as yet abandoned. Further, Douglas's translation included the Thirteenth Book by Mapheus Vegius, the fifteenth-century continuer of the *Aeneid*, who had depicted Aeneas being taken into heaven as a reward for having established Rome,[11] thereby removing from the *Aeneid*, and its English versions, any taint from its being a pagan work.

Marian politics must also have figured in the first printed edition of the Earl of Surrey's *Aeneid*. In 1554, John Day printed (for William Awen) Surrey's *Aeneid*, Book IV, with a dedication to Thomas Howard, Surrey's son. In 1547 Henry VIII had ordered Surrey executed for forwarding his own claim to the throne against that of Edward VI, and had imprisoned his father Thomas. On her accession Mary released Thomas and restored him to his title as third Duke of Norfolk; he died in 1554. The date of Day's publication marked that death and the date that Surrey's son Thomas came into the title of Duke of Norfolk.[12] We do not know why Awen published only one of the two books that Surrey had translated. But, given the suppression of *A Mirror for Magistrates* during the reign of Mary[13] and how Surrey met his end, we might surmise that Book II, the story of the fall of Troy, was deemed inappropriate. But Book IV, which narrated Aeneas' departure from Dido to resume his public life and destiny, could have seemed just right, for the Howards and for Mary.[14]

The third English *Aeneid* printed during Mary's reign was that of Thomas Phaer, the first seven books of which were printed in 1558 by John Kingston for Richard Jugge.[15] Identifying himself on the title-page as 'sollicitour to the king and quenes majesties', that is, to Mary and Philip II, Phaer dedicated the edition to Mary as 'Quene of Englande, Spaine, Fraunce, bothe Scicills, Hierusalem and Irelande, defendoure of the faithe, Archeduchesse of Austriche, Duchesse of Burgundie, Millain and Brabant, Countesse of Habsburg, Flanders and Tyroll.' This acknowledgement of the titles Mary had acquired through her marriage made explicit the imperial goals of an England allied with the major Catholic European powers. During the reign of Elizabeth, these systems of representation would be turned to other ends.[16]

Following Elizabeth's succession and prior to his death in 1560, Phaer left instructions that subsequently his *Aeneid* should be dedicated to Nicholas

Bacon,[17] whom, as William Wightman acknowledged in presenting the 1562 edition, Phaer 'tooke for a speciall Patrone and Frendly favorer bothe to him and hys doings.' A Protestant who had acquired wealth from the dissolution of the monasteries, Bacon had been retained by Mary as Attorney of the Court of Wards. On the succession of Queen Elizabeth, Bacon, William Cecil and Matthew Parker led the restoration of England to Protestantism. Toward that end, Cecil and Parker promoted research into English antiquities in order to demonstrate the authority of the Protestant religion, a project that included a reappropriation of the Troy and Brute legends.[18] The printing of the 1562 edition of the *Aeneid*, dedicated to Bacon, coincided with the beginnings of this project.[19]

Whatever the Protestant reappropriations, Catholic rejoinders were never far in the distance. In 1572, following the execution of Thomas Howard, Duke of Norfolk (the dedicatee of the 1554 edition of Surrey's *Aeneid*), for his having attempted marriage to Mary, Queen of Scots, John Leslie, Bishop of Ross, wrote *A treatise of treasons against Q. Elizabeth and the Croune of England*, in which his defence of Mary involved casting Cecil and Bacon as Sinon characters, 'these two synons' (M1v). Like the Greeks who feigned 'religious devotion to Pallas' (e4r) and thereby crept into 'old Troy' and caused its downfall, so had the Sinons of 'new Troy' turned the young Queen Elizabeth away from true religion (e3r). What we may assume to have been the Protestant reply was swift: the Phaer–Twyne *Aeneid* was reprinted in 1573, with twelve books, and again dedicated to Bacon.

Bacon died in 1579, just prior to the years of increased severity in the persecution of Catholics. Meanwhile, the tug-of-war over the cultural authority invested in the *Aeneid* continued. In the 1580s two English Aeneids appeared in rapid succession, the new translation by Richard Stanihurst and a new edition of the Phaer–Twyne translation. An Old English colonizer whose *Chronicle of Ireland* revised a draft by his mentor Edmund Campion and who was suspected of colluding with the Spanish, Stanihurst left for the Continent prior to Campion's execution.[20] His translation of the first four books of the *Aeneid* was printed in Leiden in June 1582, and in London in 1583 by Henry Bynneman, who had printed Latin editions of the *Aeneid* in 1570 and 1572, the 1577 edition of Holinshed's *Chronicles*, and the Gabriel Harvey–Edmund Spenser correspondence, in which Harvey had referred to Stanihurst's use of quantitative metre. Details about the self-presentation of other printed editions of the *Aeneid* clarifies the extent to which Stanihurst calculated the presentation of his *Aeneid* for referentiality to religious, political, colonial and European-British contexts. Appending to the end of his *Aeneid* translations of Psalms 1–4, poems about Thomas More, poems praising the Virgin Mary and eulogies of deceased relatives and countrymen, Stanihurst dedicated his *Aeneid* to his brother-in-law in Ireland, Patrick Plunket, seventh Baron of Dunsany.[21] As self-consciously situated as previous editions of the English *Aeneid*, Stanihurst's version deserves recognition as a protest against current English royal ecclesiastical and colonial policy, a demonstration of his rightful place in elite English culture, and virtually an announcement by one forced into exile that, having fled the British Troy and the Irish Carthage, he too had now travelled toward Rome.[22]

Given the patterns we have seen emerging in the publication of the English *Aeneid*, we would be amiss not to speculate that Stanihurst's edition was the impetus for the next edition of the Phaer–Twyne translation, whose politics would be suitably ambiguated. In the 1584 edition (the final page is dated 26 October 1583), Twyne added Book XIII of Mapheus Vegius; he also changed the dedication from Bacon to Robert Sackville, 'Sonne and heire-apparant to the Right honorable Syr Thomas Sackevill Knight, Lorde Buckehurst'. To affiliate the Phaer–Twyne edition with the Sackvilles would seem to be only an updating of the dedication previously assigned to Bacon. Author of the Virgilian Induction to the *Mirror for Magistrates* and co-author of *Gorbuduc*, Buckhurst rose in favour with Queen Elizabeth throughout the 1580s and 1590s; in 1599 he would succeed Burghley as Lord Treasurer.[23] Nevertheless, there has been speculation regarding Buckhurst's Catholic sympathies,[24] and, in 1580, his son Robert had married Lady Margaret, the daughter of Thomas Howard, fourth duke of Norfolk – to whom the edition of Surrey's translation had been dedicated in 1554 – in whose trial Buckhurst had participated. Like her brother Philip Howard, Earl of Arundel, Margaret was a Catholic. In 1583, the year that Stanihurst's London edition of the *Aeneid* was printed, Buckhurst turned inquisitor and informer against Margaret by recording reports of her celebrating Mass with Lady Arundel.[25] As possibly an answer to Stanihurst's polemical stance, Twyne's 1584 dedication may have represented a public acknowledgment that Robert's first commitment was to his father, who had followed the official Protestantism of Burghley, Bacon and Whitgift, however complicated his or his family's private devotional lives were.

In imitating the *Aeneid* in *The Tempest*, Shakespeare had available what was by then a national practice of appropriating the *Aeneid* for moments of controversy. For this rôle, Jacobean politics of 1611 easily qualified nationally and internationally. From early in his reign, King James's efforts to create an ecumenical council were aligned with his interest in choosing mates for his children from both Catholics and Protestants. Prospects for papal involvement in an ecumenical council faded in the aftermath of the Gunpowder

Plot and assassination of Henri IV.[26] Meanwhile, the anti-Habsburg coalition led by 'the third Earls of Essex, Southampton and Pembroke and the fourth of Bedford' had joined in support of a Protestant marriage for Princess Elizabeth.[27] In eventually settling on Frederick V, Elector Palatine of the Rhine, for his daughter, King James aligned her with a prince from a Calvinist territory who was 'in dignity . . . second to the Emperor' and 'the senior Elector of the Holy Roman Empire'.[28] The Tempest was first performed at a moment when the decision as to Elizabeth's future, a decision that would shape England's position in relation to Europe, was on the brink of being made.[29] Simultaneously, at home and alongside the imperial models that England was cultivating for its position in Europe was the contestatory situation that James's absolutist language and style had produced in his own Parliament. The interrogation of royal power to which the Parliament of 1610 had subjected the King focused on his proclaimed absolutism as having fearful implications for English subjects. Contemporary disagreements about colonial policy in Ireland and America were availing themselves as well of this constitutionalist, subject–monarch language.[30]

As I have tried to show, the history of the printed English *Aeneid* maps rather concretely the politics of post-Henrician England. Similarly, *The Tempest* – which both alludes to the *Aeneid* and, in narrative and phrase, is constituted of its parts – maps the politics of its own time. The play's replication of narrative kernels that imitate (often by reversing) aspects of the fall of Troy, the journey to and from Carthage, and the love of Dido and Aeneas – in combination with the play's representations of rule and subjection, revolt, and reconciliation – are richly homologous to contemporary events in English national and international politics. But, given the degree to which it reinvents the Trojan mythology for a new time, even allowing Prospero to reclaim power in Europe, the play is nowhere more astonishing than in the boldness with which it represents the limitation and withdrawal of royal power, namely the moments when the masque dissolves into '*confused noise*' and when Prospero gives up his magic.[31]

As the English *Aeneid* has been considered here, these moments should seem less puzzling than instructive. The challenge in 1611 was to define a politics that would promote both national and international cooperation. Relying on the *Aeneid* as its operating system, *The Tempest* incorporates the epic's cultural codes, while at the same time remaining open to new exigencies. Aeneas left Troy, taking his gods with him, and journeyed toward the founding of Rome. Mapheus Vegius continued the story by showing Aeneas in heaven. Prospero, triumphant in the union of Miranda and Ferdinand, completes his journey by preparing to return to the place from which he came; to prepare for that return, he discards the magic with which he had tormented Caliban. In this domesticated, pastoral, masque-inflected version of Virgil, the playwright grants that the old politics of the Old World is anachronistic – for both the national and international realms. From the perspective of establishing England's place in Europe by finding a proper husband for Princess Elizabeth, England must choose a Protestant husband; that is, England cannot go to Rome.[32] From the perspective of national politics and thus of those subjected to rule at home, the ruler cannot continue as a magician; he must give up some of his power. On the former point, Shakespeare joins his patrons, including the King; on the latter, he criticizes the King. Remade for its own time, the *Aeneid*, once the exemplary text of empire and of the absolutism promulgated by the Habsburgs,[33] thus became by way of *The Tempest* capable of representing an anti-absolutist position.

10 The Mediterranean and Shakespeare's Geopolitical Imagination

ANDREW C. HESS

The first question a Mediterranean historian will ask after reading *The Tempest* is why Shakespeare chose to offer such a resonant set of Mediterranean geographical referents in his play, but then made little reference to the violent rupture of Mediterranean unity that redefined political and cultural borders at the time and location of his play. The island is roughly situated off the coast of Tunis, at the geographical convergence of Christian and Muslim civilizations. And references to events in the New World suggest that Shakespeare was not opposed to having his audience place the action at the turn of the seventeenth century – shortly after the armies and navies of the powerful Ottoman and Habsburg Empires engaged in a bloody global conflict whose Mediterranean sector ranged from the shores of Morocco to the gates of Vienna. Shakespeare's Mediterranean plays also appeared during an era when European and Muslim rulers marshalled both the religious passions of Mediterranean societies and the sectarian emotions of the Reformation to recast the divisions among Christians as well as between Islam and Christianity.[1] And finally, these powerful events were connected in a complex fashion to a period of social, intellectual, artistic and technical innovation, the Renaissance, during which Europeans broke away from an old cultural order to create new frontiers in space and in imagination.

What follows is an attempt to explore the early modern Mediterranean frontier so as to obtain a deeper understanding of how *The Tempest* was – and was not – part of these processes. I shall make two points. First, colonial readings of the play have tended to obscure the significance of the Mediterranean world for Elizabethan and Jacobean England. But, second, in the play itself there is an avoidance of detailed engagement with the Ottoman Empire that is, perhaps, best explained by England's foreign policy and Shakespeare's participation in a movement to re-frame European culture during an era of ocean-spanning change.

One of the reasons why there has been a tendency in studies of *The Tempest* to avoid stressing the island's location between Tunis and Naples is that for European scholars the centrality of the Mediterranean world in human affairs declined rapidly after the end of the sixteenth century. Not only do historians with visions built on the oceanic expansion of Europe push the politics of the Mediterranean world to one side, they also forget the long history of Christian–Muslim competition and cultural exchange in this region since the rise of Islam in the seventh century. This modern view of the rise of Europe was, however, not the vision of audiences during Shakespeare's lifetime.

European leaders, and especially Philip II of Spain, felt that after the Christian victory at the battle of Lepanto in 1571, the Ottoman Empire could no longer mount a serious threat to the western Mediterranean flank of the Christian world. However, contrary to Spanish and Papal judgements, the Ottomans rebuilt their navy after the battle of Lepanto and proceeded to project their power into the western Mediterranean basin through the recapture of Tunis in 1574. But the Christians were right in their judgement on Ottoman imperial ambitions in North Africa: it was too far away from Istanbul, too close to Spain, and too poor to yield the taxes needed to finance major campaigns at the western end of the Mediterranean. Meanwhile Philip II's decision on where to concentrate his forces was influenced by the conquest of Portugal in 1580 and the continued expansion of the Protestant movement in northern Europe. Above all, war on two frontiers regularly put Spain on the edge of bankruptcy.[2]

Fortunately for the Habsburgs, the Ottoman Empire found itself in an astonishingly similar shape. Faced with expensive and unproductive campaigns on its Balkan, Russian and Mediterranean borders, the viziers turned their armies against a sectarian enemy in the east, the Shiite Empire of Safavid Persia. Thus the political economy of late-sixteenth-century Mediterranean warfare encouraged the Habsburgs and the Ottomans to arrange a truce in 1580. This stand-off between the two empires marked the end of large-scale imperial conflict in the Mediterranean Sea and a shift in the attention of court historians to other spaces.[3]

This decentralization of Christian–Muslim relations after 1580 substantially changed the way Christian Mediterranean writers, and especially Spanish and Italian authors, thought about the frontier between the two civilizations. During Shakespeare's youth the Mediterranean conflict between the Ottoman and Spanish empires dominated the political history of the Mediterranean world and Europe. However, between 1571 and 1580 both empires abandoned imperial ventures on their common frontier in order to address major problems elsewhere. Thus, Shakespeare settled on the location of The Tempest just after the rulers of the Ottoman and Habsburg empires reduced the level of military and ideological conflict in the Mediterranean region. Moreover, they also drew a dividing line between Islamic and Christian civilizations that placed Tunis solidly beyond the boundaries of Renaissance Europe at the dawn of English commercial entry into the Mediterranean world.

Spanish and English authors at this time employed a negative stereotype of the Turk, Moor, African and Muslim as a means of complimenting the civilized nature of their own societies. The net effect of this literary development not only confirmed the cultural boundaries of the Mediterranean world, it increased the geographical range of imagination to include frontier regions of the previously dangerous Ottoman Empire.[4] As Jack D'Amico's study of the Moor in English Renaissance drama demonstrates, this genre was well developed in England before the staging of The Tempest.[5] And as Nabil Matar's recent work on the description of Islam in Britain from 1558 to 1685 testifies, its authors remained hugely uninformed about the Islamic world, let alone the Ottoman Empire.[6] When joined with the place of Tunis in the history of the Roman Empire, the early modern literature reinforces this city's resonance in Shakespeare's geographical imagination.

Finally, European scholars created, over the next three centuries, a way of studying Islam that limited discussion to elite subjects in a manner that tended to discourage a practical understanding of Muslim affairs. While this Orientalist mode of thinking spread in Europe, Muslims followed an intellectual path that also restricted their understanding of European affairs.[7] Rather than encouraging travel to lands to the north and west of the Empire, they confined their knowledge of European matters to military affairs on land frontiers where the Ottomans increasingly found it difficult to achieve territorial conquests. But these conquests did not open new intellectual spaces for Muslims; and military success confirmed a sense of superiority that found expression in a reworking of classical Islamic culture.[8] In the years following the staging of Shakespeare's Mediterranean plays both Orientalists and Turko-Muslim leaders moved away from the idea that it was necessary to learn in a practical sense about each other through widespread human interaction.

The extraordinary success of the British and Dutch naval empires that followed established modern European imperialism and laid the foundation for the anti-colonial readings of The Tempest. Here scholars have suggested that Shakespeare anticipated the inequalities of European colonialism in terms of the master–slave relationship between Prospero and Caliban. It is true that he drew a negative contrast between the cultural background of Caliban and the civilizational heritage of Prospero. But his objective, I would argue, was not to predict the future but rather to delimit the cultural boundaries of Europe in the face of chaos and strong competition from an Islamic civilization whose political leadership had paradoxically become an ally of England.

THE MEDITERRANEAN LIMITS TO EARLY MODERN CULTURE

The emphasis on the power of Europe that runs through the colonial critique of *The Tempest* pushes aside a discussion of the central question in the intellectual history of the sixteenth-century Mediterranean world: why did the Ottoman Empire not keep pace with the development of modern science and technology in Europe? There are many explanations for the spectacular changes that overtook the Mediterranean world between the Hispano-Ottoman truce of 1580 and the death of Shakespeare in 1616. A full development of the historical context for *The Tempest* is beyond the scope of this essay. I will, therefore, limit the information in the discussion that follows to some of the political and cultural events in Mediterranean history that seem most pertinent to Shakespeare's handling of the multicultural setting of *The Tempest*.

Recent studies of late-sixteenth-century Mediterranean politics make it increasingly difficult to exclude the Ottoman Empire from the framework of early modern European politics, let alone other fields of historical and literary research. The work of S. A. Skilliter and Geoffrey Parker both leave no doubt that the Turkish Empire occupied a major position in the sixteenth-century European relations that pitted Spain against England.[9] This was certainly the case after 1570 when the Pope excommunicated Elizabeth I a year before the Holy League managed to defeat the Ottoman navy at the battle of Lepanto in 1571. Philip II of Spain thought this defeat of the Turks would permit him to consolidate his position in the Mediterranean – he fortified Tunis and began negotiations with the Ottomans – in order to put down the Protestant rebellion in northern Europe. The Ottomans, meanwhile, promptly strengthened their negotiating position when they rebuilt their navy, drove the Spanish out of Tunis in 1574 and helped the Saadien rulers of Morocco to defeat a Portuguese crusade in the summer of 1578. These last events marked the defeat of the Iberian effort to extend the Reconquest into North Africa and convinced Elizabeth's policy makers that the Ottoman

Empire was a natural ally of England – despite the fact that for England, as for France earlier in the sixteenth century, an alliance with the Ottomans presented a number of serious problems (not the least of which included the still powerful idea among Europeans that, regardless of current divisions among Protestants and Catholics, the common enemy was Islam).

On the Ottoman side the viziers had a number of reasons for an alliance with England. Long before the second half of the sixteenth century the Turks learned through their intelligence networks of the religious divisions within the Christian community. In 1569 their agents attempted to encourage a Lutheran revolt against the Habsburgs in order to aid the near simultaneous uprising of the Moriscos (Spanish Muslims who were forced to convert to Christianity) in Spain. These same spies probably informed their masters of the Pope's excommunication of Elizabeth I in 1570. An Ottoman alliance with England, then, made good political sense.[10]

There was another very important military reason for the Ottoman interest in England. War on the Persian frontier required great quantities of arms, ammunition and clothing that were not available in Ottoman domains. English merchants had already developed a reputation for their armaments trade with Muslims in North Africa since the mid-sixteenth century; and during the last two decades of the sixteenth century they discovered a much bigger market for their goods in Istanbul.[11]

By 1578, Queen Elizabeth, perhaps on the recommendation of Sir Francis Walsingham, decided that her realm would benefit from a policy of *realpolitik* – by establishing relations for the first time with the Ottoman sultan. In that year she dispatched William Harborne to Istanbul to begin discussions with the Ottomans on the encouragement of trade between the two states.

As Skilliter has observed, the English initiative was bound to be successful. The Ottomans agreed rather promptly to a capitulation treaty with the English in May 1580: the details of this agreement concerned the establishment of English commercial outposts in the Ottoman Empire. These places are located along the coasts of North Africa and at the eastern end of the Mediterranean: Alexandria, Tripoli in Syria, Algiers, Tunis, Tripoli in Libya, and Cairo.[12]

Philip II's naval defeat at the hands of the English in 1588 confirmed the political advantages for the Ottomans of an alliance with England. The victory at sea also demonstrated the technological superiority of England's armaments and naval forces. In terms of the armaments trade with the Ottomans, the way was now open for enterprising captains from both England and Holland to enter the Mediterranean to trade their goods on a large scale.

However, by the turn of the seventeenth century the commerce in armaments began to threaten the legitimacy of England's ruler. Ottoman viziers found that the great difficulty of conducting warfare on distant frontiers against well-fortified positions and well-armed opponents dramatically increased the Empire's demand for munitions and clothing. As a result, English merchants unhesitatingly expanded their supply of clothing and armaments to the Ottoman military establishment. At this stage, however, the business was so robust it became quite difficult for the state to deny that it was violating the old canon law that forbade the sale of military equipment to Muslims. To compound matters the Ottomans redirected their military activities toward the Balkans at the end of the sixteenth century and thereby revived a culturally entrenched hostility in Europe toward the Turks and Islam. With the aid of the printing-press, English exiles working for the Roman Catholic cause promptly stimulated public opposition in England to the Crown's alliance with the Turk.

What brought this problem to a head at the beginning of Shakespeare's career was the charge that Queen Elizabeth incited the Ottomans to attack Christendom when her agents encouraged the Ottomans to go to war with the Hungarians in 1593. The goal of English policy was to divert the energies of Spain away from northern Europe by encouraging the resumption of warfare with the Turks. While this did not particularly alarm the Protestants of Central Europe, when the Ottomans decided that attacking Spain meant a campaign against Balkan Christendom, they joined the Roman Catholic critics in condemning English foreign policy. Finally, at the start of the war in 1596 the Catholic propagandists' cause received a major boost when the English ambassador Edward Barton accompanied Sultan Mehmet III to Hungary, where the Ottoman army defeated their Christian opposition in two major battles. The news of this event spread through Europe to Russia in a manner that forced Elizabeth to mount a diplomatic campaign aimed at convincing European rulers that England was not supplying the Turkish forces with munitions and that the Sultan had forced Barton to witness the Ottoman campaign.[13] It is hard to believe that Shakespeare was unaware of the propaganda fireworks this event stimulated and of how dangerous it would be to put the politics of the English alliance with the Ottomans on the stage.

In the decade after 1580 the English launched a naval revolution in the Mediterranean Sea.[14] Well before their naval prowess became visible in the defeat of Spain in 1588, the English had perfected the design and armament of the ocean-going *bretoni*. The English innovations were, however, not just in ship and cannon design; they also involved the creation of a sophisticated maritime community of experienced captains, cannoniers, boatswains and common crew. When this combination of tested equipment and experienced personnel entered the Mediterranean world after the truce of 1580, they encountered a technologically obsolete maritime culture. Since their superior naval ability was not recruited or deployed in a struggle for religious or imperial hegemony, the Northern sailors simply looked for work. This rapidly meant engaging in lucrative corsair ventures. By the end of the sixteenth century the technological advantages of new ships, combined with a decline in the ability of Spanish and Ottoman empires to control their Mediterranean coastlines, ushered in a phase of decentralized naval warfare. Dutch and English captains who engaged in this form of violence promptly discovered North African ports where they found local Ottoman officials eager to participate in joint ventures – or, at the least, prepared to ignore the origin of the goods the freebooters often sold in their cities. Major consequences of this development were the destruction of Venetian naval commerce and the English and Dutch capture of the internal Ottoman coastal trade.

During the first decade of the seventeenth century England's corsairs ruled the waves in the Mediterranean Sea. The bases of their strength lay in the skill of their sailors, the ability of their ships to sail in all seasons, and the capacity of their crews to perform effectively in both war and commerce. Because their mother country's main opponent was Spain, the English corsairs did not hesitate to raid the rich Spanish trade with the New World.

Soon the Ottomans discovered that their Mediterranean opponents had begun to purchase and use northern European shipping. This prompted the Sultan to send an envoy to England to complain about placing this weaponry in the hands of his enemies. Meanwhile the Ottoman Empire only made token efforts to acquire the maritime skills of the European corsairs. As provincial representatives of the Sultan in Algeria, Tunisia, Libya and other coastal regions of the Empire became aware of the technical superiority of the English and Dutch corsairs, they began to lease northern ships and crews for their own privateering operations. They employed English ships to carry pilgrims on their way to Mecca and Medina; and they allowed the Northerners to capture the maritime trade in core agricultural items.[15]

By 1604 chaotic naval violence in the Mediterranean reached a zenith. In that year Shakespeare produced *Othello*, a play about the fate of an African *condottiere* whom the Venetians had recruited for the purpose of defending their naval bases in the eastern Mediterranean.[16] At that same time Tunis had become the major port for twenty English vessels engaged in privateering. A year later the English corsair, Captain John Ward, organized the Tunisian freebooters into a fleet that raided both Muslim and Christian shipping throughout the Mediterranean. Venetian complaints about the devastating impact on their economy of this revolution in naval technology emphasized how state and religion counted for nothing compared to the booty of the privateers. Moreover, the failure of Mediterranean states to respond to this decentralized challenge to trade stimulated the growth of other piratical strongholds. And soon a Mediterranean-wide trade in stolen goods and in the ransoming of captives drove up the costs of protection and discouraged commercial trade.[17]

There is plenty of information on the English rôle in this new page in Mediterranean naval history. This is especially the case for those captains who used North African ports. At the turn of the century the most flamboyant of these individuals was Captain Ward. Not only did he command a fleet of his own ships, he also flaunted his wealth by maintaining an expensive residence and lifestyle in Tunis. Although his exploits enlivened popular ballads about England's sailors, it was his conversion to Islam that put him on the London stage. In Robert Dadborne's *A Christian turn'd Turke, or The Tragicall Liues and Deaths of the two Famous Pyrates, Ward and Danisker* (1612), Ward's acceptance of Islam is described as an evil equal to Doctor Faustus's sale of his soul to the Devil.[18] The larger stage, however, for this affair is that Ward raised, in a naval framework, the important cultural problem of how to prevent a crossover on the frontier to the other side – 'turning Turk'.[19]

Shakespeare's response to disorder on the North African frontier is not to celebrate imperial conquests but to reinforce the cultural cohesion of Renaissance Europe. The most conspicuous event in the play that can give some insight into *The Tempest*'s cultural project is the marriage of Claribel to the King of Tunis before the play begins. During the early modern period the most familiar barrier separating Christians from Muslims was marriage. Early on in the play, the fate of Claribel begins Shakespeare's discussion of the appropriate Renaissance structure for marriage with negative reference to Africa. Not long after he recovers his senses on Prospero's island, Alonso is drawn into a conversation on the wisdom of his daughter's marriage, and he does not hesitate to remark how much he regrets his decision to make such a union and laments the thought that he will never see her again. Later in *The Tempest* Shakespeare does offer his audience an appropriate marriage. Caliban, the African, is firmly rejected as a suitor for Prospero's daughter; and the appropriate union is a love-match between Miranda and Ferdinand that links the ruling families of two Italian city-states.

Italian and Ottoman sources on inter-civilizational marriage in the early seventeenth century support the argument that the imaginative purpose of Claribel's wedding for Shakespeare was only to provide a negative contrast for Miranda's marriage, being – at that moment – a deeply unlikely occurrence. There were three trends, each of which required conversion to Islam, that would all but have ruled out a political marriage between Naples and Tunis. First, the sixteenth century witnessed a disappearance of dynastic marriages at the centre of the Ottoman Empire: imperial success on the battlefield removed the need for what Ottomans came to regard as an alliance based on weakness. Second, as a corollary, ruling-class members increasingly married among themselves. And finally, the single generation character of the elite-building slave system for Ottoman males and the parallel practice of concubinage in the harems made impossible the marriage calculations common to the landed and commercial nobility of Europe.[20]

Seen in this Mediterranean context, Shakespeare's avoidance of the Ottoman question, of religious issues, and his defence of Renaissance values simply made both good theatre and smart politics.

CODA: PROSPERO AND THE REFASHIONING OF MEDITERRANEAN IDENTITIES

In April of 1616 both Miguel de Cervantes Saavedra and Shakespeare died. These two authors left monumental works of imagination devoted to Renaissance ideals. These early modern writers also made foundational contributions to the creation of a modern literature of imagination in the European languages of their homelands. Their work, therefore, became a fundamental part of the identity formation process for the modern societies of Spain and England.

Sixteen years before the death of these two European authors the most famous of the sixteenth-century Ottoman writers died. In contrast to the modern literary reputations of Cervantes and Shakespeare, the poet Baki is virtually unknown among European scholars and even among those who read modern Turkish literature. It is extraordinarily difficult to compare his work with the achievements of Cervantes and Shakespeare. Baki's poetry is not part of a 'Renaissance' literature; rather it is connected to a medieval Islamic tradition that began in the thirteenth century and ended in the late nineteenth century. This literature is governed by a conservative mentality based on the revealed religious scriptures of Islam. Therefore, the product of this most influential of early modern writers for the Ottomans consisted of poems that displayed respect for authority, tradition, inherited social order and the importance of form over empirical detail. Ottoman poetry, therefore, left little room for the play of imagination that runs through the literary products of modern European writers.

These imaginative expressions in European literature of a human ability to reject the past and determine the future became part of a larger division between the two regions of the ruptured Mediterranean world. That is, the European creation of imaginary human beings who would manipulate nature and recast their position in society was substantially at odds with the wide agreement in the Islamic religious establishment that an all-powerful God determined one's destiny.[21] Similarly, the emphasis on secular accomplishments in Renaissance literature diverged greatly from the Muslim ideal that found merit only in the degree to which one served God. Thus, from the point of view of the Ottoman literary establishment, Shakespeare began *The Tempest* with a sacrilegious act.

This citie is called by the Latines Tunetum, *and by the Arabians* Tunus, *which name they thinke to be corrupt, because it signifieth nought in their language: but in old time it was called* Tarsis, *after the name of a citie in Asia. At the first it was a small towne built by the Africans vpon a certain lake, about twelue miles distant from the Mediterranean sea. And vpon the decay of Carthage Tunis began to increase both in buildings and inhabitants. For the inhabitants of Carthage were loth to remaine any longer in their owne town, fearing least some armie would haue beene sent out to Europe: wherefore they repaired vnto Tunis, and greatly enlarged the buildings thereof.*

. . . And so while all those regions were at mutuall dissension, the dominions of Tunis began mightily to encrease . . . the king of Tunis returning home conqueror from Telensin, was receiued with great triumph, and was saluted king of all Africa, because indeed there was no prince of Africa at the same time comparable vnto him. Wherefore he began to ordaine a roiall court, and to choose Secretaries, counsellers, captaines, and other officers appertaining to a king; after the very same manner that was vsed in the court of Maroco. And from the time of this king euen till our times, the kingdome of Tunis hath so prospered, that now it is accounted the richest kingdome in all Africa. The said kings sonne raigning after his fathers death, enlarged the suburbes of Tunis with most stately buildings. Without the gate called Bed Suvaica he built a streete containing to the number of three hundred families: and he built another streete at the gate called Bed el Manera consisting of more then a thousand families. In both of these streetes dwell great store of artificers, & in the street last mentioned all the Christians of Tunis, which are of the kings garde, haue their aboad. Likewise there is a third streete built at the gate next vnto the sea, called Beb el Bahar, and being but half a mile distant from the gulfe of Tunis. Hither doe the Genoueses, Venetians, and all other Christian merchants resort, and here they repose themselues out of the tumult and concourse of the Moores: and this street is of so great bignes, that it containeth three hundred families of Christians and Moores, but the houses are verie low, and of small receit. The families of the citie, togither with them of the suburbs, amount almost to the number of ten thousand.

This passage from the narrative of Leo Africanus, translated into English by John Pory in 1600, demonstrates the contemporary resonance of Tunis – the city and the king. Joannes Leo, *A Geographical Historie of Africa* (London, 1600), p. 247.[1]

11 Carthage and Tunis, *The Tempest* and Tapestries

JERRY BROTTON

The quarrel between Gonzalo, Sebastian and Adrian over the relationship between contemporary Tunis and classical Carthage in Act II, scene i has invariably been dismissed as an obscure and possibly ribald gloss on Virgil's *Aeneid*.[1] It is not immediately obvious as to how the dramatic action of *The Tempest* is assisted by this pedantic quibble on historical geography. I want to suggest that such an apparently abstruse reference to the classical geography of the *Aeneid* invites a reconsideration of the more contemporary significance of the Mediterranean geography of the play for a seventeenth-century audience. It is this Mediterranean world, and its invocation of not only seventeenth-century Tunis, but Algiers too, the birthplace of Sycorax, and Naples, 300 miles north of Tunis, which has become what Andrew C. Hess has called the 'Forgotten Frontier' of seventeenth-century culture and politics.[2] To reintegrate this world into the geographical fabric of *The Tempest* is not to dismiss the New World dimension of the play, but to suggest that the play has a much more complex and overdetermined awareness of geography than has often been thought.

This geographical complexity lies in the play's historical allusions to a past – but still culturally influential – classical world. The magical, masque-like quality of *The Tempest* comes from the sense that its voyaging is partly though time, partly through space. As Alonso's voyage to and from Tunis echoes Aeneas' journey to Italy via Carthage, so the allusion to a classical topography confers a sense of the play as shuttling between the weft of the present and the warp of the past. Such a temporal slippage was consistent with early modern perceptions of the Mediterranean world. This was the world that provided the backdrop for the narratives of the writers who were to exercise such a decisive influence on sixteenth-century humanism.[3] Not just Virgil, but Homer, Strabo and of course Ptolemy all took the geography of the Mediterranean as the inspiration for their writings. The books of which Prospero admits 'I prize above my dukedom' (I.ii.166) would undoubtedly have included some of the greats of the classical world, which allow Prospero a heightened understanding of his position in relation to space and geography, as well as time and history. Prospero recalls that he is not only furnished with valuable books by Gonzalo as he sails into exile. He is also provided with 'Rich garments, linens, stuffs, and necessaries' (I.ii.164). Textual learning and awareness of the interface between the contemporary world and the classical world was a vital dimension of Renaissance humanism, but its corollary was the sumptuous and visually arresting display of wealth and esoteric learning.[4] Nowhere can this be seen more clearly than in the visually dramatic display of Renaissance tapestries. I would suggest that in its dramatization of travel and geography, *The Tempest* is analogous to the visual symbolism of narrative tapestries, from their rise in the late fifteenth century right through to the early seventeenth century. This is reflected in the similar geographical scope of both play and tapestry, as well as the ways in which tapestries of the period represent a geographical 'doubling' in terms that are strikingly similar to those encountered in *The Tempest*.

Tapestry 'was the most expensive movable artistic production of the period',[5] involving a series of highly skilled craftsmen, expensive materials such as silk, gold, silver and precious dyes, and invariably specially commissioned designs or cartoons. Many of the most lavish tapestries involved narrative cycles of sometimes up to twelve separate panels, which adorned churches and courts throughout Europe. The stories they depict appear to offer standard moralized stories from the Bible and the ancient world. Some of the most popular designs included *The Prodigal Son, The Apocalypse, The Story of Alexander the Great, The Golden Fleece, The Trojan War,* and *Hercules*, which supplemented numerous tapestries illustrating more straightforwardly decorative *millefleurs, verdure* and hunting scenes.[6] It is particularly striking that many of these tapestry cycles dramatized different states of travel and voyaging. Either at the moral and symbolic level of the story of the Prodigal Son, or at the more strictly literal level of the fascination with the space of the Mediterranean *ecumene* portrayed in the stories of Alexander the Great and the Trojan War, these tapestries foregrounded an interest in space and travel that was mediated through the narratives of the classical world. As Anthony Grafton and Lisa Jardine have suggested, the texts of the classical world were 'studied for action'[7] by artists, scholars and diplomats eager to apply the lessons of the past to the present. Tapestries were particularly evocative in offering a visually compelling image of both the moral and the practical implications of travel. The courts of late-fifteenth-century Europe tested the limits of their own world in relation to the *ecumene* of the classical world, which was vividly displayed in the tapestry cycles adorning their walls.

The threads that tie tapestries and travel together are borne out by the extent to which such tapestries began to represent the contemporary expansion of the Mediterranean-centred Renaissance world picture. As early as the 1470s the Portuguese court had commissioned a set of four Tournai tapestries known as *The Taking of Arzila*, celebrating the successful Portuguese military campaign in Morocco in 1471.[8] Whilst the topography and military paraphernalia of the tapestries is studiedly contemporary, their design and iconography is almost identical to contemporaneous tapestries depicting the Trojan War.[9] In 1504 King Manuel of Portugal commissioned a series entitled *The Voyage to Calicut* from the Tournai tapestry maker Gilles le Castre.[10] The tapestries were intended to celebrate the daring of Portugal's breaching of the boundaries of the classical *ecumene*, in establishing a sea route to India via the Cape of Good Hope in the aftermath of Vasco da Gama's first voyage in 1498. As a result their composition drew heavily on earlier tapestries portraying that other heroic traveller, Alexander the Great. By 1525 the Portuguese court had commissioned a remarkable series of three tapestries entitled *The Spheres*, showing the astrological, celestial and terrestrial worlds, with the final tapestry exhibiting the global pretensions of an increasingly powerful Portuguese maritime empire.[11]

Perhaps the most significant tapestry series of the period, and certainly the most expensive and innovative cycle to be produced in the sixteenth century, was Willem de Pannemaker's series of twelve tapestries based on the cartoons of Jan Vermeyen, entitled *The Conquest of Tunis*. Completed in 1554, the tapestries celebrated the victory of the Habsburg Emperor Charles V over the Turkish forces at Tunis in 1535. Costing a contemporary fortune, they took eight years to complete. The remarkable first tapestry in the cycle portrays a bird's-eye topographical view of the theatre of military operations, the Mediterranean basin, but could also act as a map of the geography of *The Tempest*. Alongside the geographical precision and complex military logistics recorded in such incredible detail, the tapestries also contained the threads of a ghostly classical past into which the Habsburg forces self-consciously stepped. In the third tapestry in the cycle, entitled 'The Disembarkation Before La Goleta', the description of the scene remarkably adumbrates the dispute over Tunis and Carthage between the courtiers in *The Tempest*:

> Here they enter the port of Utica; ancient Carthage receives them in her ruins. Caesar [Charles V] goes with a small body-guard to explore Goleta . . . He pitches camp beside the walls of Carthage once illustrious, today again a village of small cottages.[12]

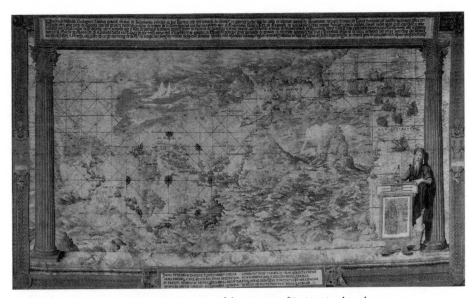

'Map of the Mediterranean Basin', first tapestry of the *Conquest of Tunis* series, based on cartoons by Jan Cornelisz Vermeyen, woven in Brussels by Willem de Pannemaker, 1549–51, wool and silk, 520 x 895 cm.

This is an acute level of geographical specification, clearly distinguishing the topography of contemporary Tunis from ancient Carthage. Yet in its historical invocation of Carthage it creates a series of analogies between past and present that reverberated well beyond the tapestries. Charles was styled the *Tertio Africano*, emulating the great Roman victories in Africa of Scipio Major and Minor.[13] This analogy had already been anticipated in a monumental tapestry cycle designed in 1544 entitled *The Story of Scipio*, which portrayed the victory of Scipio Africanus over Hannibal outside Carthage at the Battle of Zama in 202 BC. The similarities to the *Conquest of Tunis* tapestries are striking; as Roy Strong has pointed out, 'the victories were of valiant Romans over Carthaginians, not of invading knights over infidel Turks'.[14]

Such historical doubling is given an added dimension in the choice of tapestry designs made by Charles V's admiral of the Tunis campaign, Andrea Doria. By 1536, when Charles visited Doria at the Palazzo Doria in Genoa, the admiral had installed a series of tapestries in his Neptune Salon designed by Perino del Vaga entitled the *Navigatione d'Enea*.[15] The parallels between Aeneas and the exploits of both Charles V and his admiral were obvious. If Charles assumed the mantle of Scipio Africanus in his Roman exploits, then he could go even further back into classical history to also claim a direct link with the founder of the Roman Empire. Meanwhile Doria, rather like his descendant Prospero, could also mobilize the figures of Aeneas and Neptune as tamers of the sea; as Bernice Davidson points out, 'the admiral of the imperial fleet calmed the storm, bringing peace and safety to the seas. Just as Neptune conducted the Trojans safely to Italian shores and the conquest of Latium, so Doria carried the emperor's men to their victory over Genoa',[16] not to mention Tunis. Like the *Conquest of Tunis* tapestries, Doria's *Navigatione d'Enea* tapestries drew on the classical topography of Carthage, Rome and the treacherous storm-tossed waters of the Mediterranean to legitimize the military actions of the Habsburg Empire. The actions of the present neatly dovetailed with the feats of the classical past, and conferred a veneer of legitimacy and continuity on the conduct of the Habsburg forces. They also conveniently elided the reality of the Ottoman presence in North Africa; Tunis soon became an isolated Habsburg stronghold along an otherwise Ottoman-dominated coastline, and by 1569 the city had fallen back into Ottoman hands.[17]

The events of Tunis were not lost on the English court. On their completion in 1554, the *Conquest of Tunis* tapestries were packed up and dispatched to England, where they were destined to make their first appearance at the wedding of Charles V's son Philip II to Mary Tudor at Winchester. Mary's father, Henry VIII, had amassed over 2,000 pieces of tapestry, including, significantly, a set of *Dido and Aeneas* tapestries that are still housed at Hampton Court Palace.[18] However, the Tudors possessed nothing to compare with the magnificence of *The Conquest of Tunis* tapestries, although Mary herself was not averse to encouraging cultural production that looked to the past as a strategy for underwriting the present. Under Mary's literary patronage Thomas Phaer published *The seven first bookes of the Eneidos of Virgill* in 1558, and by 1573 Thomas Twyne completed Phaer's translation of all twelve books of the *Aeneid*.[19] As with the visual interweaving of past and present so vividly represented in the tapestries, Phaer and Twyne's translation is studded with anachronistic references to Aeneas being 'driven from *Italy* an extreme course, to the countrye of whyte *Moores* in *Affrike*,'[20] to marginal glosses on Dido noting that 'Of her came Hannibal that after plaged Rome'.[21] As English commercial activities extended into the eastern Mediterranean from the late 1570s onwards, these models were necessary to come to terms with places that were imbued with an intimidating classical aura. However, such ways of dealing with the region were also used to confront the fact that these territories were now under the control of the Islamic Ottoman Empire.

The suggestion of an analogy between tapestries and *The Tempest* is not just based on the extent to which tapestries like *The Conquest of Tunis*, or the other tapestries and painted hangings that appear throughout Shakespeare's work,[22] focus on the Mediterranean world that structures the action of the play. It is also based on the iconographic similarities between the two forms. The action of *The Tempest* – in its romance structure, its carefully staged tableaux and its masque-like quality – give it the feel of a dramatic tapestry. The play displays before its audience a peculiar entwining of a past and present Mediterranean geography, and of the morality of voyaging into territories that can become distant, terrifying and bewildering places; or as Antonio describes Tunis itself, 'Ten leagues beyond man's life' (II.i.245).

The New World is not absent from this perspective, but it is still far distant simply in terms of the inherited and available models for understanding the vicissitudes of travel. This is precisely what so many of the tapestry cycles of the period explored in scene after scene. Their focus remained fixed on the magical but dangerous activity of long-distance voyaging, whereby travellers laid themselves open to fate, chance and accident. In many of these tapestries fate and chance are often invoked through recourse to storms and tempests – recalling the opening action of *The Tempest*. By the time that *The Tempest* was performed, Tunis and Algiers were back in the hands of the Ottoman authorities. Vigorous English activities throughout the Mediterranean were characterized by unprincipled privateering, pragmatic alliances with the Ottomans, and an enthusiastic participation in a burgeoning slave trade that included Muslims and Christians alike. As this particular geographical thread of the play begins to unravel, it becomes ever clearer that the geography of *The Tempest* breaches far more boundaries than has previously been appreciated.

12 Island Logic

ROLAND GREENE

In the fourteenth century, Sir John Mandeville's *Travels* represented the peoples and societies of Asia in terms of islands: islands where the natives have faces on the fronts and backs of their heads or gems in their eyes; islands where the sick are hung from trees to be eaten by birds; and of course an island atop a mountain, the earthly paradise. In 1562 the scientist and translator Richard Eden concocted in a glass 'a little rounde Iland as brode as [a] riall or sumwhat more, with at least a hundred syluer trees abowt an ynche high, so perfectly formed with trunkes, stalkes, and leaves . . .that I suppose no lymne[r] or paynter is able to conterfecte the like.'[1] And in 1651 the Spanish writer Baltasar Gracián published the first part of his *El Criticón*, a philosophical dialogue between the intellectual Critilo and the natural Andrenio, which is set on the desert island where Andrenio has spent his entire life. All these productions participate in an early modern outlook that touches much of the history, cosmography and literature of the period, in which insularity comes to stand for a kind of knowledge, a distinctively partial knowledge that counters the totalities of institutions and regimes. Like *Don Quixote* and *New Atlantis*, *The Tempest* belongs to the final episode in this convention, before it becomes totalizing itself, and before the knowledge it conveys becomes systematic (as has already happened in the *Criticón*) rather than local or leveraged.

Moreover, *The Tempest* is not only a function of insularity but a play of encounters. To say it another way, the play adapts the attitude of masque or farce to a social and cultural milieu beset by change, one in which the givenness of the unitary, European-centred world around it has exploded into fragments. Worldmaking is very much in this play's sights, and major characters are defined in part by their involvement with the making of worlds. Between Tunis, Milan, Naples, Bermuda, Carthage and the strategic no-place of Prospero's island, Shakespeare posits a plurality of worlds – that is, symbolic orders that represent social, religious and political regimes – that can scarcely be bridged in human experience, and across which the only suitable bridge is magic, with Prospero as worldmaker. On its island *The Tempest* delivers a sequence of staged encounters among these worlds where the encounter itself, not a conventional plot in the fashion of other plays by Shakespeare, is the business of the drama. But what is schematic in dramatic terms may lend itself to what is critical or predictive in geopolitical terms. Prospero's rôle as protagonist posits a singular figure who can draw the world together again into a unity – he is the protoglobalist, though whether he represents the capitalist, the humanist, the patriarch, or all of these is left tactically uncertain. However, he can be depicted only within and from the horizon of the island. A mainland Prospero would challenge representation: he would be power itself, seen without shadings or perspectives. Accordingly, *The Tempest* uses the vantages of encounters and islands to offer predictions about the magic of early modern worldmaking.

ENCOUNTERS

What is an encounter? *Encounter*, in its various versions in the principal languages of western Europe, is a studiously vague term that crops up often but without much attempt at systematic definition; like any number of other terms coming into importance in this period, it functions as a stop-gap for evoking a wide array of ideas and events. In trying to recover some of the early modern meanings of 'encounter' I will make two related stipulations: the first is that an encounter is discontinuous in time, involving by implication two distinct phases. Incorporating the Latin *computare*, 'encounter' remains close to both the economic and narrative senses of 'count', as in 'account' and 'recount'. Encounters are two-staged events: something happens, and then it is counted, recounted, interpreted. Further, 'encounters' have a palpable investment in alterity because the first sense of the term, going back to its vernacular roots in Old French, is adversarial: at its most basic level an encounter happens between a subject and an other who are, and go, against one another – 'in contra'. Encounter is therefore tied to the making of identity: it is assumed to take place between agents who are opposites in some degree (including, in many humanist texts, the self as other), and this factitious opposition establishes identity on both sides. The term and concept of encounter thus lead us toward Renaissance reflections on alterity even where a particular western European text seems to stand far from literal Indians, Africans, Jews or Moors.

What is an island? Insularity in early modern thought is hardly the literal fact that it has since become – where to a modern observer, something plainly is or is not an island – but an ideologeme, a conceptual formation that proposes an imagined resolution to a social contradiction.[2] While the figurative island goes back to Mandeville and beyond, Thomas More's *Utopia* is perhaps the text that establishes insularity as an early modern vantage: it introduces a way of thinking that is properly called utopian, and opens the prospect of a more dispersed and multifarious phenomenon which I will call island logic.[3]

The dichotomy between islands and continents is a feature of the modern worldview that is so entirely naturalized, it comes to seem inseparable from the world itself – from the way things are.[4] But the profusion of islands in sixteenth- and seventeenth-century European fiction, philosophy and natural history suggests that the dichotomy was often actively undone even as it was in the process of formation. Islands make possible the observation of their own constructedness, and the constructedness of other measures of the world, because they enforce a certain clarity: they have definable borders, they are conceptually autonomous from the world at large, and they encourage attention to the conditions of indigeneity and importation. In this last-mentioned dimension especially, islands often undermine some of the mystifications of capital and power. Suddenly, in the light of island logic, the exertions with which capital fashions a world according to its own unquestioned values come to look like exertions; we are encouraged to notice the trail of investment that furnishes the island with people and materials, and – quite simply – those whose power is untraceable and natural elsewhere are much more easily questioned. When Shakespeare chooses his first and only island setting for an entire play, then, he is finding his own way through a trope that reliably undoes the world as his audience knows it. He and the play are undertaking an exercise in island logic, a way of thinking that is counterposed to worldmaking.

If More gives island logic its discursive heft, Bartolomeo dalli Sonetti's *Isolario* gives it scope. This portolan atlas, published at Venice in 1485, founds a short-lived cartographic genre that depicts islands in autoreflexive terms, as self-regulating entities to be represented in discrete blocs of text, whether sonnets or columns, which can either reflect their corresponding islands or surround them with a 'sea' of information.[5] As Tom Conley observes, this cartographic genre – which had disappeared by *circa* 1570, 'under the advent of the far more voracious shape of the Ortelian atlas that commands the

European market' – has a critical project, namely the 'digestion of a world that can never be completely explored or broken down into assimilable units', making feasible a 'modular thinking' according to which 'wholes and parts become coextensive, but endowed with an infinite possibility of difference'.[6] In an age that sees new worlds insistently built up for commercial, imperial, philosophical or poetic purposes, island logic breaks them down again, undoing the entirety from the standpoint of the part. Celebrated in productions such as utopias, romances and *isolarii*, islands are held at a premium in the sixteenth century not merely out of geographical curiosity but because they afford a perspective that can have only an oblique relation to the accumulating and totalizing worldview of the imperial and economic centres. How many fiction-writers from Rabelais to Cervantes have an island book in their repertory? How many historians from Oviedo to Guicciardini to Stow have an island episode in their histories? In this light, *The Tempest* is Shakespeare's island play, and it applies island logic to its contemporaneous world as well as to its own models and procedures.

FROM WORLDVIEW TO ISLAND LOGIC

Drawing on two early modern conventions, then, *The Tempest* is constructed out of a series of encounters in the setting of an island, not only the fictional one but the literal one inhabited by Shakespeare and his audience. Certainly the collaboration of these two dynamic elements is indispensable. In a mainland *mise-en-scène*, a play dominated by encounters of all sorts may exploit these for dramatic potential while keeping them ideologically in check according to the logic of a worldview whose terms are not seriously in doubt: at the other end of Shakespeare's canon, *The Comedy of Errors* is this kind of play of encounters. In the later play, however, encounters unregulated by a stable world horizon introduce the prospect of something new – radical masque or farce, the play as instigation to island logic.

The leap from the established worldview of the European travellers to a logic conditioned by their island experiences is made in several episodes of the play; the drive toward, and away from, insularity motivates much of the action as well as the outlook of the play. First, the main plot renders literal the resort to island logic. Having been displaced from metropolitan Milan and experienced insularity himself, Prospero is understandably eager to witness his fellow Europeans in the same condition, to see what further displacements ensue. Meanwhile, his purpose for himself is to return to Milan having absorbed the partial vantage of the island for his art, where the contents of a 'full poor cell' overgo the purchase on 'all the world' he had as Duke of Milan (I.ii.20, 69). To occupy an island perspective is often to see reality as built, imported and contingent; to have the 'art' and power to realize that perspective is to bring the island to bear on the mainland. This is the itinerary Prospero envisions for himself, while he intends incomplete renditions of it for his adversaries and inferiors. Accordingly, many scenes are infused with an emergent island logic, as the several standpoints – transported rulers, courtiers and servants; honest and evil men; Miranda as Creole, Caliban as indigenous – are tested against one another, and their earlier logics rendered partial, exposed for the interests that might have seemed natural and inevitable in Europe, and searched for contradictions.

One of these scenes is the passage in Act II.ii in which Antonio first broaches to Sebastian the possibility of the latter's becoming King of Naples. Here, the world literally looks different from – and because of – the island vantage, a fact acknowledged when Antonio says that space speaks:

> ANTONIO   Who's the next heir of Naples?
> SEBASTIAN   Claribel.
> ANTONIO   She that is Queen of Tunis; she that dwells
>   Ten leagues beyond man's life; ...
>   she that from whom
>   We all were sea-swallow'd, though some cast again –
>   And by that destiny, to perform an act
>   Whereof what's past is prologue; what to come,
>   In yours and my discharge.
> SEBASTIAN   What stuff is this? How say you?
>   'Tis true my brother's daughter's Queen of Tunis,
>   So is she heir of Naples, 'twixt which regions
>   There is some space.
> ANTONIO   A space whose every cubit
>   Seems to cry out, 'How shall that Claribel
>   Measure us back to Naples? Keep in Tunis,
>   And let Sebastian wake'. (II.i.243–58)

How does space speak? On the island they are perhaps closer to Tunis than they are when in Europe, and almost certainly closer to Tunis than to Europe, but what matters is that their removal makes for a different measure of known, objective distances. Space that had been conceived within an established political order now seems open and unscripted. Barbara Fuchs has interpreted this passage in view of 'the incredible amplification of space that Antonio imagines', containing the threat of an imperial Islam under the figure of an impossibly distant female 'Tunis': 'in a perverse metonymy, the

European woman, instead of her threatening husband, becomes "Tunis".' Crucial to Fuchs's argument is that the two conspirators think here as Europeans, for 'the very urgency of the conspiracies on the island would indicate that the Italians have little doubt they will eventually return home.'[7] To this latter point I would add that they think as displaced, or out of place, Europeans: while the island setting sees the same plots that might have been undertaken in Milan or Naples – indeed, Prospero was overthrown by such a plot – it also embeds them in speculations that are a function of the island setting. Without having been nearly 'sea-swallowed', these two dishonest brothers would not see their possibilities in quite this way. One of Prospero's motivations in subjecting the Europeans to island logic is to restage the conditions of his own overthrow, but in a wider world in which he will control the return to the mainland order. The unsettling of Antonio's and Sebastian's protocols – the loosening of their scruples against a fresh horizon of the possible – is key to his project.

Their plans represent island logic in the service of error, as Prospero knows. It is possible to occupy an unforeseen perspective, to question certainties, and still be wrong. But *The Tempest* also gives voice to island logics that extend outside the play and raise real questions for anyone situated on the mainland of received thought. One of these voicings has often been treated as a crux, when it is nothing less than a partial perspective with a purchase on a truth of its own:

ADRIAN   'Widow Dido' said you? You make me study of that. She
    was of Carthage, not of Tunis.
GONZALO   This Tunis, sir, was Carthage.
ADRIAN   Carthage?
GONZALO   I assure you, Carthage.
ANTONIO   His word is more than the miraculous harp.
SEBASTIAN   He hath raised the wall, and houses too.
ANTONIO   What impossible matter will he make easy next?
    (II.i.80–87)

This passage calls for an audience that will recognize the shadings of literal and figurative truth here, discriminating which is more true, Gonzalo's assumption of a historical continuum joining ancient, mythic, storied Carthage and modern, commercial, threatening Tunis, or the others' conviction that these places belong to separate worlds. Modern Tunis is nine miles southwest of the site of Carthage, and the two cities were involved in a complicated relationship of mutual dependency for over 1,000 years, Tunis becoming the descendent of its antique neighbour.[8] Following island logic,

Gonzalo's observation is too broad and yet strangely true in a way that many of the worldliest early modern humanists would endorse: think of Garcilaso de la Vega (1501–36), the Toledan poet who undertook the 'impossible matter' of reconciling the classical and modern worlds as an agent of the Holy Roman Empire, and who died from wounds suffered in battle at La Goleta, near Tunis.[9]

Commentators have typically been immune to the confrontation of mainland and island logic here, preferring the literality of the former and branding the latter mistaken. In his revised Arden edition of the play, Frank Kermode overconfidently asserts that Gonzalo's 'statement about the identity of Tunis and Carthage is a mistake at once pointed out'.[10] But the play asks whether there exists a worldview capacious enough to accommodate both the historical Carthage and the contemporary Tunis, the classical touchstone and the Muslim other; perhaps it is only from an insular standpoint that one can see the continuity of Western history, which its heirs have forgotten. The end of the exchange seems to accept that this is insularity speaking:

> ANTONIO   What impossible matter will he make easy next?
> SEBASTIAN   I think he will carry this island home in his pocket and give it his son for an apple.
> ANTONIO   And sowing the kernels of it in the sea, bring forth more islands. (II.i.87–91)

The ethical challenge of island logic, of course, is in accepting someone else's: in a climate of unending encounters, in which partial perspectives jostle one other, the world is in danger of being reduced to a collocation of islands. In a Renaissance that has discovered island logic, how do we return to a holistic worldview while accommodating the renovative character of insularity?[11] If the movement from mainland to island was the play's first dramatic problem, this return is its concluding project.

FROM ISLAND LOGIC TO WORLDVIEW

In his classic essay, 'Prospero's Wife', Stephen Orgel asks a question that ought to figure in any discussion of The Tempest, and which proceeds from island logic: 'What is the nature of Prospero's authority and the source of his power?'[12] Within the confines of the play, Prospero controls both how island logics are let loose and how they will be reconciled back into a comprehensive European worldview. The capacity to submit others to alternative logics and bring them back again is what the play calls 'magic', and Prospero is the only magician in sight. Moreover, the least powerful character, Caliban, is not only unable to control the provision of logics but has no mainland to return to: he is all partial perspective. The conclusion of *The Tempest* sees Prospero managing the reintegration of the European characters, obviously excluding Caliban, into an inflected version of the world they started from. When they linger over what they have experienced in the play, Prospero reassures them that 'You do yet taste / Some subtleties o'th' isle, that will not let you / Believe things certain' (V.i.123–5), and promises their restoration. This denouement is intellectually successful if dramatically ineffective.

But outside *The Tempest* – and this is the factor that accounts for a considerable part of its unquantifiable power – we spectators are encouraged to apply an island logic to the play itself, with no Prospero to guide us back; what we might make of the play by these lights is its most radical aspect, for it introduces the method of its own unmaking. Island logic leads us to ask of *The Tempest* questions that it will not ask itself – an ethical imperative in a world of encounters. In testimony to the urgency of that imperative, perhaps the play's most visible legacy is the literature that island logic has generated out of it: Rodó's *Ariel* and Fernández Retamar's *Caliban*, Césaire's *Une tempête*, innumerable productions that break open and reconceive the play, critical interrogations such as 'Prospero's Wife', postcolonial meditations on insularity such as Antonio Benítez-Rojo's *The Repeating Island*[13] – and many other refractions documented in this volume. Its extraordinary fertility must have something to do with giving itself over entirely to a mode or outlook that elsewhere is supplementary, eccentric, and of course insular: the play obliges us to elaborate it, criticize it, and – what is illusory – complete it. As Peter Brook explains the power of island logic, 'one is rapidly caught in a frightening trap: anything that one does after a first moment of enthusiasm is soon inadequate and beside the mark. The opposite, however, is even worse, as one cannot escape by doing nothing ... So while one must intervene, one must also remain harshly critical of one's attempts at intervention.'[14] If *The Tempest* is indeed Shakespeare's last work, he closed his career by leaving us not so much another play as a set of instructions based in one of the emergent outlooks of his time.

ON THE WORLD STAGE

'We have not arrived at ourselves as long as Shakespeare is writing our plays for us' (Heiner Müller, 'Shakespeare a Departure')

This inter-section offers a snapshot of recent productions which take The Tempest *as their point of departure – short pieces on three versions of the play which appeared in European theatres between the summer of 1998 and the spring of 1999. The three titles suggest the relationship with Shakespeare's original text: Aimé Césaire's adaptation is* Une tempête *(A Tempest), the Cuban play is* Otra Tempestad *(Another Tempest), and the Terra Nova production is* Tempest(s).

Césaire's *Une tempête* at The Gate

'We live in an age of brilliant Tempests . . .Yet this Tempest, from the great Martinican poet and politician Aimé Césaire, is not simply a new reading of Shakespeare but an original play of astonishing power.'[1] When Aimé Césaire's Une tempête opened at The Gate theatre in London's Notting Hill in October 1998, it received unanimous acclaim. Remarkably, it was the first production in England of Césaire's 1969 play, and used a new translation by Philip Crispin in a performance which matched Césaire's poetry with contemporary visual language and ensemble performance. While reviewers paid homage to Crispin's translation and to the inventiveness of Mick Gordon's direction and Dick Bird's scenography, they also spoke of the intended significance of the cultural moment in staging this particular re-imagining of The Tempest; for 1998 marked the 150th anniversary of the abolition of slavery in the French colonies and the 50th anniversary of the arrival of the first wave of post-war immigrants from the West Indies to Britain on board the Windrush (many of whom settled, in fact, in Notting Hill).

Césaire's play was already well known within the French-speaking world. First produced at an international festival in Hammamet, Tunisia, in the summer of 1969 before playing in Paris in January 1970, it was directed by Jean-Marie Serreau, with whom Césaire had worked very closely on most of his theatrical writing. Serreau's death in 1973 brought Césaire's career as a playwright to a close.[2] In terms of the themes of this book, that first production was of special interest: a Caribbean rewriting of The Tempest, produced in Tunisia, close to Sycorax's origins and to Claribel's destiny (though neither, interestingly, feature much in the play); which reads the play in part through the US black politics of the Civil Rights period (affiliating Caliban with Malcolm X and Ariel with Martin Luther King); and which adopted the manners and dress of an American Western. Another notable recent production was that by Elie Pennont in Martinique in 1992, where the actor playing the African God Eshu became the unifying image: while he appears in only one scene of Césaire's text, Pennont's Eshu remained on stage throughout the performance, watching silently from a distance, 'the incarnation of the fragmented psyche that must be acknowledged before any healing can take place.'[3]

The Gate production had its own emphases, departing from Césaire's stage direction that the play should have the 'ambience of a psychodrama' with actors choosing masks as they enter the stage (something taken up, in interesting ways, in the Cuban *Otra Tempestad*). The play's racialization of the difference between Caliban and Ariel – black and mulatto – was represented by a difference of physique and accent. Finally, director Mick Gordon and designer Dick Bird investigated the relationship between visual and verbal poetics, using size and scale as well as visual puns and transformations of style to explore Césaire's manipulation of Shakespeare's language.

Lucy Rix's essay in this volume offers a new study of the play. Here we reproduce two scenes from Philip Crispin's translation and two of Pau Ros's photographs of the production.[4]

[*The first extract is the entirety of Act II, scene I.*]

Caliban's cave. Caliban is singing while he works when Ariel appears. He listens to him for a moment.

CALIBAN (*singing*)
>May he who eats his corn without thinking of Shango
>be cursed! Shango will slip under his nails
>and into his every pore!
>Shango, Shango oh!
>
>Refuse him a seat! On your own head!
>He'll establish his tribunal right on your nose!
>
>No room under your roof! That's your look-out!
>He'll grab the roof and stick it on his head!
>Whoever wants to try it on with Shango
>plays an ill-fated game!
>Shango, Shango oh!

ARIEL Hello, Caliban. I know you don't think much of me, but after all we are brothers, brothers in suffering and slavery. Brothers in hope as well. We both want our freedom, only our methods vary.

CALIBAN Hello to you. But you haven't come to see me just to make that profession of faith. Come on, Alastor![5] The old man's sent you, hasn't he! A fine job: carrying out the lofty thoughts of the Master!

ARIEL No, I've come on my own account. To warn you. Prospero is planning appalling acts of revenge against you. I felt duty-bound to give you fair warning.

CALIBAN I am resolved to face up to him.

Caliban (Andrew Dennis) confronts Ariel (Michael Wildman), in Césaire's *Une tempête* at The Gate, September–October 1998.

ARIEL   Poor Caliban, you're doomed. You know well that you aren't the stronger, that you'll never be the stronger. What use your struggle?

CALIBAN   And you? What good has your obedience done you, your Uncle Tom patience and all your toadying! You must see that the man grows more despotic and demanding by the day.

ARIEL   Nevertheless, I've achieved one thing, at least: he's promised me my freedom. In the long run, I don't doubt, but it's the first time he's promised.

CALIBAN   Idle talk! He'll promise you a thousand times and betray you a thousand times. Besides, tomorrow doesn't interest me. What I want is *(shouting)* 'Freedom now!'

ARIEL   Very well. But you know well you cannot grasp it right now, and that he's the stronger. I'm well placed to know what he has in his arsenal.

CALIBAN   The stronger? What do you know about it? Weakness disposes of a thousand means that cowardice alone keeps us from counting.

ARIEL I don't believe in violence.

CALIBAN What do you believe in, then? In cowardice? In resignation? In crooking the knee? That's it. You're struck on the right cheek, you offer the left. You're kicked on the left buttock, you offer the right. That way, there's no jealousy. Well, not Caliban!

ARIEL You know very well that isn't my philosophy. Neither violence, nor submission. Listen to me. It's Prospero we must change. Trouble his calm until he finally acknowledges his own injustice and puts an end to it.

CALIBAN Oh dear! dear! That's a good laugh! Prospero's conscience! Prospero is an old bully who has no conscience.

ARIEL Exactly. We must strive to give him one. I'm not just fighting for my freedom, for our freedom, but for Prospero too, so that a conscience can well up inside him. Help me, Caliban.

CALIBAN Listen, my sweet Ariel, I sometimes wonder if you aren't cracked. So that a conscience can well up inside Prospero? You might as well wait for a stone to burst into bloom!

ARIEL You drive me to despair. I've often dreamt a rapturous dream that one day Prospero, you and I would set out as brothers to build a wonderful world, each contributing his own qualities: patience, vitality, love, will-power too, and rigour, not to mention the eddying dreams without which humanity would suffocate to death.

CALIBAN You don't understand Prospero, at all. He's not the collaborative type. He's a man who only feels alive when he's crushing someone. A crusher, a grinder to pulp, that's what he is! And you talk of brotherhood!

ARIEL So what's left? War? You know at that game, Prospero is invincible.

CALIBAN Better death than humiliation and injustice. Besides, the last word shall be mine. Unless it belongs to nothingness. The day I feel all's lost, just let me filch a few barrels of your infernal powder and – from high in the empyrean where you love to soar – you will see this isle, my inheritance, my work, all blown sky high, with, I hope, Prospero and me amongst the debris. I hope you'll enjoy the firework display, it will be signed Caliban.

ARIEL   Each of us hears his own drum. You march to the beat of yours. I march to the beat of mine. I wish you courage, brother.

CALIBAN   Farewell, Ariel, my brother, and good luck.

[*These are the final exchanges between Prospero and Caliban, from the play's final scene.*]

CALIBAN

>You must understand, Prospero:
>for years I bowed my head
>for years I stomached it,
>stomached all of it:
>your insults, your ingratitude,
>and worst of all, more degrading than all the rest,
>your condescension.
>But now it's over!
>Over, do you hear!
>Of course, for the moment you're still
>the stronger.
>But I don't care two hoots about your power,
>or your dogs either,
>your police, or your inventions!
>And do you know why I don't care?
>Do you want to know?
>It's because I know I'll have you!
>You'll be impaled! And on a stake
>you'll have sharpened yourself!
>You'll have impaled yourself!
>Prospero you're a great illusionist:
>you know all about lies.
>And you lied to me so much,
>lied about the world, lied about yourself,
>that you ended up by imposing on me
>an image of myself:
>underdeveloped, in your words,
>incompetent,
>that's how you forced me to see myself,
>and I hate that image! And it is false!
>But now I know you, you old cancer,
>and I also know myself!

Prospero (Michael Hadley) goads Caliban (Andrew Dennis).

And I know that one day
my bare fist, my bare fist alone
will be enough to crush your world!
The old world is falling apart!

Isn't it true? Just look!
It even bores you to death!
And by the way, you have a chance to finish it off:
you can get the hell out.
You can go back to Europe.
But there's no hope of that!
I'm sure you won't leave!
That makes me laugh – your 'mission',
your 'vocation'!
Your vocation is to get on my wick!
And that's why you'll stay,
like those men who established the colonies
and can no longer live elsewhere.
An old addict, that's what you are.

PROSPERO Poor Caliban! You're well aware that you're heading toward your own perdition. That you're rushing toward suicide! That I will be the stronger, and stronger each time! I pity you!

CALIBAN And I hate you!

PROSPERO Beware! My generosity has limits.

CALIBAN (*chanting*)
> Shango marches with strength
> across the sky, his covered way!
> Shango is a fire-bearer,
> each step he treads shakes the heavens
> shakes the earth
> Shango, Shango oh!

PROSPERO
> I have uprooted the oak, roused the sea,
> shaken the mountain, and baring
> my breast against adversity,
> I have exchanged thunder with Jupiter, bolt for bolt.
> Better still! From the brute monster I made man!
> But oh!
> To have failed to find the path
> to the man's heart, if that really is where man is to be found.

(*To Caliban*)
> Well, I hate you as well!
> For you are the one who
> made me doubt myself
> for the first time.

(*Addressing the Lords*)
> ... Understand me well.
> I am not, in the ordinary sense
> the master, as this savage thinks,
> but rather the conductor of a vast score:
> this isle.
> Teasing out voices, myself alone,
> and coupling them at my pleasure,
> arranging out of the confusion
> the sole intelligible line.
> Without me, who would be able

to derive music from all this?
Without me, this island is dumb.
Here then, my duty.
I will remain.

[…]

PROSPERO

And now, Caliban, there's only us!
What I have to tell you will be brief:
Ten times, a hundred times, I've tried to save you,
above all from yourself.
But you have always answered me with rage
and venom, like
the opossum that hoists itself up by its own tail
the better to bite the hand
that pulls it from the darkness.
Well, boy, I shall spurn my indulgent nature
and, from now on, I will answer your violence
with violence!

Time passes by, symbolized by the curtain's being lowered halfway and then being taken up again. In semi-darkness, Prospero appears, aged and weary. His gestures are stiff and automatic, his speech weak and listless.

PROSPERO   Funny, for some time now, we've been invaded by opossums. They're everywhere . . . Peccaries, wild boar, all those unclean beasts! But, above all, opossums. Oh, those eyes! And that hideous leer! You'd swear the jungle wanted to invade the cave . . . But I'll defend myself . . . I will not let my work perish . . . (*Roaring*) I will defend civilization! (*He fires in all directions.*) They've got what was coming to them . . . Now, this way, I'll have some peace for a blessed while . . . But it's cold . . . Funny, the climate's changed . . . Cold on this island . . . Have to think about making a fire . . . Ah well, my old Caliban, we're the only two left on this island, just you and me. You and me! You-me! Me-you! But what the hell's he up to? (*Roaring*) Caliban!

In the distance, above the sound of the surf and the mewing of birds, snatches of Caliban's song can be heard.

LIBERTY, OH-AY! LIBERTY!

Otra Tempestad at The Globe

In July 1998, Teatro Buendía brought to The Globe (London) its Otra Tempestad – written by Raquel Carrió and Flora Lauten, directed by Flora Lauten, and produced by Rachel Clare. Teatro Buendía was founded in Havana in 1986 and has established itself as one of the leading theatre companies in the Caribbean, winning prizes and critical acclaim throughout the world. Of all the modern productions of The Tempest, this Otra Tempestad is probably the most extravagant: its title suggests an 'otherness' which is fully borne out by the expanded narrative and character-list.

Otra Tempestad clearly goes further than other adaptations of The Tempest through its introduction of two new sets of characters, several from Shakespeare's other plays as well as the orishas (Afrocuban deities) who double the European parts.[1] As a consequence, the Italian noblemen disappear from the cast list as do the sailors with their comic sub-plot, and the nymphs with their classical masque, although political plotting, comic business and spectacle are all retained, even enhanced. The script preserves relatively little of Shakespeare's play (much less, for example, than Césaire's Une tempête), with the result that the Shakespearean lines have special resonance – especially when, as happens on several occasions, they are spoken by different characters. 'This island's mine' shouts Prospero at one point, while Miranda has the line 'I will people this isle with Calibans'. Both lines were, of course, originally Caliban's and, although Caliban ends the play as king, and although he gets to frolic with Miranda before her tragic death, he is a strangely silent figure in this production – given that Cuba's main contribution to Tempest criticism has been Fernández Retamar's defiant question: 'what is our history, what is our culture, if not the history and culture of Caliban?'[2]

To underline the American dimensions of the play, Prospero becomes a Columbus figure on a voyage – financed by Shylock – to discover a New World in which he can put his utopian visions into practice. His ideals quickly fall short, in scenes which echo Antonio and Sebastian's mockery of Gonzalo's 'utopia' but which also carry an undertone of contemporary comment on the ideals of the Cuban state. Otra Tempestad has been tolerated in Cuba, playing to much acclaim in small venues, but not reviewed in the press. However, Otra Tempestad is not an overtly political production. Where Third

World responses have often written back against The Tempest, Otra Tempestad
*seeks cultural synthesis within the Cuban tradition of transculturation, perhaps ironically
finding common ground between the masquerades of the Cuban orishas and Prospero's
masque at the heart of Shakespeare's play.*

*Here we present two extracts from an essay about the play by one of its authors which,
along with the three photographs by Rachel Clare, should give some sense of its intertextual ambition and cross-cultural spectacle.*

RAQUEL CARRIÓ, ON OTRA TEMPESTAD[3]

Structured into fifteen scenes, *Otra Tempestad* tells the story of the encounters
in the Caribbean, both imaginary and dreamed, between Shakespearean
characters and figures from African mythology. From the streets of the Old
World – as if from a puppet-theatre – emerge Macbeth, Hamlet, Shylock,
Othello, the magician Prospero and his daughter Miranda, in a game of
masks in which all take on their characters. Meanwhile, on the island,
Sycorax conjures the oracle. Through this ritual, Sycorax – mother of
Caliban by the orisha Shango – unleashes the tempest. Prospero's expedition
to the New World is wrecked on the island's coast and the passengers
rescued by Sycorax's daughters: Oshún, queen of the rivers, Oyá, queen of
the dead, and Elegguá, who opens and closes paths for the other orishas.

The encounters and enchantments controlled by Sycorax create a
labyrinth in which the characters 'do not know if they are dead or
asleep'. Prospero confuses Elegguá with the Ariel of his lost kingdom;
Hamlet hallucinates Oshún as Ophelia; Othello re-encounters Desdemona;
Oyá seduces Macbeth through her transformation into Lady Macbeth;
and Miranda and Caliban fall in love in a curious subversion of their
play's plot.

Transformations and mirrorings undermine the logic of the original
stories and transgress the limits of their characters and action. However, in
the crisscrossing of references, echoes, and European and African images,
there are no 'winners' and 'losers' but rather that interchange of rituals and
actions which characterizes the cultural syncretism of Latin America and
the Caribbean. 'Prospero's Laboratory' is the kingdom of the American
Utopia: the Dream of the Ideal Republic and the universe of contradictions
unleashed together in a mythic space where all the characters are condemned to re-enact their illusions over and over again. From this follows the
ritual deaths and the symbolic use of masks in an ending which warns us: 'I
have inherited a land razed by utopia and blood.' Nevertheless, the spectacle
breaks through the tragedy implicit in those references by taking on the

Prospero's ship and Sycorax's
daughters.

Sycorax (Dania Aguereberez)
and her daughters Oyá (Ivanesa
Cabrera), Oshún (Sandra
Lorenzo) and Elegguá (Giselle
Navaroli), in Teatro Buendía's
Otra Tempestad.

form of a masque, which creates the possibilities inherent in mutation, intertextual play, irony, parody and the hybridization of genres.

It is this counterpoint which makes *Otra Tempestad* a reflection on cultural
tradition and appropriation; but also a 'fiesta of body and soul', a strange
carnivalesque and self-cannibalistic ritual, and, definitively, a framework full
of metaphors, confessions, and surprising stories.

[…]

There is a first *Tempest* written by Shakespeare over three centuries ago. A
second, by the Martinican, Aimé Césaire, in the twentieth century, already
subverts the terms of the Prospero / Caliban opposition and underlines the
contestatory meaning of the action. But towards the end of the century, the
plot becomes more complicated. It is now no longer a matter of negating the
language of the conqueror, but rather of investigating how, from the crossings of cultures and ethnicities comes *another culture*, a third language which
is not that of the victor nor that of the defeated but a product of their
syncretism. This term alludes to the mixing, the interaction of elements, the
intertextual value of artistic productions in America, but also to the particular way in which these crossings and interchanges take place. It seems that
Shakespeare knew about 'distant islands' through the books and stories of
travellers, so that Caliban becomes an archetypal *stranger*, his mother

Sycorax no more than a brief reference, and the island constitutes throughout the text a space which is *magical* but unknown.

What can we do on this side of the world which wouldn't simply repeat the images of a playwright whose work has been staged thousands of times? How can we find a language which respects the beauty and profundity of the material but which does not simply translate the themes and forms of representation? The starting point of our investigation was . . . the magic universe of the text conceived as an American, Caribbean world, inhabited by myths, fables, sounds, spells, and enchantments rooted in a culture full of other spirits and legends. Two questions: *What is the island? Who are its inhabitants?* An investigation of this kind implies a comparative study and works with different reference points. On the one hand the work of Shakespeare (his plays and poems, the iconography, art and music of the period); on the other, the whole universe of Afro-Cuban culture through its systems of representation (the so-called *patakins* (stories about the orishas) and the mass of its songs, dances, masks and symbols).

This is not a matter of reproducing folklore: any backward glance from the contemporary world to a classical heritage – European or African – presupposes from the beginning an alteration of the signs. What exactly do we inherit from the encounter? What is the properly voracious, irreverent, transgressive, parodic, and festive way for the 'conquered' to appropriate myths and to model them (represent them) as their own? The idea of the masque is common to all cultures. Was *The Tempest* not presented as a wedding masque? In African traditions does there not exist the dance of the masks as incitement to and unveiling of change, the transformation of the seasons and the signs? Don't we find the masque at the centre of *Romeo and Juliet* or in Hamlet's play to catch the conscience of a King? Is not festivity, the Fiesta, at the origin of theatricality and of the forms of representation which we try to subvert or rescue? From this point of view, the Masque creates the subterfuge, the poetic entity which makes possible transgression, change, the mutation of the canon. It is in the masque tradition where what is essential is hidden and revealed, where status and class differentials disappear and where the actor acquires the condition of being *inhabited, visited* by archetypes which act *through*. This strangeness defines the encounter. Theatre, island, mixing: gradations of being or place (like Prospero's laboratory) where the act of representation is truthful only when in play – as quotation, parody, laughter, irony – empty of the references which, as they integrate, *forget*, erasing the traces of any causality (in a linear or chronological narrative) and create an analogous ambivalence or symbolic mutation of the initial signs. In this way the totality of the discourse –

A tableau of the island's inhabitants Caliban/ Macbeth (José Juan Rodríguez), Miranda (Juana García), Shylock/Romeo (Pablo Guevara), Othello (Carlos Cruz), Sycorax (Dania Aguerreberez), Oyá/Lady Macbeth (Ivanesa Cabrera), Oshún/Ophelia (Sandra Lorenzo), Elegguá/Ariel/Juliet (Giselle Navaroli).

the idyllic images of an (im)possible primitivism in the island gods – functions by *contamination*: this much-feared word which none the less expresses our only real inheritance, and of which we are made.

So it is not by chance that Sycorax unleashes the tempest by means of her daughters; that behind Ariel hides Elegguá from the Cuban mountains; that Oshún, orisha of the rivers, provokes Ophelia's illusions in *Hamlet*; or that Oyá is transformed into the the passionate Lady Macbeth. Given these alterations, or rotation of the signs, is it possible to deny that the rich merchant Shylock could once have been young Romeo or the hypnotic daughter of Prospero a Moorish captive, or Othello a forgetful melancholic, all condemned to play out, over and over again, the actions through which they have been bewitched? Beneath their disguises, all of them hide some passion or crime, from the Player to the Warrior, which they act out under the ironic gaze of the illusionist Monk.

translated by Peter Hulme

Tempest(s) at Terra Nova Theatre Institute

Tempest(s) was staged at the Terra Nova Theatre Institute in Copenhagen during April and May 1999. The production was created with and performed by Borderland, directed by Phillip Mackenzie, and co-ordinated by Antonio Cots Macia, with scenography by Luca Ruzza. This account is by Ric Allsopp, the production's dramaturg, with photographs by Jan Rüsz.

> Already a fictitious past has supplanted in men's memories that
> other past, of which we now know nothing certain – not even that it
> is false.[1]

One by one the audience is brought down a steep metal staircase into a large dimly lit industrial space. A man sits alone at a bare table in the centre of the space, facing the staircase, a pencil in front of him. On a wall behind him a large looped video projection shows documentary footage: a coastline thronged with people, an overcrowded ship departing. Individual figures separate themselves from the audience and approach the table. On a side wall another looped projection shows the identity papers and photographs of each figure. The man does not speak. A small gesture – a nod of the head, a movement of the pencil – either sends them through or back into the crowd. Those who pass through stand in line against the projection of the ship. For the displaced arrival and departure are one and the same.

Tempest(s) was staged in Copenhagen in the spring of 1999 as part of a five-year cultural and arts development plan initiated in Denmark in 1997 by Terra Nova Theatre Institute. The dramaturgy of *Tempest(s)* sought to examine relationships between the framework of an aesthetic model (Shakespeare's *The Tempest* and its themes of cultural meetings and confrontations); contemporary urban multicultural and intercultural social experience; and the placing of contemporary artwork as a cultural catalyst in such contexts. The social models of a monocultural society and the

'Crossing the Border', from *Tempest(s)*, Terra Nova Theatre Institute/Borderland, Copenhagen, April 1999.

aesthetics of a traditional illusionist theatre or performance 'object' no longer easily reflect the cultural and social realities that typify contemporary urban experience. This is not to say that 'traditional' cultural expressions no longer have a place. Shakespeare's *The Tempest* opened issues of cultural confrontation and of illusion as a power structure within the world that Shakespeare was writing in at the end of the Renaissance. The dramaturgy of *Tempest(s)* sought to translate these issues into our own contemporary terms.

Seeking cultural analogues in the themes and imagery of Shakespeare's text, *Tempest(s)* imagines a contemporary Caliban, displaced from his now 'uninhabited', or recently decolonised island, negotiating the borders and cultures of 'Fortress Europe' – the former colonial 'heartland' or 'homeland'. In trying to find a place for himself within a world that is at once both alien and familiar, Caliban discovers that his attempts to negotiate identity and values on his own terms are still shaped by Prospero's 'art'. Prospero's means of maintaining power and control over his enemies, over Caliban and Ariel, and over his daughter Miranda, are imagined as projections – the 'virtual', mediating and invisible power structures that pervade social and political life in Europe, that regulate its geographical and cultural borders. This virtual world of projections is contrasted with the actualities and pressures of a localised everyday world, in particular as seen through the experience of immigrants and refugees. Within this 'brave new world' Caliban rediscovers the difficulties of making a place for himself and the impossibility of a return in any sense to the island home from which he came.

The reality of the situation that Tempest(s) imagines does not only confront immigrants or refugees attempting to find security or asylum in contemporary Europe. Our individual perspectives on questions of gender, class, race, and sexuality are also contested areas of social and cultural negotiation. Our experiences of displacement, insecurity, mobility and difference are framed within increasingly globalized cultural images of security, prosperity, identity and idealized or normalized behaviours. It is this tension that sustains the displaced and displacing conditions of contemporary life, provides the ideas and relationships upon which the performance of Tempest(s) was built and gives the dramaturgy of Tempest(s) its central trope of 'displacement' in both the actual world of social and cultural experience, and in the aesthetic world of representation.

The dramaturgy links a reading of the The Tempest with contemporary ideas of 'otherness' as experienced by migrants, refugees, the homeless and immigrant communities; and also in terms of the everyday exclusions experienced by individuals in contemporary society – where we can go, how we can meet others and so on. The experience of potential displacement and exclusion is clearly intensified in certain locations and situations, such as national borders, immigration control, social security structures. In such situations physical spaces (the spaces of bureaucracy, the spaces of news-media, the negotiation of public space and private space) are intimately linked with language and the individual's abilities to negotiate languages of all types – from sign-systems to 'body-language' codes to language groups.

Displacement in terms of aesthetics can be read through the shifts and slippages of the conventional elements of a classical Aristotelian aesthetics. It is used structurally at all levels of the performance itself, affecting narrative lines, the use of text, of language, of characterizations, of objects and time, and of spatial sequencing. This affects aspects of how we see the artwork (visuality); how we read the artwork (textuality); how the elements (here in theatre terms) of character, object, space, time are used within the production. The performance imagery of Tempest(s) operates in both linear and non-linear terms, setting up both narrative and causal sequences, as well as non-linear, hypertextual parallels and linkages.

In *The Tempest* both Caliban and Miranda are displaced – the former through the effects of 'colonization', the latter through exile and separation. In *Tempest(s)* the characters of Caliban and Miranda are shown as a single shifting identity that may be recognized in each of us, and in the everyday social and cultural interactions we are involved with. The coherence and status of the dramatic character (at least in classical terms) is displaced with each performer as both Caliban and Miranda negotiating the projected images that are the illusions and power structures (happy families, ideal homes, social controls and legislation) of a disembodied Prospero, sometimes duplicating, sometimes subverting, always representing and merging with the 'live' presence of the performers. Ariel is the (sometimes reluctant, sometimes willing) agency of Prospero's authority and its idealizations in the form of the mechanics of projection.

The displacement of 'character' and personae as a strategy in *Tempest(s)* is paralleled in the use of text, both as speech (live, recorded, mixed) and as writing. The 'originary' fragments of text from *The Tempest* are either erased – literally written in chalk on the walls of the performance space and rubbed out – or projected unsubstantially as light; or removed from the mouths of

'Caliban's ground', from *Tempest(s)*, Terra Nova Theatre Institute/Borderland, Copenhagen, April 1999.

the performers and replaced on multiple channels available to the audience on walkabout headsets. Thus the text of *Tempest(s)* becomes multiphonic, 'full of noises', inviting its audience to make choices between what is seen and what is heard, to alter and transform meanings through selection, to construct a montage of live and projected performance image. The channels included a 1960s radio version of *The Tempest*; a female voice quietly whispering increasingly provocative aphorisms and commonplaces around cultural attitudes to 'otherness'; a series of interviews with people living and working in the locality of the performance space (the multi-ethnic immigrant area around Istedgade and Vesterbro in Copenhagen); a series of recorded 'live' phone conversations home from the performers to their families or extended families both in Denmark and abroad. In the rare instances where performers 'took pains to [. . .] speak' the texts they utter reflect the difficulties of language – mutual incomprehension, the use of invented languages or of 'minority' languages, the difficulties experienced by the immigrant placed outside a language, the place and status of 'native' languages. At the centre of all these displacements and tensions is the exchange between Caliban and Miranda (I.ii.350–64) with its cultural assumptions and sense of unresolved confrontation.

Memory and utopia form two additional themes within the dramaturgy of *Tempest(s)*. These are informed not only by *zeitgeist* – by the kinds of cultural reflection that the turn of the millennium sets going – but more specifically through intertextual readings of Shakespeare's text and *Tempest(s)*; and through exposure to particular contemporary artists – for instance Christian Boltanski, whose ideas of 'little memory' ('an emotional memory, an everyday knowledge') and 'small utopias' ('sweeping in front of your own door') seemed apposite for a project that is attempting to bring the local (the discourses of multi-culturalism and interculturalism in Denmark) and the global (discourse around power structures, immigration etc.) into relationship.

Tempest(s) was created with a group of people from very diverse ethnic, social and cultural backgrounds who, in proposing that the process and dynamics of theatre and performance parallels and interacts with the dynamics and operations of the contemporary world, recognized that theatre and performance do not simply reflect the world through establishing an 'other scene' or fictional world through which the relationships of the real world can be read.

Interculturalism implies the recognition of difference as a dynamic rather than as a category, an openness of discourse that moves beyond multi-culturalism. Theatre and performance are increasingly 'interdisciplines' drawing from a diverse range of processes and influences. The terms of engagement with performance, with artworks, are also being redefined along lines of difference: social and political dynamics are reflected in aesthetic dynamics. Simply put, the dynamics and processes of intercultural relations are paralleled in the dynamics and processes of performance work. The assumption is that artworks and performances exist not only as self-contained or self-reflexive entities within social or cultural contexts (the singular vision of late modernism) but in a shifting and dynamic relation to cultural, social and political realities. This change of perspective affects cultural and aesthetic assumptions and moves towards interdisciplinary and intercultural forms that act against the grain of both aesthetic and social monocultures.

Tempest(s) is shadowed throughout by the text of The Tempest. To read back into and through the text of The Tempest is to open up the conditions within which Shakespeare was writing and to open up our own readings of those conditions and understanding of how we read. As a dramaturgical project Tempest(s) reads The Tempest outwards into the specifics and particularities of a contemporary urban situation, outwards into the transforming structures of performance, into the placing of a project in a particular situation, for a particular audience. At the end of Tempest(s) the audience leaves down a long narrow corridor – a corridor of memory – lined and dimly lit by nine black glass-topped plinths containing various texts or personal objects – for example a set of milk teeth, a blank sheet of paper and a pencil, a photograph of a railway line with a pair of compasses. On the wall beside each plinth is a photocopy of the identity papers and photos seen at the beginning of the performance. As in The Tempest there is no resolution here – only ambivalence and ambiguity. The return home is a return to somewhere that is no longer home – is itself displaced, is in turn idealized and mythicized, a place from which we once again must depart. The Tempest – like the Boatswain's ship appearing 'tight and yare and bravely rigged' – is always 'freshly beheld'. But as it travels so it transforms. John Berger has spoken of displacement as the impossibility of return for the migrant, for the refugee: 'Unchanging as the village is, he will never see it as he did before he left. He is seen differently and he sees differently'.[2] In so far as The Tempest travels, it can never return.

(Preceding page) *Vespucci 'Discovering' America*, late sixteenth century. Theodor Galle, after Stradanus (Jan van der Straet).

In line with European conventions, the 'new' continent was allegorized as a woman and surrounded with what were seen as typically American features: parrots, tapirs, bows and arrows, and cannibal feasts.

Introduction

No issue has dogged *Tempest* criticism more insistently than that of the play's relationship to the Americas. As the previous section discussed, the explicit geography of the play is mostly Mediterranean. Nevertheless, it is widely accepted that Shakespeare read, and drew on, at least one of the contemporary accounts of the Virginia Company's voyages; that Gonzalo's famous speech, beginning 'Had I plantation of this isle' (II.i.141), is closely based on a passage in Montaigne's essay concerning Brazilian Indians, 'Of the caniballes'; that there are a handful of other references to American material; and that the play's transatlantic travels have been responsible for some of its most interesting critical and creative appropriations. However, despite a broad consensus on the *existence* of this material, opinion has been divided about its significance. The play's two most distinguished editors differ sharply. 'It is as well to be clear', wrote Frank Kermode, 'that there is nothing in *The Tempest* fundamental to its structure of ideas which could not have existed had America remained undiscovered . . .'[1] For Stephen Orgel it was equally clear that 'the Americas were in Shakespeare's mind when he was inventing [Caliban]. The significance of the literature of exploration strikes me as both deeper and less problematic than has generally been argued.'[2]

[1]

Three overlapping strands of critical opinion have argued for the importance of the American dimension of the play. The most purely 'Americanist' reading of *The Tempest* – which argued that the play is directly and unproblematically *about* the New World – was developed more than a century ago during the period of Anglo-American *rapprochement* by those who were interested in establishing at least one of Shakespeare's plays as having direct links with the American colonies that would later become the United States.[3] The first – and perhaps last – unequivocal identification of Caliban as a portrayal of an American Indian came in Sidney Lee's biography of Shakespeare in 1898: *The Tempest* became for Lee, 'a veritable document of early Anglo-American history'.[4]

From 1960, the play's Caribbean travels have come to the fore, in readings which tend to empathize with Caliban. George Lamming, author of the inaugural Caribbean reading, is the subject of Peter Hulme's essay here, which also traces the broader Caribbean context, while Aimé Césaire's 1969 play, *Une tempête*, is analysed by Lucy Rix. The Caribbean reading is, by definition, postcolonial – alert to the colonial dimensions of the play and suspicious of Prospero's power over Caliban, and both Lamming and Césaire are seen as offering deliberately rude interruptions of Prospero's narrative. However, the postcolonial reading is not necessarily Caribbean, nor even American, in orientation. There are readings that focus on Africa, India, Ireland, and even – as we explored in our first section – Britain itself.

At a certain point the Americanist reading began to merge with the postcolonial. Leslie Fiedler's important book, *The Stranger in Shakespeare* (1972), marks this key moment in the 1970s, along with Terence Hawkes's chapter from *Shakespeare's Talking Animals* (1973), James Smith's 'journey through and about *The Tempest*' (1974) and Stephen Greenblatt's 'Learning to Curse' (1976).[5] Greenblatt's work has been the most influential, and the reading of the play stemming from it has established itself as a new critical orthodoxy in recent years – although its arguments are far from as univocal or reductive as its critics generally make out.

[2]

The Tempest's special relationship with America did not begin, of course, with Malone's assertion – at the beginning of the nineteenth century – of the play's connection with the Bermuda pamphlets. The general relevance of its themes for the colonial situation may have led to *The Tempest* being the first Shakespeare play printed in the New World and the largest and most ambitious theatrical production mounted in the pre-war colonies. Strikingly, the only allusion to Shakespeare in the writings of George Washington comes in a letter written from the camp at Fishkill in 1778 where he describes the British Army as a Prospero, whose grand strategies are about to dissolve, 'like the baseless fabric of a vision' – leaving Washington and the rebellious colonists to occupy the position of a Caliban, who will on this occasion be successful.[6]

Even as late as 1960, Leo Marx could see *The Tempest* as Shakespeare's 'American Fable' in the sense of the play's connections, as pastoral romance, with the early English experience of America as wilderness.[7] This is a reading which, developed through the work of Perry Miller, became central to the self-styled 'American Studies' of the 1960s and '70s. While Marx's reading bears no trace of any postcolonial dimension,[8] other early Americanizers of *The Tempest* 'highlighted the play's prophetic lessons for the Americas, especially the United States . . .'[9]

It is not accidental that major Latin American interest in *The Tempest* – with a sense of its relevance to current political circumstances – should date from the turn of the twentieth century, when the play was being most aggressively claimed for America. It was then, especially in the war against Spain in 1898, that the United States emerged as the dominant military and political power in the region, displacing both Spain and Britain. The range of allegorical possibilities meant that identifications were going to be various, as Gordon Brotherston's essay here shows.

That *The Tempest* could be seen as dealing with colonial relationships was also recognized in nineteenth-century Britain, in readings that fully identified with Prospero's imperial burden. After all, Shakespeare had recently assumed his place as the great *national* poet, and therefore as an emblem of the values that the British Empire was exporting to those parts of the globe where civilization had yet to penetrate. *The Tempest* was probably the most important play of all for this idea of Shakespeare. The play seemed to represent in the relationship between Prospero and Caliban the colonizing process that had its beginnings in Shakespeare's day, but which was in its heyday in the mid-nineteenth century. Prospero is the teacher of Caliban; and, if the outcome of that education is not altogether successful, then that only goes to show – so the argument went – that gratitude is not to be expected from native populations, that the civilizing burden is a heavy one to bear. In 1876 *The Tempest* was published in a new series called The Rugby Edition, founded to make Shakespeare accessible to the school population, precisely as a way of moulding a sense of national culture, with the nation at the centre of a huge empire. About Caliban the editor wrote:

> The character of [Caliban] may have had a special bearing on the great question of a time when we were discovering fresh colonies . . . Even if there were special dangers to savage races when first brought into contact with civilisation, yet we might justify the usurpation of power by those who were mentally and morally the stronger, as long as that usurpation was only used to educate and humanize the savage.[10]

It would certainly be possible to argue an essential continuity in critical language between 1876 and, say, 1947, when G. Wilson Knight's *The Crown of Life* was published. Knight's framework is, to put it mildly, Shakespearean, since *The Tempest* is understood as a reworking and interpretation of all the previous plays. Prospero is seen therefore as controlling not just the plot of the one play, but the whole Shakespearean world: 'he is thus automatically in the position of Shakespeare himself, and it is accordingly inevitable that he should often speak as with Shakespeare's voice'.[11] Knight's reading of events is entirely consonant with Prospero's, while Caliban 'condenses Shakespeare's concern ... with the animal aspect of man'.[12] Knight too is tempted by the national allegory, with Britain's imperial efforts 'to raise savage peoples from superstition and blood-sacrifice ... to a more enlightened existence' offering much fuel for correspondences with Prospero, Ariel and Caliban.[13]

Exactly a century after the Rugby Edition, and exactly two centuries after the United States's Declaration of Independence, Stephen Greenblatt's 'Learning to Curse' inaugurated the *postcolonial* readings of *The Tempest* within the academy. These readings were informed by critical theory and political radicalism, and they would, in the course of the 1980s, gradually intersect with the equally postcolonial readings undertaken by the likes of Mannoni and Lamming as contributions to the anti-colonial struggles of the postwar period.

In 'Learning to Curse' and in subsequent essays Greenblatt has diverted attention from the Bermuda pamphlets as potential *sources* for *The Tempest*, material that Shakespeare may have read and drawn on, towards a consideration of the larger discursive contexts that the play seems to share with such documents from the colonial archive. As Greenblatt puts it in his introduction to the play in the Norton edition:

> Shakespeare's play seems constantly to echo precisely the issues raised by the Bermuda shipwreck and its aftermath. What does it take to survive? How do men of different classes and moral character react during a state of emergency? What is the proper relation between theoretical understanding and practical experience or between knowledge and power? Is obedience to authority willing or forced? ... If there are natives to contend with, how should colonists establish friendly and profitable relations with them? What is to be done if relations turn sour? ... And – in Montaigne's more radical question – what is the justification of one person's rule over another? Who is the civilized man and who is the barbarian?[14]

A large number of postcolonial readings of *The Tempest* have been published since 1976: enough, certainly, for the 'postcolonial' reading to become dominant in textual studies (though not in productions) and for that reading to be attacked by critics offering new approaches and defending earlier ones. Two trends can be noted here. Postcolonial readings have recently spread out from *The Tempest* into Shakespearean studies more widely, encompassing *Othello* and *Antony and Cleopatra*, *The Merchant of Venice* and *Titus Andronicus*, as well as many of the history plays with their representations of the struggle for national unity.[15] This has had the benefit of providing a broader canvas against which the relationship between Prospero and Caliban can be seen as just one of many Shakespearean explorations of cultural difference, albeit the one that still seems to retain the most powerful resonance.

At the same time, historically based studies of early English colonialism, especially in Ireland and the Americas, and of the literature associated with it, have begun to produce a more nuanced picture of how a play such as *The Tempest* might actually relate, as text and performance, to colonial practices, and to the conceptual language in which America was made comprehensible for Europe during the sixteenth and early seventeenth centuries.[16] John Gillies's essay contributes to precisely that project, suggesting that the discursive homologies to be found argue for *The Tempest*'s vital rather than casual implication in the discourses of America in general and of the Virginia colony in particular.[17]

Gillies tracks the discourse of the New World through two stages, between which the term is disassociated from its native inhabitants. Patricia Seed provides a detailed background to this process, based on an investigation of Caliban's claim, 'This island's mine'. The relation of *The Tempest* to questions of possession and dispossession is still as contested as the disputes about indigeneity in the USA, Australia and New Zealand – and even those about nationality within Europe, as the Terra Nova *Tempest(s)* showed. Seed sets these debates in the context of the origins of international law, pointing out – among other things – the irony that both Caliban's and Prospero's claims to the island are dependent on women.

[3]

Caliban has become a potent symbol within writing and criticism from the 'Third World' – the name often employed in a loose sense to denote those who present themselves as finding their voice in a world dominated by Prosperos. Janheinz Jahn uses the term for much of what he calls 'neo-African literature'; José David Saldívar offers a 'Calibanic frame of reference' for reading contemporary texts from the Americas; and Margaret Joseph takes Caliban as simply 'synonymous with the colonized human being'.[18]

But a label that can include Kamau Brathwaite and Jean Rhys, Lemuel Johnson and Margaret Laurence, may well have exceeded its usefulness as a critical tool.

The poets and artists who have made use of the figure of Caliban have tended to marshal its resources more narrowly and therefore more creatively, engaging with the play, recasting its elements and rewriting its language in ways subtle enough to make Derek Walcott's description of self-styled Calibans as 'enraged pupils' who limit their language 'to phonetic pain, the groan of suffering, the curse of revenge' now seem outdated.[19] In the early 1990s Jimmie Durham (an artist and writer of Cherokee descent) created a series of diary entries, drawings, paintings and sculptures from Caliban's years as Prospero's pupil (see below, p. 179). Their tone is disarmingly naïve, the voice of a humble student discovering himself and demonstrating his gratitude to his teacher; but the language is laced with irony and violence. Many of the pieces relate to Caliban's quest to discover the shape of his nose: 'I don't know what I look like, since Dr. Prospero came there's nothing here that reflects me. I don't know what my nose looks like, for example, I can't touch it because Dr. Prospero says it's not nice to touch yourself.' One of Caliban's artworks is a small 'action painting', made with paint and dirt on paper: a crude pair of eyes stare out from a red smear where the nose should be, and a note from Caliban explains, 'One time Prospero was going to spank me because I was playing with mud. When I resisted I caused him to accidentally hit me in the nose.'[20]

The poetry of Lemuel Johnson presents us with a 'Caliban Agonistes', who uses the Creole dialect and the calypso form to explore the 'geography of his imagination'.[21] His 'Calypso for Caliban' ends with the lines, 'be present / while and still I am ready, / if the revel end, / to wake and cry to dream again.'[22] Refusing Caliban's (con)trite exit from the play after his failed rebellion ('I'll be wise hereafter, / And seek for grace'; V.i.294–5), Johnson leaves him poised in the musical dream-life of the island, which he had described earlier to his co-conspirators:

> Sometimes a thousand twangling instruments
> Will hum about mine ears; and sometimes voices,
> That if I then had waked after long sleep,
> Will make me sleep again, and then in dreaming
> The clouds methought would open and show riches
> Ready to drop upon me, that when I waked
> I cried to dream again. (III.ii.135–41)

Kamau Brathwaite has for some time been pushing the boundaries of written, printed and spoken language and struggling against the standards of Standard English and its institutions. In several engagements with *The Tempest* he has created 'a poetic rhetoric which attempts to outwit the restraints of the book'[23] as well as the constraints of Prospero – as in his 'Letter Sycorax', which begins,

> *Dear mamma*
>
> i writin yu dis letter/*wha?*
> guess what! pun a computer o/kay?
> like i jine de mercantilists?
>
> *well not quite!*
>
> *. . . say*
> *wha? get on wid de* same ole
>
> story?
>
> okay
> okay
>
> okay
> okay
>
> *if yu cyaan beat prospero*
> whistle[24]

Suniti Namjoshi's 'Snapshots of Caliban' sequence, finally, shifts between voices and identities ('From Caliban's Notebook', 'M's Journal', Prospero's Meditations'), exploring the new dynamics that result from making Caliban female:

> There's something wrong with Caliban.
>   Is it her shape? Is it her size?
> If I could say that Caliban is stupid,
> then that might help, but she can read and write
>   and sometimes her speech is so lucid.
> . . . Yet she is Caliban. I've seen her gaping
>   at the blue heavens, or at me,
> and I fear her dream. For there is something
> I dislike thoroughly about Caliban:
> if she had her way, she would rule the island,
>   and I will not have it.[25]

This book's travels through these complex contact zones are exemplified in the last few pieces in the section. David Dabydeen traces his Caribbean reworking of the *Tempest* in some of his poems back to an early fascination with Hogarth's painting of a scene from the play, of which he now offers an insightful reading suggesting Hogarth's deep fascination with, and even sympathy for, Caliban.[26] And whereas most late twentieth-century responses to the play have involved identification with Caliban, Ariel and Miranda, H.D.'s *By Avon River* (1949) is remarkable for taking Claribel as the subject of her imaginative quest. This work was the last of the three poetic tribute volumes she wrote in the 1940s (following *The Gift*, for her mother, and the *Tribute to Freud*); and it emerged from visits to Stratford-upon-Avon in the wake of both a personal breakdown and the wreckage of World War II. Once again, the geography gets complicated as an Anglo-American modernist poet chooses to pursue a character who relates Europe to North Africa, while showing a deep awareness of the American dimensions of the play. Here we reproduce the first part of this little-known work along with an introduction by Martha Nell Smith.

Our phrase 'transatlantic routes' tries at least to hint at something less than a radical division between the European and American dimensions of *The Tempest*. British ships leaving the English Channel to the west sailed out into the Atlantic to reach the Mediterranean, and crossed many thousands of Atlantic miles before rounding the Cape on their way to the east; and those routes, with possible calling points in the Canaries or Madeira or the Cape Verde Islands, overlapped with the routes taken from Britain and other European countries to various parts of the Americas. The Mediterranean and the Atlantic were not distinct navigational, trading or cultural systems – as Charles Verlinden's formulation, 'the Atlantic-Mediterranean', suggested many years ago.[27] The 'triangular trade in slaves, sugar and capital'[28] connected northern Europe with the African coast and the Americas; and it traces the itinerary of Shakespeare's characters in and after *The Tempest*.

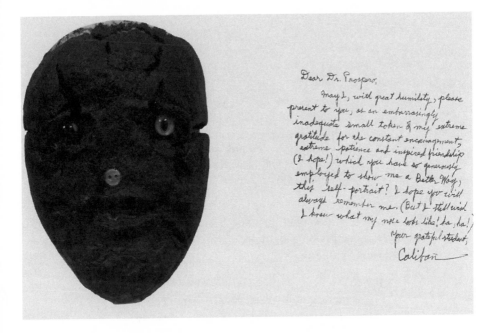

Jimmie Durham, *Untitled (Caliban's Mask)*, 1992, glass eyes, button, PVC, glue.

'Caliban finally completes an image of himself and he makes a gift of it for Prospero. It is a mask, the skin appears to be made of cracking earth, the eyes asymmetrical, brown and yellow, seemingly from different species. The mask attempts an uncertain smile over which hovers a button nose . . . In Caliban's unfinished skin we find the contemporary crisis of identity. This notion allows for the serious playfulness that characterizes Durham's work in general and the Caliban series in particular. Caliban's quest for identity is really a search for a proper mask to wear in his dance with Prospero.'[1]

'In this process of catching our gaze and turning it back on ourselves, and by other linguistic procedures that treat the 'insider/outsider' paradigm as a dubious cultural standard, Durham's art tries to help us understand why we continue to find such machinations necessary at all.'[2]

13 The Figure of the New World in *The Tempest*

JOHN GILLIES

> The projected creations of primitive men resemble the personifica-
> tions constructed by creative writers; for the latter externalise in the
> form of separate individuals the opposing instinctual impulses strug-
> gling within them.[1]

The question of precisely how *The Tempest* touches on the New World is
nowhere more pressing or more elusive than in this exchange between
Miranda and Prospero:

> MIRANDA   O wonder!
>   How many goodly creatures are there here!
>   How beauteous mankind is! O brave new world
>   That has such people in't!
> PROSPERO 'Tis new to thee. (V.i.181–5)

A 'close reading' will help to a certain extent. Raised in isolation from
European society, Miranda looks on human beings as a species for the first
time, recognizing in them a 'world' of beauty, goodliness and utopian
possibility. With no direct experience of 'human' (as distinct from native)
depravity, she misses what Prospero sees: creatures whose potential is perpetually cancelled by their history.

It is a moot point which of these visions is privileged, that of 'wonder' (an
emotion which Renaissance artists associated not merely with children but
with poetry as prophecy), or that of 'irony' (the 'knowing' response to history
purchased at the price of being perpetually consumed by it). What we are
left with is a stand-off: each vision defining, haunting, provoking, yet disal-
lowing the other. For a play in which prophecy has been the controlling
mode, the moment is especially disturbing. How far back does Prospero's
irony reach? How much of his own prophetic, masque-like design is called
into question? Potentially, all of it. In the play's most puzzling moment, we

have already seen Prospero effectively abdicate his rôle of *vates* – or prophetic maker of visions of chastisement and renewal – when abruptly terminating his masterpiece, the betrothal masque of Act IV. Logically, then, the power of irony is all but complete. And it would be complete in an aesthetic sense too, but for the fact that we experience the play from start to finish not in reverse, such that the irony is too belated and understated to cancel the effect of the previous four acts.

There is, however, something about the metaphoric structure of Miranda's 'brave new world' which goes uncomprehended and unchecked by Prospero's apparently all-embracing irony. This is that Miranda's phrase is displaced from its own historical and tropological roots, from precisely what a contemporary audience must have recognized as its primary referential horizon: the New World as historico-geographic trope. In addition to the words themselves, the very construction of this moment (a species of 'first encounter' scenario) inscribes it within New World discourse. Whereas in voyage literature from Columbus to Hariot, the encounter is between Europeans and New World natives, in Shakepeare it is an exclusively European affair. There are other differences. Where in voyage literature, the natives wonderingly see the Europeans as gods, in Shakespeare Miranda looks on the Europeans as 'mankind'. Where in the voyage literature, the Europeans wonder at the natives for their Edenic quality, their 'otherness', or in some way for bearing the mystery of the New World (its promise, wealth or horror); in Shakespeare, the Europeans view Miranda essentially as one of themselves.

This is not to say that the figure of the native is excluded from *The Tempest*, nor indeed from other versions of 'first encounter' in the play. In spite of the fact that 'the scene' of the play is described above the cast-list as 'an uninhabited island', images of the native are everywhere. Shortly after this moment, Caliban too gazes on the same group of Europeans, with the words, 'O Setebos, these be brave spirits indeed' (V.i.261); thus echoing his earlier wonder at Stephano as 'a brave god' (II.ii.112) and, as it were, reciprocating Gonzalo's earlier wonder at the 'strange shapes' (III.iii.19-20) who proffer a 'banquet' to the famished European castaways. But if 'natives' wonderingly encounter Europeans in fictional moments that shadow the 'encounters' of the voyage literature, such moments are effectively divorced from the theme of renewal and from any 'prophetic' or rhetorically privileged order of 'wonder'. The exultant cry, ''Ban, 'Ban Ca-Caliban / has a new master – get a new man' (II.ii.179–80), with which Caliban follows Stephano, must, we know, end in the same disappointment as Caliban's earlier infatuation with Prospero.

In the very moment of being cited, therefore, the trope of the New World is subtly re-engineered. To employ an Aristotelian distinction, Shakespeare splits the *pathos* (or feeling) of the 'first encounter' scenario from its *ethos* (or meaning) which is accordingly recast. The *pathos* (wonder) is further 'sublimed' (to use an alchemical term) by its linkage to the theme of renewal and the prophetic or masque-like idiom in terms of which that theme is enacted. We may think of it as the idiom of Miranda –the name represents a gerundive form of the Latin *miror/mirari*, thus 'fit to be wondered at'. But the *ethos* of that wonder is altered in the sense that the native has been removed from its content, and is thus no longer part of its meaning. In Julia Kristeva's terms, he has been 'abjected', plucked from the heart of the mystery of renewal and left in a realm of the monstrous or farcical.[2] The historico-geographic trope of the New World becomes a purely fictional trope, but one that is intimately parasitic on its original, one in which the original energies undergo a sea-change into 'something rich and strange', but not something without historic and geographic meaning. It is this deep act of occultation at the metaphoric core of Miranda's 'brave new world' that escapes Prospero's irony. I am suggesting that the real relationship between Shakespeare's 'brave new world' and the historical New World is veiled in a way that requires an 'archaeological' reading rather than a 'close' reading to unpack (that is, to comprehend with a species of historicising irony beyond the ken of Prospero's irony). This in turn must begin with the 'invention' of the New World as a trope, a verbal and conceptual object.

As various accounts of it have now argued, the New World was a deeply unstable figure by the early seventeenth century. In his study of the evolution of the New World as concept, the Mexican historian Edmundo O'Gorman finds it harbouring two essentially contrary orders of value and meaning.[3] The first derives from the earliest usages of the term by Peter Martyr and Amerigo Vespucci. In Peter Martyr's redaction of Vespucci's *mundus novus* as *novus orbis*, the new geographic entity was posited as a 'world' in the ancient sense of being humanly inhabited.[4] While both *mundus* and *orbis* carried the same literal sense of habitation, the eventual preference for the term *orbis* further stressed the uniqueness of the new entity by its association with the ancient title for 'the world' proper, the *orbis terrarum* (or inhabited earth). As such, 'New World' strongly implied an *orbis alterius*, that species of entirely separate human and animal creation posited in ancient philosophy and outlawed by the Christian doctrine of the unity of creation.[5] For such reasons, the term 'new' was left deliberately vague. The New World might have been 'new' in a genuinely ontological sense, but then again it might have been 'new' merely in the contingent sense of only recently having come to European notice.

The second value which O'Gorman finds in the idea of the New World dates from the invention of the name 'America' by Martin Waldseemüller in the *Cosmographiae Introductio* (1507), where the New World is defined as a 'fourth part' of the world on the assumption of its comprising a 'continent' (America) in addition to the three continents of the ancient world.[6] This represented a novel (indeed contradictory) use of the term 'continent' (*terra continens*) because America was an island rather than a large land-mass abutting other large land-masses. Why then did America continue to be called a 'continent'? By virtue, O'Gorman argues, of the deep elemental and ontological connection thereby implied between the two 'worlds'.[7] As one of four continents (as distinct from two worlds), America's unsettling novelty was brought under control. It was not an entirely 'other' geological and biological creation, just an unexplored part of the old one. Far from dropping out of currency, however, the term 'New World' persisted, though at the price of a semantic occultation. The New World now began to take on an historical and teleological dimension in the sense of fulfilling or completing the lost potentialities of the Old World – a sense anticipated by Columbus in a letter written during his third voyage when, drawing on the prophetic language of St John and Isaiah, he speaks of himself as a divine messenger chosen to make 'a new voyage to the new heaven and world, which up till then had remained hidden'.[8] While this second value of the term 'New World' might be modified in respect of various colonial projects at different places and times, its burden was to stress its ontological continuity, rather than its alterity.

In the long view of history, the second valency would eventually drive out the first. In the northern European experience, however, for all of the sixteenth century and much of the seventeenth, the two values would remain in tension. In world maps of the early to mid seventeenth century, the tension is harmonious.[9] America characteristically comprises a second 'world' in the sense of occupying the left half of the map and balancing the three continents of the Old World on the right. But it is also visually personified as a 'continent' in the iconographic border of the map, where it is joined by the personifications of Europe, Africa and Asia (the usual scheme is for the four continents to be arranged at the four corners of the sheet). The 'otherness' of America is further blunted by the frequent inclusion of the four Elements and/or the four Seasons in the iconographic programme, the implication of which is that the four continents and two worlds are linked by a fundamental 'natural' rubric. In voyage literature and colonial discourse (and their literary offshoots), however, the tension between the two values is more unstable, more dynamic, and more agonized. Earlier discourse tends to emphasize and even idealise the 'otherness' of the New World, whereas later discourse tends to elide – and, finally, bury – it. As this process (a process bearing uncanny similarities to the deep occultation within Miranda's 'brave new world') is best appreciated in a long historical view, I would like to illustrate it by reference to two studies of the iconographic shift within the New World trope.

E. McClung Fleming shows how the standard sixteenth-century European image of the Indian queen becomes (specifically in the context of North America, and in the course of the seventeenth and eighteenth centuries) an Indian princess, and finally (in the eighteenth century) a Greek goddess.[10] In the first stage of this evolution, America is an Indian queen: an heroic and gorgeous female nude, often with a feather headdress, jewellery, weapons (club or bow and arrow), and exotic and/or monstrous beasts (parrot, armadillo or alligator). In some versions of the iconography she is depicted in association with images of wealth (gold or silver), and in some she is depicted beside a severed head (suggestive of cannibalism). If the preponderance of savage (and generally Caribbean) attributes suggest her 'otherness', her attraction for Europeans is explicitly signalled by her wealth (in Anverian and London pageantry, she obligingly offers such wealth to the reigning monarch). Less explicitly, her interest for Europeans is suggested by her sexual allure. Of the psychic content of such iconography (as ambivalent compound of horror and desire), McClung Fleming has little to say. He is equally reticent when explaining the shifts to the second and third stages, beyond venturing the thought that some attributes were more pertinent than others to differing historical circumstances and geographic locations. Thus, the Indian queen's Southern American attributes – club, parrot, doubloons and silver-mine – were dispensed with because of their irrelevance to North America. When the queen becomes a princess, resigning her splendid independence to become a 'ward of the state' (a daughter or step-daughter to Britain) this is merely a recognition of contemporary colonial reality. McClung Fleming is likewise incurious about the loss of sexual frisson involved in the domesticating change from queen to princess.

What deeper pressures might lie behind such transformations? While not about personification as such, another study of New World iconography is enlightening in this regard. In her analysis of iconographic formations within the visual programme of the De Bry family's *Great Voyages* (a thirteen-volume compendium of major European discovery narratives, published serially between 1590 and 1634), Bernadette Bucher offers a kind of struc-turalist–psychoanalytic account.[11] For Bucher, the graphic image of the Indian throughout this compilation evolves according to an informal but entirely consistent 'mythology' with its roots in the Protestant unconscious. While such images derive in the first instance from eyewitness drawings (such as the work of Jacques Le Moyne de Morgues in Florida and John White in Virginia), they develop according to a logic which is independent of those sources. Thus, at a certain stage in the series, we find images of Indian women with sagging breasts. At later stages, we discover Indians (male and female) with other types of physical deformity – ranging to outright monstrosity. Where do these doctorings of the visual record originate? For Bucher, there are roughly two levels of explanation. In the process of copy-ing the original drawings into copperplate engravings, much characterizing information (colour, visual freshness and idiosyncrasy, emotional toning) was lost. Accordingly, a complex and nuanced visual record became flat-tened into a monochromatic formula based on a simplified version of the Renaissance classical nude. In this form, the Indians are classicized and idealized (their bodies invariably young and graceful) in line with the myth of New World infancy. While such images are in sympathy with the more lyrical (and in general earlier) encounter narratives, they clash markedly with narratives of a more aggressively colonial character. Physical deformi-ties such as sagging breasts originate in illustrations of these later narratives as ways of suggesting the depravity of the Indians – as, for example, in a series of engravings of Indian women preparing cannibal feasts illustrating the narrative of Hans Staden's capture by the Tupinambas of Brazil. What is interesting about such alterations for Bucher, however, is that they are sys-tematic rather than opportunistic: that they appear in connection with a range of different narratives as distinct from randomly varying according to the requirements of individual narratives. Moreover the system is increas-ingly word- rather than picture-driven; which is to say that an original (and relatively small) stock of ethnographic images is increasingly plundered, fractured and recombined in the context of increasingly remote narrative and discursive pressures:

> Old materials going back fifty years and more are thus separated from
> their original settings and turn up again in new arrangements. We are,
> then, confronted with a sort of Tower of Babel of the Amerindian
> peoples. Physical types, articles of ornamentation, and hairstyles, all
> borrowed from different cultures appear together quite incongruously
> in a single plate.[12]

World map with allegorical representations of the four corners of the earth: Petrus Plancius, *Orbis Terrarum Typus* (Amsterdam, 1594).

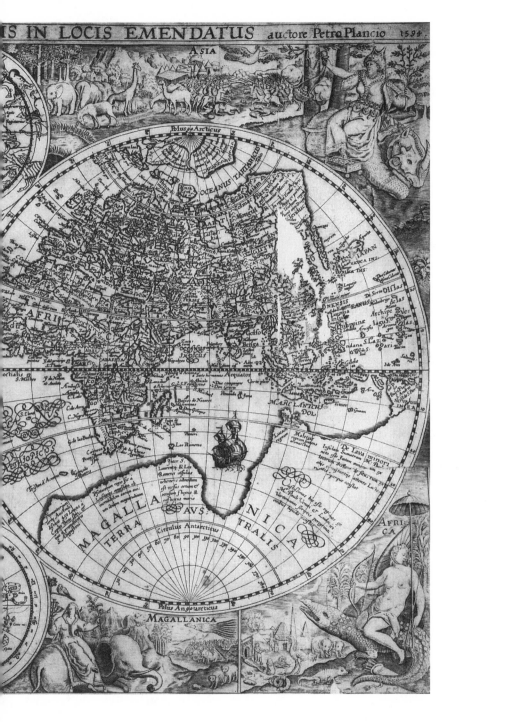

The babelesque image of the Indian is driven by a kind of unconscious taboo mechanism whereby the Indian, originally imagined as a potential partner in relationships of exchange, alliance and marriage, is rejected via a mythological transformation affirming 'mutual incompatibility between the two peoples and a taboo of miscegenation and intercultural marriage.'[13] Several aspects of this conclusion are of particular interest for our purposes. In the first place, the progressive deformation of the pristine Amerindian female body opens up a rift within the ambivalence (horror and desire) figured by America as cannibal queen. Second, where the Amerindians are originally taken to be endemic to the New World (they are what make it a 'world' in the human sense, and their conversion by the European and potential partnership with him, justifies the Protestant colonization by contrast with the forcible seizure – or 'rape' – of the Spanish), they end by being extirpated from it. But the Protestant vision of the New World nevertheless remains that of a 'world', rather than a geographic blank indifferent to whether it is unpopulated or populated, or to the character of any population it may have.

Quite apart from the interest of their explanations, Bucher and McClung Fleming significantly bear out O'Gorman's elucidation of the bipolarity in the New World as representative object. All three posit a process whereby the New World is first apprehended as both *alter-* and *mundus-orbis* (a compound of 'lands and peoples'), and next apprehended as ontologically *idem* (same), though in the sense of a teleological extension (old–new). This second stage itself evolves through two stages. The teleological vision of renewal begins by including 'lands and peoples', but ends by excluding 'peoples'.[14] In the end only these are *alter*, but by this stage the land is supplied with new peoples (Europeans), and together they comprise another species of new world which can be less problematically viewed as an offshoot of the old one.

This process is exemplified over the long term in the Jacobean discourse of Virginia. Between 1610 (the probable year of composition of *The Tempest*) and 1623 (the date of its publication in the First Folio), 'Virginia' can be seen to undergo a figurative evolution anticipating that traced by McClung Fleming. Moreover, this evolution appears to have been pushed by the same order of unconscious mythologization – roughly the same psychic tectonics – as that detected by Bucher.

The historical 'moment' of *The Tempest* (*c.*1610) coincides closely with a burst of sermons and pamphlets sponsored by the Virginia Company, promoting the colony as an object of messianic national destiny and spiritual renewal.[15] In one of the most elaborate of these, the Reverend William

Crashaw's sermon on 21 February 1609 – before 'The right honorable the Lord Lawarre' on his departure as governor (in the *Sea-Venture*, whose shipwreck is echoed in *The Tempest*) – the goal of the colony is identified as 'the plantation of a church of English Christians there, and consequently the conversion of the heathen from the divel to God.'[16] This messianic destiny, insists Crashaw, arises from England's own providential conversion in the distant past by the 'Apostles and their disciples' (following on the civilizing of Britain by the Romans). It is for such reasons that, even though Crashaw flags the possibility of contextualizing Virginia in the genocidal discourse of the Old Testament Canaan, he prefers to do so in the messianic idiom of the Acts of the Apostles. Hence, instead of arguing that the Indians be justly extirpated as the Canaanites were by the Israelites, he argues that they should be converted in line with the covenant of Grace that Christ made with Peter. The sermon ends with a kind of messianic apostrophe to Virginia:

> And thou Virginea, whom though mine eies see not, my heart shall love; how hath God honoured thee! Thou hast thy name from the worthiest Queene that ever the world had: thou hast thy matter from the greatest King on earth: and thou shalt now have thy forme from one of the moste glorious nations under the sunne ... But this is but a little portion of thy honour: for thy God is coming towards thee, and in the meane time sends to thee, and salutes thee with the best blessing Heaven hath, the blessed Gospell. Looke up therefore, and lift up thy head, for thy redemption draweth nie.

Appended to the sermon is a kind of Blakean dialogue between God and the nations, a scripturally inspired prophetic masque entitled 'A New Yeere's Gift to Virginea' (which I here reproduce in full):

> *God to Europe*: The Kingdome of God shall bee taken from you and given to a Nation that shall bring forth the fruits thereof.
> *God to England*: But I have praied for thee that thy faith faile not: therefore when thou art converted, strengthen thy brethren. (Luk, 22.32)
> *England to God*: Lord heere I am, send me. (Essay, 6.7)
> *God to Virginea*: He that walketh in darknesse and hath no light, let him trust in the name of the Lord, and stay upon his God. (Essay, 50.10)
> *Virginea to God*: God be mercifull to us, and bless us, and cause the light of (y)our countenance shine upon us: let thy waies be knowen upon earth, and thy saving health among all Nations.' (Psal.67.1.2)
> *England to Virginea*: Behold I bring you glad tidings. Unto you is borne a Saviour, even Christ the Lord. (Luk.1)

> *Virginea to England*: How beautifull are the feet of them that bring glad
> tidings, and publish salvation! (Es.52.7)
> *England to Virginea*: Come children, hearken unto me: I will teach you
> the feare of the Lord. (Psal.34.11)
> *Virginea to England*: Blessed be he that cometh in the name of the Lord.
> (Psal.118)

What is particularly striking about both of these passages is the depth at
which the separate identities of land and people are elided within the figure
of 'Virginea'. This personification is of neither land nor people, but a neophyte 'nation' conscious of itself as newly emerging from darkness into
light. As a national personification 'Virginea' corresponds to McClung
Fleming's Indian princess rather than his Indian queen, having exchanged
her barbarous independence for tutelage in Christianity from a patriarchal
'England'. However ominous 'England's' promise to the 'children' of
Virginea (the Indians) to teach them 'the feare of the Lord', the Indians are
not only included within the vision of renewal but constitute its origin and
justification.

In Samuel Purchas's *Virginias Verger* of 1623, however, 'Virginia' is very differently imagined.[17] While ostensibly just another 'discourse shewing the
benefits which may grow to this Kingdome from American English
Plantations', Purchas's tract reconstitutes the English title to Virginia independently of any ongoing tie with the Indians (patently in response to the
Indian uprising of 18 April 1622). While an ongoing duty to proselytize is
acknowledged (where that is feasible), the stress here is on Virginia as a
vacant land rather than a compound of land and people. Considering that
'every man by Law of Nature and Humanitie hath right of Plantation' from
God's command to the children of Noah to 'replenish the whole earth', the
English are allowed to replenish the greater part of Virginia which is not
occupied by the Indians, and to hold those parts which they have already
purchased.[18] In view of the uprising, moreover, they are allowed a right of
'forfeiture'. At exactly this point in the argument, Virginia is personified
anew:

> ... howsoever since they have beene perfidious ... this perfidiousnesse
> of theirs hath further warranted the English Title. Temperance and
> Justice had before kissed each other, and seemed to blesse the cohabi-
> tations of English and Indians in Virginia. But when Virginia was vio-
> lently ravished by her owne ruder Natives, yea her Virgin cheekes dyed
> with the bloud of three Colonies ... Temperance could not temper her
> selfe, yea the stupid Earth seemes distempered with such bloudy

potions and cries that shee is ready to spue out her Inhabitants.[19]

While Purchas still wants to 'espouse Virginia to one husband, presenting her as a chast Virgin to Christ', the quasi-nuptial imagery which had once functioned within a millennial discourse of conversion now becomes a coy invitation to repopulate:

> But looke upon Virginia; view her lovely lookes (howsoever like a modest Virgin she is now vailed with wild Coverts and shadie Woods, expecting rather ravishment then Mariage from her Native Savages ... and in all these you shall see, that she is worth the wooing and loves of the best Husband.[20]

As a personification of the land only, we cannot tell exactly what this Virginia would look like in terms of a graphic image, except that she would not have any Indian attributes. We notice that her relationship to the colonizer has also changed. She is no longer ward or neophyte or convertee, but a prospective spouse – not so much of Crashaw's 'England' but of whichever English choose to settle. The sexual allure of the Indian queen has returned but with an entirely new logic: this Virginia is to be sexually possessed through legal espousal.

Where does *The Tempest* stand in relation to the New World trope, and the symbolic shift we have found within different stages and instances of it: 'invention' (O'Gorman), formal personification (McClung Fleming), informal visual iconography (Bucher), and finally the Jacobean Virginia discourse? I suggest that the resonance is powerful and many-layered.

The earlier valency of the trope is ironically cited – 'historicized' we might almost say – at various points of the play. Thus, in Act I, scene ii, Gonzalo imagines himself governing a 'plantation' of New World natives according to the ancient formula of the 'golden age' that had been routinely invoked in first encounter discourses. Two specifically literary spin-offs of such discourse are registered here. The phraseology of Gonzalo's primitivist fantasy is that of a passage in Florio's English translation (1603) of Montaigne's 'Of the Caniballes' (1578/80). Its situation – a counsellor to a European prince suddenly conceiving the possibility of using the celebrated communism of the New World Indians as the basis for a radical critique of European institutions – is that of More's *Utopia* (1516). As Arthur J. Slavin has argued, the radical thought experiments of More and Montaigne are predicated on an 'American principle': the perception that ideal prehistoric forms of political organization posited in ancient poetry, philosophy and Natural Law thinking (and completely at odds with the contemporary or historical European political order) actually existed in the New World, and were therefore pertinent to political thought in a way that they had never been before.[21] Aside from the fact of its very existence, the quality that More and Montaigne most respond to in the New World is its radical alterity. Only in the glass of this *orbis alterius* – a space and a population unmortgaged to European history – is a 'utopian' critique of European society imaginable. Cited in *The Tempest*, however, the utopian mode becomes old-hat and just plain wrong-headed – their founding proposition (that the New World really is different) seemingly disproved by common sense and subsequent contact.

Successively later New World scenarios are also echoed in the play. In the 'several strange shapes' who prepare a banquet for the European castaways, we appear to have a variation on a slightly later type of encounter discourse. While these islanders are still able to call European society into radical question (as befits their utopian pedigree), their powers of question are limited. This is because, while 'different' from the Europeans – monstrous, speechless and yet of more gentle 'manners' – their difference is measured on an implicitly European scale of values, in terms of which they are judged to be inferior on the first two counts and superior on the third. What has happened here, then, is that the image of the native has shifted from being radically 'other' to being merely 'different' within a broad assumption of parity – putting the native in the position of European neophyte. Caliban's apprenticeships to Miranda, Prospero and Stephano echo yet later versions of this positionality. Miranda's efforts to teach Caliban language and Prospero's efforts to foster him as a kind of ward, seem to echo the Indian policy propounded by Virginia Company sermons contemporary with the play's composition. In this succession of 'moments', the position of the Indian shifts from being that of a radical 'other' capable of a wholesale interrogation of European social norms, to that of an apprentice European (a neophyte at the altar of civilization), to that of the apostate neophyte (Caliban).

The radical opposition of Miranda and Caliban, however, represents something beyond the citations of earlier moments within the New World discourse, and beyond the Virginia discourse of 1610. What it figures is something like the final state of the New World trope in which the dream of a 'brave new world' is defined against rather than with or through the Indian. Neither 'historicizing' citation nor contemporary colonial ideology, it is more like a 'mythological' activity in Bucher's sense, the willed transformation of an existing repertory of meanings. The opposition has a peculiar character: on the one hand so 'natural' as to defeat question, but on the other hand provoking question by means of its very over-insistence. What I am suggesting is that Caliban's 'abjectness' and Miranda's 'sublimity' need not be taken at face value. The symbolism is open to a decoding, a reading such as that to which Bucher subjects De Bry. In place of Bucher's structuralist paradigm however, I prefer to make use of Julia Kristeva's theory of 'abjection' and 'sublimation'. Like Freud, Kristeva thinks of the 'personifications of creative writers' in terms of a 'primitive' projection outwards of internal emotional content (where 'primitive' has the sense of the psychologically archaic and occult).[22] Again, like Freud, she takes such projection to be motivated by an intolerable emotional ambivalence. Kristeva, however, understands 'projection' in far more radical terms than Freud. For her, the founding division between self and other has the character of a projection. The external world is only knowable once the self has been split off from engulfment within its own abjection: 'in the symptom, the abject permeates me, I become abject. Through sublimation, I keep it under control. The abject is edged with the sublime.'[23] It is then on the basis of the emotional economy made possible by this constant dialectic of affirmation and denial that the world becomes knowable – and acceptable. (An object which is too emotionally ambivalent is not acceptable to the subject and thus not properly knowable.) Roughly this, I suggest, was behind the metamorphosis of the New World object in the course of the sixteenth and seventeenth centuries. In the sheer shock of its original novelty, the New World was figured as ontologically 'other' and emotionally ambivalent in ways too disturbing to endure. The inherent instability led to a transformation whereby ontological otherness was refigured as ontological affiliation, and the ambivalent became split into figures of desire (the land, the dream of renewal, Miranda) and figures of abjection (the dispossessed savage, Caliban). Kristeva is suggestive for another reason: namely that while the self represses the dialectic of sublimation and abjection by which its world comes into existence as an already cathected object, it is also condemned in some shadowy sense to remember.[24] What I should now like to suggest is that the sheer energy invested in stating the opposition between Caliban and Miranda, is in some sense haunted by a remembering – a faint but definite suggestion that the two figures share a common imaginative element, a common root.

Let us begin with how the opposition is declared within the play. Miranda is 'sublime' (a 'goddess' to Ferdinand, a 'nonpareil' to Caliban), beautiful, associated with a thematic of temperance, nurture, education, renewal, and finally with a masque in which nuptial imagery harmonizes with agricultural imagery, fertility with temperance, and Spring with Harvest. By contrast, Caliban is abject, physically and morally monstrous, intemperate, ignorant, futile, lustful and violent. Where Miranda's symbolism culminates in the masque of Ceres, Caliban's culminates in the 'filthy-mantled pool' (IV.i.182) by Prospero's cell. The very symmetry of these oppositions, however, bespeaks a shadowy alliance, a primordial togetherness. Thus each is more 'natural' than the visiting Europeans (Caliban in a 'wild' sense and Miranda in a 'pristine' sense). Both inhabit the emotional element of 'wonder' (as wonderers and as objects of wonder to Europeans), both are structurally speaking children, both are wards of Prospero within his project of education and renewal. Their paths have crossed twice: first when Miranda teaches Caliban 'language' with the intention of conscripting him within the project of moral renewal; second when Caliban attempts to violate Miranda and is driven from her presence.

What, we might ask, is the burden of this earlier alliance up to the moment of its rupture? It points to a relationship of filiation of the order envisioned by Crashaw in 1609, a species of potential partnership such as that represented in the earlier volumes of the *Great Voyages*. Even in these terms however, the affiliation is highly ambiguous and correspondingly unstable. The project of teaching Caliban 'language' potentially inducts him into the civilized order itself, and from there into a potential marital partnership with Miranda. Even though already figured as conspicuously ineligible, his status as ward gives him a kind of parity with Miranda, and indeed with Ferdinand, the successful marital partner with whom Caliban is clearly juxtaposed (each is figured as a 'natural man', each is situated within a redemptive ordeal, each is shown bearing wood, each is figured as inherently lustful). Yet if the potential nuptial relationship between Caliban and Miranda in some senses suggests that of contemporary Virginian discourse, there is also a striking difference: the sexual polarity is reversed. Whereas in Crashaw (and the historical marriage of Pocahontas with John Rolfe) the native is female and the European male, here the European is female and the native male.

Miranda, however, is not just any European. As an embodiment of wonder and exemplar of renewal she is heavily suggestive of New World symbolism – and not least for feminizing and sexualizing these themes. If her lack of savage 'otherness' is discounted, Miranda's first encounter with Ferdinand can read like a bowdlerized version of Theodore Galle's engraving of Vespucci encountering a naked female 'America': there is the same sense of mutual wonder, the same sexual polarity, the sexual magnetism (though without the sexual threat), the sense of mutual 'discovery', the sense of radical difference and mutual destiny, and the sea-shore setting.[25] There may indeed be a direct New World echo in this encounter. If it is true, as Frank

Kermode suggests, that the 'curious burthen of Ariel's first song (*bowgh wawgh* in F) may derive from James Rosier's account of a ceremonial Virginian dance', then it would appear that this particular echo has undergone the order of alienating 'sea change' I have suggested in the case of Miranda's 'brave new world'.[26] The ceremonial dance of the Other is translated into a European courtly ceremony (hand-taking and curtsying). To adapt the description of 'altogether Estrangefull, and *Indian* Like' torchbearers in Chapman's *Memorable Masque* (1613), Ferdinand and Miranda are wonderfully 'Estrangefull' here, but hardly '*Indian* Like'. Again, if the imagined *mise-en-scène* rather suggests Inigo Jones's 'Sceane of an Indian shore and a sea' from *The Temple of Love* (1634), there is no equivalent for 'Indamora', Davenant's Indian queen. Masque indeed is highly suggestive here. Prospero stages the encounter literally as a 'discovery' within the idiom of spectacle ('the fringéd curtains of thine eyes advance'; I.ii.408) and frames it within a masque-like symbolism of death, transformation and rebirth. In its prophetic register, the theme of New World discovery was more generically at home in masque than the popular theatre.[27] Thus, Crashaw had inveighed bitterly against the stage representation of 'Virginea' in his sermon, before fancifully staging her encounter with England as a masque.

While her discursive intertext is hazier than Caliban's, Miranda resonates far more strongly with the evolving discourse of the Virginia plantation than with earlier stages of New World discourse. Various aspects of her rôle point in this direction. The imagery of temperance and fruitfulness associated with Miranda suggests a similar imagery in the Virginia discourse.[28] Nuptial symbolism is common to both. Miranda's attempt to educate Caliban corresponds with Crashaw's idea of educating the Indians. Most important perhaps is the Patriarchal and 'Natural Law' character of her own 'training', for which, in Prospero's account, geographic isolation is a positive advantage (I.ii.171–4). More so than a conventional education in 'the liberal arts', this education takes the 'nature' of the pupil as its primary focus. What appears to be at work here is a Protestant philosophy of 'Natural Law' whereby education is envisaged as a process of emphasizing the innate inscription of 'Natural Law' in the heart, at the expense of a conventional socialization.[29] Thus, Miranda is educated in ignorance of identity, rank or privilege; heavily against the grain of a conventional aristocratic socialization. She responds to people for their 'natural' or moral qualities alone: Caliban himself she has cared for simply on the assumption of an answerably 'natural' receptiveness to the 'print of goodness' (I.ii.351) – and with no hint of the socialized contempt which is the reflex response of the visiting Europeans. Ferdinand's ordeal on the island also has a Natural Law character, its added harshness explained by its function as a 're-education'. Authorizing all these educational projects is the patriarchal figure of Prospero.[30] The same complex of Natural Law ideas makes sense of the masque of Ceres, with its vision of an earthly paradise in which nature is simultaneously perfected by nurture but is also strenuously unfallen. (Ceres, mother of Proserpine, is gratified to hear that Venus and Cupid have not been allowed to re-enact the rape of her daughter – and hence the classical version of the Christian Fall.) It also seems behind the dream of renewal (nature is renewable if its primitive virtue is 'educable').

Natural Law thinking may explain the curious mix of failure and success in Caliban's education. Significantly, Caliban's overall failure seems to hinge not on an absence of intellectual ability but on the absence of any counterpart of 'Natural Law' in his nature ('thy vile race – / Though thou didst learn – had that in't which good natures / Could not abide to be with'; I.ii.357–9). It is no accident that it should be Miranda who pronounces the rationale of Caliban's slavery, nor that this rationale should be modishly Aristotelian (Caliban is a 'slave by nature').[31] The idea that the native is beyond Natural Law would of course directly contradict the root assumption of the utopian writing characteristic of an earlier stage of New World discourse: that the New World peoples were actually closer to Natural Law than the Europeans were. But if Shakespeare contradicts Montaigne here, he also contradicts the thrust of the contemporary Virginia discourse, based as it was on the assumption that the savages were reclaimable.[32] Denial of any Natural Law status to the Indian is fully in line with the transformation within the New World trope that we have been positing. By covertly Europeanizing this status in Miranda, indeed, Shakespeare manages to have his cake and eat it. The 're-education' of Ferdinand and his fellow visitors to the island suggests that the utopian function of the New World (as a 'natural' touchstone of civilization) is retained in spite of the reassignment of Natural Law status from the native to Miranda. The importance of Natural Law to Miranda's character – specifically the peculiar quality of her 'innocence' – is perhaps best illustrated by comparing her to her counterparts in Dryden's adaptation of The Tempest in 1670. Here Miranda's rôle is multiplied by three in order to furnish multiple opportunities for erotic titillation. Effectively, the Natural Law theorem of educated innocence has been translated into the Restoration syllogism of Wycherley's 'country wife'.[33] 'Natural Law' becomes the law of nature, or the commonplace sex drive. In the absence of a climate receptive to Natural Law belief, Miranda's higher innocence collapses into the merest pretext. Prospero's 'Temperance' league becomes a bit of a joke.

While Miranda's imaginative being corresponds to the most fully evolved

stage of New World tropology – its most sublime and 'prophetic' possibility –
Caliban's seems rooted in a much older imagery. Like the 'tower of Babel of
Amerindian types' that Bucher finds in De Bry, Caliban has no coherent
ethnographic model. The sole principle of coherence lies in his abjectness. It
is this that accounts for the dominance of the older Caribbean and
Patagonian elements over the newer Virginian. The Caribbean element
shows up in his name, an anagram of 'cannibal'. But we may well ask why, as
'cannibalism' is not part of his character or action. His mother's god,
'Setebos', derives from Antonio Pigafetta's narrative of Magellan's encounter
with the Indians of Tierra del Fuego – for centuries, the most primitive and
forlorn of Indian types (a type particularly influential in the De Bry iconography). Where Virginian elements do emerge, they seem either alienated
from Caliban (as in Ariel's 'bowgh wawgh') or retrojected through the older
imagery. Thus, the ironic conversion tableau in which Caliban 'kisses'
Stephano's bottle – as though it were a font of 'language' (II.ii.79) – would
appear to echo a passage from Hariot's *Report*:

> Many times and in every towne where I came . . . I made declaration of
> the concepts of the Bible . . . And although I tolde them the booke
> materially and of it selfe was not of any vertue, as I thought they did
> conceive, but onely the doctrine therein conteined: yet woulde many
> bee glad to touche it, to embrace it, to kisse it, to holde it to their breastes
> and heades, and stroke over all their body with it, to shewe their hun-
> grie desire of that knowledge which was spoken of.[34]

Behind the strange Machiavellian ambivalence of this passage (so much
more naked in Stephano), however, lies an older conversion scenario from
Magellan's encounter with the Patagonians. In Richard Eden's translation it
is subtitled 'The gyantes language . . . the gyant is baptised':

> The other gyante which remayned with them in the shyp ... spoke al
> his wordes in the throte. On a tyme, as one made a crosse before him
> and kyssed it, shewynge it vnto him, he suddeynely cryed *Setebos*, and
> declared by signes that if they made any more crosses, *Setebos* wold
> enter into his body and make him brust. But when in fine he sawe no
> hurte coome thereof, he tooke the crosse and imbrased and kyssed it
> oftentymes, desyringe that he myght be a Chrystian before his death.
> He was then baptysed and named Paule.[35]

Shakespeare, we know, took the name 'Setebos' from this account. Whether
he used Harriot as well, he appears to have drawn the same moral: the savage is capable only of a debauched and Papist form of Christianity, even

when it is preached by Protestants. Conversion thus becomes a farce on one side and 'policy' on the other.

One Virginian detail, however, stands out in Caliban's iconography. In the course of his exultant celebration of 'freedom', Caliban cries out: 'No more dams I'll make for fish' (II.ii.173). Of this line, Sir Sidney Lee remarks that 'Shakespeare's very precise mention of Caliban's labours as a fisherman is the most literal of all transcriptions in the play from records of Virginian native life', and significant moreover as 'a vivid and penetrating illustration of a peculiar English experience in Virginia'.[36] Lee points out that Eliza-bethan and Jacobean colonists had expressed 'amazement at the mechanical skill which the natives brought to the construction of their fish-dams'; also that 'the secret of construction was well kept . . . and European visitors to their embarrassment, never learned it'.[37] More than embarrassment was at stake: Lane, Smith and Strachey all remarked on the colonists' dependence on the dams for food. Dam failure meant starvation, and 'was a chief cause of the disastrous termination of the sixteenth century efforts to found an English colony in Virginia'. The significance of this for Lee is that 'Caliban's threat . . . consequently exposed Prospero to a very real and a familiar peril.'[38] While this is true, the real significance is surely greater – namely that the logic of the idea is never registered in the play. The reasons are obvious. If taken seriously, the notion that Caliban possesses a technology unmas-tered by Prospero must have deconstructed the hierarchy of skill, power, value and right which is presupposed in Prospero's subjection of Caliban. It would, moreover, have made nonsense of Caliban's symbolic association with evil-smelling fens and filthy mantled ponds, which (particularly in the context of the imagery of artful land-drainage in the masque of Ceres) epitomize nature in its wild and potentially malevolent state (the fens supply Sycorax with her 'wicked dew'). For such reasons the idea is not developed. It is elided with Caliban's refusal to 'fetch in firing at requiring' in the very next line, and buried beneath numerous suggestions of Caliban as hunter-gatherer; one who snares 'the nimble marmoset', who gathers 'berries, 'crabs', 'pignuts', 'jay's eggs' and 'clustering filberts'. Finally, it vanishes into the common European impression that Caliban is himself a fish: he smells like a fish, looks like a fish and might be sold as a fish. The way in which the text suppresses what it also adverts – the Virginian discourse of Indian dams – is akin to a repression.

'History', writes Michel de Certeau in a reading of Freud strikingly comple-mentary to Julia Kristeva's, 'is "cannibalistic", and memory becomes the closed arena of conflict between two contradictory operations: forgetting, which is not something passive . . . but an action directed against the past; and the mnemic trace, the return of what was forgotten . . . an action by a past that is now forced to disguise itself.'[39]

While generically a romance rather than a history, The Tempest (in de Certeau's metaphor) 'bites' the subject which it represents.[40] What is bitten or cannibalized? The earlier ethnographic repertory, the 'beautiful' Amerindian body which Montaigne projects from that repertory, any possibility of representing the Amerindian without projection or 'prejudice' (which is to say outside of the available language).[41] What need is fed by this 'biting'? The inner compulsion of the New World trope to divest itself of the savage 'Other', precisely the dissimulation which escapes Prospero's ironic surveillance. If all this is to suggest that the play is a strategic 'forgetting' or (worse) propaganda in the service of early European colonialism, it is also to suggest something more.[42] There is, as Peter Hulme reminds us, a 'difference' between Prospero's play and Shakespeare's: namely that 'The Tempest stages Prospero's staging of his play'.[43] To the extent that this is so, we have an uncanny sense of the repressed content of Prospero's play returning to 're-bite' (to de-form, undo, haunt) that which represses it.

Suggestions of this are legion. Prospero is linked to Sycorax by a subterrene set of correspondences: each a sorcerer, each an enslaver of Ariel, each an echo of Medea, each in some sense a parent of Caliban. Prospero's gnomic acknowledgement of Caliban ('this thing of darkness I / Acknowledge mine'; V.i.275) hints at deeper wells of complicity, of remorse – both personal and historical – than we can ever say (De Certeau's 're-bite', re-mordre, puns directly on 'remorse', remords).[44] Miranda too seems haunted, her notional sublimity jarring with her invocation of the Aristotelian argument for 'natural' slavery. For his part, Caliban's very abjectness calls forth poetry, beauty, pathos – and a devastating sense of 'natural' justice. The sheer overdetermination of Caliban's monstrosity leads to the continuing enigma of his appearance. Behind the enigma lurks something deeper: the physical appearance which is the master sign of Caliban's existence is actually a relational term whereby Caliban appeals over the heads of his fellow characters to audiences past and present, First World and Third.

The most telling of all disjunctions between Prospero's play and Shakespeare's, however, is provided by Prospero himself. Famously, the symbolic centre of the play enshrines an enigma: the 'strange hollow and confused noise' (IV.i.138–9) to which the masque of Ceres 'heavily' dissolves. If the masque of Ceres represents the crowning moment of the theme of renewal – the high point of its prophetic mode – then the failure to consummate it represents something deeper, unplumbable, a deliberate *aporia*. The moment is unpackable to certain levels. There is Prospero's own explanation: 'I had forgot the foul conspiracy / Of the beast Caliban and his confederates / Against my life. The minute of their plot / Is almost come' (IV.i.139–42). But a scheduling error is hardly sufficient. Then there is a formalistic explanation to the effect that the masque has to be truncated to allow the play to continue as a play. Yet this explanation fails to take account of the fact that masque has been the dominant mode of the play in any case up to this moment, and it ignores the deliberate inversiveness of the moment – the way in which Prospero's 'beating mind' and 'distempered' visage represent a resurgence of the chaotic imagery of tempestuousness and disordered passion over the hard-won victory of music, harmony, temperance and 're-education'. Finally, there is the 'our revels now are ended' speech (IV.i.146–63), in which human life and 'the great globe itself' are likened to a masque, but from a counter-masque standpoint in which vision collapses into its 'baseless fabric' and prophecy shrinks into a dream. We are left, then, with the *aporia*, the figure of unknowing. We can, however, say two things. First, the ambition to raise human nature to some prelapsarian yet millenial status is exposed as 'utopian' (an effect reinforced by the prayerful entreaty of the Epilogue). Second, Caliban's intrusion is in some way material to this new humility, this grounded refusal of the language of vision.

What this building-up and emptying-out of utopia also suggests is that there is no going back. The dream of renewal, once entertained within history – that of Prospero's island or Caliban's nature or the New World – is irreversible. The haunted utopia is still utopia. The ground once having been cleared will never revert to forest. The New World, once having been conjured forth, will never collapse back into the Old. It is in the depth at which this most romance-like of Shakespeare's plays encodes the metahistorical logic of the New World trope as a process of continual historical becoming that it outstares (out-bites?) the remorseful and nostalgic archaeologies of the twentieth century.

O THOU MINE HEIR
OF NAPLES AND MILAN, WHAT STRANGE FISH
HATH MADE HIS MEAL ON THEE? (I.ii.110–11)

'Nibbled swimmer', from Conrad Gesner, *Historiæ Animalium, Liber IV*, 2nd edn (Frankfurt, 1604), p. 800.

In sixteenth-century Europe, images of strange fish were plentiful: they filled the edges of maps and the tops of broadsides (such as the one published in 1569, containing 'The true descripcion of this marueilous straunge fishe . . . taken between Callis, and Douer'). Gesner's volumes on the history of animals – translated for English readers by Edward Topsell in 1607–8 – offered a veritable catalogue.

For Alonso, his son and heir Ferdinand is not just drowned but eaten, food for strange fish. Caliban is probably an anagram of 'canibal', but he seems to have no anthropophagous characteristics attributed to him – until Trinculo's conclusion to his examination of Caliban's figure ('A strange fish!'; II.i.26–7) provides a textual link.

14 'This island's mine': Caliban and Native Sovereignty

PATRICIA SEED

'This island's mine', claims Caliban to Prospero near the beginning of *The Tempest*. And he adds the characteristic anti-colonial complaint 'which thou tak'st from me' (I.ii.331–2). Was the island his? And did Prospero take it from him? The answers to these questions lead in two sharply different directions – one connecting the play to claims of colonial ownership, the other echoing the increasingly masculine character of inheritance rights in England.

Perhaps the most important dimension of Caliban's claim is its enunciation. During the sixteenth and seventeenth centuries Europeans no longer shared a common concept of international law. Prior to Martin Luther's and Henry VIII's break from the Church, the dominant form of international law in Europe had been Catholic. But the growing antagonism between Catholics and Protestants left neither a single body nor single doctrine to govern the European community and its actions overseas. Instead, leaders of the separate European states proposed their own versions of international rules, each claiming as universal principles those that suited their own interests best.[1]

The trend to separate histories of international law within the European community remains in place to this day. In the Anglo-Dutch world, the history of modern international law is customarily said to have begun with Hugo de Groot (Grotius). However in the Iberian world, the history of international law is narrated with a separate beginning spearheaded by Francisco Vitoria and Bartolomé de Las Casas, with Grotius rarely, if ever, mentioned.[2] Therefore, at the time of *The Tempest* there was no common European conception of how to claim an island. Different Europeans performed different ceremonies to establish legitimate political possession – and rationalized their occupation in different ways.[3] As a result, Caliban's interactions with Prospero and Miranda over claims to the island closely resemble what would become the conventional narratives of English colonizers in the Americas: the preoccupation with seizing productive farmland, the aim of resettling the land with Europeans, and the denial of responsibility for native violence against the colonisers.

[1]

As Caliban tells it, their initial contacts were full of hospitality and Prospero's apparent affection for him. When Prospero had first arrived, he had treated Caliban well: 'When thou cam'st first, Thou strok'st me and made much of me . . . and then I loved thee' (I.ii.332-6). And in return for all this flattery and petting, Caliban 'showed thee all the qualities o'th' isle, / The fresh springs, brine pits, barren place and fertile' (I.ii.337–8), in short all the essential places for maintaining human existence – locales where food could be grown, fresh water found, as well as salt for preserving food.

In Caliban's version of the events following the arrival of the first Europeans, Prospero masked his initial dependence on Caliban for information about the island with displays of often-physical affection. Prospero's abrupt abandonment of that affection for Caliban has left Caliban angry and deceived, as the apparent kindness revealed itself to have been less than caring, merely a pretence of humanity in order to find out all the knowledge of the island. Once found, that knowledge is put to Prospero's use while Caliban is confined: 'And here you sty me / In this hard rock, whiles you do keep from me / The rest o'th' island' (I.ii.342–4). Once petted, Caliban now remains penned like a pig, but on a rock barren of all food.

Tales of initial native hospitality and the sharing of food and resources were the stock-in-trade of English colonizers. Whether composed by Shakespeare in *The Tempest*, William Bradford at Plymouth, Walter Ralegh in Guyana or Francis Drake in South America, English narratives of arrival in the Americas characteristically record their approach to the natives as benevolent and the natives' response as placidly or enthusiastically welcoming. These English formulaic accounts of initial contacts differ from more varied Spanish and Portuguese reports that describe a credible mixture of encounters – some initially hospitable, others of weapon-brandishing hostility.

Yet there was a politically exonerating message implicit in the English set accounts. As Peter Hulme pointed out in *Colonial Encounters*, English colonists reaching Jamestown described their arrival as a coming in peace, consistently explaining the subsequent hostility solely as a result of the natives' bad behaviour.[4] In *The Tempest* Prospero declaims: 'I have used thee . . . with humane care, and lodged thee / In mine own cell, till thou didst seek to violate / The honour of my child' (I.ii.345–8). Prospero is initially gracious and kind, albeit in the patronizing way of a European aristocrat. He has treated Caliban well, housing him in his own room. Only a wicked, seemingly inexplicable, act by Caliban halted Prospero's continued graciousness – 'till thou didst seek to violate / The honour of my child.' Such is the basic colonial structure of Shakespeare's account of the interaction of Prospero and Caliban: initial hospitality is followed by a 'wicked deed' of the native (Caliban), resulting in the expected punishment.

Echoing her father's distaste in a line often editorially attributed to Prospero, Miranda adds, 'Abhorrèd slave, / Which any print of goodness wilt not take, / Being capable of all ill! . . . therefore wast thou / Deservedly confined into this rock, / Who hadst deserved more than a prison'(I.ii.350–52, 359–61). The conduct of Caliban in seeking to violate the sexual honour of Miranda was criminal and results in a standard English consequence: gaol. But there is a further consequence to the imprisonment of Caliban, namely his loss of dominion over the island that once was his. 'Deservedly confined into this rock' in fact also means Prospero's expropriation of the entire island by restricting Caliban to a barren and unproductive place. Thus, responsibility for his loss of the island lies wholly with Caliban himself, with Prospero blameless for the original act of colonial expropriation.

Nearly identical tales of initial hospitality followed by 'inexplicable' violence on the part of the natives dominated the English colonial narratives of the occupation of many overseas dominions. In mainland North America, as well as in Australia and New Zealand, the most popular colonial and postcolonial narratives of occupation detail these same steps. The English settlers were initially cordial and hospitable, their behaviour courteous and without reproach. The popular American accounts of Thanksgiving – peaceful exchange over food – continue to be the politically dominant tales of English arrival. In these stories, only the inexplicably violent conduct of the natives initiated the eventual colonization process. In addition, Shakespeare introduces several other distinctively English colonial actions, also tied to Prospero's rationale for both imprisoning Caliban and seizing his land.

While the attempted assault on Miranda clearly merited a punitive consequence, although not necessarily loss of the island, Shakespeare introduces the colonial context once again in presenting Caliban's motives for this seemingly unprovoked attack. In order to explain why Caliban was intent on raping Miranda, Shakespeare has Caliban remark: 'Thou didst prevent me – I had peopled else / This isle with Calibans' (I.ii.348–9). In other words, in preventing the assault before it happened, Prospero was also forestalling Caliban's intent 'to people this isle' with those like himself. Seventeenth-century English audiences would have readily understood why

Caliban's desire to people the island with others like himself was horrifying. For the goal of populating was in fact the primary agenda of English colonizers overseas.

English settlement overseas was frequently rationalized in terms of population disparities. The images of the sceptred isle as 'full' and the New World 'empty' echoed throughout English literature advocating colonization. Believing themselves entitled (as inhabitants of more populated lands) to take over those less settled, English colonists understood their right to people the New World (with people resembling themselves) as God-given.[5] Therefore English colonists in the New World believed that they alone (rather than the indigenous inhabitants) had a right to people the land.

Even today 'peopling' is the most frequently occurring word in histories of the English conquest of the New World. Bernard Bailyn's immensely popular account of the English occupation of North America is called *The Peopling of British North America*, and scores of other modern English-language titles invoke the identical phrase for colonial settlement. Carl Bridenbaugh's history of the English Caribbean, *No Peace Beyond the Line*, begins with 'Peopling the English Colonies.'[6] Postcolonial historians writing in English thus continue naïvely to perpetuate this English colonial premise that the central objective of overseas settlement was to people (resettle) the New World with the English. But the uncritical belief in the intent to 'populate' becomes problematic when contrasted with the overseas ambitions of other Europeans. Only rarely does peopling emerge as an important ambition in Spanish and Portuguese colonial literatures. Not until after independence from Spain did the idea of 'peopling' with Europeans gain support in Ibero-America – and even then only in three South American nations.[7] Thus the intent to 'people' with Europeans is a uniquely English colonial ambition in the Americas.

Shakespeare therefore imputed to Caliban a motive for the attempted rape that reflects the specifically English colonial desire for 'peopling'. Caliban is rendered guilty of what were in reality English colonial ambitions. Shakespeare's projection of colonial ambitions onto Caliban allowed English audiences of the time to understand the character's motives, but to identify with their fellow colonizer's horror at the possibility of a colonial island peopled with Calibans. Since Caliban is the colonial subject, English audiences would not perceive him as having symmetrical rights with colonizers to 'people' the isle.

But while Caliban is saying that he would desire to people the isle with those like himself, he was choosing Miranda, daughter of Prospero, as his means of reproducing himself. In this curious monogenetic origin (rather like modern-day cloning), the children would be 'Calibans', not a mixture of Caliban and Miranda, a statement which touches on English folk beliefs in the determining character of the father. But this twist also leads straight to the gendered complexities of Caliban's and Prospero's respective claims to the island, for both men's rights turn out to operate through women.

[2]

Historically, European recognition of native sovereignty in the Americas divided into the two traditions of international law noted earlier, Spanish and Anglo-Dutch. According to Spanish jurists, sovereignty over land resided with the aboriginal people themselves in perpetuity. However, Spanish conquerors and their national successors claim ownership of valuable subterranean mineral resources such as gold, silver or emeralds, while allowing indigenous communities to retain their surface farmlands. Even today native communities in places such as Chiapas can reclaim farmland on the grounds that they held such terrain centuries ago. This enduring right to own their own farms, and transmit them according to indigenous rules, was among the earliest principles of Spanish jurisprudence in the New World. In the law codes and popular culture of nearly every nation of modern Spanish America native communities have retained in theory ownership of their land.[8] By contrast, English colonizers claimed the natives' land – even though it would take several centuries to actually dispossess them.

Both Spanish and English colonizers rationalized the natives' loss of ownership rights – whether to minerals or surface land. English colonists in the Americas during the seventeenth and eighteenth centuries would justify seizing land by self-servingly proclaiming that natives were not using the land profitably (which they themselves would indeed do). They also claimed, equally self-servingly, that the natives' land was simply 'waste'. But at no time did colonists ever have to prove that the land was 'waste' or that the natives were not making profits. Rather they needed only to assert such claims (to other Englishmen). Such statements were simply rationalizations for taking the natives' possessions.[9]

Nor did English colonists have to demonstrate that they had any particular capacity to farm or pasture that was superior to native Americans. To accomplish this end, English colonists invented an identity for themselves as 'farmers', that is the inhabitants of settled agricultural villages. And they classified the native inhabitants of the Americas and Australasia as their opposites, 'hunter-gatherers'. These two artificially created contrary identities allowed English colonizers informally at first and later legally to systematically deny land ownership rights to all people they classified as hunter-gatherers, on the grounds of the superior rights of permanent villagers. (This policy would continue to be observed even in India where only inhabitants of settled communities became British subjects, while the semi-nomadic peoples remained 'tribes'.) While English colonists encountered many hunter-gatherers in Australasia and the Americas (the aboriginal people of Australia for example), they also found many others – the Maori in New Zealand, the Apalachees in the United States – whom they mythically cast as hunter-gatherers despite their permanent farming practices. Settlers thus sustained the myth of encountering hunter-gatherers because it justified their denying natives any ownership of their lands.

'Native title' – the understanding current in the former English colonies of Australia, New Zealand, Canada and the United States – had not emerged at the time of the composition of *The Tempest*: it is a legal construction that surfaced in former British colonies only after their courts became independent of the English judiciary. As long as legal appeals could still be made to the Privy Council, settlers could assert a title to their land from the Crown. But once the legal systems of Australia, the United States, Canada and New Zealand were released from Crown authority, they had to find a new way to rationalize their legal title to the land, one that necessarily did not include the Crown's grants.[10] That novel justification became the doctrine of native title.

'Native title' in English postcolonial legal systems means a limited right to possess but not to own the terrain on which native peoples reside. Under common law, a wide variety of forms of land rights, collectively called 'tenures' existed: copyhold, fee simple and a host of other equally quaintly named and now seldom used tenures. But in formerly English colonial states, nineteenth- and twentieth-century judges would categorize natives' land-holding practices outside any of these traditional tenures of the common law because many traditional common law categories required procedures and formal hearings before any expropriation could take place. The doctrine of native title imposed no such requirements. It assumed that Native Americans had no real ownership of the land.

Thus the judges and lawyers rewrote the history of English occupation of colonial terrain. Native Americans lost their land not because of Crown grants, but because from the very beginning of colonization they never had any real ownership of their land. Their limited residual possessory rights could be and indeed were terminated by English settlers and their successors without the consent of the natives. All judges had to do was explain that colonists had begun to farm or pasture animals on the land, given the natives currency, and thus made it their own. Furthermore there was no need for natives to understand the treaties or written texts that they signed; fraud, coercion and misrepresentation were common and indeed usually legal under postcolonial systems, because the natives had never had the right to own their land. Because these ideas – including the right to own aboriginal grounds – were uniquely *English* myths, only English colonists invented the doctrine of native title (the loss of land ownership to colonizers). Hence only in post-English colonial societies – the United States, Canada, Australia, New Zealand – has such a doctrine become the national standard today.[11]

However, not surprisingly, this postcolonial legal orthodoxy for the English occupation of North America does not appear in *The Tempest*. None of the myths justifying occupation are asserted in *The Tempest* – the idea of a 'vacant' or relatively unpopulated land, the idea of terrain going to waste that could be used more profitably by the colonizers. Nor is Caliban the mythical 'hunter-gatherer' who enabled English colonization in the name of farming – even though there is an allusion to this possibility later in the play (II.ii.152-65). Rather, Shakespeare tortuously detours Caliban's claim to the island through a maternal line, using the usual English narrative of seemingly inexplicable violence caused by Caliban's possessing a colonial desire of his own, to people the island with Calibans.

In *The Tempest* Caliban asserts his original ownership of island rather oddly: 'This island's mine by Sycorax my mother,' he claims to Prospero. And the reasons for Sycorax's appearance on the island are unusual. She has been banished as a witch from Algiers, a suitably remote but not entirely obscure place in North Africa. North Africa, and the Algerian coast in particular, was home to the Barbary Coast pirates, raiders who periodically attacked English, Spanish and other European shipping in the Mediterranean and eastern Atlantic. Hence the association of Sycorax, Caliban's mother, with the group of people most likely to attack European shipping brings to the Caribbean the theme of piracy; though in Caribbean waters around 1,600 pirates were principally English, and secondarily French and Dutch, roaming in a sea claimed by Spain.

Yet the association with piracy, through the birthplace of Sycorax, raises another question about the sometimes legal, but often illegal occupation of islands deserted by the Spanish once the gold was gone. Towards the close of the sixteenth century, English, French, and Dutch pirates established bases throughout the Caribbean that would enable them to tend the wounded, rest and recuperate in between attacks on Spanish ships. Since the Spanish vessels assembled bi-annually in large convoys whose departures were timed to avoid the hurricane season in the Caribbean, there were long periods of slim or little pickings in the Caribbean. During those intervals, the pirates waited out the hurricanes on islands such as St Kitts, St Martin and St Domingue.[12]

Beginning two decades after *The Tempest*'s composition, several pirate bands decided to attempt to legalize their position on the islands. Facing increasing competition from bandits of other nations in the still highly lucrative assaults on Spanish vessels in the Caribbean, several groups of brigands petitioned the political leaders of the societies from which they were formally outcast, calling for official recognition of their political status. In these petitions, pirates offered Europe's governments the possibility of establishing a formal political base in the Caribbean, complete with an armed, if rag-tag, assortment of ready-made defenders. European powers readily acceded. They decided that the occupation of the Caribbean islands by pirates originally from their shores provided an excellent opportunity for claiming their own little spaces in the Caribbean's many locales. Thus began the process of recognition, and the claiming of the islands where castaways and pirates had toe-holds as new parts of the French, English and Dutch empires in the Caribbean. English officials claimed St Christopher (St Kitts) in this fashion, and even more notoriously seized Jamaica, placing as deputy governor the infamous pirate Henry Morgan who had been led off in ostentatiously deceptive chains the year before.[13]

On the islands where pirates and shipwrecked Englishmen landed, earlier visitors had only left behind pigs, which Spaniards abandoned everywhere in the Americas. Thus the allusion 'And here you sty me / In this hard rock' (I.ii.342–3) also connects Caliban's island to the Spanish desertion of the Caribbean, leaving behind one of their favourite sources of animal protein in an environment lacking in natural predators. Here too, the overtones of Elizabethan gender preoccupations re-emerge, for pigs in the Elizabethan world were often identified with witches. But the willingness to treat Caliban as an animal – 'to sty him up' – foretells the understanding of future generations of American colonists, who would pen Native American peoples up on reservations, like pigs in a sty, on places made only of 'this hard rock', and rest with their consciences fully at ease.

So, Caliban's claim, 'This island's mine by Sycorax my mother', ironically underpins what would become the formal claims of several European powers to Caribbean bases. Whether Caliban's claim to own the island through his mother would have held up at the time of *The Tempest*'s composition is debatable, but the future of such assertions was different. The claims of banished exiles and criminals would indeed be advocated by European powers eager for formal toe-holds in the geographically central location of the Caribbean, crucial for the launching of the Atlantic passage and for the continuation of the still lucrative pirate attacks against Spanish convoys. But since the first of those episodes was still over ten years away – the English seizure of St Christopher in 1623 – the idea of seizing an island based on the claim of a castaway had yet to become policy. Only in the light of the subsequent history of English practice in the Caribbean would the claim of the son of a castaway like Caliban be justified.

But it is the gender of Caliban's parent that creates the most profoundly undermining dimension of Caliban's claim to the island. While anyone familiar with the bilateral inheritance systems of Spain and Portugal would find the claim to inherit the island through Sycorax, his mother, to be totally unexceptional, in the reality of Shakespeare's England such a claim was extraordinary. English inheritance systems were determinedly patrilineal, that is to say passing valuable goods and property through the male line. Caliban's claim that he aimed to people the island with Calibans might be biologically improbable (for the offspring would necessarily be mixtures of Caliban and Miranda), but it would be culturally plausible because valuable property was increasingly handed down strictly along the male line.

Only in the counter-culture of Shakespeare's day, the culture of witches, was there a widely-known counterpoint to the dominant patrilineal system with a system of bilateral inheritance of traits. For English folklore acknowledged that witches could pass their gifts on to both female and male offspring. Caliban's claim to inherit through his maternal line is illegitimate according to English understanding, but consistent with that maternal ancestor supposedly being a witch.[14] Thus the association with witchcraft allowed Shakespeare – or at least Prospero – to produce a recognizably illegitimate female claim that could be easily dismissed by English audiences.

From this perspective the greatest irony of the play is that while Caliban's claim comes through Sycorax his mother, Prospero's own claim to the island also comes through a female, indeed from a thoroughly unsavoury and opportunistic response to the sexual attack on his daughter. Prospero claims that the reason why he has become entitled to take over the entire island for himself is that 'thou [Caliban] didst seek to violate / The honour of my child' (I.ii.347–8). But as the phrase carefully notes: 'thou didst *seek* to violate'. There was no actual rape: Miranda has to pass intact to her husband. Shakespeare fails to specify whether Caliban used force against Miranda or whether he communicated his intention by threatening her. All we know from the text is that no rape occurred. But Prospero takes the father's right to defend his daughter against unwanted sexual advances into another realm altogether.

Instead of simply condemning Caliban for his mistreatment of his daughter, punishing him, and making sure that he is never left alone with her again (to prevent the reoccurrence of the attempted sexual attack), Prospero opportunistically uses this moment as the pretext to seize the island. Thus Prospero manages to use his own daughter's near-rape as an opportunity to justify an advantage for himself. Thus the colonially inclined father/colonist turned a threatened act of abuse into an act of legitimate claim to a colonial possession.

While Prospero has not prostituted Miranda in order to achieve his goal, he has taken advantage of a sexual threat in order to benefit from his daughter's vulnerability. It is not quite the same thing as pimping, the receipt of financial advantage from a sexual attack, but the willingness to explain that his daughter's near-rape is a legitimate source of his own rightful title to the island comes very close to a cynical use of the threat of sexual contact to explain colonial entitlement. While Prospero's claim comes by an opportunistic exploitation of his own daughter's near-rape, Caliban's comes from what in English culture would be seen as a subversive right to inherit from a maternal line.

So, perhaps surprisingly, both claims seem weak according to English law, although Prospero's corresponds, at least discursively, to the manner in which English claims to native land were often made.[15] Prospero secures his own prosperity, backed up by the 'admirable' or 'lovely' Miranda, who joins in her father's taunt – 'therefore wast thou / Deservedly confined into this rock, / Who hadst deserved more than a prison' (I.ii.359–61) – echoing her father's wish for Caliban's colonial incarceration. Caliban's claims and desires conform to the theme in the English narratives of colonization of the always potentially violent and therefore treacherous native who offers a fearsome threat to the sexual integrity of white women – and hence implicitly to the English *man* overseas. The theme of dangerous sexual relations between colonizer and colonized reflects a final distinctively English colonial anxiety – one that stretches across several continents and several centuries. This preoccupation with preventing sexual connections (or even the threat of such contact) between English women and native men – later metamorphosed into fear of contact between white women and African men – has remained an enduring and often frightening characteristic of former British colonies where it has continued to justify displays of violence.

15 *Arielismo* and Anthropophagy: *The Tempest* in Latin America

GORDON BROTHERSTON

In the wake of the Independence movements that began in Latin America in the early nineteenth century, Shakespeare's *The Tempest* caught the attention of many writers there, not least because of the play's supposedly Caribbean or New World setting. In particular, reference to the foursome Prospero, Miranda, Ariel and Caliban has served to bolster a range of arguments, in which Caliban has been both neglected and exalted as one born in America and the prior owner of the island appropriated by Prospero.

In Spanish America, interest in the play first concentrates around the year 1898, the time of the conflict between Spain and the USA that resulted in the latter taking over Cuba, Puerto Rico and the Philippines. Various writers associated with the *modernista* movement of that period alluded to or drew on the play, among them the Cuban José Martí (1853–95), the Nicaraguan Rubén Darío (1867–1916), and the Uruguayan José Enrique Rodó (1871–1917), author of *Ariel* (1900) and *El mirador de Próspero* (1913). Indeed, after the appearance of *Ariel* it became hard for Spanish Americans to invoke *The Tempest* without alluding to Rodó.

In Portuguese-speaking Brazil there was no equivalent engagement, although Caliban features to notable effect in the final poem of Joaquim Maria Machado de Assis's *Occidentaes* ('western' poems first published in his *Poesias completas* (1901). This is 'No alto' ('at the top'), where, having guided the poet to the top of the hill Ariel disappears in a haze of music and leaves him to be taken down the western slope by Caliban, who appears in the unprepossessing shape of the 'other' (*o outro*). As late as the 1920s, and rather despite Machado de Assis's insight, Ronald de Carvalho continued to celebrate Ariel simply as the 'airy spirit' of (Old World) classical beauty (in *O Espelho de Ariel*, 1923), without a thought for Caliban.

More significantly, in the 1920s Oswald de Andrade and other members of the Brazilian *Antropofagia* movement stayed closer to Machado in revaluing the Carib Caliban's cannibalism as a cultural phenomenon that was indispensable to true American consciousness. In so doing, they anticipated the similar re-readings of Caliban subsequently made by English- and Spanish-speaking writers in the Caribbean, in which Martí's work was critical. The Brazilian *antropofagistas*, however, tended to have recourse less to Shakespeare's play than to its sources in Montaigne – the case of Gonzalo's 'Utopian fantasy' early in the play, has been amply noted,[1] as well as the Tupi and Carib traditions of South America which had so intrigued Montaigne in the first place. Montaigne, the Carib and the Tupi are all writ large in the revolutionary manifesto published by Oswald in the first number of the *Revista de Antropofagia*, published in São Paulo in 1928.

One of the *antropofagistas* and wife to Oswald de Andrade, Patricia Galvão (Pagú), looked to Ariel anew during the bleak years of the Vargas dictatorship and World War II. As a socialist she was tortured by Vargas and, on the very day that Brazil was drawn into the war (22 August 1942), she took Ariel as a pseudonym on initiating a regular column in the São Paulo newspaper *A Noite*, where very much against the mood of the time she defended poetry as an indispensable element in human life.

The figure who is celebrated as the leader of the Spanish American *modernista* movement, Rubén Darío, often alluded to Shakespeare's play. His hardest-hitting response is perhaps 'El triunfo de Calibán', written in the heat of the moment, in May 1898, right after Spain's humiliation at the hands of the United States. Already before the war, enthusiasm for the USA had been tempered in many quarters of the continent, first in Mexico, by the annexation of Texas and the 'South West', and was virtually extinguished at the time of the Pan American Conference of 1889-90 by the churlish behaviour of such statesmen as President Hayes and Richard Olney. With the US 'triumph' of 1898, feelings of animosity crystallized and a sense of Latinity became more admissible in the emotions of the inhabitants of Spain's former possessions in America. This is the message of Darío's essay, which in denouncing US aggression and greed takes up speeches made in Buenos Aires earlier in that same month of May 1898 by 'Latin' intellectuals, writers and politicians. Prominent among them was Paul Groussac, who is said by Darío to have emerged from a book-lined cave (like Prospero's) to reprehend the monstrous US–Caliban. Darío likewise decries this dangerous and all-devouring beast of terrifying energy and greed; and he closes by comparing his 'Latin soul' to Miranda, 'who will always prefer Ariel'.

Before the conflagration of 1898, the Spanish American *modernistas* whom Darío was seen to typify had invoked *The Tempest*, prompted in part by Edgar Allan Poe (whose 'The Mask of the Red Death', 1847, features an embattled Prospero), and Poe's translator Charles Baudelaire, as well as by influential French thinkers like Ernest Renan. In his posthumous novel *De sobremesa*, José Asunción Silva, who committed suicide in 1896, imagines a conversation between a Colombian poet such as himself and an English doctor who advises him never to attempt to be a Prospero in a New World land of Calibans. In Darío's own work, *The Tempest* is a repeated reference in *Los raros* (1893), an early manifesto of the *modernista* movement that consists of portraits of nineteenth-century figures, not least Poe.[2] Darío makes the link with Shakespeare via Joséphin Peladan (1858–1918), a high-ranking Rosicrucian and French man of letters, who captured the (for him) overpowering vulgarity of the United States by calling it the land of 'féroces Calibans', which victimized Poe at the same time as it threatened Latin culture. Darío refers to Poe (whom he also mentions in 'El triunfo') as an 'Ariel in human form', persecuted and misunderstood by the hordes around him. Ariel reappears as a term of comparison in Darío's piece on another of 'los raros', the overtly decadent poet Augusto de Armas, who abandoned Cuba for Paris: the vulnerability of this vanishing 'airy spirit' indicates concerns with specifically Latin-(American) decadence that had been voiced by Peladan.

Yet what Darío has to say in *Los raros* about Poe and *The Tempest*, when he is dealing with the actual plot of Shakespeare's play, takes us in a different direction. For here we see the beginnings of a certain contradictory admiration for the American Caliban, one who is vigorous, sensual and bacchic, as Darío wished poets to be, the wronged son of Sycorax who has thrown off the slavery imposed by Prospero and escaped at last the ceaseless taunts of Ariel (who reciprocally had been obliged to serve Sycorax). Indeed, for Darío, the faintly sadistic Ariel is at this point displaced by fair Miranda as the emblem of finer values. Although only hinted at in Darío's portrait of Poe, this reading of Caliban diverges radically from that of the aristocratizing European Peladan and could be seen rather to anticipate the depths of native American solidarity that Roberto Fernández Retamar would later discover in his homage to fellow Cuban José Martí, appropriately entitled *Calibán*.

As Latin America's best-known devotee of *The Tempest*, Darío's contemporary and critic José Enrique Rodó returned repeatedly to that play, and over time his Ariel came to inspire nothing less than a cultural and philosophical movement, known as *arielismo*, which gained notice in all parts of the continent. Like Darío's, Rodó's initial involvement with the English text appears to have been indirect, spurred by the thoughts and commentaries of late-nineteenth-century French writers, in his case chiefly Ernest Renan, Paul Bourget and Alfred Fouillée, who had already expounded their own firmly philosophical readings of the play. These touched principally on contemporary debates about the rôle of education as a means of regenerating France after its defeat in 1871 (the year of Rodó's birth), and about the strengths and menaces of democracy, in which Prospero, Ariel and Caliban were given major parts.

Renan's play *Caliban, Suite de 'La Tempête'* (1878) was more immediately important than Shakespeare's play to Rodó's *Ariel* (1900). The debt to Renan is obvious and acknowledged in repeated references, which outnumber those made to any other writer. The questions at stake, like the struggle between utilitarian democracy (Caliban) and spiritual values (Ariel), belong not to Elizabethan times but to the nineteenth century. Yet it is worth defining Rodó's angle on his French antecedents more closely since yet another writer was more important to Rodó than either Renan or Shakespeare: Alfred Fouillée.

If we accept that Rodó carried on in *Ariel* where Renan had left off at the end of *Caliban*, then we can see that he was faced with the prospect of demagogy and Ariel's disappearance into even thinner air, while Prospero looked on, grudgingly having to accept the situation. Rather than compromise, Renan's Ariel had chosen to dissociate himself from worldly politics, leaving the twice-dethroned Prospero to defend himself against the plebs, who, now educated and led by Caliban, were no longer so readily susceptible to the power of aristocrat magic. Renan even hints that, in order to protect himself and his intellectual elite, Prospero is ready for an alliance with the triumphant Caliban. This apparent indifference to the fate of Ariel irritated many French thinkers, among them Fouillée. His upbeat response, *L'Idée moderne du droit* (1878), which appeared in Paris in the same year as *Caliban*, censured Renan for his adherence to a new, dangerously cynical style of politics, and pleaded for Ariel's resurrection, expressing the hope that one day Caliban could even become Ariel.

Renan's own response to all this was *L'Eau de jouvence: Suite de 'Caliban'* (1880), a play ironic in the extreme, and in some respects as ominous as Aldous Huxley's *Brave New World*, that other continuation of *The Tempest*. In the preface to *L'Eau de jouvence*, Renan urges sympathy for Caliban, who is shown to be assuming agreeable and even aristocrat attitudes now that he is supreme, and asks that we endeavour to 'attach' Ariel to life again, so that he not be tempted to abandon the body politic at the merest provocation. In the play itself, however, we are asked to believe that Renan is willingly sacrificing the devotion to culture and finer values which he himself had formerly advocated, in favour of the egalitarian hedonism fostered by Caliban's regime. The only practical demand made by Prospero in this regard is that Ariel be given a sinecure as warden at the castle of Sermione.

Unpreoccupied by the subtleties of Renan's thought in these matters (which sprang from his ambiguous feelings towards the Church and towards Gambetta in the France of the 1870s), Rodó goes straight back to the questions Fouillée had said were prompted by the denouement of *Caliban*; for in *L'Idée moderne du droit*, which like *Ariel* treats Shakespeare's *dramatis personæ* more as symbols than as characters, Fouillée had found Renan's ideas in that play both authoritarian and fear-inspired. Rodó not only adopted this reading but went so far as to censor, as if for the first time, Renan's dictum about democracy being at odds with God's design, when in fact Fouillée had already censored it in his work. Above all, it was Fouillée who inspired in Rodó the meliorist/gradualist notion that, as society evolved, so the law of natural selection would somehow become less brutal, as the rigour of social hierarchies was attenuated (and so on). In practice, it is Fouillée, in responding to Renan's response to *The Tempest*, who guides the Uruguayan Rodó through the maze of contemporary European political thinking.[3]

In all, this is a far cry from the still partly medieval parameters of Shakespeare's play; and hence from the tradition of knowledge to which Prospero is said to have adhered as the scholar–aristocrat of Milan. The route from Shakespeare's English to Rodó's Spanish was indeed a long and circuitous one. The process of successive translation is perhaps nowhere more evident than at that moment when Ariel, about to regain his freedom, sings his little song 'Where the bee sucks, there suck I'. By the time it reaches Montevideo, via Paris, this has become:

> He will traverse human history chanting, as in Shakespeare's play, his melodious song, to encourage those who work and those who struggle, until the fulfilment of the mysterious plan which he is part of enables him – just as in the play he is freed from Prospero's service – to break material bonds and return forever to the centre of his divine light.[4]

Above all, through the work of Rodó and his fellow Latin Americans, Shakespeare's story was transposed (back) to a home in America. In Rodó's case, this was now not to an unmapped island in the Caribbean realm of Caliban, but to Montevideo, which lies at the southern end of the American continent, under a sky dominated by just the constellations named at the end of *Ariel*, chief among them the Southern Cross. In his work, Rodó became Prospero, a persona he adopted with so little hint of irony that Prospero may be said to have become Rodó. That is, he is updated to become the Uruguayan scholar of *Ariel*, who rounds off the (southern hemisphere) university year in November by delivering a homily to his students, just as he later becomes the critic of *El mirador de Próspero*, whose book-lined study (formerly but a 'cell') becomes the vantage-point or oriel (*mirador*) for views on another, New World landscape and history.

In *Ariel*, the figure of that 'airy spirit' is caressed by Prospero as he delivers his homily, cast in very solid bronze yet in the posture of one about to take flight, ready to carry the authorized word far afield. In reaffirming Ariel as his messenger and agent, Prospero charges his class of students now to believe in the *cause* of Ariel, in the name of America's future, and to resist the lower impulses of sensuality and materialist greed, synonymous (in his eyes) with Caliban, which he was beginning to find ever more evident in the USA. Appearing as it did in 1900, *Ariel* could not help being heard as a continuation of the cries against the monster Caliban raised by Darío and others at the time of Spain's defeat in 1898. It was read as a powerful message and a continental warning at a critical time in American history, at the turn of a century that the USA was already wanting to call its own.

This denunciatory part or aspect of Rodó's 1900 essay echoed and provoked similar cries, along with some serious modifications, throughout Spanish America among the most apparently diverse groups, including fellow Uruguayan intellectuals and the Ateneo group in Mexico (which brought together figures such as Alfonso Reyes and the celebrated literary historian from the Dominican Republic, Pedro Henríquez Ureña). In 1914, launching the first number of a journal named after his *Ariel*, Rodó was able to declare, in more or less Olympian fashion:

> In the development of the ideas which have steered the course of current Hispanic American thinking, the name Ariel means the affirming of an idealist sense of life against the limitations of utilitarian Positivism; the spirit of quality and selection, as opposed to the equality of false democracy; and the feeling of *raza*, of Latin ancestry, as a source of the energy needed to save and sustain the personality of our nations before the triumphal expansion of others . . .Those pages had the virtue of appearing at the right moment, which explains their extraordinary diffusion and the wave of sympathy which has multiplied them in a thousand echoes.[5]

After Rodó's death in 1917 and the horror of World War I (in which he served the French as a 'Latin' propagandist), enthusiasm for his style of philosophizing perceptibly dimmed.[6] Even so, *Ariel* continued to be read and pondered, not just by liberal politicians in countries like Venezuela and Panama (signally by university rector Octavio Méndez Pereira in the late 1940s), but by such unlikely others as the founders of the Cuban Communist Party, Waldo Frank in the USA, and the Mexican Octavio Paz.[7]

Overall, the starkest reactions to *arielismo* have come from those parts of the Americas – notably the Andes and the Caribbean – which are culturally least like Rodó's homeland, the small, largely white and officially 'Indian-free' Republic of Uruguay. In 1941 the Peruvian Luis Alberto Sánchez deplored *Ariel* in his *Balance y liquidación del 1900*, taking Rodó to task for recommending the cultivation of the spirit and an Old World sense of ease to a subcontinent rich with cultural traditions of its own and at the same time beset by poverty and nightmarish social injustice. Then in 1971 the Cuban Roberto Fernández Retamar went further still, actually dethroning Ariel as cultural icon and installing Caliban in his stead, in his fine study of José Martí's *Nuestra América*.[8] Through Martí's own words, Fernández Retamar shows how 'Latin' Americans can in some sense recover a more meaningful heritage by imbibing the 'classics' not just of Europe but of the continent's native cultures (for example, the *Popol Vuh*, which Martí discusses at some length), and by contemplating with due reverence the Carib blood of Caliban that was so wantonly spilt by European adventurers. In pointing via Martí to American roots, Retamar's *Caliban* diverges interestingly from the line followed by the Caribbean francophone writers of *négritude*, who sooner point to Africa.[9]

Through Rodó, *The Tempest* was carried all over America, and even beyond. Indeed, it was returned to its first source in Britain, strikingly in the rich and curious case of Aneurin Bevan, whose twin mentors turn out to have been 'Marx & Rodó'. Unlikely as the pairing may now seem at first sight, its extremes are also echoed in the full name of the well-known Chilean writer Ariel [i.e. Rodó's work] Vladimir [i.e. Trotsky] Dorfman. Bevan got to know Rodó through the English translations of *Ariel* (1922) and of *Motivos de Proteo* (1929), an edition which has a commentary by Havelock Ellis on the range and significance of all Rodó's work but especially *Ariel*, and which had originally been published in Ellis's *The Philosophy of Conflict* (1919), probably Bevan's first source.[10] Bevan habitually recited passages at length to (hapless) dinner guests, and turned to *Ariel* for substantial quotation in his 1950 Fabian lecture.

There is plentiful reference to Rodó in Michael Foot's massive two-volume biography of Bevan, along with lengthy epigraphs from the translations of his work. Foot goes deeply into how Rodó, always basically a democratic gradualist who (thanks to Fouillée) believed in the eventual transformation of Caliban into Ariel, tempered Marx's dismissal of the parliamentary path, and so effectively shaped blueprints for British socialism when Bevan eventually became a minister in the Atlee government. Foot takes particular pleasure in showing how Rodó's distaste for hero-worship (again, Fouillée-inspired) helped Bevan to disbelieve the idea, much touted towards the end of World War II, that Churchill would necessarily triumph in the 1945 elections. Liking Rodó's rhetoric a good deal less, John Campbell has recently taken a more caustic line in *Nye Bevan and the Mirage of British Socialism* (1987) and indeed comes close to suggesting that Bevan's unswerving enthusiasm for *Ariel* was precisely the mark of his intellectual limitation.[11]

Over the last century or so, *The Tempest* has made some intriguing journeys through Latin America, chiefly as a result of interest inspired by the characters Ariel and Caliban. The former, suitably affected by the experience, was even sent back to haunt post-war British socialism. The latter, by contrast, has tended to put down roots as if in an American homeland regained, significantly modifying thereby dominant Euro-American images of him as purely African or, worse, bestial slave.

16 Reading from Elsewhere: George Lamming and the Paradox of Exile

PETER HULME

In retrospect, it can be seen as highly appropriate that the most radical re-readings and re-writings of *The Tempest* came, in the years of decolonization, from the Caribbean. Not because the play is in any easy sense *about* the Caribbean, but because it seems likely that the name Caliban rearranges the letters of the word 'canibal', the indigenous original of which had also over the course of the sixteenth century produced the Spanish 'caribe' and the English 'Caribbean'. For Caribbean writers, then, there could be a sense that the play was associated with the Caribbean, at least in a way that no other Shakespearean play was, nor indeed any other canonical English text apart from *Robinson Crusoe*. This undoubtedly mattered most in the English-speaking Caribbean, although writers on the French- and Spanish-speaking islands also had their own contributions to make. It is easy to underestimate the novelty of these readings, especially from the British Caribbean islands, still colonies in the 1950s, places where English literature came from England and was interpreted from England. When the Barbadian writer George Lamming came to write about *The Tempest*, he did so with a clear sense that he was blaspheming: it had not previously been the place of the West Indian to offer anything other than the most orthodox and respectful comments on canonical authors.

[1]

The three great landmarks of the reading of *The Tempest* from the Caribbean come from three different language traditions, those of Barbados, Martinique, and Cuba: George Lamming's essay 'A Monster, A Child, A Slave', which appeared in his collection *The Pleasures of Exile* (1960); Aimé Césaire's play *Une tempête* (1969); and Roberto Fernández Retamar's essay 'Calibán', first published in the Havana journal *Casa de las Américas* in 1971. All three, however, have a precursor in Octave Mannoni's 1950 book, *Psychologie de la colonisation* (later translated as *Prospero and Caliban: The Psychology of Colonization*).[1] In particular, Césaire's adaptation may have been provoked by the passages in Mannoni that offer the figures of Prospero and Caliban as exemplars of the dependency complexes. Mannoni had taught Césaire in Martinique during the mid-1920s and, since the other literary text he devotes space to is *Robinson Crusoe*, there could be grounds for seeing *Psychologie de la colonisation* as a book owing something to the Caribbean as well as to Madagascar – another island situated (from a European perspective) across a long stretch of Atlantic waters – where Mannoni wrote it in the late 1940s. Césaire had touched – critically – on Mannoni and his theories in his *Discourse on Colonialism* (1950), as, two years later, had Frantz Fanon (Césaire's pupil, also from Martinique) in *Black Skin, White Masks* (1952), through which those themes eventually entered the mainstream of postcolonial theory.[2] But *Une tempête* is a more serious and complex involvement with the Shakespearean play, an 'adaptation' that keeps close enough to its original for the variations to be striking, and which also responds to Ernest Renan's famous continuation of the play, *Caliban: Suite de 'La Tempête'* (1878), set in Europe in the mid-nineteenth century. Césaire moves 'back' to the Caribbean (and back to Shakespeare), and therefore away from Renan's concern with European politics. Lamming actually has it both ways, tracing the triangular route which took Caliban from Africa to the Caribbean – allegorically in the slave trade and dramatically in Sycorax's belly – but also insisting that the tide of colonial aftermath washes up on metropolitan shores, as it does in particular in Lamming's novel, *Water with Berries* (1971), in which a version of the *Tempest* story forms a violent colonial prehistory to the struggles of West Indian immigrants to make lives for themselves in London.

The intertexts of Roberto Fernández Retamar's 1970 essay, 'Calibán', stretch back most significantly to the Uruguayan essayist José Enrique Rodó's *Ariel* (1900), to which 'Calibán' is openly a response, and therefore also to Renan and his followers, to whom Rodó was indebted. Much of the debate in which these writers are involved has to do with how to characterize such large-scale entities as the United States or Latin American culture: characters from *The Tempest* provide allegorical figures, although not necessarily with the identifications to which we've become accustomed, as Gordon Brotherston's essay in this volume makes apparent. Both Renan and Rodó were, in general terms, making use of the play's possibilities rather than offering original reflections back on it. However, both helped keep alive the sense that *The Tempest* is a vibrantly *political* play, in contrast to late-nineteenth-century English readings which tended to stress its spectacular or autobiographical nature.

Fernández Retamar participates in that debate, as well as offering a learned summary of it, but he is also keen to position himself as giving a reading of the play, at least initially. To that end, he situates Shakespeare historically, tracing in particular the history of the term 'canibal', noting the number of Spanish names in the play drawn from the chronicles of the Spanish voyages, and being in no doubt 'that *The Tempest* alludes to America'.[3] However, ultimately, and in keeping with the subtitle of the essay – 'Notes Towards a Discussion of Culture in Our America' – Retamar is interested in offering Caliban as a *symbol* of *mestizo* America, replacing Rodó's Ariel. The rest of his essay has little to say directly about *The Tempest*, and nor have either the ensuing debate or Retamar's own further essays, however illuminating they have been about the circumstances of the writing of 'Calibán'.[4] Bearing in mind the way in which Retamar remembers how José Martí deconstructed Domingo Sarmiento's opposition between 'civilization' and 'barbarism', it might be thought that Retamar's championing of the figure of Caliban was a similar rhetorical strategy aimed at inducing outsiders to see Latin American culture for its own qualities rather than boxing it within imported categories.[5] It is also worth observing that Retamar's Caliban is a resolutely mixed or *mestizo* figure, part Native American, part African, part European.[6]

As far as can be judged, Lamming's approach to *The Tempest* was more 'internal' in the sense that he developed his reading out of an engagement with the play as part of his colonial education, alongside a reading of early Caribbean history. What followed was a dual recognition: that the play could be read as a kind of colonial history, with specific Caribbean reverberations, and that he himself was a Caliban-like figure, educated by Prospero but rebelling against that education. His essay on *The Tempest* seems to have been produced, understandably enough, without reference to Mannoni's work;[7] however, Lamming often refers to Césaire's poetry in *The Pleasures of Exile*, with a passage from 'Return to My Native Land' serving as epigraph to the chapter on *The Tempest*. In turn, Césaire's *Une tempête* has been seen as a response to Lamming, while Fernández Retamar makes brief references to both Lamming and Césaire.[8] The different language traditions of the Caribbean often act in ignorance of each other, but in this case there seems to have been a rather full awareness, amounting to a significant – and ongoing – dialogue.

All three Caribbean writers introduce the issue of race. The more general American reading had not done so, in this period of the 1950s and 1960s, with the exception of Leslie Fiedler's pioneering work. The matter of race in *The Tempest* is by no means straightforward. It is true that, when approached through the optic of colonizer / colonized (as found in Mannoni or Fanon) it is easy to read Prospero as white and Caliban as black. Such a distinction would hardly have been available to Shakespeare in the context of this play. Indeed, if Caliban is associated, through 'canibal', with the aboriginal inhabitants of the West Indies, then he is red or olive, or whatever colour Indians were supposed to be. Yet we are told in the play that Caliban is the son of Sycorax, who comes from Algiers, which might make him tawny or whatever colour North Africans were supposed to be.[9] Lamming and Retamar both give attention to Caliban as mixed, culturally and possibly racially, and therefore not easily definable in terms of race or colour. Michael Dobson notes that Caliban was seen as black as early as 1774, so that identification is not postcolonial in origin – although its most powerful articulation is probably Aimé Césaire's, with Ariel identified as 'mulatto'.[10]

[2]

Like much West Indian writing, George Lamming's work has at its centre the image of the middle passage, the transatlantic shipping of millions of black slaves from Africa to the Americas. Yet, for Lamming, the middle passage and its imagery is far from singular. There is a middle passage for Europeans too, which, though metaphorical and psychological, would often also involve long voyages across water – which is one of the reasons why he's interested in *The Tempest*. And there is also a 'voyage in' – to England – of the kind discussed by Edward Said in *Culture and Imperialism*, one of his examples being C.L.R. James's *The Black Jacobins*, a history of the Haitian revolution at the end of the eighteenth century.[11] However, whereas James, after coming to England, reflected back on Caribbean history, Lamming conceived of his book, *The Pleasures of Exile*, 'as a descriptive reflection on the predicament of a group of writers who originated in the English-speaking Caribbean and who arrived in Britain as part of a larger migrating labour force.'[12]

Lamming, born in Barbados and later living in Trinidad, travelled to England in 1950. Soon after reaching London, he began writing his autobiographical novel, *In the Castle of My Skin* (1953), and had published two further novels before the appearance of *The Pleasures of Exile*, a collection of critical and autobiographical pieces published in 1960. Eleven years later, his novel *Water with Berries* provided perhaps the most challenging and radical of the re-writings of the play.[13] While Lamming has always been included in the tradition of what Rob Nixon calls the 'transgressive appropriations' of *The Tempest*, the colonial allegories produced by postcolonial writers, the aim of this chapter is to position his work as also a *reading* of Shakespeare's play, a reading widely ignored for many years, though one whose reverberations within literary institutions can now be firmly felt. *The Pleasures of Exile* engages at both levels – appropriation and reading – without obvious changes of gear. However, I will distinguish between the allegorical level, where the address is outwards, either historically or politically, and the textual, addressed back, both to the text that Lamming actually studied and to the institution of Shakespeare criticism and performance. There is no evidence that this distinction was important for Lamming himself. Indeed he 'admits' to the likelihood that he will be seen to be 'wrong in the parallels which I have set out to interpret', though replying 'that my mistake, lived and deeply felt by millions of men like me – proves the positive value of error.'[14] The simplest way of putting my argument here is to say that Lamming was not wrong, and that his reading of *The Tempest* deserves a place at the centre of Shakespeare criticism, not just at the centre of what that institution regards as the outpost of the Third World allegory.

[3]

The Pleasures of Exile is a book both deeply personal and deeply collective, qualities which have helped – slowly – make it a classic of postcolonial criticism, a status it achieved when an extract ('The Occasion for Speaking') appeared as the very first passage in *The Post-Colonial Studies Reader*.[15] When it was first published, in 1960, *The Pleasures of Exile* offered a set of readings and meditations made through and as part of a deep engagement with a long imperial history, focused – though not exclusively – on the Caribbean. It was a reading from elsewhere, produced at a time when the location of hegemonic readings was completely unmarked, simply not an issue. But *The Pleasures of Exile* was never going to isolate itself as merely peripheral, as a book from the colonies. It was a reading that was coming 'home', to the place from which Shakespeare had been made such a meaningful authority.

The Introduction to *The Pleasures of Exile* involves an extraordinary piece of self-positioning, which is also distinctly unsettling to readers' attempts to position themselves. Lamming describes a 'ceremony of the Souls' which he had witnessed in Haiti four years previously. He sees parallels with *The Tempest*, announcing his intention 'to make use of *The Tempest* as a way of presenting a certain state of feeling which is the heritage of the exiled and colonial writer from the British Caribbean.'[16] Noting that the ceremony is sometimes forbidden by the authorities, Lamming goes on to imagine a trial that might have resulted. This introduces the familiar theatre of the law but, confusingly, the roles of accused, prosecutor, witness and judge shift constantly, along with the personal pronouns 'I' and 'you' and the position of the characters Prospero and Caliban, both of whom seem at different moments to be on trial. The witness who arrives 'claiming extraordinary privileges' would seem to be the author himself:

> [H]e sees himself as Caliban, while he argues that he is not the Caliban whom Prospero had in mind . . .He thinks he is, in some way, a descendant of Prospero. He knows he is a descendant of Caliban. He claims to be the key witness in the trial; but his evidence will only be valid if the others accept the context in which he will give it.[17]

As described, the trial seems like something out of *Alice in Wonderland* – one of the great realist novels when it comes to English institutions; but Lamming sees himself as a potentially privileged witness, descended from both Prospero and Caliban, if the courtroom and jury will only allow themselves to listen to his evidence. Never mind that it remains unclear who is on trial or what the charge is, the trial must proceed, and the witness must have the absolute privilege to interpret his own evidence. Asking the impossible, no doubt. 'Agreed,' he says. 'But it is the privilege of his imagination to do so.'[18] The idea of the colonial trial had a particularly strong resonance in 1960. Nearly 100 people had just been accused in the South African 'Treason Trials' of 1958–9. Closer to home, a series of trials had followed the Notting Hill riots of August and September 1958. The law often provides a dominant metaphor for historiographical and literary work: here, to set the scene, Lamming offers his work as a kind of hybridized trial, part Old Bailey, part a ceremony of the Souls conducted on a back street in Port-au-Prince.

When Lamming finally reoccupies the first person singular, it is to address the reader, or at least his imagined reader in 1960, directly:

> This book is based upon the facts of experience, and it is intended as an introduction to a dialogue between you and me. I am the whole world of my accumulated emotional experience, vast areas of which probably remain unexplored. You are the other, according to your way of seeing me in relation to yourself. There will be no chairman.[19]

In this version of the confrontation, the rôles are clear: Lamming is the descendant of Caliban, 'you' (the reader) of Prospero, who makes his first appearance as 'John Haukins, sometimes treasurer of her Majesties navie Roial', on what is often regarded as the first English slaving voyage, in 1562 – 'that tremendous Voyage which swept Caliban from his soil and introduced him to Heaven through the long wet hell of the Middle Passage.'[20] Hawkins's voyage into the Caribbean from Sierra Leone led to landfall on Dominica, 'an

Island of the Canybals'. The African slave and the Carib Indian thereby become identical, 'both seen as the wild fruits of Nature, [they] share equally that spirit of revolt which Prospero by sword or Language is determined to conquer.'[21]

There is a sense of a personal history here, which invests these parallels with great dynamism; but the argument is not simply personal – there is also a larger history, one that associates Hakluyt with *The Tempest*, reads the play 'against the background of England's experiment in colonisation', and assumes, in the light of Shakespeare's known curiosity, and the fact that these matters were being 'feverishly discussed' in England at the time, that 'they would most certainly have been present in his mind'.[22]

Much of Lamming's emphasis is on Caliban as a *slave*, which he is called in the *dramatis personæ*, a status which has been surprisingly little discussed:

> I am a direct descendant of slaves, too near to the actual enterprise to believe that its echoes are over with the reign of emancipation. Moreover, I am a direct descendant of Prospero worshipping in the same temple of endeavour, using his legacy of language – not to curse our meeting – but to push it further, reminding the descendants of both sides that what's done is done, and can only be seen as a soil from which other gifts, or the same gift endowed with different meanings, may grow towards a future which is colonised by our acts in this moment, but which must always remain open.[23]

The dialogue with Prospero is a dialogue with England, in England, about the nature of English society, culture, and history. But, as *The Tempest* shows, Prospero always refuses dialogue with Caliban: slaves learn and obey, they do not converse; and so the descendant of Caliban cannot take it for granted that Prospero will even hear the remarks he makes. This 'dialogue' has never really materialised. Lamming's work on *The Tempest* has been discussed within a postcolonial context by critics such as Janheinz Jahn and Rob Nixon, but Shakespeare criticism has rarely noticed Lamming's work and given it no serious attention.[24]

Still operating within the allegory, Lamming analyses Prospero's situation, in England, in 1960:

> It was a divine recognition of privilege which made Prospero's past, the divinity which gave him the right to colonise the unarmed and excluded Caliban is the witness which waits for this decision. He cannot deny that past; nor can he abandon it without creating a total suicide of all those values which once sanctified his acts as a coloniser.

He cannot commit his name and history to the unforgivable vice of ingratitude against the dumb conscience of the Infidel; the grace which still promises to wash him clean of any crime resurrected in the name of colonisation . . . He must act; and he must act with Caliban; or he must die, not so much from spears, as from the slow and painful diminution of an energy he used to call human dignity . . . Colonised by his own ambition, Prospero's role is now completely reversed. Prospero is once again face to face with what is urgent and near-impossible. And he is terrified.[25]

When these words were published, Frantz Fanon was in the midst of writing what was to be his final book, *The Wretched of the Earth*, in which he uses a very similar formulation in describing decolonization:

The extraordinary importance of this change is that it is willed, called for, demanded. The need for this change exists in its crude state, impetuous and compelling, in the consciousness and in the lives of the men and women who are colonised. But the possibility of this change is equally experienced in the form of a terrifying future in the consciousness of another 'species' of men and women: the colonisers.[26]

The scenarios that Lamming and Fanon are here sketching differ in many ways. Most obviously Fanon, writing in the midst of the Algerian war for independence, is discussing violence: the colonizers' 'terror' is of what might happen to them, a fear which prompts the violence directed at Algerians, as it had been at Madagascans a generation earlier. Although British decolonization was not without similar violence, Lamming's own expectation, from the West Indies, was of a peaceful transition to independence – an expectation which makes the use of the word 'terrified' to describe Prospero's state of mind particularly interesting.

Lamming's writing does not shrink from describing the violence associated with colonialism, and even here he notes the military aspects of Prospero's takeover – Caliban was 'unarmed'. Nor of course does Shakespeare so shrink, although Prospero's physical power over Caliban is an aspect of his magic, and therefore distinctly 'clean', while Caliban has to resort to the threats of the unarmed – to burn Prospero's books and drive a nail into his head. However, as Lamming says, in 1960 Prospero's terror springs less from the threat of the native spears than from the thought that he must now act *with Caliban*. Lamming notes that he shares with Prospero the status as 'colonial': 'For it is that mutual experience of separation from their original ground which makes both master and slave colonial. To be colonial is to be in a state of exile.'[27] This emphasis on 'mutual experience' puts Lamming into the tradition which has its roots in the post-war work of French intellectuals such as Georges Bandelier and Octave Mannoni, a concern for the 'colonial situation' itself which, whatever their differences, is what Prospero and Caliban – within the allegory – have in common.[28]

As a prediction about the development of racial politics in Britain over the last 40 years of the century, Lamming's paragraph is remarkably prescient. More relevant here, though, are its emphasis on the psychological effects of colonialism, not just on Caliban (as explored by Fanon) but also on Prospero (an emphasis Lamming shares with Mannoni), and its insistence that the nub of the matter lies in Britain itself, where Caliban has followed Prospero, as if to say that matters cannot be brought to a conclusion simply by Prospero leaving the island, that there is a sixth act still to be written, and that Caliban and Prospero must write it together. If *Water with Berries* is this sixth act, it makes it very clear that Lamming was suffering from no utopian delusions about how this future collaboration might play out in practice.[29]

One reason for Prospero's terror, which casts an intriguing light back on the play, is the extent to which Caliban is Prospero's own creation. In the colonial allegory, Caliban is stolen from Africa by Prospero. In the play, and in Lamming's present, the relationship between the two is more complicated. Caliban is in exile, not just from Africa, involuntarily, and from the West Indies, but 'from his gods, ... from his nature, ... from his own name!'[30] This increasingly sounds like an exile from which there can be no possible return, no recovery of previous identity. So Prospero is afraid of Caliban because 'his encounter with Caliban is, largely, his encounter with himself'.[31]

One might expect from Lamming, as from the other Caribbean critics, some particular insight into the character of Caliban, with whom they are, to a degree, identifying, and from whose subject position they approach the colonial allegory. What is surprising, however, is the extent to which Lamming analyzes Caliban as it were from a distance, as he has been created within the play – leaving open the question as to whether such understanding is intended as to any degree a self-analysis:

> Caliban cannot be revealed in any relation to himself; for he has no self which is not a reaction to circumstances imposed upon his life . . . In all his encounters with his neighbours – whether they be Kings or drunken clowns – Caliban is never accorded the power *to see*. He is always the measure of the condition which his physical appearance has already defined. Caliban is the excluded, that which is eternally below possibility, and always beyond reach. He is seen as an occasion,

a state of existence which can be appropriated and exploited for the purposes of another's own development.[32]

This is by no means the heroic Caliban as Third World hero, as found even in Lamming's own versions of the allegory elsewhere in *The Pleasures of Exile* as Toussaint L'Ouverture or C. L. R. James or Fidel Castro. Caliban is even, Lamming suggests, 'outside the orbit of Human'. This is not his own fault, nor even Prospero's: 'It is some original Law which exists even beyond Prospero's seeing';[33] an original Law which it is hard not to equate either with Shakespeare as author or with some aspect of what, since Lamming wrote, has come to be called 'colonial discourse'.

For this Caliban, the heart of the matter, as Lamming calls it, is education, the most important of the parallels between the play and Caribbean history, and the one which brings Lamming and other West Indian writers most closely into the play's thematics: 'There is no escape from the prison of Prospero's gift.'[34] The teaching of language to Caliban may not have had the desired effect but, as Lamming suggests, 'It has a certain finality. Caliban will never be the same again. Nor, for that matter, will Prospero.'[35] This suggestion that the change has been irrevocable, that some identity has quite simply been lost and must be forged anew in new circumstances, has often led Lamming to be viewed rather equivocally by those standing (as it were) within the colonial allegory, firmly committed to the contemporary identification with the figure of Caliban as oppressed by Prospero. Lamming's position is, I think, more interesting. He writes as someone educated in the English literary system, deeply aware of 'the whole tabernacle of English names', 'this ancient mausoleum of historic achievement' whose foundations he is determined to shake.[36] This may, on most grounds, seem a less radical move than hammering a nail into Prospero's head. However, the implication of Lamming's dense meditations on these matters, if I read them correctly, is that the postcolonial response must involve at least a partial disidentification with Caliban on the grounds that Caliban is Prospero's creature, and postcolonial intellectuals, whilst having to recognize themselves in Caliban, should at the same time refuse any full identification and find another ground on which to stand. Part of that ground might be as readers and interpreters of *The Tempest*, ground which Prospero had long thought of as rightfully his. He will expect the nail in the head and take precautions, as the play shows; but he will not expect to be displaced as a literary commentator. Always take the enemy by surprise.

[4]

Lamming's discussion of *The Tempest* in the chapter of *The Pleasures of Exile* called 'A Monster, A Child, A Slave' begins with parallels and similarities of the kind raised in his Introduction. Ariel's account of the shipwreck recalls the Middle Passage; Prospero's sadism towards his slave Caliban recalls accounts of the torture of slaves in Haiti; Caliban's imprisonment is a form of emergency regulation restricting movement; Miranda has no recollection of her mother, 'like many an African slave child'.[37] Within the politics of the island, Prospero has absolute power, with Ariel as his 'privileged servant', 'the archetypal spy'.[38] Lamming's analysis of Prospero is very much in line with Mannoni's, associating the imperialist (even 'by circumstance') with psychosis: 'Sadism is characteristic of this type . . . His imperialism is like an illness, not only in his personal relationships, but in his relation to the external and foreign world.' The memory of Sycorax 'arouses him to rage that is almost insane'. His version of past events is certainly not to be taken as authoritative: 'We begin to distrust this Duke.'[39]

In 1960 Lamming's concern for both the politics of the island situation and for the human relationships on the island blithely ignores the contemporary formalism of much English criticism, expressed so damningly in L. C. Knights's sarcastically entitled essay 'How Many Children Had Lady Macbeth?'[40] It is precisely family questions of this kind that provide Lamming with an entry point into the racial and sexual politics of the play: Miranda's failure to remember much about her childhood prompts Lamming's surprise 'that she has, it seems, absolutely no recollection of her mother'.[41] Prospero's ambiguous reply to Miranda's innocent question about whether he is really her father ('Thy mother was a piece of virtue, and / She said thou wast my daughter') initiates speculation about the woman who was, presumably, Prospero's wife: 'Is she alive? Or did she die in the treacherous *coup d'état* which led to Prospero's exile?' 'Who, we are left to wonder, was really Miranda's mother? And what would she have had to say about this marvellous monster of a husband who refuses us information?'[42]

The prehistory of the characters in the play is an area to which Lamming gives full rein. After all, the preservation of the unities allows the audience to see little narrative extension on stage, but the characters themselves, and none more so than Prospero, are obsessively concerned with what has gone before, and offer us a good number of historical narratives; so discussion of the play's pre-history hardly involves the introduction of a subject irrelevant to the announced themes of the play. Lamming is especially interested in the relationship between Miranda and Caliban, respectively – and again the play provides us with this information – around three and twelve years of age when Prospero and Miranda reached the island: 'As time passed, and Prospero grew more and more occupied with his Book, Caliban and the child, Miranda, must have grown closer by the necessary contact of servant and mistress', a relationship Lamming again reads through the prism of African servant and European child in the Caribbean.[43]

However, the nub of Lamming's analysis, inasmuch as it offers a reading of the play itself, comes in his discussion of Prospero's accusation of rape ('thou didst seek to violate / The honour of my child') and Caliban's response: 'O ho, O ho! Would't had been done! . . . I had peopled else / This isle with Calibans' (I.ii.346–8).

> Is there a political intention at work? Does he mean that he would have numbers on his side; that he could organise resistance against this obscene and selfish monster. But why, we wonder, does Caliban think that the population would be Calibans? Why would they not be Mirandas? Does he mean that they should carry the father's name? But these children would be bastards and should be honoured no less with their mother's name. Or were there other possibilities?
>
> Did Caliban really try to lay her? This is a case where the body, in its consequences, is our only guide. Only the body could establish the truth; for if Miranda were made pregnant, we would know that some-one had penetrated her. We might also know whether or no it was Caliban's child; for it is most unlikely that Prospero and his daughter could produce a brown skin baby. Could Prospero really have endured the presence and meaning of a brown skin grandchild? It would not be Miranda's own doing. It would not be the result of their enterprise. It would be Miranda's and Caliban's child. It would be theirs: the result and expression of some fusion both physical and other than physical: a fusion which, within himself, Prospero needs and dreads![44]

The 'attempted rape' seems to have been little discussed in Shakespearean criticism before 1960: it was simply a fact, as reported by Prospero – and not of course actually denied by Caliban. Some recent criticism has felt the need to defend Caliban from that charge, as if he were a person falsely accused rather than a character in a play. The matter has become an issue only because the attempt is *reported* rather than enacted, and reported by a witness who can hardly be considered impartial, whatever the assumptions of earlier criticism; indeed, doubly reported, since what Prospero throws at Caliban is presumably his version of what Miranda has told him. Lamming is prepared to speculate that Miranda might have accused Caliban falsely, perhaps on the basis of a dream; but he is also prepared to assume that Caliban, created as 'outside the orbit of the Human', 'would think no more of raping Miranda than he might of eating her if she were alone, and he was hungry'.[45] Such speculation slights the 'colonial other' only if Caliban is assumed to be an autonomous individual *represented* by Shakespeare rather than a literary character produced by means discursive. Caliban's gleeful acceptance of the charge could easily be read, Lamming suggests, as his acute realization that the very idea of an attempted rape of his daughter could hurt Prospero more than anything else. The question of whether Caliban *actually* attempted to rape Miranda is of course meaningless. Within the dramatic fiction of the play, Shakespeare leaves the question open: what we know for sure is how the very thought rankles with Prospero.[46]

It is this passage in the essay which corresponds most closely to Lamming's sense of blasphemy, offering a transgression of all kinds of boundaries about the 'proper' way in which to conduct literary-critical discussion. Flip through *Shakespeare Quarterly* for 1960 to get some sense of how distinct Lamming's language and thematics were for the time. Of course, his language *still* has the capacity to offend: we are not now likely to respond positively to the idea of 'the man in Caliban', if that phrase is meant to imply some universal masculine principle.[47] Strings of questions are hardly more usual now than they were in 1960, but they work with considerable effect to raise new issues. Why Caliban thinks that the population would be Calibans must be as a result of what he has been taught about political dynasty by Prospero, a man who is, after all, in the process of manoeuvring his daughter into a marriage that will allow Prospero's progeny to govern Naples.[48] Prospero's evident exasperation with Caliban makes much more sense once one realizes that Caliban is speaking Prospero's language not just in his use of English but, even more disconcertingly, in the arguments he is putting forward. Caliban is, to put it in familial terms, the typical adolescent son. To adapt and to answer L. C. Knights's rhetorical question about Lady Macbeth, Prospero has two children, one natural, one fostered, with 'Miranda [as] the innocent half of Caliban; Caliban [as] the possible deformity which Miranda, at the age of experiment, might become.'[49]

This familial complexity, deeply Oedipal in its implications, was only really explored by the new wave of psychoanalytical criticism in the 1970s and 1980s – which rarely if ever mentioned the pioneering work of Mannoni and Lamming.[50] But, however happy this new criticism was to tackle questions about Prospero's sexuality and the theme of incest, it steered well clear of the topic of miscegenation, the truly unthinkable, if not – given Caliban's evident humanity – the inconceivable. Within the allegory,

Lamming's speculation is now fully readable: indeed we have seen the Cuban *Otra Tempestad* develop a love relationship between Caliban and Miranda, and a 'brown skin baby' is the final outcome of Marina Warner's *Tempest*-based novel, *Indigo*, when Miranda Everard and the black George Felix (an actor who plays Caliban) have a child together.[51] Prospero's need and dread is thereby associated with his earlier 'terror', which can be read metaphorically as the realization that he needs to embrace a future in which Miranda and Caliban are lovers. But put this way, and with attention paid to the unconscious of the text, Lamming's insight can also be read as directed towards the play itself, offering an explanation for aspects of the plotting, the relationships between the characters, the parallels – intended or not – between sets of characters, and in particular for the disturbances that punctuate the play's surface: none more troubling than Prospero's own perturbation which brings a premature end to his masque-like betrothal celebration.

[6]

I have tried to suggest that Lamming's essay on *The Tempest* offers a reading of the play, placing the essay within the institution of Shakespearean criticism as well as within the tradition of Third World allegory, its more usual location. This is not to suggest that such an approach is the only way of engaging with *The Pleasures of Exile*, or that it is necessarily the *best* way from a pedagogical or political point of view.[52] Rather, the three stages of the argument are, firstly, that the institution of Shakespeare studies has too easily been able to sidetrack 'anti-colonial' readings of *The Tempest* by putting them in the category of 'appropriations' or 'allegories' (in effect saying 'very interesting, but not actually speaking to the *real* Shakespearean text'); that, second, if these 'anti-colonial' readings do actually, as in Lamming's case, speak to the *real* text, we should listen to what they say and write a place for them in Shakespearean criticism; and that, third, this approach does have significant pedagogical and political advantages – intervening in a key area of the educational system and tackling mainstream literary criticism on that criticism's own chosen ground.[53]

The sea-change in readings of *The Tempest* during the second half of the twentieth century does not centrally involve, it should be stressed, a move from Europe to America, however often it may have coincided with an attention to American materials. We read differently now at least in part because we occupy a different world. Discussing Caliban's famous retort, 'You taught me language; and my profit on't / Is, I know how to curse'

(I.ii.366–7), Stephen Greenblatt speaks of how 'what we experience', in these lines, 'is a sense of their devastating justness.'[54] He says this not to claim that Shakespeare was unjust to Caliban, but that Prospero was – although many of Greenblatt's hostile readers have seemed incapable of understanding the difference. And, although 'we experience' that sense of devastating justness, we do so not because we are imposing on the play our late-twentieth-century concerns. Rather, for Greenblatt, the lines 'refuse to mean' otherwise, refuse to be taken as the self-indictment that Prospero would read them as. The ending to the play remains open, Caliban's fate, as Greenblatt says, 'naggingly unclear'. But Greenblatt's argument, although open to the play's complexity, rejects the view that the reading through Prospero's eyes is just as valid as the reading which listens to, and is moved and persuaded by, the arguments that Caliban makes. This does not immediately lead us to an overall interpretation of the play or even of the respective parts that Prospero's and Caliban's voices have in the play. However, it does suggest that the postcolonial reading claims to locate its local analyses in the words of the text, not in its own decision to find postcolonial themes present, to land a seventeenth-century play with a late-twentieth-century agenda. The lines themselves 'refuse to mean' otherwise. The claim, in other words, is an historicist one, whether new or old, a claim which has no truck with the radical indeterminacy usually associated with the notion of the postmodern. This, after all, is a crucial component of the political nature of postcolonial readings: they claim to discover something of significance about the play that was obscured or ignored for many years. That discovery may have been in some sense enabled by the whole process of decolonisation, but the readings invent nothing, whatever the supposed political motivation for them doing so. George Lamming's essay on The Tempest, although widely ignored at the time of its publication, read the play in ways which foreshadow and chime with the readings which now dominate Tempest criticism. Just as Mannoni's brief remarks on The Tempest might now strike us as more illuminating than those of his exact contemporary, Wilson Knight, so Lamming's understanding of The Tempest has outlasted that of Leo Marx, published in the same year.

These comparisons are not made to belittle, but rather to suggest how sharply different circumstances and different places could, at the same time, produce such startlingly different readings of The Tempest, which have then had such different histories. It would be tempting, but mistaken, to think that the critics were reading different plays: they were not. And in the struggles over the meaning of The Tempest, which have been a significant aspect of literary culture in the last half century, Mannoni and Lamming have moved from their once-peripheral positions to occupy something like centre-stage. Rather like Eshu, in Césaire's play, they have move uninvited into the masque, spoken their lines, and made a new generation of readers see the play differently.

17 Maintaining the State of Emergence/y: Aimé Césaire's *Une tempête*

LUCY RIX

> The Martinican malaise is the malaise of a people that no longer feels responsible for its destiny and has no more than a minor part in a drama of which it should be the protagonist.[1]

> What is this distinctive *force* of Fanon's vision that has been forming even as I write about the division, the displacement, the cutting edge of his thought? It comes, I believe, from the tradition of the oppressed, as Walter Benjamin suggests; it is the language of a revolutionary awareness that the state of emergency in which we live is not the exception but the rule. We must attain to a concept of history that is in keeping with this insight. And the state of emergency is also always a state of emergence. The struggle against colonial oppression changes not only the direction of Western history, but challenges its historicist idea of time as a progressive, ordered whole.[2]

ADAPTATION FOR A BLACK THEATRE

Aimé Césaire's last play, *Une tempête*, was written for a festival in Tunisia in 1969. After a period of exhilaration and optimism as African states began to gain their independence, Césaire used the process of adaptation as a method by which to probe emerging debates concerning colonialism. As can be seen from the first epigraph, Césaire believed that it was crucial for the colonized Martinican peoples to relocate themselves at the centre of the stage. *The Tempest* was adapted so as to 'protagonize' the colonized and to ensure that their voices were heard loud and clear from within the hushed citadel of Western culture. At the time, the very act of rewriting *The Tempest* was seen as an audacious literary siege; for Césaire it provided a potent strategy by which to throw aside the rules of colonial culture and to dramatize the destinies of the colonized. He rudely thrusts into Shakespeare's text in the same way that Eshu bursts, uninvited, into the prudish circle of Roman gods and goddesses.

Strangely, the first performance of *Une tempête* was set in pioneer America, using the motifs of the Western.³ Although this may seem incongruous in view of the play's references to Africa and, more specifically, to the Caribbean, the decision to set the play in America demonstrates the possibilities of alluding to, or even of integrating, a number of colonial dramas on one stage. Thus, Césaire's adaptation is as open to a variety of times and locations as Shakespeare's text. Despite attacks on Césaire's essentialist vision of *négritude*, the play itself displays flexibility and plurality. Although it is clear that *Une tempête* was written with the particular political situation of Martinique very much in mind, rather than reducing *The Tempest* to a series of closures, Césaire's adaptation opens up further possibilities of history, interpretation and location. As Césaire has said,

> Demystified, the play [is] essentially about the master–slave relation, a relation that is still alive and which, in my opinion, explains a good deal of contemporary history: in particular, colonial history, the history of the United States. Wherever there are multiracial societies, the same drama can be found, I think.⁴

'TURN WHITE OR DISAPPEAR': INTERNALIZED RACISM

Césaire grew up within the particular colonial situation of Martinique, where he was born in 1913. French Caribbean colonies differed from those of Britain in that, after abolition (which occurred in Martinique in 1848), adult male ex-slaves were immediately made citizens of France. The right to vote was intermittently removed, but the concept of Frenchness came to be seen as a positive and integral part of 'freedom'. The minority of powerful white settlers in Martinique had made every effort to create an abyss of difference between themselves and the black slaves whom they imported to work on the sugar plantations. The settlers' laws and attitudes worked to prevent slaves from in any way comparing themselves to whites. As Lilyan Kesteloot comments:

> They [slaves] were not allowed to wear the same clothes as whites nor to work as anything but farm labourers, domestics etc. As a result, it became the main object of coloured men to resemble their masters as closely as possible. As long as the slave's condition was associated with a differentiation between slave and master, the black man would associate *this idea of freedom with resemblance*. Thus, after the emancipation of 1848, those few slaves who had the opportunity undertook by all and any means a race toward the assimilation represented by money, studies, marriages, intrigue.⁵

This drive towards self 'whitening' was, and perhaps still is, one of the most insidious obstacles to decolonization. Richard Burton points out that it was the French West Indians themselves who desparately sought to pay the 'blood tax' (*l'impôrt de sang*) by enlisting in the French army in 1914 and again in 1939. It was surely the pinnacle of assimilation: to die for *la mère-patrie*. In order to assert any sort of authority or authenticity in any aspect of life, blacks were forced to seek the validation of European culture, European customs, European politics.

Unlike many other Caribbean colonies, Martinique, from a very early stage, had a large mulatto population: by 1850, there were more mulattos than whites. This had a significant effect on future racial relations. In a process which is in some ways comparable to the racial situation in Brazil, Martinican mulattos made every effort to dissociate themselves from 'blacks'. Carl Degler has named this phenomenon 'the mulatto escape hatch',[6] and there is a similar phrase in Martinican Creole: *peau chappé* (escape skin). This was further complicated by class: to be rich, or to hold a high-status job, was to become 'whiter'. The ideal of a colour-blind society was thus nothing but the ideal of assimilation to white French culture.

During the occupation of France in World War II, Admiral Georges Robert arrived in the island as representative of the Vichy government. Ten thousand European sailors were stationed in Martinique for four years. It has been suggested that it was the racism of these sailors that finally fuelled underlying resentment and facilitated the birth of a black Martinican consciousness. Most black Martinicans at this time believed themselves to be first and foremost French. The European servicemen, however, treated them as 'niggers'. In 1943, in the face of massive demonstrations, Admiral Robert was forced to resign. Despite the unrest caused by the occupation, and the racism that black Martinicans faced both in their homeland and, particularly, when they travelled to France, the racial ideology of Martinique seems to have been deeply-seated in not only whites, but within the mulatto and black communities as well. The myth of racial harmony and the absence of legal segregation prevented black Martinicans from uniting in a focused struggle for racial equality. (The dispersal of French West Indian families on both sides of the Atlantic has also been discussed as a major obstacle to the formation of nationalist movements: Edouard Glissant, the Martinican cultural critic, has termed this 'genocide by substitution'.)[7] As Michel Giraud notes, there was no substantial difference in the way in which each racial group in Martinique perceived itself (auto-stereotype) and the way in which it was perceived by other racial groups (hetero-stereotype), which leads him to conclude that racism in Martinique was firmly internalized.[8] It is easy to criticize the essentializing elements of the concept of *négritude* that Césaire employed as a means of overcoming this 'escape hatch' ideology, but the specific racial history that Césaire was confronting makes matters less straightforward.

'TO HELL WITH HIBISCUS': FINDING A CULTURAL SPACE

The Martinican literature produced during Césaire's childhood was, almost without exception, 'traditional' French literary production, what Léon Damas has termed 'tracing-paper poetry'. This was one of the first aspects of black Martinique to be attacked in the *Légitime Défense* (1932), a journal published by a group of Martiniquan students at the Sorbonne that would have a profound impact on their struggle for cultural identity. It provided a clear indication of its opinion of the current West Indian literary tradition:

> The West Indian writer, stuffed to bursting with white morality, white culture, white education, white prejudice, fills his little books with a swollen image of himself. Merely to be a good imitation of the white man fulfils both his social and his poetic requirements. He cannot be too modest or too sedate. Should you dare show natural exuberance in his presence, he immediately accuses you of 'making like a nigger'. So naturally, he does not want to 'make like a nigger' in his poems. It is a point of honor with him that a white person could read his entire book without ever guessing the author's pigmentation.[9]

Even when writers were not employing traditional French imagery or classical subject-matter, they continued to express themselves in traditional 'poetic' French language, style, form and vocabulary. The poetry written specifically about Martinique was restricted to the view of the colonizer, who spoke only of the paradise of the island, thus textually erasing the squalor, poverty and racism caused by colonialism. This cultural bleaching culminated in an exhibition held in Paris in 1945 by the Ministry of Colonies. It was entitled 'The Happy Antilles: in honour of all those who have dreamed of the Islands with a poet's heart', and included poems from which the following quotations have been taken:

> Ah! all the sweetness of my early childhood
> Those languid nights in the port of Fort-de-France
> A vegetable paradise
> Long do you enchant me with your captivating play.
> . . .
> Coffer of kisses

Hummingbird to tourists
Geographic gem

Dear garden of small gifts
Ground for the supple footsteps
And ample stride of coloured women
Small circus of the hallway of my heart
Familiar jack-in-the-box.[10]

It was poetry of this type that Césaire wished to expose as blatantly perpet-
uating the colonial myth. He believed that it was essential to reveal the agenda
of 'colour-blind literature' and to begin to create a cultural form in which to
express the reality of racism and poverty that was lived by the majority of
Martinican blacks. Published in a 1941 issue of *Tropiques*, Suzanne Césaire's
poem 'Misère d'une poésie: John-Antoine Nau', epitomizes the attack on
traditional French and exotic 'touristic' writing which she condemns as
'Littérature de hamac. Littérature de sucre et de vanille. Tourisme littéraire...'
(Literature of the hammock. Literature of sugar and vanilla. Literary
tourism).[11] Eventually, and perhaps paradoxically, it was a European literary
movement that Césaire appropriated in his search for a poetry of defiance:
Surrealism. The Surrealist movement temporarily seemed to fit neatly with
Césaire's requirements for a movement of cultural resistance: it aimed to
shock the prim bourgeoisie with a production of humorous, vulgar gestures
that attempted to undermine the validity and authority of high-brow
Western culture. As R. M. Albères states:

> Surrealism set dynamite under these conventions and blew them up.
> New foliage grew in the ruined palaces of sentiment and rhetoric. A
> jungle of wild plants, their roots drawing strength from the uncon-
> scious and their strange shapes breaking all known rules of botany,
> fertilized the fields of rubble – the ruins of the ever heavier construc-
> tions of a civilization which, from a surfeit of rational humanism, had
> drowned in the habitual.[12]

This new literary credo offered Césaire a great variety of ammunition to
turn against stagnant European traditions. The innovative method of forag-
ing into the unconscious, and particularly the 'black unconscious', seemed
an ideal way in which to start to delve into the 'black memory' and rediscover
the beginnings of 'black history'. Although today these terms are frequently
branded as essentialist and therefore highly suspect, for Césaire and his contemporaries such categories provided a framework and a much-needed
space within which black Martinicans could question their Euro- and

ethnocentric education and begin to envisage a new and positive awareness of being 'black'. As Sartre said of Césaire, 'surrealism, a European movement in poetry [has been] stolen from the Europeans by a black man who turns it against them and gives it a well defined purpose.'[13]

THE LATER STAGE: TURNING TO THEATRE

After completing a model assimilationist education, mainly in Paris, Césaire returned to Martinique in 1939. After the war, he was invited to run on the Communist party ticket in the municipal elections and was elected mayor in 1945. The following year he successfully oversaw Martinique's transition from a colony to a department of France. This was something that he had long struggled for, and which he believed to be a positive change. However, it was to be the first disappointment in a long and often disillusioning political career. It actually resulted in the loss of the limited, but real influence that local people could bring to bear on colonial governors and officials. The whole decision-making process was transferred to Paris, and the colonial governors, who were often residents of Martinique, were replaced by prefects who were less sensitive to local needs. From 1958 to 1964, the sugar industry, which had produced almost all of Martinique's exports, went into serious decline and unemployment rose to 25 per cent. The riots of 1959 in Fort-de-France were directed 'not against the local white Creoles, but against metropolitans . . . the metropolitan had, in scarcely more than a decade, become a popular scapegoat for the disruptions and disappointments of departmentalization'.[14] Césaire formed the Parti Progressiste Martiniquais in 1958: its aim was not independence, but autonomy. The colonial legacy of social, economic and psychological destruction has left Martinique significantly dependent on France for financial support (in the 1970s, France was supplying half Martinique's revenue). Although nominally it has been abandoned, colonialism remains both overtly and insidiously in place, as Susan Frutkin notes: 'French assistance has been along social rather than developmental lines, and, while a higher standard of living has accompanied the infusion of public funds, in reality it reflects an inflated state of welfare living rather than any improvement in the island's productive capabilities.'[15]

This was the political climate in which *Une tempête* was written, Césaire having turned to theatre for a more accessible cultural channel through which to communicate his views:

> Blacks from now on must make their history. And the history of the
> blacks will truly be what they will make of it . . . a black writer cannot

enclose himself in an ivory tower. There are things to be understood . . . it is necessary to speak clearly, speak concisely, to get the message across – and it seems to me that the theatre can lend itself to that.[16]

Although Césaire here stresses the importance of transmitting 'the message', the particular form of theatre to which he turned was actually one of great flexibility. It seems that what may be interpreted as a desire to find a more transparent medium resulted in the discovery of a highly diverse and shifting site of performance. Jean-Michel Serreau, who collaborated with Césaire on all three of his plays (Césaire has said that Serreau's death contributed to his decision not to continue writing drama), sought 'an open or exploded scenic space, overtly constructed rather than self-enclosed, an environment for registering rhythmic movement rather than capturing a static scene'.[17] In making explicit the process of construction and impermanence, this theatre could be mobile and provisional: it could adapt itself to an individual environment rather than the audience adapting themselves to the institutional stasis of traditional theatre. The message, then, becomes an integral part of the dramatic process, as Césaire highlights in the opening masking scene of *Une tempête*. In this scene, what was originally intended to be an entirely black cast dons masks in order to designate the race of each character. Césaire suggests that the allocation of masks (and therefore race) is an arbitrary process by showing each actor to be choosing his or her mask:

> Come gentlemen, help yourselves. To each his character and to each character his mask. You, Prospero? Why not? His is an unfathomable will to power. You, Caliban? Well, well, that's revealing. You, Ariel! I have no objections. And what about Stephano? And Trinculo? No takers? Ah, just in time! It takes all sorts to make a world.[18]

One of Césaire's pointed changes to Shakespeare's cast list was to specify Caliban as a black slave and Ariel as a mulatto slave. Prospero's race and nationality are left unspecified and, although the obvious assumption is that the actor will don a white mask, Césaire avoids any assumption that 'white' is a neutral or normative race – because every actor wears a mask, the white race is displayed as equally constructed and performed. As Robert Eric Livingston comments: 'The effect of the maskplay is to de-essentialize the construction of race, to set up a tension between the racial script and its performance'.[19] From the outset, therefore, Césaire undermines his own racial stereotyping of a black Caliban as the violent rebellious slave (the 'Malcolm X' figure) and Ariel as the 'whitened', Christian 'Uncle Tom' mulatto, who hopes to assert change through non-violent means (the Martin Luther King figure). The overlaying of a specifically American colonial situation (which Césaire himself posited and which is evident in the echoes of the US black leaders' speeches in the speeches of Caliban and Ariel) adds to the play the contemporary politics of the Black Power movement. This compression of colonial history (remembering that the first performance of the play was set in pioneer America) produces a reinforcing of the simultaneous commentary offered by the play on both the historical condition of slavery and its effect on contemporary Martinique. Universal themes of power and colonialism are shown to be locked in constant combat with specifics of time and locality. As Homi Bhabha points out in this essay's second epigraph, the disruption of the traditional Western teleological conception of history offers one way of levering open the holes and voids of the colonial story.

Re-tracing 'black history' on the stage reveals what Glissant has observed to be a vertiginous process: 'For history is not only absence for us, it is vertigo. The time that was never ours we must now possess. We do not see it stretch into our past and calmly take us into tomorrow, but it explodes in us as a compact mass, pushing through a dimension of emptiness where we must with difficulty and pain put it all back together.'[20] Césaire's choice of dramatic form destabilizes authorial control and rejects the concept of uncontaminated reading. As Helen Gilbert and Joanne Tompkins note, 'most postcolonial criticism overlooks drama, perhaps because of its apparently impure form: playscripts are only a part of theatre experience, and performance is therefore difficult to document.'[21]

Despite Césaire's achievement of both beginning to develop a specific space for 'black' culture and, at the same time, highlighting the constructed nature of racial identity, there remain apparent racial clichés in the play that are less straightforward to explain or justify. For example, Western culture is characterized as the height of Enlightenment rationalism (epitomized by the measured dance and mannered speeches of the prudish Olympian goddesses) and 'black culture' is portrayed in an equally hackneyed manner, as a vibrant glorification of chaos and untamed nature, personified by Eshu (the Yoruba god of boundaries between worlds):

ESHU   ... Eshu is a feisty lad,
     and with his penis he smites,
     He smites
     He smites ...
CERES   Well! Iris, don't you find this song obscene?
JUNO   Disgusting! Intolerable ... If he carries on, I'm leaving!

This opposition feels uncomfortable because it seems to perpetuate stereotyping that was, and continues to be, employed by colonialists. However, read within the context of a play that Césaire specified as having the 'ambience of a psychodrama', to simplify his treatment as stereotyping or essentialism would be reductive. In fact, by placing such blatant stereotypes on the stage, Césaire reveals and displays internalized and entrenched racial images, and thereby provokes discussion.

Additionally, the manner in which Césaire juggles and undermines rôles and characters ensures that an atmosphere of impermanence and humour is maintained. From the very start of the play, Prospero's role as theatre director is usurped by the mysterious 'Messeur de jeu' who supervises the random distribution of actors' parts and who also generates the tempest itself. Thus, despite Prospero's later rantings about conducting the score of the island, during the first scene we see him relegated to an anonymous actor. Not only are racial rôles displayed as being constructed through masking, but the play is also frequently interrupted by characters usurping the rôles of others: Césaire himself takes Shakespeare's place; Eshu intrudes into the Western pantheon; Ferdinand plays at being a slave and Stephano and Trinculo at being kings and generals. Rôles and subjects are exploded and temporary, they can be taken or handed out; despite Césaire's desire to write the black subject into existence, the play's self-conscious treatment of performance tends repeatedly to shake off the potential solidification of racial essence.

Une tempête is also an urgent play of protest, written at a time when Césaire could see the possibility of autonomy for Martinique (let alone independence) slipping further and further out of reach. Although *négritude* and its association with a return to African roots has been heavily criticized for its reductionism, Césaire needed to maintain the momentum of a waning struggle. He was well aware that *négritude*'s creation of Africa was a textual process: 'Of course my knowledge of Africa was bookish; I and my whole generation were dependent on what whites wrote about it'.[22] The very textuality of Africa enables its appropriation to an anticolonialist cause. As Benita Parry observes:

As I read them [Césaire and Fanon], both affirmed the invention of an insurgent, unified black self, acknowledged the revolutionary energies released by valorizing the cultures denigrated by colonialism and, rather than construing the colonialist relationship in terms of negotiations with the structures of imperialism, privileged coercion over hegemony to project it as a struggle between implacably placed forces, an irony made all too obvious in enunciations inflected, indeed made possible, by these very negotiations.[23]

Frantz Fanon's *Black Skin, White Masks* (1952) provides an analysis of the dilemma of *négritude* that offers much to supplement a reading of Césaire. As Bhabha points out, it is particularly surprising that in *Black Skin, White Masks*, Fanon rarely historicizes the colonial experience:

> There is no master narrative or realist perspective that provide a background of social and historical facts against which emerge the problems of the individual and the collective psyche. It is through image and fantasy – those orders that figure transgressively on the borders of history and the unconscious – that Fanon most profoundly evokes the colonial condition.[24]

This observation could productively be applied to *Une tempête*, in which the use of masks and the specified atmosphere of 'psychodrama' create the preconditions for a gap between performer and rôle, thus undermining a realist perspective. Similarly, location and historical moment are implied by Césaire, but never made explicit. As Parry suggests, *négritude* was not the regression to, or recovery of, a pre-existent state, but a textually invented history, 'an identity effected through figurative operators, and a tropological construction of blackness as a sign of the colonized condition and its refusal'.[25]

Fanon's frustration with Sartre's critique of *négritude* as being 'anti-racist racism' is telling: 'I needed not to know', Fanon tells us, 'I needed to lose myself completely in *négritude*'.[26] Sartre, in an essay entitled 'Black Orpheus' had written:

> *négritude* appears as the minor term of a dialectical progression: the theoretical and practical assertion of the supremacy of the white man is its thesis; the position of *négritude* as an antithetical value is the moment of negativity . . .Thus *négritude* is the root of its own destruction, it is a transition and not a conclusion, a means and not an ultimate end.[27]

Although both Fanon and Césaire may have sympathized with the last part of this critique, negating *négritude* as the minor antithesis of white supremacy was a formation that undermined *négritude*'s potential for opening a space (albeit transitory) in which black culture could develop. Furthermore, it seemed to destroy any sense of the agency of black resistance. Sartre continued, 'Today let us hail the turn of history that will make it possible for the black men to utter 'the great Negro cry with a force that will shake the pillars of the world (Césaire)'. To which Fanon responded

> And so it is not I who make a meaning for myself, but it is the meaning that was already there, pre-existing, waiting for me. It is not out of my bad nigger's misery, my bad nigger's teeth, my bad nigger's hunger that I will shape a torch with which to burn down the world, but it is the torch that was already there, waiting for the turn of history.[28]

However, although Fanon does not comment on this point, it is Sartre's distinction between race and class that seems to be the most problematic part of his argument. 'The first (race) is concrete and particular, the second (class) is universal and abstract; the one stems from what Jaspers calls understanding and the other from intellection; the first is the result of a psycho-biological syncretism and the second is a methodical construction based on experience.'[29] This hierarchization of class over race employs adjectives that are close to those frequently used in describing white superiority. Sartre seems to suggest that race is subordinate because it is a 'particular' issue – that of non-whites – whereas class is a universal issue. This distinction falls easily into the statement that everybody has a 'class' whilst only non-white people have a 'race'.

REPLAYING THE CANON

In 'Misére d'une poésie' Suzanne Césaire writes: 'La poésie martiniquaise sera cannibale ou ne sera pas!' (Either the poetry of Martinique will be cannibalistic or there will be no poetry in Martinique). The word 'cannibale' is coyly translated by Ellen Conroy Kennedy as 'done with them', which ignores its most literal connotations and force. The term suggests not merely that the 'cannibal' could be appropriated as a symbol of colonized people, but goes further to imply that the poetry itself should be 'cannibalistic'. For writers so long force-fed European literature, the time had come to devour and digest this same literature in a self-conscious manner and be empowered to spew out whatever they chose not to swallow. When Prospero asks Caliban what he would do alone on the island, Caliban answers: 'I'd rid myself of you, first of all . . . I'd vomit you up, all your pomp and designs! Your white poison!' This can be seen as an analogy for the very process of adapting canonical texts. Taking the canon to task enables writers to destroy any apparent European monopoly on representation and, like Eshu, to interrupt and intervene in established social conditioning. Cannibalistic intertextuality allows a replaying of fiction that rejects claims to transcendence or to the supposed universality of Shakespeare's self-evident worth.

Césaire highlights the issues of hunger, consumption, force-feeding and power during the scene in which Prospero torments Alonso, Gonzalo and Sebastian by tempting them with a delicious meal and then removing it. The first time the food vanishes, Alonso says, 'I firmly believe that we have fallen into the hands of powers that are playing cat and mouse with us. It's a cruel way of making us appreciate our helplessness.' But, as soon as the unfortunate men decide not to touch the meal, Prospero asserts his control:

> PROSPERO   (*Invisible*) I don't like this refusal, Ariel. Torment them
> until they eat.
> ARIEL   Why should we put ourselves out for their benefit? It's
> their look-out if they won't eat; they'll die of hunger.
> PROSPERO   No, I want them to eat.
> ARIEL   That's despotism. A while ago you made me snatch it away
> from their drooling mouths; now that they refuse, you are
> ready to force-feed them.
> PROSPERO   Enough quibbling! My mood has changed! They would
> wrong me by not eating! Let them experience eating out of my
> hand like chicks. I insist upon this sign of their submission.
> ARIEL   It's as evil to play their hunger as it is their anguish and
> their hope.
> PROSPERO   That is how power is measured. I am Power.

Here, the hungry trio are forced, unknowingly, to submit to Prospero's crazed desire for power. The process of being forced to consume Prospero's language and culture leads Caliban to want to vomit Prospero's 'white poison'; and Césaire's text, in a comparable gesture, is produced through a controlled consumption of Shakespeare's text.

Peter Hulme has suggested that Shakespeare's *Tempest* is structured by a series of replays or re-enactments, most signally Prospero's staging of a fantasized version of the original conspiracy that overthrew him with the difference that, this time, he will defeat the conspirators, led by Caliban.[30] What happens, then, when a writer who has forged a political identification with Caliban, adapts the play, thus replaying the replays? If, for Prospero, a psychopathic series of repetitions placates him with the satisfaction of victory over a powerless subject, for Césaire the replay is not so simple. When Prospero sets in motion his re-enactment, he is certain that his plan to resume his dukedom will be successful (although at times his grand plan seems fragile and superficial). However, as Césaire replays Shakespeare, the end to colonialism in Martinique was not close at hand. Thus Césaire, unlike Prospero, does not even appear to 'win' at the finish of *Une tempête*: the struggle between colonized and colonizer remains unresolved. Significantly, Césaire appears to allow Caliban the chance to defeat Prospero, which he refuses to take. Whereas Shakespeare's Caliban is portrayed as completely powerless against Prospero, Césaire's Caliban faces a crucial moment in which destiny appears to be in his hands. In a complex twist, Césaire suggests that at this moment Prospero is both fallible and simultaneously invincible. He is not purely a magician (Césaire stresses this by transforming the majority of his powers into military and technological ones), and yet his power and its aftermath are strong enough to prevent a reversal of his position. Caliban is unable to wave goodbye to the oppressors and reclaim his freedom because he and Prospero remain trapped together on the island ('PROSPERO: Ah well, my old Caliban, we're the only two left on this island, just you and me. You and me! You-me! Me-you!'). Joan Dayan links this reciprocity with the strategy employed by Césaire to undermine the notion of Shakespeare's *Tempest* being the 'original'. Césaire refuses to give his work any illusion of primariness, and thus avoids a reductive reversal. 'Instead, he recognises the force of mutuality, the knot of reciprocity between master and slave, between a prior "classic" and his response to it. This labour of reciprocity accounts for the complexities of Césaire's transformation: a labour that defies any simple opposition between black and white, master and slave, original and adaptation, authentic and fake.'[31]

Here, Dayan is also alluding to the 'dependency theory' promulgated by Octave Mannoni, to which Césaire had strongly objected in his *Discourse on Colonialism*. But, despite Césaire's complete rejection of the concept that particular races were inherently predisposed either to the rôle of colonizer or the rôle of colonized, he was influenced by the idea that dependency established following colonization could be psychological and not exclusively economic. An economic dependency due to de-forestation and soil erosion of the island is implied in the text ('SEBASTIAN: A pity that the ground's barren in places. CALIBAN: That isn't mud . . . It's something Prospero's conjured up'), but complex psychological reasons are also suggested for Caliban's refusal to murder Prospero. It is not clear whether Prospero is genuinely physically defenceless, but in any case he manages to paralyse Caliban's action merely with words. Firstly, he orders Caliban to strike him. This immediately maintains the master–slave relation: Caliban's act of freedom would thus be to obey his master's orders. Second, Prospero refuses to arm himself, placing Caliban not only in the rôle of slave, but also in that of assassin – he allows Caliban no civilized way out. By denying him the typically Shakespearean duel, he also refuses to treat Caliban as an equal human being. Unlike Prospero, who is content with a sham victory over a powerless and unaware victim, Caliban yearns for a 'real' victory. Despite his scorn for Ariel's struggle to 'free' Prospero and give him a conscience, in the final hour it seems that Caliban is not content with a cold-blooded murder that would implicate him in a reductive reaction rather than any genuine solution. Caliban is nearer to approaching a positive position with his lucid articulation of the process of colonization and his verbal attack on Prospero that finally leads Prospero to admit: 'you are the one who made me doubt myself for the first time'. But Césaire makes it quite clear that lengthening colonial dependence, in whatever form (Gonzalo's speech suggests the neo-colonial behaviour of the tourism industry: 'They must stay as they are: savages, noble savages, free, without complex or complication. Something like a pool of eternal youth where we would come at intervals to revive our drooping urban spirits'), cannot be seen as a victory for the colonizer. Prospero's final degeneration and loss of the precious order of his 'civiliza-tion', the disintegration of his mind and of his language, reveal Césaire's belief in what he called the 'boomerang effect' – the phenomenon by which colonialism poisons and dehumanizes both sides. As Fanon puts it, 'The Negro enslaved by his inferiority, the white man enslaved by his superiority alike behave in accordance with a neurotic orientation.'[32] While Caliban has found a reductive form of freedom and Prospero's rantings are drowned by the noises of the island, a rotting colonialism continues to fester, reminding us, in Dayan's words, that for many peoples the era of 'postcolonialism' has not yet dawned, and for Martinique Une tempête serves as a 'painful reminder of what has not happened'.[33] Furthermore, the form of neocolonialism that remains in Martinique is particularly entrenched because racism and finan-cial dependence are masked by an apparent understanding and unity between colonizer and colonized.

18 H.D.'s 'The Tempest'

MARTHA NELL SMITH

> H.D. is a poet of color heightened by color, of overtones of sound
> and meaning – e.g., Rosemary, Rose-of-Mary and ros maris; and of
> uninsisted upon implications (Marianne Moore, on the dust-jacket of
> H.D.'s *By Avon River*)[1]
>
> I am almost 63 & have been writing for 40 years but *Avon* is the first
> book that really made me happy (H.D. to George Plank, 2 July 1949)[2]
>
> Remembering Shakespeare always, but remembering him differently.
> Reach from your bed in dark night, half in a dream or delirium.
> What do you seek? (H.D., 'The Guest')[3]

Shakespeare went home to Stratford after *The Tempest*. H.D. comes home to herself in *By Avon River*, and consecrates that journey by beginning with her own 'The Tempest', Part I of the three-part poem that serves as the first half of the book that was her darling. In this extended response to Shakespeare, often assumed to be the greatest poet of the English language, Hilda Doolittle is preoccupied not so much with what her artistic forebear wrote and said, but with what he didn't say. She chooses Claribel, who exists only outside the action of Shakespeare's play, who cannot be found in the *dramatis personæ* but in the remembering conversations of those shipwrecked on their return from her nuptials. On this magical island, his counsellors remind her father Alonso that fair Claribel is 'now queen', married to the King of Tunis, and he pines that his daughter is 'so far from Italy remov'd'. His brother Sebastian readily reminds him that 'you may thank yourself for this great loss, / That would not bless our Europe with your daughter, / But rather loose her to an African.' All of this remembering repeatedly reminds the audience that Claribel will likely 'ne'er again' be seen, having been 'banish'd' from sight (II.i.116–32). Birthed to English literary tradition by a stroke of Shakespeare's pen, where is Claribel's story written down, H.D. wonders –

for the dramatist only gives her a name. Does her tale abide in the 'old pamphlet[s]' (7) from which the bard stole his plot? The play finished, does the playwright – who gave her no roundelay, no rôle, even as audience – does he himself remember her while fingering the script? Since she is virtually unscripted, will she hold a place in his memory?

H.D. asks the question for her readers, 'why did I choose / The invisible, voiceless Claribel?' (14). Why not choose Miranda and her 'brave new world' as her subject? H.D. seeks newness of mind, rejuvenation, hope and inspiration for strong female character, and one expects her to plumb the scripts of Shakespeare's strong women whom she has loved. Instead, she makes a rôle for the woman whom the writer names but whom he does not imagine uttering a word, much less a refrain. Indeed, his Claribel has no authority as an actor. She neither outsmarts, claims, eschews nor raises her hand in action; in his textual fact, she cannot even act as audience in a play within a play (14–17). Unlike T. S. Eliot's *The Wasteland*, H.D.'s *By Avon River* does not repeat its introductory allusions to the lines of *The Tempest* but dwells on the woman between the lines, the woman whose wedding precipitates the shipwreck, thus the play's action, but on whom Shakespeare himself dwells hardly at all. Unlike Caliban, H.D. does not plot to destroy books and literary conventions but to overwrite them, and their plots which so often only glance at the lives of women. And doing so, she moves Claribel, on Shakespeare's periphery, to the centre of her text.

Like Eve, who introduced critical inquiry into the world by enacting her question, 'Why not eat of the Tree of Knowledge?', H.D.'s Claribel displays her 'passion for philosophy' (20). Asking questions of prelates and scholars, H.D.'s Claribel gives birth to herself beyond her name, an existence beyond that of 'emblem' and 'marriage token' (14, 22) to which Shakespeare had consigned her. Writing powerfully as a woman, H.D. demonstrates a 'vigorous and varied invasion of the sanctuaries of existing language', and thereby 'subvert[s] and transform[s] the life and literature' she inherits from Shakepeare. His name-only figure Claribel and the tempest of a tale that excludes her are 'appropriated for altered ends, the old vessel filled with new wine', as it were. Writing in this way, H.D. accesses what the poet and critic Alicia Ostriker has called material that has 'a double power. It exists or appears to exist objectively, outside the self. Because it is in public domain, it confers on the writer the sort of authority unavailable to someone who writes 'merely' of the private self.' Shakespeare's writings are 'high' culture, and have been handed 'down' to us through cultural, literary and educational authorities. Yet at the same time, his works act on individuals so that they are 'quintessentially intimate material, the stuff of dream life, forbidden desire, inexplicable motivation'. Revising his script, H.D. satisfies first her individual thirst, but in a way that ultimately makes 'cultural change possible'.[4]

By rewriting him, by overwriting, H.D. connects to her readers and her text in very personal terms, yes, but terms that are also of the public domain. Doing so, she demonstrates that 'every statue, as every person, draws out of us a different song. Therefore our songs, had we (or have we) the gift of singing, are never at a loss for some worthy object.'[5] In that, she reminds each of us that literary and cultural histories teem with Claribels. But of course those powerful women are often known only in name. H.D. gives Claribel the power of voice, and makes her capable of action. Doing so, she makes even Shakespeare himself complicit so that, authorized by H.D., he regards her Claribel as if she 'were the play, / Players and a great company' (22). Indeed, the copyright page of *By Avon River* witnesses the risks of forgetting what is in a name and haunts her text to underscore just what is at stake. Copyrighted to 'Hilda Aldington', and thus to a name acquired by her short-lived marriage, the book bears a trace of the legal authority that threatens to erase every woman's existence. Yet authorizing herself for herself and every woman who might disappear between the lines, Hilda Doolittle writes as H.D., inscribing herself on the dust-jacket, the title-page and in literary history, enacting, then, the 'laughter heard and song and history, / Unrolled further into the past, / Unrolled mysteriously / Into the future' (17). H.D. thereby exemplifies that cultural change is possible, 'When One is Three and Three are One, / The Dream, the Dreamer, and the Song' (25). When, in other words, writer, reader and text are acting as one.

THE TEMPEST
H.D.

I

Come as you will, but I came home
Driven by *The Tempest*; you may come,

With banner or the beat of the drum;
You may come with laughing friends,

Or tired, alone; you may come
In triumph, many kings have come

And queens and ladies with their lords,
To lay their lilies in this place,

Where others, known for wit and song,
Have left their laurel; you may come,

Remembering how your young love wept
With Montague long ago and Capulet.

II

I came home driven by *The Tempest*;
That was after the wedding-feast;
'Twas a sweet marriage, we are told;
And she *a paragon ... who is now queen,
And the rarest that e'er came there*;

We know little of *the king's fair daughter
Claribel*; her father was Alonso,
King of Naples, her brother, Ferdinand,
And we read later, *in one voyage
Did Claribel her husband find at Tunis*:

Claribel was outside all of this,
The Tempest came after they left her;
Read for yourself, *Dramatis Personae*.

III

Read for yourself, *Dramatis Personae*,
Alonso, Sebastian, Prospero,
Antonio, Ferdinand, Gonzalo,
Adrian, Francisco, Caliban
(Whom some call Pan),
Trinculo, Stephano, Miranda,
Ariel, Iris, Ceres, Juno;

These are the players, chiefly,
Caliban, a savage and deformed slave,
Ariel, an airy Spirit, Miranda,
The magician's lovely daughter,
The magician – ah indeed, I had forgot
Boatswain, Mariners, Nymphs and Reapers,

And among these, are other
Spirits attending on Prospero.

IV

Read through again, *Dramatis Personae*;
She is not there at all, but Claribel,
Claribel, the birds shrill, Claribel,
Claribel echoes from this rainbow-shell,
I stooped just now to gather from the sand;

Where? From an island somewhere . . .
Some say the *Sea-Adventure* set out,
(In May, 1609, to be exact)
For the new colony, Virginia;
Some say the *Sea-Adventure* ran aground
On the Bermudas; but all on board
Were saved, built new ships
And sailed on, a year later;

It is all written in an old pamphlet,
Did he read of her there, Claribel?

V

The flagship, the *Sea-Adventure*
Was one of nine ships; it bore
Sir Thomas Gates and Sir George Somers;
So the poet read, some say
Of the five hundred colonists;
(O the wind, the spray,
The birds wheeling out of the mist,
The strange birds, whistling from strange trees,
Bermuda); there was more than one pamphlet,
(The newspaper of his day),
He searched them all;
Gates, Somers – who were they?

Englishmen like himself, who felt the lure
Of the sea-ways – here we are in London –
A new court festival, a masque?
Elizabeth, our princess, is to wed
The Elector Palatine – who's that?
Frederick, I think. And where's the place –
Bohemia? I don't think so,

But anyhow it doesn't matter,
A foreign fellow is to wed our princess,
The grand-daughter of Scotland's Mary;
Occasion – compliment – another play!

VI

That was yesterday or day before yesterday;
To-day (April 23, 1945, to be exact),
We stand together; it always rains
On Shakespeare's Day, the townsfolk say,
But to-day, there is soft mist only . . .

Slowly, there are so many of us,
We pass through the churchyard gate,
And pausing wait and read old names
On the stones under our feet;
Look – there's a Lucy – O, the hunter's heart,
The hunter's stealth,
But listen to this,
He's caught at last – who?
John Shakespeare's lad – up to no good –
Sir Thomas Lucy caught him at it –
Poaching – (O feet of wind,
O soul of fire, so Lucy caught you
Stalking deer?) – poaching?

VII

He stole everything,
There isn't an original plot
In the whole of his plays;
They're scattered everywhere, hotchpotch;
A little success with the old Queen?

Well, yes – by patching up
Other men's plots and filling in
With odds and ends he called his own,
But now – he's gone back home,

And time he went;
He couldn't compete with the new wits,

New fashions – that last, he called *The Tempest*,
Was taken out of the news-sheet,
Stale news at that and best forgot,

The *Sea-Adventure* and that lot,
Gates, Somers – who are they anyway?
Or who *were* they? They'll come to no good,
(No one ever did) in that colony,
What d'you call it? Virginia?
Look at Drake, Raleigh.

VIII

Awkwardly, tenderly,
We stand with our flowers,
Separate, self-consciously,
Shyly or in child-like
Delicate simplicity;

Each one waits patiently,
Now we are near the door;
Till sudden, wondrously,
All shyness drops away,
Awkwardness, complacency;

Ring, ring and ring again,
'Twas a sweet marriage,
So they say, *my beloved is mine
And I am his*; Claribel
The chimes peel;

Claribel, the chimes say,
The king's fair daughter
Marries Tunis; O spikenard,
Myrrh and myrtle-spray,
'Twas a sweet marriage;

Tenderly, tenderly,
We stand with our flowers,
Our belovèd is ours,
Our belovèd is ours,
To-day? Yesterday?

19 Hogarth and the Canecutter

DAVID DABYDEEN

[1]

I came to Caliban in the 1980s, not through Caribbean re-inventions of the play but through William Hogarth's painting *A Scene from the Tempest*.[1] It was, and still is, perhaps the most neglected of Hogarth's major paintings, receiving a few cursory lines from art historians and next to nothing from Shakespeare scholars. Given the compartmentalization of the study of the humanities in the West, the silence of the latter is understandable. That of the former is inexplicable. Typical of the refusal to look at the painting is Mary Webster's one-liner, ignoring content altogether and making a vacuous comment on style: 'Hogarth has given himself a greater freedom of invention, which the smoother, more free-flowing paint accentuates.'[2] Lawrence Gowing ignores both content and style, giving the barest of information, then immediately looks away to someone else's art: 'the picture shows, Act I, Scene 2. Shakespeare provided a source for history painting. The subject was later adapted, probably by Hayman, for one of the decorations in the Princes' Pavilion at Vauxhall'.[3] Even Ronald Paulson, whose work on Hogarth amounts to monumental scholarship, turns a blind eye to the painting, making a cursory comment on its 'Conversation Piece' structure.[4]

Hogarth is a masterful painter of the ugly, grotesque and deformed, and Caliban is his first and finest specimen of beast. Caliban's emergence onto Hogarth's stage is utterly dramatic, his earth-coloured skin glowing against a gloomy background, lit up by desire as much as by the rich red drapery of Miranda's chair. He is half-man, half-fish, his feet webbed, his legs leprous with scales. The growth on his shoulder, like clipped or embryonic wings, suggests an inability to fly, an enslavement to the weight of his flesh. He is indeed gross in the proportions of his massive arms and legs, his swollen belly and his huge hands, one of which is clenched in rage. That he is a creature from the bowels of the earth is suggested by the snake – ancient Christian icon of sin – knotted around his burden of sticks. His evil and retaliatory nature is symbolized crudely in the white dove he stamps on, preventing it from flying. Caliban's warped intellect is indicated in the swelling on his forehead, which no doubt mirrors the swelling underneath his loincloth. Mary Webster is right in one respect: Caliban's loincloth is a masterpiece of free-flowing brushstrokes, revealing his capacity for copious ejaculation. The size and shape of the loincloth are a measure of Caliban's monstrous sexuality.

Meanwhile a cherubic Ariel flies effortlessly, serenading Prospero, Ferdinand and Miranda. If Caliban's hands curl in hatred or reach threateningly for a stick, Ariel's pluck gently at a lute's strings. If Caliban is a gargoyle, a figure from Gothic art, then Prospero, Ferdinand and Miranda are his neoclassical opposites. Ferdinand clasps his hands and bows gracefully before Miranda as before the Virgin Mary. Prospero is the picture of a venerable magus or prophet or patriarch. The wand he holds delicately contrasts with Caliban's rough-hewn phallic sticks. If Caliban is the exposed nerve of lust, the others are fully and decorously clothed. On their side of the picture lies Prospero's book, its pages open at philosophical and scientific formulations, and an armillary sphere. Neither Prospero, Ferdinand nor Miranda speak – their delicate lips are closed – for they communicate through Ariel's heavenly music. Caliban's mouth is open, exposing broken teeth and the capacity for howling and cursing.

And yet they have no vivid life, there is no drama to their presence. They could have stepped out of any of a 1,000 Renaissance paintings of the Holy Family. Any competent artist could have painted them, copying previous models. Not so Caliban. He bears on him the stamp of Hogarth's originality, which is his mastery of the degraded form. (Hogarth's only obvious nod to the past is in Caliban's Rubensesque belly.) Lewd and cackling whores, vomiting drunks and the like excited Hogarth's imagination. He despised grand historical art and religious paintings with their abstractions and well-lit, stiffly formal figures. Caliban is an extreme and mythological version of the low-life specimens he later painted, those who actually lived in the dark spaces of brothel and gaming house. The dribble escaping Caliban's mouth is Hogarth's own relishing of his self-made creature. 'This thing of darkness I acknowledge mine', he is saying, with open fervour. Hogarth's sympathy for Caliban is suggested in the coloration of his skin. A conventionally religious light falls on the Virgin-Miranda, but Caliban is lit in a complex way. The monotony of Miranda's porcelain whiteness contrasts with the rich terracotta texturing of

William Hogarth, *A Scene from the Tempest* (*c.*1735).

Caliban's skin. The effect of richness is created by hints of golden hues. His deformed forehead, for instance, gleams like a nugget of gold. The scales on his leg are like chipped and loosened gold leaf. The gilded tassel hanging from the gilded shoulder of Miranda's chair (or throne) echoes Caliban's colour. Caliban is primeval earth, but seamed with gold, such as Ralegh hoped to discover in Guiana.

As to Caliban's lack of intellect, his inability to fly, the faggot he bears explains all. He is simply weighed down by Prospero's cruelty. On reflection, the crushed dove, its wings splayed in aborted flight, signals Caliban's own condition. Caliban stamps upon the dove, not in a gesture of innate cruelty, but to signify (since he has none of Prospero's language in which to address Prospero) the crushing force of Europe.

Caliban's capacity for fine feeling, such as evoked by Ariel's lute, is suggested in his prominent and exaggerated ear, the duct of which is echoed in the shape of his exposed navel and in the shape of the aperture made by his clenched hand.

Be not afeard, the isle is full of noises,
Sounds, and sweet airs, that give delight and hurt not.
Sometimes a thousand twangling instruments
Will hum about mine ears; and sometime voices,
That if I then had wak'd after long sleep,
Will make me sleep again . . . (III.ii.133–8)

It is Caliban who is open-eared to Ariel's celestial music, even as enslavement to Prospero makes him open-mouthed in protest and pain (as in the beak of the squashed dove).

Prospero and Ferdinand are, by contrast, closed to the redemptive possibilities of music, even as it is being played to them, and for them. Hogarth, famous for the most careful deployment of detail, covers over their ears with thick hair. Only Miranda's ear is noticeably exposed, Hogarth making a subtle connection between her and Caliban. Her ear is tilted in Caliban's direction, as if the two are connected by Ariel's gentle music but also by Caliban's anguished cry. Ronald Paulson asserts that

> If Miranda is the protagonist, Hogarth has arranged the composition
> to emphasise the contrast between her true lover and her pseudo-lover
> Caliban, who weaves fantasies of raping her, and the structure of
> choice is here a true and not a parody one, since all indications point
> to Miranda's making the proper judgement.[5]

Paulson is wrong. On close inspection, all indications point to Miranda's suspension of judgement. In moral terms Miranda is equidistant between Ferdinand and Caliban but a trick of perspective makes her appear, in spatial terms, closer to Caliban. Her gesture in holding up her hand in protest is as much aimed at Ferdinand as it is at Caliban: her thumb beckons towards Ferdinand but her little finger points towards Caliban. Her other hand fumbles and spills the liquid being fed to the (Christian) lamb, the spillage echoing in pointed detail the escape of spittle from Caliban's mouth. Typically, spillage in Hogarth's art signifies sexual desire: here, Miranda is as aroused by Ferdinand's presence as Caliban is aroused by hers. Miranda's ambivalent sexuality is suggested in the detail of her exposed ankle and feet (her gown is deliberately upturned), which endow her with a certain coquetry. Such nakedness, echoed in her half-exposed breast, allies her with Caliban as it distances her from her garbed suitor. Her feet are pointed in the direction of Ferdinand as if out of heightened desire, even as her hand protests such desire. Miranda then is not the bland or conventional Virgin she appears to be, Hogarth endowing her with ambivalent character. Caliban is the embodiment of her sexual desire. She is an 'open book', unlike Prospero's book which lies open at her feet but which paradoxically contains knowledge of how to imprison and enslave. On reflection, Prospero's elegant wand is more sinister than Caliban's crude sticks. Miranda is caught between a honey-tongued Prospero fingering his wand and Caliban wielding curse and cudgel. The structure of the painting makes no neat divisions between Caliban, Prospero, Ferdinand, Miranda and Ariel. Spatially they are distributed within the painting in a series of overlapping structures. The upright triangle of Ariel, Ferdinand and Miranda overlaps the upturned triangle of Ariel, Miranda and Caliban as well as the upturned triangle of Prospero, Miranda and Caliban, such patterning reflecting Hogarth's sense of the complex moral connections between the various characters.

[2]

My preliminary comments should suggest that a complete dissertation can be written on the painting, relating it to the iconography of Caliban in European, Latin American and Caribbean art. My doctoral dissertation on William Hogarth (University College, London, 1982) made the briefest of comment on the *Tempest* painting. I limited myself to making a connection between Caliban and the black man in Hogarth's *Marriage à la mode*. At the time of my doctoral dissertation I was writing poems that were eventually published in two collections, *Slave Song* (1984) and *Coolie Odyssey* (1987). My response to Hogarth's *Tempest*, unspoken in the dissertation, was fleshed out in poetry. Why? I don't know, but perhaps it was a youthful feeling, excited by too much reading of the Romantics, that academic prose 'murders to dissect', and that Hogarth's complex art demanded poetic utterance.

What my poetry does is to echo the moral ambivalence in his painting by presenting the mistress of the plantation as being simultaneously virginal and voracious. In 'The Canecutters' Song' she watches the nakedness and ardour of the canecutters, repelled and seduced by their squalor. In 'Nightmare' she is terrorized by the dream of rape and ritual humiliation, yet 'wet she awake, cuss de daybreak'; that is, she curses the *aubade* tradition which imprisons her in virtuousness. Of course I have been soundly whipped by male and female critics (Benita Parry foremost!) for seeming to say that women secretly want to be possessed and mutilated in the mud.[6] By and large I have taken my chastisement silently, since to yelp is to apologize for what I have written, and I am genuinely unsure as to whether there are grounds for apology. The deeper vision in *Slave Song* and *Coolie Odyssey* is of the possibility of tenderness between Miranda and Caliban, between the oppressor's daughter and the broken slave (see 'Miranda' on the page opposite). Here the sun is Prospero, the tyrant enlightenment, the incandescence of the branding iron.

As to the canecutters I depict them as foul-mouthed, aggressively obscene, wielding their cocks like cutlasses. And yet they are no more than Hogarth's squashed dove, expressions of stunted and frustrated love. Their true desire is not to rape Miranda and people the isle with mulatto monsters, but simply the freedom to dream of the possibilities of romance (that is, love and poetry):

> White hooman walk tru de field fo watch we canecutta,
> Tall, straight, straang-limb,
> Hair sprinkle in de wind like gold-duss,
> Lang lace frack loose on she bady like bamboo-flag,
> An flesh mo dan hibiscus early maan, white an saaf an wet
> Flowering in she panty.[7]

What I wanted my canecutters to do was to aspire to and arrive at lyrical words, their final emancipation from Prospero's definition of them as grunting brutes and people without a literature.

MIRANDA

His black bony peasant body
Stalk of blighted cane
In dry earth.

I will blot out the tyrant sun
Cleanse you in the raincloud of my body
In the secrecy of night set you supple and erect.

And wiped him with the moist cloth of her tongue
Like a new mother licking clean its calf
And hugged milk from her breast to his cracked mouth.

That when he woke he cried to dream again
Of the scent of her maternity
The dream of the moon of her deep spacious eye

Sea-blue and bountiful
Beyond supplication or conquest
A frail slave vessel wracked upon a mere pebble of her promise.

And the sun resumed its cruelty
And the sun shook with imperial glee
At the fantasy.

David Dabydeen, from *Turner: New and Selected Poems* (London, 1994), p. 51.

Envoy

Envoy (f. OF envoy {mod. envoi} . . . f. phrase en voie on the way)
Sending forth.

The action of sending forth a poem; hence, the concluding part
of a poetical or prose composition; the author's parting words;
a dedication, postscript . . . (*Oxford English Dictionary*)

'The Word – In the Beginning'

MERLE COLLINS

But why Caliban? We're talking about literature from the Caribbean,
about writers who often have an anti-colonial perspective. So why
this privileging of Shakespeare, literary giant of the colonial over-
lords? Why The Tempest? Can't we find another, anti-colonial frame?

These were the kinds of questions coming from one of my Caribbean
literature classes. We were talking about *The Tempest* and its influences on
the shaping of a critical dialogue on Caribbean literature. Many
Caribbean writers have found intersections between their own work and
the themes of *The Tempest*. It is part of probing the psychological shaping
of an arguably postcolonial Caribbean. Caribbean writer George Lamming
has written about his perceptions in *The Pleasures of Exile* (1960) and his 1971
novel, *Water with Berries*, takes its title from *The Tempest*. Caliban states that
Prospero, when he first arrived on his island, had given him (Caliban)
water with berries to eat:

> When thou cam'st first,
> Thou strok'st me and made much of me; wouldst give me
> Water with berries in't, and teach me how
> To name the bigger light and how the less . . . (I.ii.332–5)

Lamming notes that Caliban recalls this as he is experiencing Prospero's
mistreatment. Caliban is enraged because he considers that he has

welcomed Prospero, educated him about the island and to some extent also welcomed the exchange between them. According to Lamming, as he considered the matter of Caliban's response to Prospero's peculiar gifts, 'the whole question has always been raised for (him) of the rôle of language as a gift.'[1]

In that encounter, he feels, Caliban received not only words, but 'language as symbolic interpretation, as instrument for exploring consciousness. Once he had accepted language as such, the future of his development, however independent it was, would always in some way be inextricably tied up with that pioneering aspect of Prospero. Caliban at some stage would have to find a way of breaking that contract, which got sealed by language, in order to restructure some alternative reality for himself.'[2] In *Water with Berries*, Lamming claims to be trying to reverse the journeys, so that Caliban is in the role of visitor to Prospero's island. The characters in *Water with Berries* visit and discover the reality of Prospero's land first-hand. So that the journey and the experiences consequent upon the journey become part of the disintegration of an idea. I am fascinated by this theme of the journey and of the role of language. Like my students, one might well ask, why use *The Tempest* as a point of departure at all? But that is as easy (or as difficult) a question as: Why speak English? The response is a history lesson. English, Lamming claims, is a West Indian language and it's up to the West Indian what he does with it.

All of those connections leave me very interested in the theme of the journey and, untiringly, in the theme of language. These are some reasons that the two 'The Word' poems presented here will be at the beginning of a forthcoming collection, *Lady in a Boat*. They beg the question, or hopefully move some way towards answering the question: what have been the shaping influences informing how the essence of (my) Caribbean experience is expressed? What forces have helped me to name the bigger light, and the less? My grade school teacher encouraged me to approach this naming using methods she had also been taught to employ. Her first 'R,' Reading, emphasized, among other things, the tight quatrains of the ballad form and the narrative poetry which I found attractive perhaps partly because what was considered the more everyday, less academic culture, also emphasised narrative(s):

> I met a little cottage Girl:
> She was eight years old, she said;
> Her hair was thick with many a curl
> That clustered round her head.
> (from William Wordsworth, 'We are Seven')[3]

My first 'The Word' poem might be described as my 'Water with berries' poem, remembering the kinds of naming in the *Royal Readers*, a near-regurgitation of *something* of the form of the ingested water with berries. The second, 'The Word – In the Beginning (2)' represents early attempts to break that contract and move also – though not necessarily exclusively – to other modes of expression. It re-presents formulations and ideas used in my first novel, *Angel*. But it is about more than form. It emphasises the Grenadian Creole language, but it also suggests the importance of understanding a way of being which is not the way of Prospero's *Royal Reader*. The two poems together are meant to emphasize, not an anguished rebuttal that may be thought to be Caliban's cry of rejection, but a consideration of the differing approaches of this double inheritance which, valued according to a hierarchical system by academia then and now, are both parts of my double inheritance.

THE WORD – IN THE BEGINNING (1)

In the beginning, a schoolhouse crouched
at the curve of one craggy hilltop
Lenorice, teacher, tall, tough, remote
and parents reaching for the commandments

Twice times tables, the bumpy brown ground
under the tree, chant of ABC
the long wooden bench, the shouted word
Royal Reader Book One, Book Two, Three

Chanted poetry, The Rain *lesson*
Spider and the Fly, The Beggar Man
wailing stories, The Lost Child
The Child's First Grief, The Better Land

Chattering, The Parrot in Exile
eyes on The dog at his master's grave
story time with Meddlesome Matty
poem story. Chant. We are seven

Evening time come, word leave mountain top
racing down from Teacher's nutmeg trees
at the curve of that craggy hilltop
In front, the valley. Beyond, the seas.

THE WORD – IN THE BEGINNING (2)

In the beginning, a little house facing the road
sitting down in the crooked elbow of a hill
cousins, uncles, aunts, macomeres slowing down to call out
How thing going? Sa ki fèt. You holding on? Child, God is love
We making it. God don't give more than you can handle
Papa God make he world uneven. Watch the fingers of yu hand
Gadé. You see how all of them different length? But never mind
The next generation to raise we nose. You talk to Teacher yet?

Oh you buy reading book. They know the ABC and their numbers already?
God don't sleeping. Pu them in Teacher hand. Teacher going shape them up
So macomere what not happening? Ay! Come come come
You don't know what I hear down the road this selfsame morning?
Come, siddown by here little bit let me tell you the story
I won't take up too much of yu time. I know master work waiting

Child, go and pick up yu reading book

She could hear too much, you know. Palé Patwa
Ou ba konnet . . .? Eh! When I hear I say, èmbè oui!
Sit down, sit down, sit down let me pinch you
this thing. Ay!
Wéspé. Wéspé. Wait.

You reading yu book, Madam?

References

PREFACE

1 For a good sense of what such 'translatability' entails, see Sanford Budick and Wolfgang Iser, eds, *The Translatability of Cultures: Figurations of the Space Between*, (Stanford, 1996); for a useful survey of the play's movements, see Virginia Mason Vaughan and Alden T. Vaughan, 'Introduction: *The Tempest* Transformed', in their *Critical Essays on Shakespeare's 'The Tempest'* (New York, 1998), pp. 1–14.

2 Russell Hoban, 'Some Episodes in the History of Miranda and Caliban', in *The Moment Under the Moment* (London, 1992), p. 83.

3 *Caliban*, ed. and with an introduction by Harold Bloom (New York, 1992), p. 1.

4 This term has become increasingly prominent in *Tempest* criticism. See, for instance, Rob Nixon, 'Caribbean and African Appropriations of *The Tempest*', *Critical Inquiry*, 13 (1987), pp. 557–78; Michael Dobson, '"Remember / First to possess his books": The Appropriation of *The Tempest*, 1700–1800', *Shakespeare Survey*, 43 (1991), pp. 99–107; Lemuel A. Johnson, *Shakespeare in Africa (and Other Venues): Import and the Appropriation of Culture* (Trenton, 1998); Thomas Cartelli, *Repositioning Shakespeare: National Formations, Postcolonial Appropriations* (London, 1999).

5 Jean Marsden, ed., *The Appropriation of Shakespeare: Post-Renaissance Reconstruction of the Works and the Myth* (London, 1991), p. 1.

6 Stephen Orgel, Introduction to the Oxford edition of *The Tempest* (Oxford, 1987), pp. 64–76; Dobson, 'The Appropriation of *The Tempest*', p. 101.

7 Orgel, Introduction, p. 11.

8 Nigel Wood is one of those who sees the play's gaps as 'deliberate' (Nigel Wood, ed., 'Introduction' to *The Tempest*, Buckingham, 1995, p. 1). José Antonio Maravall has drawn attention to the play's affinities with a Baroque aesthetic that preferred the suggestive and the unfinished ('The Technique of Incompleteness', in *Culture of the Baroque: Analysis of a Historical Structure*, trans. Terry Cochran, Minneapolis, 1986, pp. 207–24). W. H. Auden, on the other hand, simply felt that 'Shakespeare really left it in a mess' (cited by John Fuller in *W. H. Auden: A Commentary*, London, 1998, p. 357).

I LOCAL KNOWLEDGE

INTRODUCTION

1 See Stephen Orgel, Introduction to the Oxford edition of *The Tempest* (Oxford, 1987), for a concise performance and publication history (pp. 1–4, 56–64).

2 On *The Tempest* as a ritual response to the annual descent into winter, see John Bender, 'The Day of *The Tempest*', *ELH*, 47 (1980), pp. 235–58. On the possible relevance of the royal wedding, see Orgel, Introduction, pp. 30–31; David Bergeron, *Shakespeare's Romances and the Royal Family* (Lawrence, 1985); David Scott Kastan, '"The Duke of Milan / And His Brave Son": Dynastic Politics in *The Tempest*', in Virginia Mason Vaughan and Alden T. Vaughan, eds, *Critical Essays on Shakespeare's 'The Tempest'* (New York, 1998), pp. 91–103.

3 Douglas Bruster, 'Local Tempest: Shakespeare and the Work of the Early Modern Playhouse', *Journal of Medieval and Renaissance Studies*, 25 (1995), pp. 33–53.

4 Glynne Wickham, 'Masque and Anti-Masque in *The Tempest*', *Essays & Studies*, n.s. 28 (1975), pp. 1–14.

5 Curt Breight, '"Treason doth never prosper": *The Tempest* and the Discourse of Treason', *Shakespeare Quarterly*, 41 (1990), pp. 1–28; cf. Frances E. Dolan, 'The Subordinate('s) Plot: Petty Treason and the Forms of Domestic Rebellion', *Shakespeare Quarterly*, 43 (1992), pp. 317–40.

6 Paul Brown, '"This thing of darkness I acknowledge mine": *The Tempest* and the Discourse of Colonialism', in Jonathan Dollimore and Alan Sinfield, eds, *Political Shakespeare: New Essays in Cultural Materialism* (Manchester, 1985), pp. 48–71.

7 Terence Hawkes, *That Shakespeherian Rag: Essays on a Critical Process* (London, 1986), p. 3.

8 See David Baker, 'Where is Ireland in *The Tempest*', in Mark Thornton Burnett and Ramona Wray, eds, *Shakespeare and Ireland* (New York, 1997), pp. 68–88; Barbara Fuchs, 'Conquering Islands: Contextualizing *The Tempest*', *Shakespeare Quarterly*, 48 (1997), pp. 45–62, esp. 46–54.

9 W. B. Whall, *Shakespeare's Sea Terms Explained* (London, 1910), p. 95.

10 Cf. Margaret Tudeau-Clayton, 'Shaking Neptune's "dread trident": *The Tempest* and Figures of Virgil', in her *Jonson, Shakespeare and Early Modern Virgil* (Cambridge, 1998), chap. 6.

11 Julie Robin Solomon, 'Going Places: Absolutism and Movement in *The Tempest*', *Renaissance Drama*, n.s. 22 (1991), pp. 3–45.

12 John Gillies, *Shakespeare and the Geography of Difference* (Cambridge, 1994), pp. 45–9.

13 See John Gillies's introduction to John Gillies and Virginia Mason Vaughan, eds, *Playing the Globe: Genre and Geography in English Renaissance Drama*, (Madison, NJ, 1998); Jerry Brotton, *Trading Territories: Mapping the Early Modern World* (London, 1997).

14 See Orgel, Introduction, pp. 32, 62–3. The connection between *The Tempest* and the Bermuda pamphlets was first proposed by Edmond Malone in 1808: it excited little attention at the time, but is now generally accepted, and Strachey's letter is often reproduced in editions of the play (it is Appendix B in Orgel's edition).

15 See his earlier article, 'Shakespeare's Indian: The Americanization of Caliban', *Shakespeare Quarterly*, 39/2 (1988), pp. 137–53.

16 Frances A. Yates argued that Prospero was not only based on Dee but used by Shakespeare to defend Dee's reputation; see her 'Prospero: The Shakespearean Magus', in *The Occult Philosophy in the Elizabethan Age* (London, 1979), pp. 160–61. For critiques of Yates's argument, see William H. Sherman, *John Dee: The Politics of Reading and Writing in the English Renaissance* (Amherst, 1995); Barbara A. Mowat, 'Prospero, Agrippa, and Hocus Pocus', *ELR*, 11 (1981), pp. 281–303. In new research presented at the conference connected to this book, Mowat proposed an alternative source for Prospero's magic (and a new candidate for 'Prospero's Book') in medieval and Renaissance 'grimoires', or manuals for invoking spirits and enforcing their service.

17 Robert Grudin makes a case for Drebbel (and Emperor Rudolf II, who employed

both Drebbel and Dee) in 'Rudolf II of Prague and Cornelis Drebbel – Shakespearean Archetypes', *Huntington Library Quarterly*, 54/3 (1991), pp. 181–205.

18 Jennifer Drake-Brockman, 'The *Perpetuum Mobile* of Cornelis Drebbel', in W. D. Hackmann and A. J. Turner, eds, *Learning, Language and Invention: Essays Presented to Francis Maddison* (Aldershot, 1994), p. 125.

19 Geoffrey Bullough, *Narrative and Dramatic Sources of Shakespeare*, vol. 8 (London, 1975), p. 250.

20 William W. E. Slights, 'A Source for *The Tempest* and the Context of the *Discorsi*', *Shakespeare Quarterly*, 36 (1985), pp. 68–70.

21 E. H. Gombrich, '"My library was dukedom large enough": Shakespeare's Prospero and Prospero Visconti of Milan', in Edward Chaney and Peter Mack, eds, *England and the Continental Renaissance: Essays in Honour of J. B. Trapp* (Woodbridge, 1990), pp. 185–90.

22 Henry James, 'Introduction to *The Tempest*', in *Shakespeare's 'The Tempest'*, a casebook edited by D. J. Palmer (London, 1991), pp. 67–81.

23 Vaughan and Vaughan, *Shakespeare's Caliban*, p. 103. Cf. Michael Dobson, '"Remember / First to Posses His Books": The Appropriation of *The Tempest*, 1700–1800', *Shakespeare Survey*, 43 (1991), pp. 99–107; Trevor R. Griffiths, '"This Island's mine": Caliban and Colonialism', *Yearbook of English Studies*, 13 (1983), pp. 159–80. For the sharp political relevance of Fuseli's striking engraving of a scene from *The Tempest*, see the essays by Marcia Pointon and Grant F. Scott in Walter Paper and Frederick Burwick, eds, *The Boydell Shakespeare Gallery*, (Bottrop, 1996), pp. 103–12, 113–24.

24 Jonathan Bate calls Hazlitt's response a reading against the grain, which he distinguishes from a misreading, furnishing us 'with an account of *The Tempest* as an affair of imperialism and power politics' (*Shakespearean Constitutions: Politics, Theatre, Criticism, 1730–1830*, Oxford, 1989, p. 179), though Hazlitt's 'defence' of Caliban is in fact a parody of the arguments to legitimacy brought forward on behalf of the Bourbons rather than a forerunner of postcolonial readings.

25 Vaughan and Vaughan, *Shakespeare's Caliban*, pp. 191–2, 197.

'THE GREAT GLOBE ITSELF' (IV.1.153)

1 Helen Wallis, *Sir Francis Drake: An Exhibition to Commemorate Francis Drake's Voyage around the World, 1577–1580* (London, 1977), pp. 80–81.

2 John Gillies, *Shakespeare and the Geography of Difference* (Cambridge, 1994), *passim*.

1 CRYSTAL BARTOLOVICH: 'BASELESS FABRIC': LONDON AS A 'WORLD CITY'

1 Andrew Sullivan, 'There Will Always Be An England', *New York Times Magazine*, 21 February 1999, pp. 39–45, 54, 70–73, 78–9. The phrase cited is the article's teaser on the cover.

2 Sullivan, 'England', p. 40.

3 *Ibid.*, p. 79.

4 Roland Robertson, *Globalization: Social Theory and Global Culture* (London, 1992), p. 6.

5 The escalator image is borrowed from Raymond Williams, *The Country and the City* (New York, 1973), pp. 9–12.

6 David Harvey, 'Globalization in Question', *Rethinking Marxism*, 8/4 (1995), pp. 1–17. Major early modern cities were linked in what Lawrence Manley, in *Literature and*

Culture in Early Modern London (Cambridge, 1995), calls a 'transnational grid' (p. 136), but these links were hardly the instantaneous, computer- and media-facilitated, advanced capitalized connections of today.

7 *Spectator*, 19 May 1711. Addison's (and Steele's) journalistic essays on The Exchange are conveniently collected in *The Royal Exchange*, ed. Ann Saunders (London, 1997), pp. 206–8. The passage cited appears on p. 206.

8 Cf. Vanessa Harding, 'Early Modern London 1550–1700', *London Journal*, 20/2 (1995), pp. 34–45.

9 Cicero complained, for example, of the 'degeneration' of Greek cities which 'receive[d] a mixture of strange languages and customs, and import[ed] foreign ways as well as foreign merchandise, so that none of their ancestral institutions can possibly remain unchanged'. He did not, however, see this as at all as a generalized world condition – and certainly not as one which could be simply taken for granted, as in the Dekker passage cited below. See *The Republic*, trans. Clinton Keyes, Loeb Classical Library (Cambridge, 1961), p. 117.

10 Thomas Dekker, *The Black Rod: and the White Rod* (London, 1630), in F. P. Wilson, ed., *The Plague Pamphlets of Thomas Dekker* (Oxford, 1925), p. 199.

11 Roy Porter, *London: A Social History* (Cambridge, 1995), p. 42.

12 See Theodore Rabb, *Enterprise and Empire* (Cambridge, 1967); Robert Brenner, *Merchants and Revolution: Commercial Change, Political Conflict, and London's Overseas Traders, 1550–1653* (Princeton, NJ, 1993). Within the 'transition debate' in Western Marxism, the rôle of 'trade' has been much contested. Its major advocate has been 'world-systems'-orientated theorists, who argue that 'the distinction between "trade" and "production" is not as clear-cut as it is often assumed to be' (Giovanni Arrighi, *The Long Twentieth Century*, London and New York, 1994, p. 177). The question remains, however, to what extent 'trade' involves the extraction of 'surplus value' through relations of exploitation as typically understood by Marxism. For a discussion of some of these issues with a focus on the early modern period, see Alan K. Smith, *Creating a World Economy: Merchant Capital, Colonialism, and World Trade 1400–1825* (Boulder, 1991).

13 Henry Fitzgeffrey, *Certain Elegies, Done by Sundrie Excellent Wits* (London, 1620), excerpted in A. M. Nagler, ed., *A Source Book in Theatrical History* (New York, 1952), pp. 138–140.

14 Edmund Spenser, *The Shepherd's Calendar* (New York, 1932), p. 5.

15 John Earle, *Microcosmography* (1633), excerpted in Alexander M. Witherspoon and Frank J. Warnke, eds, *Seventeenth-century Prose and Poetry, Second Edition* (Fort Worth, 1982), p. 315.

16 John Lyly, 'Midas', in R. Warwick Bond, ed., *The Complete Works of John Lyly, III* (Oxford, 1902), p. 115.

17 Donald Lupton, *London and the Country Carbanadoed*, in Saunders, *The Royal Exchange*, p. 98.

18 Thomas Platter, 'Travels in England in 1599', in *The Journals of Two Travellers* (London, 1995), p. 32. On tobacco, see Jeffrey Knapp, *An Empire Nowhere* (Berkeley, 1992), chap. 4; Douglas Bruster, *Drama and the Market in the Age of Shakespeare* (Cambridge, 1992), chap. 6.

19 Platter, 'Travels', pp. 35–6.

20 Wa[lter] Hamond, *A Paradox* (London, 1640), fol. 2r.

21 In *A Paradox*, Hamond applauds the inhabitants of Madagascar for not being 'contaminated with the vices and evill customes of strangers' (fol. 2r), as the English, from his perspective, most manifestly are.

22 Thomas Dekker, *The Gull's Hornbook* (London, 1609), excerpted in Nagler, *Source Book*, p. 133.

23 John Dryden, 'Prologue' to Aphra Behn's *The Widow Ranter*, in *Oroonoko, the Rover and Other Works*, ed. Janet Todd (London, 1992), p. 251.

24 Platter, *Journals*, p. 31.

25 Thomas Heywood, *If You Know Not Me, You Know Nobody: The Dramatic Works of Thomas Heywood, I* (New York, 1964), p. 254.

26 See Jean-Christophe Agnew, *Worlds Apart: The Market and the Theater in Anglo-American Thought, 1550–1750* (Cambridge, 1985). For a critique of the market/theatre linkage in Agnew and others, see Scott Cutler Shershow, 'Idols of the Marketplace: Rethinking the Economic Determination of Renaissance Drama', *Renaissance Drama*, n.s. 26 (1995), pp. 1–27.

27 A recent consideration of the location problem is David Baker's 'Where is Ireland in *The Tempest*', in Mark Thornton Burnett and Ramona Wray, eds, *Shakespeare and Ireland* (New York, 1997), pp. 68–88. In this essay, Baker advances the thesis that *The Tempest* 'is the result of Shakespeare's sustained meditation on the "connecting links" among, and the exchanges between, several (not entirely distinct) places in the early modern period . . . [W]hat it is "about" . . . is a dynamic relation between places, three places on the globe that Shakespeare knew: America, England and Ireland' (pp. 68–9). In his emphasis on the interconnection of places, we are at one; in his focus on authorial intention and his narrowing of the places the play is 'about' to three (Africa is most notably absent), we differ markedly.

28 Roberto Fernández Retamar, *Caliban and Other Essays*, trans. Edward Baker (Minneapolis, 1989), p. 8; Stephen Greenblatt, *Shakespearean Negotiations: The Circulation of Social Energy in Renaissance England* (Berkeley, 1988), p. 154.

29 Knapp, *Empire*, p. 7.

30 Anthony Giddens, *The Consequences of Modernity* (Stanford, 1990), p. 18.

31 Giddens, *Consequences*, p. 1. He differentiates himself from theorists such as Immanuel Wallerstein by suggesting that modernity is not an effect of capitalism alone, but rather is multiply determined by the 'nation-state system', the 'world military order' the 'international division of labor', as well as the 'world capitalist economy' on which world systems theory has often focused (pp. 65–78). One significant problem with his view of 'disembedding', however, is that he sees it as primarily affecting Europe, whereas it has characterized non-European sites as well (see Antonio Benitez-Rojo,*The Repeating Island: The Carribbean and the Postmodern Perspective*, Durham, NC, 1992).

32 Fredric Jameson, 'Cognitive Mapping', in Cary Nelson and Lawrence Grossberg, eds, *Marxism and the Interpretation of Culture* (Urbana and Chicago, 1988), p. 349. It should be noted that Jameson situates the change significantly later – with nineteenth-century European imperialism – a timeline with which I obviously take issue here.

33 In the course of her critique of them, Meredith Skura produces a good bibliography of the early 'colonial' readings of the play: 'Discourse and the Individual: The Case of Colonialism in *The Tempest*', *Shakespeare Quarterly*, 40 (1989), pp. 42–69, esp. 42, n. 1. A number of other such readings have emerged since her article was published, many of which focus on the interest of 'postcolonial' writers on the play. What these readings draw attention to is the possibility of a reverse movement or pressure to colonial conquest as peoples in formerly colonized countries 'write back', and reinscribe, literatures that Europe has claimed exclusively for itself. One of the implications for 'colonial' readings suggested by my own 'inter-

mixture' emphasis is that a focus on this counter-force needs to go back to remote origins. We need to examine the transformation not only of the colonies but of the so-called metropole, both as a result of and following the encounter.

34 Skura, 'Discourse ', p. 47. She is only able to make this claim by ignoring the 'internal colonialism' of Britain; most seriously, she apparently does not consider Ireland to have been colonized in any sense. On 'internal colonialism', see Michael Hechter, *Internal Colonialism: The Celtic Fringe in British National Development* (Berkeley, 1975).

35 Skura, 'Discourse', p. 67.

36 Fran Dolan, 'The Subordinate('s) Plot: Petty Treason and the Forms of Domestic Rebellion', *Shakespeare Quarterly*, 43 (1992), pp. 317–69.

37 Douglas Bruster, 'Local *Tempest*: Shakespeare and the Work of the Early Modern Playhouse', *Journal of Medieval and Renaissance Studies*, 25/1 (1995), pp. 33–53.

38 Sigmund Freud, 'The "Uncanny"', in *The Standard Edition of the Complete Psychological Works of Sigmund Freud*, XVII, trans. James Strachey (London, 1955), p. 241.

39 Karl Marx, *Capital*, I, trans. Ben Fowkes (London, 1990), p. 165.

40 All references to Duffett's play come from Ronald DiLorenzo, ed., *Three Burlesque Plays of Thomas Duffett* (Iowa City, 1972), pp. 57–145, and will be noted parenthetically in my text.

41 Gonzalo refers in passing to 'the merchant' (II.i.5) when attempting to cheer up Antonio by pointing out that while shipwrecks are common, surviving them is not – and (following Montaigne) he bans 'traffic' from his utopian commonwealth (II.i.146). Trinculo later muses about how much money he could make from displaying Caliban (significantly, in England); additionally, references to Caliban as 'slave' call up certain trade relationships, though they are not emphasized in the play (Prospero does not 'buy' Caliban). Commerce is simply not a major, explicit theme.

42 Freud notes that 'a great deal that is not uncanny in fiction (i.e. does not produce anxiety) would be so if it happened in real life' and suggests that humour is one of the strategies literature employs to undermine the usual emotional response to 'uncanny' material (Freud, 'Uncanny', p. 249).

43 The two plays are associated because of what is read as a reference to Shakespeare's play in Jonson's: 'If there be never a servant-monster in the Fair, who can help it? he says; nor a nest of antics? He is loth to make nature afraid in his plays, like those that beget *Tales*, *Tempests*, and such like drolleries . . .' (Induction.136–9). All references to this text are from Russell A. Fraser and Norman Rabkin, eds, *Drama of the English Renaissance II: The Stuart Period* (New York, 1976), pp. 191–239, and will be cited parenthetically in my text.

44 In their discussion of *Bartholomew Fair*, Peter Stallybrass and Allon White have reminded us that fairs are irreducibly sites of inter-mixing and hybridity, social and spatial. Men and women, masters and servants, and all the rest of the socially high and low come into a proximity that threatens to expose the instability and constructed quality of all socially imposed categories and spaces. See *The Politics and Poetics of Transgression* (Ithaca, 1986), chap. 1. More recently, Shannon Miller has called attention to the way in which the expansion of the market is figured in *Bartholomew Fair* through the 'grotesque' body of women; see her 'Consuming Mothers/Consuming Merchants: The Carnivalesque Economy of Jacobean City Comedy', *Modern Language Studies*, 26/2–3 (1996), pp. 73–98.

45 Not unlike E. E. Stoll's interpretation of the reference to the 'vexed Bermoothes' in *The Tempest*, famously dismissed by him (in the course of his refutation of the

New World reading of the play) as 'once barely mentioned as faraway places, like Tokio or Mandalay' ('Certain Fallacies and Irrelevancies in the Literary Scholarship of the Day', *Studies in Philology*, 24, 1927, p. 487).

46 Henry Peachum, *The Art of Living in London* (London, 1642), excerpted in Lawrence Manley, *London in the Age of Shakespeare: An Anthology* (University Park and London, 1986), p. 205.

47 Christopher Pye, 'The Theater, the Market, and the Subject of History', *ELH*, 61 (1994), pp. 501–22.

48 As Marx put it, 'just when they appear to be engaged in the revolutionary transformation of themselves and their material surroundings, in the creation of something which does not yet exist . . . they timidly conjure up the spirits of the past to help them' ('The Eighteenth Brumaire of Louis Bonaparte', trans. Ben Fowkes, in *Surveys from Exile*, Harmondsworth, 1973, p. 146).

49 John Donne's version from 'An Anatomy of the World' (which, like *The Tempest*, dates from 1611) mourns: 'Tis all in pieces, all coherence gone;/ All just supply, and all relation:/ Prince, subject, father, son, are things forgot,/ For every man alone thinks that he hath got/ To be a phoenix, and that there can be/ None of that kind, of which he is, but he' (A. L. Clements, ed., *John Donne's Poetry*, New York, 1966, p. 73).

50 O.E.D. While 'fabric' connotes textiles in modern usage, its definition was much broader in the early modern period, and the word was often associated with exactly the sort of built environment Prospero refers to in the ensuing lines of his speech: 'towers', 'palaces', and 'temples' – buildings that call to mind a major city, such as London, with its 'great [G]lobe' (as Bruster and others have argued).

51 'The new global cultural economy has to be seen as a complex, overlapping, disjunctive order that cannot any longer be understood in terms of existing center-periphery models (even those that might account for multiple centers and peripheries)' (Arjun Appadurai, *Modernity at Large: Cultural Dimensions of Globalization*, Minneapolis, 1996, p. 32).

52 Donald Lupton, *London and the Countrey Carbanadoed* (London, 1632), in Manley, *London*, p. 46.

53 As Frantz Fanon evocatively put it, 'European opulence is literally scandalous, for it has been founded on slavery, it has been nourished with the blood of slaves and it comes directly from the soil and from the subsoil of that underdeveloped world. The well-being and the progress of Europe have been built up with the sweat and the dead bodies of Negroes, Arabs, Indians, and the yellow races' (*The Wretched of the Earth*, trans. Constance Farrington, New York, 1963, p. 96).

2 BARBARA A. MOWAT: 'KNOWING I LOVED MY BOOKS': READING *THE TEMPEST* INTERTEXTUALLY

1 *The Tempest* is not alone among Shakespeare's plays, of course, in featuring the book. *Hamlet* and *Cymbeline* call for books as props; in *Titus Andronicus*, a schoolboy copy of Ovid's *Metamorphoses* plays an integral part in the plot; and *Pericles* openly links its stage action to the book that lies behind its story. But no play by Shakespeare gestures toward the book as pervasively and as importantly as does *The Tempest*.

2 Peter Greenaway, *Prospero's Books: A Film of Shakespeare's 'The Tempest'* (New York, 1991), p. 17.

3 Ralph G. Williams, 'I Shall Be Spoken: Textual Boundaries, Authors, and Intent',

in G. Bornstein and R. G. Williams, eds, *Palimpsest* (Ann Arbor, 1993), pp. 45–66, esp. p. 49.

4 See Claes Schaar, 'Linear Sequence, Spatial Structure, Complex Sign, and Vertical Context System', *Poetics*, 7 (1978), pp. 377–400; and *The Full Voic'd Quire Below: Vertical Context Systems in 'Paradise Lost'* (Lund, 1982), esp. pp. 11–33. Louise Schleiner's 'Latinized Greek Drama in Shakespeare's Writing of *Hamlet*', *Shakespeare Quarterly*, 41 (1990), pp. 29–48, first drew my attention to Schaar's work. Quotations from Schaar will be from pp. 16–28 of *The Full Voic'd Quire Below*.

5 See, for example, Richard Hillman, 'Deceiving Appearances: Neo-Chaucerian Magic in *The Tempest*', in his *Intertextuality and Romance in Renaissance Drama* (New York, 1992), pp. 124–35.

6 David Bevington's section on 'Sources' of *The Tempest* is representative in drawing attention to the four works named here (though he gives much less emphasis to the *Aeneid* than do most), and is also representative in adding a few new suggested 'sources', among them Spenser's *Faerie Queene*, Book 6 (*The Complete Works of Shakespeare*, updated 4th edn, New York, 1997, pp. A-55-6). While Strachey's work is in the form of a 'letter' to an 'Excellent Lady', it seems not unacceptable to include it among *The Tempest*'s 'books', in that it is some ten times longer than another extant document describing the same events (Sylvester Jourdain's *A Discovery of the Bermudas*, printed as a 'book' in 1610) and especially since the 'letter' in manuscript form (the form in which it would have been read up until 1625, when it was printed) would certainly have seemed book-sized. Similarly, Montaigne's 'Of the Cannibals', while itself an essay, would have been known in John Florio's translation of the *Essais*, a substantial folio-sized book.

7 See Barbara A. Mowat, 'The Theatre and Literary Culture', in John D. Cox and David Scott Kastan, eds, *A New History of Early English Drama* (New York, 1997), pp. 213–30, esp. 223.

8 See Barbara A. Mowat, '"A local habitation and a name": Shakespeare's Text as Construct', *Style*, 23/3 (1989), pp. 333–51, esp. 342–8.

9 Donna B. Hamilton, 'Defiguring Virgil in *The Tempest*', *Style*, 23/3 (1989), pp. 352–73, esp. 361. See also Hamilton's *Virgil and 'The Tempest': The Politics of Imitation* (Columbus, 1990), pp. 19–21.

10 Richmond Noble, *Shakespeare's Biblical Knowledge* (New York, 1935), p. 80. Noble points out that the words in the agreed-on passage, Psalm 4.8 ('since the time that their corn, and wine, and oil increased'), appear in this form only in the Psalter.

11 Jonathan Bate describes Prospero's speech as 'Shakespeare's most sustained Ovidian borrowing' and writes that the passage borrowed from Ovid 'was viewed in the Renaissance as witchcraft's great set-piece' (*Shakespeare and Ovid*, Oxford, 1994, pp. 8, 252).

12 Peter Hulme, *Colonial Encounters: Europe and the Native Caribbean, 1492–1797* (London, 1986), p. 109.

13 Hamilton, 'Defiguring Virgil', p. 360.

14 *Odyssey* 5.291–332, 9.67–78, 12.403–25; *Argonautika* II, 1097–1121. Peter Green writes in his commentary to *Argonautika* II, 1097–1121, 'This shipwreck ... gives Ap[ollonius] a chance to work variations on the two shipwrecks ... and the extra storm in the *Odyssey*' (*The Argonautika* by Apollonios Rhodios, trans. with intro, commentary and glossary by Peter Green, Berkeley, 1997, p. 249).

15 Stephen Orgel, while listing the storm among *The Tempest*'s Virgilian parallels, adds that the storm 'in its specific details seems to owe more to both the Strachey letter and Ovid's storm in the *Meta.* 11.474–572' ('Introduction' to *The Tempest*,

Oxford, 1987, p. 40). The Ovidian storm cited by Orgel, found in Golding's translation of the *Metamorphoses* at Book 11, ll. 549–665, destroys the ship of King Ceyx as he attempts to cross the Aegean from Thessaly to Lydia. (See W. H. D. Rouse, ed., *Shakespeare's Ovid, Being Arthur Golding's Translation of the Metamorphoses*, New York, 1961). Orgel is right that there are close parallels with the language in *The Tempest*. The storm in Achilles Tatius' *Clitophon and Leucippe* is at 3.1–5.5 (*Achilles Tatius* with an English translation by S. Gaselee, London, 1917, pp. 135–47).

16 H. F. Watson, *The Sailor in English Fiction and Drama: 1550–1800* (New York, 1931), pp. 47–8.

17 'Introduction', *Valerius Flaccus*, trans. J. H. Mozley (Cambridge, 1936), p. x.

18 Watson writes that 'In the creative literature of the last half of the sixteenth century nautical incidents increase in frequency . . . Strangely enough, however, contemporary accounts of voyages contribute almost nothing . . . and the increasing interest in maritime matters is expressed in terms going back to the Greek pastoral romances of Heliodorus, Longus, and Achilles Tatius in the fourth century AD' (*The Sailor in English Fiction and Drama*, pp. 46–97, esp. 46).

19 The great difference in content and emotional affect between a 'formula storm' and sixteenth-century travel narratives should not surprise us, given the authors' quite different purposes for writing. As Mary C. Fuller makes clear, authors of travel narratives wrote in order to provide records of journeys, not to provide entertainment or larger instruction. Because 'the act of writing was crucial to the navigational, commercial, and informational purposes of the voyage, principally . . . as a record', travel narratives were designed to be as 'transparent' – free of emotion and personal feelings – as possible, in order better to convey the needed facts about such matters as locations, geography, high and low tides, currents and winds (*Voyages in Print: English Travel to America, 1576–1624*, Cambridge, 1995, pp. 1–15).

20 'A voyage with three tall ships . . . to the East Indies . . . begune by M. George Raymond, in the year 1591, and performed by M. James Lancaster, and written from the mouth of Edmund Barker of Ipswich, his lieutenant in the said voyage, by M. Richard Hakluyt' (*The Principal Navigations, Voyages, Traffiques, and Discoveries of the English Nation*, ed. S. Douglas Jackson, 8 vols, London, 1926–31, IV, pp. 242–59, esp. 256; spelling modernized).

21 Watson, *The Sailor in English Fiction and Drama*, pp. 75–6; William Strachey, 'A True Reportory', Louis B. Wright, ed., *A Voyage to Virginia in 1609: Two Narratives* (Charlottesville, 1965), pp. 3–101, esp. 4–16; for the passage in *Clitophon and Leucippe*, see *Achilles Tatius*, 3.4.4–6. (trans., p. 143).

22 Strachey's discussion of the corposant (pp. 12–13) itself echoes Richard Eden; it is just possible, then, that Ariel's description of St Elmo's fire quotes Eden rather than Strachey. See 'of the bright and shynyng exhalations that appeare in the tempestes, whiche the Mariners call Santelmo, or Corpus sancti' ([M. Cortes,] *The Arte of Nauigation*, trans. Richard Eden, 1584, pt II, chap. xx, fols 51ᵛ–52).

23 See Acts 27.34: 'for there shall not an heare of the head perish of any of you' (Rheims); 'for there shall not an heare fall from the head of any of you' (Bishops and Geneva).

24 See H.H.K., 'Luke', *Encyclopedia Britannica* (1971), vol. XIV; and J.V.B., C. S. and C. W., 'The Acts of the Apostles', vol. I.

25 See Barbara A. Mowat, '"And that's true, too": Structures and Meaning in *The Tempest*', *Renaissance Papers 1976*, pp. 37–50; '*The Tempest*: A Modern Perspective', in *The Tempest*, ed. Barbara A. Mowat and Paul Werstine, New Folger Library Shakespeare (New York, 1994), pp. 185–99. Virgil's account of the harpies as

encountered by Aeneas and his men is found in the *Aeneid* 3:210–69. The pertinent section of Apollonius Rhodius' *Argonautika* is II:178–535.

26 The Harpy scene finds analogues in sixteenth-century travel literature even beyond its echoes of fantastic travellers' tales. Charles Frey, in his important 'The *Tempest* and the New World' (*Shakespeare Quarterly*, 30, 1979, pp. 29–41), cites a passage from an account of Drake's voyage in which 'the party lands upon a small island' where they are 'overwhelmed with birds'. Frey quotes the account, in which the men describe themselves as 'more and more overcharged with feathered enemies whose cries were terrible, and their powder and shot poisoned us unto even death if the sooner we had not retired'. Frey notes the parallel between this account and what happens to the court party in *The Tempest*, even to the fact that both parties 'have drawn their swords' (pp. 35–6).

27 Joseph Farrell, 'The Virgilian Intertext', in Charles Martindale, ed., *The Cambridge Companion to Virgil* (Cambridge, 1997), pp. 222–38, esp. 222.

28 Farrell, 'The Virgilian Intertext', p. 236.

29 Celaeno doubtless appears in other works between the writing of the *Aeneid* and *The Tempest* (she certainly appears in Valerius Flaccus' *Argonautica*, written in the first century AD). But the story replicated in *The Tempest* of the confrontation between the Harpy and the voyagers, with its attendant details of prophecy, etc., gives the illusion of a continuous flight from the Black Sea to the Strophades to Prospero's island. (Quotations from the *Aeneid* are from *Virgil* with an English translation by H. Rushton Fairclough, rev. edn, London, 1986.)

30 For the link between Medea and Dido, see Green's edition of the *Argonautika*, pp. 290, 300–301, 308. Richard Hunter emphasizes the connection between Medea and Nausicaa, noting that 'the scenes in Aia in Book 3 [of the *Argonautika*] contain an elaborate set of echoes of the Phaeacian scenes of the *Odyssey*; just as Jason is the Greek stranger arriving unexpectedly, so Medea is cast in the rôle of Nausicaa, and Aietes in that of Alkinoos. Whereas, however, Alkinoos was generous and welcoming to the point of wishing the stranger to marry his daughter (*Odyssey*, 7.311–316), Aietes is treacherous and scheming. Whereas Odysseus' arrival briefly brought Nausicaa into contact with another world, but his departure allowed her to retreat safely from that glimpse, the ultimate outcome for Medea will be disastrous . . .' ('Introduction', Apollonius of Rhodes, *Jason and the Golden Fleece* [the *Argonautica*], trans. Richard Hunter, Oxford, 1993, p. xxv).

31 Hamilton, *Virgil and 'The Tempest'*, pp. 107–8.

32 Schaar discusses similar contrast effects between text and infracontexts in *The Full Voic'd Quire Below*, pp. 24–6.

33 Jerry Brotton, '"This Tunis, sir, was Carthage": Contesting Colonialism in *The Tempest*', in Ania Loomba and Martin Orkin, eds, *Post-Colonial Shakespeares* (London, 1998), pp. 23–42, esp. 24.

34 *The Aeneid*, trans. Kevin Guinagh (New York, 1970), bk I, l. 12.

35 *The Argonautika*, pp. 33–5.

36 Green finds a 'systematic effort at Hellenic self-definition by contrast with the Barbarian Other' in a version of the Argonauts' story contemporary with the *Argonautika* (Dionysios Skytobrachion's *Argonautai*) and concludes that 'it is hard not to see this treatment as in some sense propaganda for Ptolemy II's vigorous program of colonial expansion' (pp. 33–4).

37 Richard Hakluyt, *Divers Voyages Touching the Discoverie of America* (London, 1582), p. 4.

38 The exhortation advises Henry that 'with a small number of shippes there may be discovered divers new landes and kingdomes, in the which without doubt your

Grace shall winne perpetual glory and your Subjects infinite profite.'

39 Thomas Greene, 'Du Bellay and the Disinterment of Rome', in his *The Light in Troy: Imitation and Discovery in Renaissance Poetry* (New Haven, 1982), pp. 220–41, esp. 228. As Greene points out, Du Bellay, in his *Les Antiquitez de Rome*, was responding to 'the enormous literature on the Roman antiquities', including Castiglione's and Raphael's letter to Leo X, in which 'Rome is represented as a lacerated corpse, little more than a skeleton, which it is the obligation of modern men to restore and flesh out.' Greene quotes Hegel's *Philosophy of History*: 'What traveller among the ruins of Carthage, of Palmyra, Persepolis, or Rome, has not been stimulated to reflections on the transiency of kingdoms, and men, and to sadness at the thought of a vigorous and rich life now departed . . .' (p. 233).

40 Greene, 'Du Bellay and the Disinterment of Rome', pp. 238–9.

41 Revelation 16.17–21, 20.11, 21.1–2. In a paper read at the International Shakespeare Conference in Stratford upon Avon in August 1998, Donaldson pointed out echoes of Revelation and of Isaiah in Prospero's lines: 'the great globe itself / . . . shall dissolve, / And . . . / Leave not a rack behind.' The passage in Isaiah is at 34.4, which reads (King James version) 'And all the host of heaven shall be dissolved, and the heavens shall be rolled together as a scroll.' As Donaldson notes in a private communication, 'The heavens "dissolve" in Isaiah, which is Prospero's word, and in the Vulgate there is an interesting *liber/folium* resonance.' (Peter Donaldson's paper has now been published as '"All Which It Inherit": Shakespeare, Globes, and Global Media', *Shakespeare Survey* 52 (1999), pp. 183–200. See esp. p. 139 and n. 20.)

42 For parallels drawn in the sixteenth century between the Native Americans and the savage ancient Britons, see Stephen Orgel, 'Introduction' to *The Tempest*, pp. 34–5.

43 Greenaway, *Prospero's Books*, p. 124.

3 ELIZABETH FOWLER: THE SHIP ADRIFT

1 But see Barbara Mowat's essay in this volume, where she shows the storm that plagues the ship to be part of a network of allusions. The crucial works on *memoria* and cognition in pre-modern European practice are Mary Carruthers, *The Book of Memory* (Cambridge, 1990) and *The Craft of Thought* (Cambridge, 1998). For the picture 'as a cognitive machine', a notion that guides my analysis here, see *The Craft of Thought*, pp. 198–203. For the *Bildeinsatz*, see also Eva Keuls, 'Rhetoric and Visual Aids in Greece and Rome', in E. Havelock and J. P. Hershbell, eds, *Communications Arts in the Ancient World* (New York, 1978), p. 128. On images in narrative, see V. A. Kolve, *Chaucer and the Imagery of Narrative* (Stanford, 1984); chapter 7 is a rich consideration of the rudderless boat in medieval religious art and literature. Surely Chaucer's Man of Law's tale, with its rudderless boat and unwilling marriage of an Italian Christian princess to a North African sultan, is recombined in *The Tempest*. Kolve includes images of Fortune's boat, an emblematic tradition to which Prospero refers at I.ii.178, and argues that the topos of the rudderless boat developed from ancient traditions (found in Roman sculpture and coins) in which Fortune stands at the rudder of a boat (327–8). On the political, rather than religious, topos of the rudderless boat, see also Elizabeth Fowler, 'The Empire and the Waif: Consent and Conflict of Laws in the Man of Law's Tale', in David Aers, ed., *History, Criticism, Ideology* (forthcoming).

2 Andrea Alciati included a similar image of a foundering ship of state in his famous collection of emblems (Antwerp, 1577); see Heather James, *Shakespeare's*

Troy: Drama, Politics, and the Translation of Empire (Cambridge, 1997), fig. 16.

3 For pictures of the seals of Ipswich, Dunwich, New Shoreham (Sussex), Haverfordwest, Winchelsea and Rye, see Ian Friel, *The Good Ship: Ships, Shipbuilding and Technology in England, 1200–1520* (London, 1995).

4 *St. Thomas Aquinas on Politics and Ethics*, trans. Paul E. Sigmund (New York, 1988), p. 14. The original reads: 'Principium autem intentionis nostrae hinc sumere oportet, ut quid nomine regis intelligendum sit, exponatur. In omnibus autem quae ad finem aliquem ordinantur, in quibus contingit sic et aliter procedere, opus est aliquo dirigente, per quod directe debitum perveniatur ad finem. Non enim navis, quam secundum diversorum ventorum impulsum in diversa moveri contingit, ad destinatum finem perveniret, nisi per gubernatoris industriam dirigeretur ad portum . . .' (Thomas Aquinas, *De regimine principum*, ed. Joseph Mathis, Rome, 1948, p. 1). In later chapters (esp. chap. 14), the allegory is elaborated further.

5 Stephen Orgel, ed., *The Tempest* (Oxford, 1987), p. 102 n.

6 For a collection of rudderless boats and the immediate legal context of punishment, see J. R. Reinhard, 'Setting Adrift in Mediæval Law and Literature', *PMLA*, 56 (1941), pp. 33–68.

7 Orgel, *The Tempest*, e.g. pp. 12, 36.

4 CHRISTY ANDERSON: WILD WATERS: HYDRAULICS AND THE FORCES OF NATURE

I am grateful to Daria Fisher, whose investigations into the rôle of water and hydraulics provided invaluable background for this essay.

1 Gary Schmidgall, *Shakespeare and the Courtly Aesthetic* (Berkeley, 1981), pp. 156–64.

2 See the discussion of Miranda's relationship to nature in Denise Albanese, *New Science, New World* (Durham, NC, 1996), pp. 59–91.

3 John Dixon Hunt, *Garden and Grove: The Italian Renaissance Garden in the English Imagination, 1600–1750* (London, 1986).

4 Werner Oechslin, '"Architectura Hydraulica" or "Showplace of the Aquatic Arts"', *Daidalos*, 55 (15 March 1995), pp. 24–37.

5 Naomi Miller, *Heavenly Caves: Reflections on the Garden Grotto* (New York, 1982), p. 61.

6 John Bate, *The Mysteries of Nature and Art. In Foure severall parts* (London, 1635), sig. A3.

7 Cyprian Lucar, *A Treatise Named Lucarsolace devided into Fovver Bookes* (London, 1590), p. 148.

8 Bate, *The Mysteries of Nature*, p. 51.

9 Roy Strong, *Henry Prince of Wales and England's Lost Renaissance* (New York, 1986), p. 107.

10 Roy Strong, *The Renaissance Garden in England* (London, 1979), pp. 87–93.

11 Salomon de Caus, *Les raisons des forces movvantes auec diuerses machines tant vtilles que plaisantes, aus quelles sont adioints plusieurs desseings de grotes et fontaines* (Frankfurt, 1615), bk II, Problesme XIII.

THE BURFORD INDIANS

1 On Edmund Harman, see Michael Balfour, *Edmund Harman: Barber and Gentleman*, Tolsey Paper no. 6 (Burford, 1988). Although he lists the Burford monument in his 'First Visual Images of Native America', William C. Sturtevant is sceptical of the first identification of the Indians as Tupinamba in an article by Stuart Piggott.

However, the link to Cornelis Bos, first made by Mr Wells-Cole of the City of Leeds Art Gallery, would seem to confirm the American Indian connection. A sceptical view of the influence of the 'Treasure of Montezuma' on European art in the sixteenth century is put forward by Nicole Dacos, who favours Etruscan sources for exotic headgear, but the upper figures on the Harman monument clearly have no classical source. See William C. Sturtevant, 'First Visual Images of Native America', in *First Images of America*, ed. Fredi Chiappelli (Los Angeles, 1976), pp. 417-54; Stuart Piggott, 'Brazilian Indians on an Elizabethan Monument', *Antiquity* 38 (1964), pp. 134-6; Sune Schéle, *Cornelis Bos: A Study of the Origins of the Netherland Grotesque* (Stockholm, 1965); Nicole Dacos, 'Présents Américains à la Renaissance: L'Assimilation de l'Exotisme', *Gazette des Beaux Arts* 6è pér. 73 (1969), pp. 57-64.

5 ALDEN T. VAUGHAN: TRINCULO'S INDIAN: AMERICAN NATIVES IN SHAKESPEARE'S ENGLAND

1 Harlow's other captives were Monopet and Pekenimme from Monhegan (or perhaps Allen) Island; Sakaweston from Nohomo Island; and Coneconam, like Epenow, from Capawick (later Martha's Vineyard): Philip L. Barbour, ed., *The Complete Works of Captain John Smith*, 3 vols (Chapel Hill, NC, 1986), II, p. 399; James Phinney Baxter, *Sir Ferdinando Gorges and His Province of Maine*, 3 vols (Boston, 1890), II, p. 20.

2 Barbour, *Works of John Smith*, II, p. 403; William Shakespeare, *Henry VIII*, V.iii.34–5 (Riverside edn).

3 Barbour, *Works of John Smith*, I, p. 433; II, pp. 399, 403; Baxter, *Gorges*, II, pp. 23–5.

4 David Beers Quinn, *England and the Discovery of America, 1481–1620* (New York, 1974), pp. 419–31. The Virginians' arrival in England in 1603 is uncertain but probable.

5 English literary and artistic representations of American Indians are beyond the scope of this essay. A useful overview is Hugh Honour, *The New Golden Land: European Images of America from the Discoveries to the Present Time* (New York, 1975).

6 Richard Hakluyt, *The Principal Navigations Voyages Traffiques & Discoveries of the English Nation*, 12 vols (Glasgow, 1903–5), VII, p. 155; also in Hakluyt's *Divers voyages touching the discouerie of America . . .* (London, 1582) and *Principall navigations . . .* (London, 1589).

7 Hakluyt, *Principal Navigations*, XI, p. 24.

8 Previous accounts – incomplete and largely undocumented – of Native Americans in England include Carolyn Thomas Foreman, *Indians Abroad, 1493–1938* (Norman, OK, 1943); Sidney Lee, 'The Call of the West: America and Elizabethan England, III – The American Indian in Elizabethan England', *Scribner's Magazine*, XLII (1907), pp. 313–30.

9 Michael Lok in William C. Sturtevant and David Beers Quinn, 'This New Prey: Eskimos in Europe in 1567, 1576, and 1577', in Christian F. Feest, ed., *Indians and Europe: An Interdisciplinary Collection of Essays* (Aachen, 1987), pp. 61–140.

10 On visual representations of this Eskimo, see Sturtevant and Quinn, 'This New Prey', pp. 73–6, 88–9.

11 George Best, *A True Discourse of the Late Voyages of Discouerie . . .* (London, 1578), p. 50 (1st pagination); Sturtevant and Quinn, 'This New Prey', p. 72; Neil Cheshire et al., 'Frobisher's Eskimos', *Archivaria*, 10 (Summer 1980), pp. 23–50.

12 Best, *True Discourse*, pp. 12, 23 (2nd pagination). The surviving records contain several variations of the Eskimos' names (Sturtevant and Quinn, 'The New Prey',

pp. 80, 115–16; Vilhjalmur Stefansson, *The Three Voyages of Martin Frobisher*, 2 vols, London, 1938, II, p. 235–6).

13   F. F. Fox, ed., *Adams's Chronicle of Bristol* (Bristol, 1910), p. 115. Adriaen Coenen encountered a similar 'wild woman with a child' in Holland, where 'one could see them for money' (Sturtevant and Quinn, 'This New Prey', pp. 132–7).

14   Best, *True Discourse*, p. 12 (2nd pagination); Cheshire et al., 'Frobisher's Eskimos', pp. 40–41; Sturtevant and Quinn, 'This New Prey', pp. 80–84.

15   David B. Quinn, ed., *New American World: A Documentary History of North America to 1612*, 5 vols (New York, 1979), IV, p. 218.

16   Sturtevant and Quinn, 'This New Prey', p. 84.

17   Manteo's career is documented in David Beers Quinn, ed., *The Roanoke Voyages, 1584–1590*, 2 vols (London, 1955), passim; and Quinn, *Set Fair for Roanoke: Voyages and Colonies, 1584–1606* (Chapel Hill, 1985), esp. 218, 233–6.

18   Quinn, *Set Fair*, p. 236.

19   Quinn, *Set Fair*, pp. 145, 236; Quinn, *Roanoke Voyages*, I, p. 495. The Indian place name may actually have meant 'you weare good clothes' (*ibid.*, I, pp. 116–17; II, pp. 853–4).

20   Walter Ralegh, *The Discoverie of . . . Guiana*, ed. V. T. Harlow (London, 1928), pp. 63, 64, 117, 122; Hakluyt, *Principal Navigations*, X, p. 353; Robert Lacey, *Sir Walter Ralegh* (New York, 1973), p. 210.

21   Samuel Purchas, *Hakluytus Posthumus, or Purchas His Pilgrimes*, 20 vols (Glasgow, 1905–7), XVI, pp. 310, 312, 319, 323.

22   Robert Harcourt, *A Relation of a Voyage to Guiana* (London, 1613), pp. 6–8, 12–15; Lawrence Keymis, *A Relation of the Second Voyage to Guiana* (London, 1596), sig. B2; Hakluyt, *Principal Navigations*, X, p. 454. According to Harcourt, John, Martyn and Leonard had become Christians.

23   Walter Ralegh, *The Discovery of . . . Guiana*, ed. Robert H. Schomburgk (London, 1848), pp. 197–200; Lacey, *Ralegh*, pp. 329.

24   James Rosier, *A True Relation of the Most Prosperous Voyage . . .* (London, 1605), sigs C4r–D, E4; Baxter, *Gorges*, II, p. 8. The spellings of the Indians' names varied widely.

25   Alexander Brown, *The Genesis of the United States*, 2 vols (Boston, 1890), I, p. 46.

26   David B. Quinn and Alison M. Quinn, eds, *The English New England Voyages 1602–1608* (London, 1983), p. 309–10.

27   Quinn, *New American World*, III, pp. 404–14; Baxter, *Gorges*, II, pp. 22–3; Brown, *Genesis*, I, pp. 114–15.

28   Baxter, *Gorges*, I, pp. 104–6, 212, 215; II, p. 8; *Dictionary of American Biography*, XVII (New York, 1935), p. 487; Neal Salisbury, 'Squanto: Last of the Patuxets', in David G. Sweet and Gary B. Nash, eds, *Struggle and Survival in Colonial America* (Berkeley and Los Angeles, 1981), pp. 228–46; William Bradford, *History of Plymouth Plantation, 1620–1647*, 2 vols (Boston, 1912), I, p. 202.

29   Barbour, *Works of John Smith*, I, pp. 79, 91, 216, 236; II, pp. 183, 248, 350; Philip L. Barbour, ed., *The Jamestown Voyages under the First Charter, 1606–1609*, 2 vols (London, 1969), I, pp. 163; II, p. 274. The evidence on Namontack is confusing, but it is unlikely that he was murdered on Bermuda by Machumps. The records probably conflate two or more natives.

30   William Strachey, 'A True Reportory of the Wreck and Redemption of Sir Thomas Gates, Knight', in *Purchas His Pilgrimes*, vol. XIX, pp. 65, 66; William Strachey, *The Historie of Travell into Virginia Britania*, ed. Louis B. Wright and Virginia Freud (London, 1953), pp. 34, 61–2, 98.

31 [John White], *The Planters Plea* (London, 1630), pp. 53–4.

32 Christian F. Feest, 'The Virginia Indian in Pictures, 1612–1624', *Smithsonian Journal of History*, II (1967), pp. 6–13; and Feest, 'Virginia Indian Miscellany III', *Archiv für Vülkerkunde*, XXVI (1972), pp. 3–5.

33 Some of the extensive evidence on Pocahontas's trip to England is in Brown, *Genesis*, II, pp. 784–9 and passim; Barbour, *Works of John Smith*, II, pp. 255, 258–62; *Purchas His Pilgrimes*, XIX, pp. 116–19; Norman Egbert McClure, ed., *The Letters of John Chamberlain*, 2 vols (Philadelphia, 1939), I, p. 470; II, pp. 12, 50 (quotation), 57, 66. An imaginative modern reconstruction is Frances Mossiker, *Pocahontas: The Life and the Legend* (London, 1977), pp. 221–81.

34 Hakluyt, *Principal Navigations*, VII, p. 155; Victor von Klarwill, ed., *Queen Elizabeth and Some Foreigners*, trans. T. H. Nash (London, 1928), p. 323; Rosier, *True Relation*, sig. B3v; Quinn and Quinn, *New England Voyages*, p. 311. Although Frobisher's captive of 1576 survived less than a month, one of the several paintings of him was 'in Englishe ap[par]ell' (Sturtevant and Quinn, 'This New Prey', p. 73).

35 Hakluyt, *Principal Navigations*, VII, p. 155.

36 Von Klarwill, *Queen Elizabeth*, p. 323.

37 Wanchese's career is documented in Quinn, *Roanoke Voyages*, passim, and summarized in Quinn, *Set Fair*, pp. 218, 235–6.

38 On Indian pigmentation, see Alden T. Vaughan, 'From White Man to Redskin: Changing Anglo-American Perceptions of the American Indian', in his *Roots of American Racism: Essays on the Colonial Experience* (New York, 1995), pp. 3–33. For William Strachey's explanation of Virginia Indians' coloration, see his *Virginia Britania*, pp. 70–71.

39 The usual explanation is that Trinculo would advertise his creature by having its image painted on a sign.

40 A vivid description of London's variety of entertainment is *Thomas Platter's Travels in England* [1599], trans. Clare Williams (London, 1937), pp. 166–73.

41 About half of the Indians known to be in England between 1564 and 1616 (not counting the Pocahontas party) returned to America, and roughly one quarter are known to have died in England; the remainder disappear from the records. The last category includes Sakaweston, one of Harlow's captives of 1611, who 'after he had lived many yeeres in England went a Souldier to the warres of Bohemia' (Barbour, *Works of John Smith*, II, p. 399).

42 Best, *True Discourse*, p. 50. That Shakespeare intended 'Caliban' to be an anagram of 'cannibal' has been widely asserted since the late eighteenth century but remains unproven. See Alden T. Vaughan and Virginia Mason Vaughan, *Shakespeare's Caliban: A Cultural History* (Cambridge and New York, 1991), pp. 26–32.

6 JOSEPH ROACH: THE ENCHANTED ISLAND: VICARIOUS TOURISM IN RESTORATION ADAPTATIONS OF *THE TEMPEST*

1 Dean MacCannell, *The Tourist: A New Theory of the Leisure Class* (New York, 1976), p. 21.

2 Tom Brown, *Amusements Serious and Comical, Calculated for the Meridian of London*, 2nd edn 'with large Improvements' (London, 1700), p. 48.

3 *Ibid.*, p. 56.

4 Jocelyn Powell, *Restoration Theatre Production* (London, 1984), pp. 62–83.

5 [Thomas Shadwell], *The Tempest, or the Enchanted Island. A Comedy. As it is now Acted at His Highness the Duke of York's Theatre* (London, 1674), p. 1. Subsequent citations of

this edition, which reprints Dryden's Preface and the 1667 Prologue and Epilogue, will be given in the text.

6　See Richard D. Altick, *The Shows of London* (Cambridge, MA, 1978); Dean MacCannell, *The Tourist: A New Theory of the Leisure Class* (New York, 1989); Barbara Kirshenblatt-Gimblett, *Destination Culture: Tourism, Museums, and Heritage* (Berkeley, 1998). For an excellent account of the ethnographic ambitions of the Restoration and eighteenth-century stage, see Mita S. Choudhury, 'Imperial Licenses, Borderless Topographies, and the Eighteenth-Century British Theatre', in Michal Kobialka, ed., *Of Borders and Thresholds: Theatre History, Practice, Theory* (Minneapolis, 1999), pp. 70–109.

7　Orest Ranum, 'Islands and the Self in a Ludovician Fête', in David Lee Rubin, *Sun King: The Ascendancy of French Culture during the Reign of Louis XIV* (Washington, D.C., 1992), p. 17. See also my 'Body of Law: The Sun King and the Code Noir', in Sara E. Melzer and Kathryn Norberg, eds, *From the Royal to the Republican Body: Incorporating the Political in Seventeenth- and Eighteenth-Century France* (Berkeley, 1998), pp. 113–30.

8　Christopher B. Balme, 'Staging the Pacific: Framing Authenticity in Performances for Tourists at the Polynesian Cultural Center', *Theatre Journal*, 50 (1998), pp. 53–70.

9　MacCannell, *The Tourist*, pp. 91–107. Cf. Erving Goffman, *The Presentation of Self in Everyday Life* (Garden City, NY, 1959).

10　Kirshenblatt-Gimblett, *Destination Culture*, p. 255.

11　Brown, *Amusements*, p. 22, pp. 56–7.

12　*Ibid.*, p. 56.

13　MacCannell, *The Tourist*, p. 41.

14　*The Diary of Samuel Pepys*, ed. Robert Latham and William Matthews (London, 1970), VIII, pp. 521–2, 527, 576; IX, pp. 12, 48, 179, 195, 422.

15　John Downes, *Roscius Anglicanus, or an Historical Review of the Stage*, ed. Judith Milhous and Robert D. Hume [1708] (London, 1987), pp. 73–4.

16　Thomas Duffett, 'The Mock-Tempest; or, The Enchanted Castle', in Montague Summers, ed., *Shakespearean Adaptations* [1922] (New York, 1966), p. 147.

17　Gerard Langbaine, *An Account of the English Dramatick Poets* (Oxford, 1691), pp. 177–8.

18　*The Diary of Samuel Pepys*, VIII, pp. 521–2.

19　See Katherine Eisaman Maus, 'Arcadia Lost: Politics and Revision in the Restoration *Tempest*', *Renaissance Drama*, 13 (1982), pp. 189–209; Matthew H. Wikander, '"The Duke my Father's Wrack": The Innocence of the Restoration *Tempest*', *Shakespeare Survey*, 43 (1991), pp. 91–8; Nancy Klein Maguire, *Regicide and Restoration: English Tragicomedy, 1660–1671* (Cambridge, 1992), esp. chap. 4, 'The Commercial Market: Genre as Commodity', pp. 131–7.

20　James Anderson Winn, *John Dryden and His World* (New Haven, 1987), p. 262.

21　Downes, *Roscius Anglicanus*, p. 55.

22　Philip H. Highfill Jr, Kalman A. Burnim and Edward A. Langhans, eds, *Biographical Dictionary of Actors, Actresses, Musicians, Dancers, Managers, and Other Stage Personnel in London, 1660–1800* (Carbondale, 1973–93), IV, p. 222.

23　*The Diary of Samuel Pepys*, IX, p. 195.

24　Alden T. Vaughan and Virginia Mason Vaughan, *Shakespeare's Caliban: A Cultural History* (Cambridge, 1991), p. 174.

25　*The Diary of Samuel Pepys*, IX, p. 422.

26　[Charles Gildon], *A Comparison Between the Two Stages* [1702] (New York, 1973), p. 17.

27　Anthony Aston, *A Brief Supplement to Colley Cibber*, in *An Apology for the Life of Mr. Colley Cibber*, ed. Robert W. Lowe (London, 1889), II, p. 305.

28 Brown, *Amusements*, pp. 51–2.

II EUROPEAN AND MEDITERRANEAN CROSSROADS

INTRODUCTION

1 See Geoffrey Bullough, *Narrative and Dramatic Sources of Shakespeare*, VIII (London, 1975), pp. 245–8; introduction to Stephen Orgel, ed., *The Tempest* (Oxford, 1987).

2 Jan Kott, 'Prospero, or the Director', in *The Bottom Translation: Marlowe and Shakespeare and the Carnival Tradition*, trans. Daniela Miedzyrzecka and Lillian Vallee (Evanston, 1987), p. 134; he cites not only the plot and the names of the characters but also 'Ariel's recitativo, Stephano and Trinculo's *lazzi*, repeated after the [*commedia*] *dell'arte* scenarios, [and] the Roman goddesses of the betrothal masque'.

3 Robin Kirkpatrick, *English and Italian Literature from Dante to Shakespeare: A Study of Source, Analogue and Divergence* (London, 1995).

4 Cf. Frank Kermode, Introduction to the Arden edition of *The Tempest* (London, 1954), pp. lix–lxiii.

5 Cf. Karol Berger's sensitive comments in 'Prospero's Art', *Shakespeare Studies*, 10 (1977), pp. 211–39. While he approaches Prospero as a Neoplatonic artist-magus in the Kermodean mould, he acknowledges that the play could be read 'as a meditation on violence' (p. 225).

6 David Scott Kastan, '"The Duke of Milan / And His Brave Son": Dynastic Politics in *The Tempest*', in Virginia Mason Vaughan and Alden T. Vaughan, eds, *Critical Essays on Shakespeare's 'The Tempest'* (New York, 1998), pp. 91–103.

7 '"What cares these roarers for the name of king?": Language and Utopia in *The Tempest*', in Gordon McMullan and Jonathan Hope, *The Politics of Tragicomedy: Shakespeare and After* (London, 1992), pp. 21–54.

8 Peter S. Donaldson, *Machiavelli and Mystery of State* (Cambridge, 1988). Cf. José Antonio Maravall, *Culture of the Baroque*, trans. Terry Cochran (Minneapolis, 1986), p. 218; R. Marienstras, 'Prospero ou le Machiavélisme du Bien', *Bulletin de la Faculté des Lettres de Strasbourg*, 43 (1965), pp. 833–917.

9 Donaldson, *Machiavelli and Mystery of State*, p. 166.

10 *Ibid.*, chap. 5.

11 *Ibid.*, pp. 148–50.

12 Gabriel Naudé, *Political Considerations upon Refin'd Politicks, and the Master-Strokes of State*, trans. William King (London, 1711), p. 24. There is a modern French edition of Naudé's *Considérations politiques sur les coups d'État* (Paris, 1989) with a useful prefatory lecture by Louis Marin, 'Pour une théorie baroque de l'action politique'. A figure worth setting alongside Naudé is the Neapolitan natural philosopher, political advisor and Dominican priest Tommaso Campanella. Best known as the author of the utopian work *The City of the Sun*, Campanella published a volume called *Monarchia Messiae* (1633), which contained aphorisms such as 'Potentia, Sapientia, & Amor sunt principia nostrae metaphys' (Power, Wisdom, and Love are the principles of our metaphysics)' (p. 8). When it appeared in English in 1659, Campanella was labelled a 'Second Machiavel' on the title-page (John M. Headley, 'Campanella, America, and World Evangelization', in *America in European Consciousness, 1493-1750*, Chapel Hill, NC, 1995, pp. 243–71).

13 See, for example, Alvin B. Kernan, *Shakespeare, the King's Playwright: Theater in the Stuart Court, 1603–1613* (New Haven, 1995).

14 Sycorax has tended to reappear in performances and adaptations – as in Peter

Brook's 1968 production and the film versions of Derek Jarman and Peter Greenaway. She plays a central rôle in Marina Warner's novel *Indigo: or, Mapping the Waters* (London, 1992), where she embodies the indigenous community of the Caribbean island soon to be devastated by English invaders. Her subsequent 'presence' reverberates through the novel and through the history of the Caribbean. The most sustained critical attempt to grapple with the absence of Sycorax is Lemuel Johnson's extraordinary essay 'Whatever Happened to Caliban's Mother? Or, The Problem with Othello's' (in his *Shakespeare in Africa (and Other Venues): Import and the Appropriation of Culture*, Trenton, NJ, 1998, pp. 17–179).

15 Diane Purkiss, 'The Witch on the Margins of "Race": Sycorax and Others', in *The Witch in History: Early Modern and Twentieth-century Representations* (London, 1996), pp. 250–73. Also see Barbara Fuchs's discussion of *The Tempest*'s 'superimposed' locations in 'Conquering Islands: Contextualizing *The Tempest*', *Shakespeare Quarterly*, 48 (1997), pp. 45–62, and Peter Hulme's formulation of the problem in *Colonial Encounters: Europe and the Native Caribbean, 1492–1797* (London, 1986), pp. 109–12.

16 In 'Forgetting the Aeneid', Mary Fuller refers to 'a nexus of Roman, English, and Caribbean sites, texts, figures' (*American Literary History*, 4, 1992, pp. 517–38).

17 In doing so, she picks up Jerry Brotton's challenge that 'Critics . . . who have acknowledged the importance of the play's Virgilian references have failed to locate such references within the contemporary context of the reception, translation and distribution of such texts' ('"This Tunis, sir, was Carthage": Contesting Colonialism in *The Tempest*', in *Post-colonial Shakespeares*, London, 1998, pp. 23–42 at 41).

18 Jerry Brotton and Lisa Jardine, *Global Interests: Renaissance Art between East and West* (London, 2000); Lisa Jardine, *Worldly Goods: A New History of the Renaissance* (London, 1996), passim.

19 'While etymologists agree that the term "trafficking" arose in the context of Mediterranean commerce, there are equally reasonable arguments for a Latin derivation from *tra/trans* (across) and *facere* (to do or make), and an Arabic origin from *traffaqa*, which can mean 'to seek profit' or *tafriq*, signifying distribution. This divided etymology makes 'trafficking' all the more attractive as a descriptive term aimed to displace unidirectional models of early modern cross-cultural encounters' (Jonathan Burton, '"A most wily bird": Leo Africanus, *Othello* and the Trafficking in Difference', in Ania Loomba and Martin Orkin, *Post-colonial Shakespeares*, London, 1998, pp. 43–63.

20 Alberto Tenenti, *Piracy and the Decline of Venice, 1580–1615*, trans. Janet and Brian Pullan (Berkeley, 1967), pp. 75, 86.

21 Richard Wilson, 'Voyage to Tunis: New History and the Old World of *The Tempest*', *ELH*, 64 (1997), pp. 333–57.

22 Brotton, '"This Tunis, sir, was Carthage"'.

7 ROBIN KIRKPATRICK: THE ITALY OF *THE TEMPEST*

1 See Peter Burke (discussing the traveller Fynes Morrison, who briefly visited Milan in 1594) in *Varieties of Cultural History* (Cambridge, 1997), pp. 101–8.

2 See esp. G. K. Hunter, 'English Folly and Italian Vice', in J. R. Brown and B. Harris, *Jacobean Theatre* (London, 1960), pp. 85–111.

3 D. Wallace, *Chaucerian Polity* (Stanford, 1996), passim.

4 Peter Donaldson, *Machiavelli and Mystery of State* (Cambridge, 1988), pp. 86–110.

5 Francis Bacon, *The Advancement of Learning*, bk II, xxxi, 8.
6 *The Prince*, trans. George Bull (Harmondsworth, 1975), pp. 87–90.
7 Donaldson, *Machiavelli and Mystery of State*, esp. pp. 111–40.
8 First translated by Sir John Dymock in 1602: *Il Pastor Fido: or the faithfull Shepheard* (London, 1602).
9 See J. W. Lever's introduction to the Arden edition (London, 1965).
10 See Louise Clubb, *Italian Drama in Shakespeare's Time* (New Haven, 1989).
11 See Agostino Lombardi, 'The Veneto, Metatheatre and Shakespeare', and Giorgio Melchiori, '"In fair Verona": *Commedia Erudita* into Romantic Comedy', in the excellent volume *Shakespeare's Italy*, ed. M. Marrapodi et al. (Manchester, 1993), pp. 143–57, 100–111.
12 See her 'Livy, Machiavelli and Shakespeare's *Coriolanus*', *Shakespeare Survey*, 38 (1985), pp. 115–29.
13 On Guarini and Shakespeare's poetics, see M. Doran, *Endeavours of Art: A Study of Form in Elizabethan Drama* (Madison, 1954).
14 See John White's important volume *The Birth and Rebirth of Pictorial Space* (London, 1987), p. 30.
15 Quoted from Ernst Cassirer et al., *The Renaissance Philosophy of Man* (Chicago, 1948), p. 249.
16 Orgel, *The Tempest*, note at V.i.322–7.
17 On the contrast between visual and aural forms of organization in the Renaissance, see Gary Tomlinson, *Music in Renaissance Magic* (Chicago, 1993), p. 50.
18 See Stephen Greenblatt's analysis of the ambiguities of wonder in *Marvellous Possessions* (Oxford, 1991).

8 MARINA WARNER: 'THE FOUL WITCH' AND HER 'FRECKLED WHELP': CIRCEAN MUTATIONS IN THE NEW WORLD

The author would like to thank Trinity College, Cambridge, for valuable research time and, most particularly, Anne Barton, William St Clair, the late Jeremy Maule and the staff of the Wren Library. David Harvey's comments on my earlier work on Circe have been much help and an inspiration in developing these further thoughts; to him many thanks.
1 Donna Landry and Gerald Maclean suggest that 'the one thing' may be her pregnancy and that the Ottoman Turks showed clemency in these circumstances. I am grateful to Landry and Maclean for reading this essay and offering this and other valuable observations.
2 Ted Hughes, *Shakespeare and the Goddess of Supreme Being* (London, 1992), p. 382.
3 Antonio Pigafetta, *Magellan's Voyage: A Narrative Account of the First Circumnavigation*, trans. and ed. R. A. Skelton (New York, 1994), pp. 48–9.
4 I am grateful to Adriana Cavarero for her talk 'Ondine Goes Away', delivered at Warwick University, 4 November 1996, and especially for her thoughts about sirens' and monsters' relation to speech.
5 Robert Graves, *The Greek Myths*, 2 vols (Harmondsworth, 1966), I, pp. 299–300.
6 *The Metamorphoses of Ovid*, trans. Mary M. Innes (Harmondsworth, 1973), bk XIV, ll. 252–6, p. 318.
7 Niccolò Machiavelli, 'L'Asino', in *Tutte le opere* (Florence, 1971), p. 971; John Baptist Gelli, *Circe* [1548], trans. H. Layng (London, 1744), first French trans. by Denis Sauvage (1550), English trans. by Henry Iden (1557). See Emmanuel Hatzantonis, 'I Geniali rimaneggiamenti dell'episodio Omerico di Circe in Apollonio Rodio e

Plutarco', *Revue belge de philologie et d'histoire*, liv/1 (1976), pp. 5–24.

8   Joost van den Vondel, *De Vernieuwde Gulden Winckel der kunstlievenden Nederlanders (The Golden Shop of Art-loving Netherlanders, Revised)* (Amsterdam, 1622).

9   Horace, *Epistles* I.2 'To Lollius Maximus', ll. 23–9, quoted by Richard Brilliant, 'Kirke's Men: Swine and Sweethearts', in Beth Cohen, ed., *The Distaff Side: Representing the Female in Homer's Odyssey* (Oxford, 1995), p. 170.

10   Bruce Thomas Boehrer, *The Fury of Men's Gullets: Ben Jonson and the Digestive Canal* (Philadelphia, 1997).

11   C. Lloyd, *English Corsairs on the Barbary Coast* (London, 1981), p. 53, quoted in Peter Lamborn Wilson, *Pirate Utopias: Moorish Corsairs and European Renegadoes* (Brooklyn, 1995), p. 67.

12   Konrad Gesner, *Curious Woodcuts of Fanciful and Real Beasts*, ed. Edmund Gillon (New York, 1971); see also Jeffrey Kahan, 'Ambroise Paré's "Des Monstres" as a Possible Source for Caliban', *Early Modern Literary Studies*, 3/1 (1997), 4.1–11.

13   Edward Topsell, *The History of Four-Footed Beasts and Serpents . . . Whereunto is now Added, The Theatre of Insects by T. Muffet* (London, 1658), pp. 343–4.

14   *Ibid.*, p. 353.

15   *Ibid.*, pp. 546–7.

16   See A. Montanus's engraving of 'South American Wildlife' from his book *De Nieuwe en Onbekende Weereld* (1671), which includes several snakes, the manticore and the baboon from Gesner/Topsell (reproduced in Hugh Honour, *The New Golden Land: European Images of America from the Discoveries to the Present Time* (London, 1976), p. 42.

17   See for example Philippe Galle, *America* (1581–1600); Maarten de Vos, *America* (1594); Crispijn de Passe, *America* (early seventeenth century); Stefano della Bella, *America* (1644), all reproduced in Honour, *The New Golden Land*, pp. 87–9.

18   Aucher Warner, *Sir Thomas Warner: Pioneer of the West Indies. A Chronicle of His Family* (London, 1933), facing p. 27, pp. 28–33. The painting has been attributed to Robert Peake, Serjeant Painter, who died some time after the accession of Charles I, or to John de Critz, who held the same office from 1610 until he died in the civil war.

19   Because it exists in two different states, the ornament gives precious clues to the printing history. See Charlton Hinham, *The Printing and Proof-reading of the First Folio of Shakespeare*, 2 vols (Oxford, 1963), I, pp. 21–4, 36–7, 340–41, 355–6; reproduced following p. 180.

20   I am indebted to William Sherman for the information about the ornament's uses, and to his insight into the connections with accounts of Elsewheres, real and imagined.

21   See Hughes, *Shakespeare and the Goddess*, pp. 438–40.

22   See *ibid.* Hughes announces that he will use the female pronoun for Ariel; in the novel *Indigo*, which I published the same year (1992), I cast Ariel as the adoptive daughter of Sycorax.

23   F. G. Waldron, *Free Reflections on Miscellaneous Papers and Legal Instruments, Under the Hand and Seal of William Shakespeare, in the Possession of Samuel Ireland, of Norfolk Street. To which are added, Extracts from an unpublished MS. play, called The Virgin Queen. Written by, or in imitation of, Shakspeare* (London, 1796), p. 22.

24   *Ibid.*, pp. 6–7.

9 DONNA B. HAMILTON: RE-ENGINEERING VIRGIL: *THE TEMPEST* AND THE PRINTED ENGLISH *AENEID*

1 See Annabel Patterson, *Pastoral and Ideology: Virgil to Valery* (Berkeley, 1987), p. 139.
2 See Donna B. Hamilton, *Virgil and The Tempest* (Columbus, OH, 1990).
3 See Heather James, *Shakespeare's Troy: Drama, Politics, and the Translation of Empire* (Cambridge, 1997).
4 See Margaret Tudeau-Clayton, *Jonson, Shakespeare and Early Modern Virgil* (Cambridge, 1998).
5 David Loades, *Mary Tudor: A Life* (Oxford, 1989); David Loades, *The Mid-Tudor Crisis, 1545–1565* (New York, 1992), pp. 25, 34, 36.
6 Anthony Kemp, *The Estrangement of the Past: A Study in the Origins of Modern Historical Consciousness* (Oxford, 1991), pp. 66, 55. The birth of Christ during the reign of the emperor Augustus, Charlemagne's acceptance of Christianity, the establishment in Rome of the papacy, and the notion of Rome 'as city, as nation, as empire' had combined to produce a 'Roman cultural identity' in which all of Christianity might hold citizenship (Kemp, *Estrangement of the Past*, pp. 56–7; see also Frances Yates, *Astraea: The Imperial Theme in the Sixteenth Century*, London, 1975, pp. 1–23).
7 Marie Tanner, *The Last Descendant of Aeneas: The Habsburgs and the Mythic Image of the Emperor* (New Haven, 1993), p. 109.
8 Andrew Wheatcroft, *The Habsburgs* (London, 1995), pp. 127–33; cf. Jerry Brotton's essay in the present volume.
9 Tanner, *The Last Descendant of Aeneas*, p. 137.
10 See *Dictionary of National Biography* entries for Archibald Douglas, Gavin Douglas and Margaret Tudor; David F. C. Coldwell, ed., *Virgil's Aeneid*, trans. Gavin Douglas, 4 vols (Edinburgh, 1964), I, pp. 1–18. For the politics of Douglas's translation, see *ibid.*, I, pp. 19–38.
11 See Anna Cox Brinton, *Maphaeus Vegius and His Thirteenth Book of the Aeneid* (Palo Alto, 1930), pp. 2–3, 26.
12 See Herbert Hartman, ed., *Surrey's Fourth boke of Virgill* (Purchase, NY, 1933), pp. xii–xiii.
13 See Scott Campbell Lucas, 'The Suppressed Edition and the Creation of the "Orthodox" *Mirror for Magistrates*,' *Renaissance Papers* (1994), pp. 31–54.
14 In 1557, in conjunction with the printing of his miscellany, *Songes and Sonettes . . .,* Tottel printed both books of Surrey's *Aeneid*.
15 Kingston and Jugge were involved in the production, respectively, of Sarum service books and of Bibles; see E. G. Duff, *A Century of the English Book Trade, 1457–1557* (London, 1905), pp. 82, 86.
16 See Yates, *Astraea*, pp. 29–87.
17 See Robert Tittler, *Nicholas Bacon: The Making of a Tudor Statesman* (London, 1976).
18 For Parker's letters to Burghley on the antiquarian project, see John Bruce and Thomas Thomason Perowne, eds, *Correspondence of Matthew Parker* (Cambridge, 1853), XXXIII, pp. 253, 424–6.
19 Over time, as William Camden and others subjected the Trojan myth to increasing scepticism, the Roman Empire and Queen Elizabeth's identification with Constantine replaced to some extent the Brute–Troy legend as the historical authority on which the Elizabethan monarchy was said to be founded; see Christiane Kunst, 'William Camden's *Britannia*: History and Historiography,' in M. H. Crawford and C. R. Ligota, eds, *Ancient History and the Antiquarian: Essays in Honour of Arnaldo Momigliano* (London, 1995), pp. 117–31.

20 Colm Lennon, *Richard Stanihurst The Dubliner, 1547–1618* (Blackrock, 1981), pp. 40–41.
21 *Two Bokes of the Histories of Ireland, compiled by Edmunde Campion*, ed. A. F. Vossen (Assen, 1963), pp. 47–48, 50.
22 Stanihurst received a pension from the Spanish government from 1586 until his death in 1618, was in residence as a physician in the court of Philip II from 1591 to 1595, visited 'his friend Justus Lipsius' on his way there, became a Jesuit priest after his wife died in 1602, and worked for the household of Albert, the archduke of Austria, and the Infanta Isabella in the Netherlands (Lennon, *Richard Stanihurst*, pp. 4, 47–8, 62, 52, 55).
23 P. W. Hasler, *The House of Commons, 1558–1603*, 3 vols (London, 1981), III, pp. 316–17; Charles Wilson, 'Thomas Sackville: An Elizabethan Poet as Citizen', in *Ten Studies in Anglo-Dutch Relations* (London, 1974), pp. 30–50.
24 See Paul Bacquet, *Un Contemporain d'Elizabeth I: Thomas Sackville, l'homme et l'oeuvre* (Geneva, 1966). The 1563 edition of *A Mirror for Magistrates* included a prose link defending Buckhurst against charges that his tale of Aeneas' journey to the underworld was touched with the Catholic notion of purgatory (see Scott Campbell Lucas, 'Tragic Poetry as Political Resistance: *A Mirror for Magistrates, 1554–1563*', PhD diss., Duke University, 1997, pp. 299–300).
25 *The Ven. Philip Howard Earl of Arundel, 1557–1595, Catholic Record Society*, XXI (London, 1919), pp. 43–45.
26 W. B. Patterson, *King James VI and I and the Reunion of Christendom* (Cambridge, 1997), pp. 89–97, 155–8.
27 Simon Adams, 'Spain or the Netherlands? The Dilemmas of Early Stuart Foreign Policy', in H. Tomlinson, ed., *Before the English Civil War* (London, 1983), pp. 79–101.
28 Claus Peter Clasen, *The Palatinate in European History, 1559–1660* (Oxford, 1963), p. 6; Roy Strong, *Henry Prince of Wales and England's Lost Renaissance* (London, 1986), p. 78. At the wedding in 1613, the use of tapestries depicting the defeat of the Spanish Armada would register the international religious-political significance of this union; see Yates, *Shakespeare's Last Plays: A New Approach*, p. 32. See also David Norbrook, '"The Masque of Truth": Court Entertainments and International Protestant Politics in the Early Stuart Period', *The Seventeenth Century*, I (1986), pp. 81–110.
29 See Stephen Orgel, ed., *The Tempest* (Oxford, 1987), pp. 30–31; Hamilton, *Virgil and 'The Tempest'*, pp. 40–43; David Scott Kastan, '"The Duke of Milan / And His Brave Son": Dynastic Politics in *The Tempest*', in Virginia Mason Vaughan and Alden T. Vaughan, eds, *Critical Essays on Shakespeare's 'The Tempest'* (New York, 1998), pp. 91–103.
30 See Hamilton, *Virgil and 'The Tempest'*, pp. 44–55, 55–66.
31 On the '*confused noise*,' see esp. the readings by David Norbrook, '"What Cares These Roarers for the Name of King?": Language and Utopia in *The Tempest*', in Gordon McMullan and Jonathan Hope, eds, *The Politics of Tragicomedy: Shakespeare and After* (London, 1992), pp. 21–54; Tudeau-Clayton, *Jonson, Shakespeare and Early Modern Virgil*, pp. 194–244. Critics who read an opposition politics here and elsewhere in the play nevertheless call that politics by different names. To Norbrook, the '*confused noise*' moment supports his reading of the play's republicanism; to Tudeau-Clayton, it supports her reading of Shakespeare's resistance politics. For a reading of the giving up of power as bespeaking the constitutionalism (i.e. republicanism) of the play, see Hamilton, *Virgil and 'The Tempest'*, pp. xii, 127–9, 133.
32 While I agree with Tudeau-Clayton on *The Tempest*'s opposition politics, we disagree on matters of religion. Tudeau-Clayton relies on a binary that associates

absolutism with Catholicism and resistance with Protestantism (what she calls the 'protestant turn'). This binary overlooks the absolutism of James's Protestant politics as well as the resistance that often characterized Catholic politics.

33 On Habsburg absolutism, see Claudio Veliz, *The New World of the Gothic Fox: Culture and Economy in English and Spanish America* (Berkeley, 1994), pp. 56ff, 79. I am grateful to Ralph Bauer for this reference and for discussion of this paper.

10 ANDREW C. HESS: THE MEDITERRANEAN AND SHAKESPEARE'S GEOPOLITICAL IMAGINATION

1 For the sixteenth-century clash of Mediterranean empires, see Andrew C. Hess, *The Forgotten Frontier* (Chicago, 1978), pp. 71–99.

2 On the strategy of Philip II after the battle of Lepanto in 1571, see Geoffrey Parker, *The Grand Strategy of Philip II* (London, 1998), pp. 77–177.

3 Andrew C. Hess, 'The Battle of Lepanto and Its Place in Mediterranean History', *Past and Present*, 57 (1972), pp. 53–73.

4 How this literary development marked a new era in the history of the Ibero-African frontier is covered in Hess, *Forgotten Frontier*, pp. 194–211.

5 Jack D'Amico, *The Moor in English Renaissance Drama* (Tampa, FL, 1991).

6 In May 1649, long after Shakespeare's death in 1616, Alexander Ross completed the first translation into English of the Koran. A more accurate version did not appear until 1734. This history of the Koran's arrival in England is only one gauge of the inadequate knowledge of the Islamic world. For a broad coverage of this issue, see Nabil Matar, *Islam in Britain 1558–1685* (Cambridge, 1998), pp. 73–119.

7 The original work is Edward Said, *Orientalism* (New York, 1978). An expansion of that study is Said, *Culture and Imperialism* (New York, 1993).

8 The success Islam had in meeting past historical challenges is a major factor in explaining why Muslims in the late sixteenth century did not feel it necessary to acquire European experience; see Andrew C. Hess, 'Islamic Civilization and the Legend of Political Failure', *Journal of Near Eastern Studies*, 44/1 (1985), pp. 27–39; Bernard Lewis, *The Muslim Discovery of Europe* (New York, 1982).

9 S. A. Skilliter, *William Harborne and the Trade with Turkey 1578–1582* (London, 1977), is a documentary study of the earliest Anglo-Ottoman relations.

10 On the Ottoman involvement in internal religious affairs on the Protestant side, see Andrew C. Hess, 'The Moriscos: An Ottoman Fifth Column in Sixteenth Century Spain', *American Historical Review*, 74/1 (October 1968), pp. 1–25.

11 The trajectory of English trade in armaments with Muslims begins in Morocco and moves eastwards along the coast of North Africa to Istanbul. While there is no major study on this important sixteenth-century trade, there is ample evidence of it. See D'Amico, *The Moor*, pp. 7–40; Dahiru Yahya, *Morocco in the Sixteenth Century* (Harlow, 1981), pp. 59–77, 151–8; Skilliter, *Harborne*, pp. 1–33.

12 Skilliter, *Harborne*, pp. 34–138.

13 The history of England's foreign policy difficulties with the Ottoman alliance is developed by V. J. Parry, 'The Successors of Sulaiman, 1566–1617', in M. A. Cook, ed., *A History of the Ottoman Empire to 1730* (New York, 1967), pp. 122–7.

14 Alberto Tenenti, *Piracy and the Decline of Venice 1580–1615* (London, 1967), pp. 56–86, describes the entry of English and Dutch sailors and merchants from the Venetian point of view. For an Ottoman experience of the same event, see Daniel Goffman, *Izmir and the Levantine World, 1550–1650* (Seattle, 1990), pp. 3–76.

15 Halil Inalcik, 'Northerners in the Mediterranean', in Halil Inalcik and Donald

Quataert, eds, *An Economic and Social History of the Ottoman Empire 1300–1914* (New York, 1994), pp. 364–79.

16 See Virginia Mason Vaughan, *'Othello': A Contextual History* (Cambridge, 1994), esp. the chapter entitled 'Global Discourse: Venetians and Turks'.

17 Ellen G. Friedman, *Spanish Captives in North Africa in the Early Modern Age* (Madison, WI, 1983).

18 While this play appeared one year later than *The Tempest*, a linkage between the Turk and the necromancer had already been made in a 1594 non-dramatic recasting of Christopher Marlowe's *The Tragicall History of Dr Faustus*.

19 On John Ward, Tunis and the serious problem of cultural chaos and conversion to Islam in English literature during the Jacobean era, see Matar, *Islam in Britain*, pp. 1–72, 120–90. Cf. Daniel J. Vitkus, 'Turning Turk in *Othello*: The Conversion and Damnation of the Moor', *Shakespeare Quarterly*, 48 (1997), pp. 145–76.

20 The details of these developments are given in Leslie P. Pierce, *The Imperial Harem* (New York, 1993); *Women in the Ottoman Empire*, ed. Madeline C. Zilfi (Leiden, 1997).

21 The traditional opposition to the Renaissance in the Islamic world is discussed in Seyyed Hossein Nasr, *Traditional Islam in the Modern World* (New York, 1987), pp. 97–113; for a study of the place of Ottoman poetry in the literary tradition of the Turks, see Kemal Silay, *Nedim and the Poetics of the Ottoman Court* (Bloomington, 1994), pp. 1–54.

A DESCRIPTION OF THE MIGHTIE CITIE OF TUNIS

1 Kim F. Hall, echoing the essays of Crystal Bartolovich and Joseph Roach in this volume, described this text as 'a safe conduit through which readers become protected tourists, enjoying the wonders and promised wealth of Africa while safely distanced from its more ominous and seductive cultural practices' (*Things of Darkness: Economies of Race and Gender in Early Modern England* [Ithaca, NY, 1995], p. 30). But Jonathan Burton has argued that, when seen in its own right, Leo Africanus provides an example 'of how Eurocentric principles such as European and Christian superiority and entitlement were challenged and even reshaped by their non-Western counterparts' ('"A most wily bird": Leo Africanus, *Othello* and the Trafficking in Difference', in *Post-colonial Shakespeares*, ed. Ania Loomba and Martin Orkin [London, 1998], pp. 43–63, at p. 44.

11 JERRY BROTTON: CARTHAGE AND TUNIS, *THE TEMPEST* AND TAPESTRIES

1 See for instance John Pitcher, 'A Theatre of the Future: *The Aeneid* and *The Tempest*', *Essays in Criticism*, 34 (1984), pp. 193–215.

2 Andrew Hess, *The Forgotten Frontier: A History of the Sixteenth-Century Ibero-African Frontier* (Chicago, 1978).

3 For the most recent and accessible account of classical learning and Renaissance humanism, see John Hale, *The Civilization of Europe in the Renaissance* (London, 1993), pp. 189–214.

4 On this dimension of Renaissance culture, see Lisa Jardine, *Worldly Goods: A New History of the Renaissance* (London, 1996).

5 Craig Harbison, *The Art of the Northern Renaissance* (London, 1995), p. 47.

6 On the history of tapestries, see W. G. Thomson, *A History of Tapestry From the*

Earliest Times to the Present Day (London, 1906), and, more recently, Barty Phillips, *Tapestry* (London, 1994).

7 See Anthony Grafton and Lisa Jardine, '"Studied for action": How Gabriel Harvey Read his Livy', *Past and Present*, 129 (1990), pp. 30–78.

8 See Jay Levenson, ed., *Circa 1492: Art in the Age of Exploration* (Washington, D.C., 1991), pp. 139–40.

9 *The Taking of Arzila* has been attributed to the studio of Pasquier Grenier, who was also responsible for at least one series of tapestries portraying the Trojan War. See William Forsyth, 'The Trojan War in Medieval Tapestries', *Metropolitan Museum of Art Bulletin*, 14 (1955), pp. 76–84.

10 See Phyllis Ackerman, *The Rockefeller McCormick Tapestries: Three Early Sixteenth Century Tapestries* (Oxford, 1932), pp. 10–44.

11 See my *Trading Territories: Mapping the Early Modern World* (London, 1997), pp. 17–45.

12 Hendrick Horn, *Jan Cornelisz Vermeyen: Painter of Charles V and His Conquest of Tunis*, 2 vols (Netherlands, 1989), I, p. 289.

13 See Roy Strong, *Art and Power: Renaissance Festivals, 1450–1650* (Woodbridge, 1984), p. 83.

14 *Ibid.*, p. 86.

15 See Bernice Davidson, 'The *Navigatione d'Enea* Tapestries Designed by Perino del Vaga for Andrea Doria', *Art Bulletin*, 72 (1990), pp. 35–50.

16 *Ibid.*, p. 38.

17 See Hess, *Forgotten Frontier*, pp. 71–99. When Charles V's illegitimate son, Don John of Austria, briefly retook the city in 1573, upon landing he immediately rode out to the site of ancient Carthage (Fernand Braudel, *The Mediterranean*, trans. and abbr. Richard Ollard, London, 1995, p. 295).

18 See the inventory in H. C. Marillier, *The Tapestries at Hampton Court Palace* (London, 1951).

19 *Dictionary of National Biography*, entry on Phaer, vol. XLV, p. 404; entry on Twyne, vol. LVII, p. 404.

20 Thomas Phaer and Thomas Twyne, *The whole xii Bookes of the Aeneidos of Virgill* (London, 1573), unpag. preface.

21 *Ibid.*, sig. L2r.

22 See *The Rape of Lucrece*, where Lucrece gazes on 'a piece / Of skilful painting made for Priam's Troy,' (ll. 1366–7), and *Cymbeline*, when Iachimo reports that Imogen's bedchamber 'was hang'd / With tapestry of silk and silver, the story / Proud Cleopatra, when she met her Roman (II.iv. 68–70). On the creation of the English tapestry industry from the late sixteenth century, see W. G. Thomson, *Tapestry Weaving in England* (London, 1915).

12 ROLAND GREENE: ISLAND LOGIC

1 Richard Eden, *The First Three Books on America*, ed. Edward Arber (Birmingham, 1885; reprint New York, 1971), p. xliv. I am grateful to Edmund Campos for bringing this island to my attention.

2 Fredric Jameson, *The Political Unconscious: Narrative as a Socially Symbolic Act* (Ithaca, NY, 1981), pp. 67, 87–8; 'Of Islands and Trenches: Neutralization and the Production of Utopian Discourse', in his *The Ideologies of Theory: Essays 1971–1986*, 2 vols (Minneapolis, 1988), II, p. 75.

3 With reference to Utopia, Louis Marin has described a poetics of the island: 'Utopia is a circular island, but it is both closed and open. It is closed off to the

outside, and engineering, *arte*, and nature have fortified the coast to such an extent that any invasion is impossible . . . It is a line closed off to itself; a centered circle . . . gives strong connotations of geometry, astronomy, and magic' (*Utopics: The Semiological Play of Textual Spaces*, trans. Robert A. Vollrath, Atlantic Highlands, 1984, pp. 102–3).

4   Martin W. Lewis and Kären E. Wigen, *The Myth of Continents: A Critique of Metageography* (Berkeley and Los Angeles, 1997).

5   Tom Conley, 'Virtual Reality and the *Isolario*', *Bolletino del Centro Interuniversitario di Richerche sul Viaggio in Italia*, 27–8 (1993), pp. 130–31. Conley treats the isolario in more detail in the chapter entitled 'An Insular Moment', in his *The Self-Made Map: Cosmographic Writing in Early Modern France* (Minneapolis, 1996), pp. 167–201. See also Christian Jacob, *L'Empire des Cartes: Approche théorique de la cartographie à travers l'histoire* (Paris, 1992), esp. pp. 174–201.

6   Conley, 'Virtual Reality and the *Isolario*', p. 138.

7   Barbara Fuchs, 'Conquering Islands: Contextualizing *The Tempest*', *Shakespeare Quarterly*, 48 (1997), pp. 45–62.

8   Perhaps the best commentaries are the brief ones of Orgel in his edition (p. 42, n. 2) and of John Gillies in *Shakespeare and the Geography of Difference* (Cambridge, 1994), p. 49.

9   Hayward Keniston, *Garcilaso de la Vega: A Critical Study of his Life and Works* (New York, 1922), pp. 142–59, describes the events leading up to Garcilaso's wounding in the presence of Charles V and his death at the home of the Duke of Savoy around 13 October 1536. See also the biographical compilation *Para la biografía de Garcilaso: Documentos completos*, ed. Antonio Gallego Morell (Madrid, 1975).

10   William Shakespeare, *The Tempest*, ed. Frank Kermode (London, 1958), p. 47, n. 78.

11   Such is the problem at the end of *Don Quixote* as well: after Sancho Panza has been governor of his imaginary island, he is obliged to return to Quixote's service in the novel's real Spain.

12   Stephen Orgel, 'Prospero's Wife', *Representations*, 8 (1984), pp. 1–13.

13   Antonio Benítez-Rojo, *The Repeating Island: The Caribbean and the Postmodern Perspective*, trans. James Maraniss (Durham, 1992).

14   Peter Brook, *There Are No Secrets: Thoughts on Acting and Theatre* (London, 1993), p. 109.

ON THE WORLD STAGE: CÉSAIRE

1   Malcolm Bowie, 'Island infamy', *TLS*, 9 October 1998, p. 22.

2   See Robert Eric Livingston, 'Decolonising the Theatre: Césaire, Serreau and the Drama of Negritude', in J. Ellen Gainor, ed., *Imperialism and Theatre: Essays on World Theatre, Drama and Performance* (London, 1995), pp. 182–98.

3   Alvina Ruprecht, 'Staging Aimé Césaire's *Une tempête*: Anti-Colonial Theatre in the Counter-Culture Continuum', *Essays in Theatre / Études théâtrales*, 15/1 (1996), pp. 59–68.

4   Philip Crispin's translation is published by Oberon Books Ltd, 521 Caledonian Road, London N7 9RH.

5   'The evil genius of a house; a nemesis, the Greek term for an avenging power who visits the sins of the fathers on their children' (*Brewer's Dictionary of Phrase and Fable*, fourteenth edn, London, 1989, p. 18).

ON THE WORLD STAGE: *TEMPESTAD*

1 Orishas are the deities of *santería*, the Afro-Cuban religion of Yoruba origin, syncretized with Catholicism; see Natalia Bolívar, 'The Orishas in Cuba', in Jean Stubbs and Pedro Pérez Sarduy, eds, *Afrocuba: An Anthology of Cuban Writing on Race, Politics and Culture* (Melbourne, 1993), pp. 137–42.
2 Roberto Fernández Retamar, *Caliban and Other Essays*, trans. Edward Baker (Minneapolis, 1989), p. 14.
3 These passages are translated from Raquel Carrió, *Teatro y Modernidad: Siete Ensayos de Ficción* (Havana, 1997).

ON THE WORLD STAGE: *TERRA NOVA*

1 Jorge Luis Borges, 'Tlön, Uqbar, Orbis Tertius', in his *Collected Fictions*, trans. Andrew Hurley (New York, 1998), p. 81.
2 John Berger and Jean Mohr, *A Seventh Man* (Harmondsworth, 1975), p. 220.

III TRANSATLANTIC ROUTES

INTRODUCTION

1 Frank Kermode, Introduction to his Arden edition of *The Tempest* (London, 1954), p. xxv.
2 Stephen Orgel, Introduction to his Oxford edition of *The Tempest* (London, 1987), p. 33.
3 See Michael Dobson, 'Fairly Brave New World: Shakespeare, the American Colonies, and the American Revolution', *Renaissance Drama*, n.s. 23 (1992), pp. 189–207; Alden T. Vaughan, 'Shakespeare's Indian: The Americanization of Caliban', *Shakespeare Quarterly*, 39 (1988), pp. 137–53.
4 Sidney Lee, *A Life of William Shakespeare* (London, 1898), p. 257; see Vaughan, 'Shakespeare's Indian', p. 140.
5 Leslie Fiedler, *The Stranger in Shakespeare* (London, 1973), pp. 199–253; Terence Hawkes, '*The Tempest*: Speaking Your Language', in his *Shakespeare's Talking Animals* (London, 1973), pp. 194–214; James Smith, 'The Tempest', in his *Shakespearian and Other Essays*, ed. Edmund Wilson (Cambridge 1974), pp. 159–261; Stephen Greenblatt, 'Learning to Curse: Aspects of Linguistic Colonialism in the Sixteenth Century', in Fredi Chiappelli, ed., *First Images of America: The Impact of the New World on the Old*, 2 vols (Berkeley, 1976), pp. 561–80, reprinted in *Learning to Curse: Essays in Modern Culture* (New York, 1990), pp. 16–39.
6 Dobson, 'Fairly Brave New World', pp. 193, 196–7.
7 Leo Marx, 'Shakespeare's American Fable', in his *The Machine in the Garden: Technology and the Pastoral Ideal in America* (New York, 1964), an essay first published in *The Massachusetts Review* in 1960. Cf. Perry Miller, *Errand into the Wilderness* (New York, 1964).
8 'The play, after all, focuses upon a highly civilized European who finds himself living in a prehistoric wilderness.' The indigenous inhabitants feature in this picture only as part of the threatening background: the fact that the island 'is the home of Caliban' heralds no dilemma as to ownership or power, but simply the difficulties that accrue to the search for a moral life in the face of one 'who embodies the untrammeled wildness or cannibalism at the heart of nature' (Marx, 'Shakespeare's American Fable', pp. 44, 69).

9   Virginia Mason Vaughan and Alden T. Vaughan, 'Introduction' to their *Critical Essays on Shakespeare's 'The Tempest'* (New York, 1998), pp. 1–14. They cite the now classic passage from Fiedler's *The Stranger in Shakespeare* that finds in the play 'the whole history of imperialist America . . . prophetically revealed to us in brief parable' (p. 6).

10 James Surtees Philpott, quoted by Howard Felperin, 'The Tempest in Our Time', in his *The Uses of the Canon: Elizabethan Literature and Contemporary Theory* (Oxford, 1990), pp. 176–7.

11 G. Wilson Knight, 'The Shakespearian Superman: A Study of *The Tempest*', in his *The Crown of Life: Essays in Interpretation of Shakespeare's Final Plays* [1947] (London, 1964), p. 208.

12 *Ibid.*, p. 211.

13 *Ibid.*, p. 255.

14 Stephen Greenblatt, 'The Tempest', in Stephen Greenblatt et al., eds., *The Norton Shakespeare* (New York, 1997), pp. 3047–54.

15 See, for example, Ania Loomba, 'Shakespeare and Cultural Difference', in Terence Hawkes, *Alternative Shakespeares Volume 2* (London, 1996), pp. 164–91, and the essays in Ania Loomba and Martin Orkin, eds, *Post-Colonial Shakespeares* (London, 1998).

16 See, for example, B. J. Sokol and Mary Sokol, 'The Tempest and Legal Justification of Plantation in Virginia', in Holger Klein and Peter Davidhazi, eds, *Shakespeare Yearbook IV* (1997), pp. 353–80.

17 See also John Gillies's earlier essay, 'Shakespeare's Virginian Masque', *ELH*, 53 (1986), pp. 673–707; Joan Pong Linton, *The Romance of the New World: Gender and the Literary Formations of English Colonialism* (Cambridge, 1998), pp. 155–84.

18 Janheinz Jahn, *A History of Neo-African Literature: Writing in Two Continents*, trans. Oliver Coburn and Ursula Lehrburger (London, 1966), pp. 241–69; José David Saldívar, 'The School of Caliban', in his *The Dialectics of Our America: Genealogy, Cultural Critique, and Literary History* (Durham, NC, 1991), chap. 6; Margaret Paul Joseph, *Caliban in Exile: The Outsider in Caribbean Fiction* (New York, 1992). See also Max Dorsinville, *Caliban without Prospero: Essays on Quebec and Black Literature* (Erin, Ontario, 1974); Vera Kutzinski, 'The Cult of Caliban: Collaboration and Revisionism in Contemporary Caribbean Narrative', in A. James Arnold, ed., *A History of Literature in the Caribbean, Vol. 3: Cross-Cultural Studies* (Amsterdam, 1997), pp. 285–302.

19 Derek Walcott, 'The Muse of History' [1974], in his *What the Twilight Says: Essays* (London, 1998), pp. 38–9. For what reads like a response, see Houston A. Baker, Jr, 'Caliban's Triple Play', *Critical Inquiry*, 13 (1986), pp. 182–96: 'Caliban's triple play . . . is a maroon or guerilla action carried out within linguistic territories of the erst-while masters, bringing forth sounds that have been taken for crude hooting, but which are, in reality, racial poetry' (p. 195).

20 Laura Mulvey, Dirk Snauwaert and Mark Alice Durant, *Jimmie Durham* (London, 1995), pp. 78–89.

21 Sylvia Wynter, 'The Poetics and the Politics of a High Life for Caliban', in Lemuel Johnson, *Highlife for Caliban* (Trenton, NJ, 1995), pp. 85–110 at 92 and 99–100.

22 Johnson, *Highlife for Caliban*, p. 42.

23 Elaine Savory, 'Returning to Sycorax/ Prospero's Response: Kamau Brathwaite's Word Journey', in Stewart Brown, ed., *The Art of Kamau Brathwaite* (Bridgend, 1995), pp. 208–30 at 209.

24 Kamau Brathwaite, 'Letter Sycorax', in his *Middle Passages* (Newcastle upon Tyne, 1992), pp. 76–7.

25 Suniti Namjoshi, 'Snapshots of Caliban', in her *Because of India* (London, 1989), pp. 85–102 at 91.
26 Dabydeen's reading of the dynamism of Hogarth's painting breaks with the traditional art-historical reading, which sees the scene as a kind of Annunciation, with Ferdinand as one of the Magi coming to pay homage, Ariel as one of the heavenly angels, and Caliban as his 'diabolical opposite' (Ronald Paulson, *Book and Painting: Shakespeare, Milton and the Bible: Literary Texts and the Emergence of English Painting*, Knoxville, 1982, p. 49).
27 Charles Verlinden, *The Beginnings of Modern Colonization*, trans. Yvonne Freccero (Ithaca, 1970).
28 Paul Gilroy, *'There Ain't No Black in the Union Jack': The Cultural Politics of Race and Nation* (Chicago, 1987), p. 157.

JIMMIE DURHAM'S CALIBAN

1 Mark Alice Durant, 'The Caliban Codex of A Thing Most Brutish', in Laura Mulvey, Dirk Snauwaert and Mark Alice Durant, *Jimmie Durham* (London, 1995), p. 87.
2 Dan Cameron, 'The Subject was Roses (But Now It's Fish)', in Jimmie Durham, *The East London Coelacanth* (London, 1993), p. 36.

13 JOHN GILLIES: THE FIGURE OF THE NEW WORLD IN *THE TEMPEST*

1 Sigmund Freud, 'Totem and Taboo', in *The Pelican Freud Library*, vol. 13, trans. James Strachey (London, 1955), p. 121, n. 3.
2 Julia Kristeva, *Powers of Horror: An Essay on Abjection*, trans. Leon S. Roudiez (New York, 1982).
3 Edmundo O'Gorman, *The Invention of America: An Inquiry into the Historical Nature of the New World and the Meaning of Its History* (Bloomington, 1961).
4 *Ibid.*, p. 84.
5 *Ibid.*, p. 86. In *New Worlds, Ancient Texts: The Power of Tradition and the Shock of Discovery* (Cambridge, MA, 1992), Anthony Grafton points out that whereas 'Columbus used his texts to make the new familiar, to locate it,' Vespucci 'did the reverse. He emphasized that . . . familiar terms could not apply. He framed his whole account . . . as something new' (p. 84).
6 O'Gorman, *The Invention of America*, pp. 122–3.
7 *Ibid.*, p. 140.
8 *Ibid.*, p. 100.
9 See my analysis of such maps in *Shakespeare and the Geography of Difference* (Cambridge, 1994), pp. 156–88.
10 E. McClung Fleming, 'The American Image as Indian Princess', *Winterthur Portfolio*, 2 (1965), pp. 65–81; 'From Indian Princess to Greek Goddess: The American Image, 1783–1815', *Winterthur Portfolio*, 3 (1967), pp. 37–66. See also Clare Le Corbeiller, 'Miss America and Her Sisters: Personifications of the Four Parts of the World', *Metropolitan Museum of Art Bulletin*, 19 (April 1961), pp. 209–23.
11 Bernadette Bucher, *Icon and Conquest: A Structural Analysis of the Illustrations of de Bry's Great Voyages* (Chicago, 1981).
12 *Ibid.*, p. 18.
13 *Ibid.*, p. 102.
14 My reference is to Richard F. Thomas, *Lands and Peoples in Roman Poetry: The*

Ethnographical Tradition (Cambridge, 1982). Conceiving a 'land' independently of its 'peoples' represented a complete departure from the authority of the ancient tradition charted by Thomas.

15 An account of these is given in Louis B. Wright, *Religion and Empire: The Alliance between Piety and Commerce in English Expansion, 1558–1625* (Chapel Hill, NC, 1943), chap. 4.

16 Short Title Catalogue 6029, University Microfilms reel 727.

17 'Virginias Verger: Or a Discourse shewing the benefits which may grow to this Kingdome from American English Plantations and specially those of Virginia and Summer Ilands' (1625), in *Hakluytus Posthumus or Purchas His Pilgrimes*, 20 vols (Glasgow, 1905), XIX, pp. 218–67.

18 *Ibid.*, p. 222.

19 *Ibid.*, p. 229.

20 *Ibid.*, pp. 231, 242.

21 Arthur J. Slavin, 'The American Principle from More to Locke', in Fredi Chiappelli, ed., *First Images of America* (Berkeley, 1976), pp. 139–64.

22 Kristeva cites the same passage I cited at the beginning of this essay (see *Powers of Horror*, pp. 60–61).

23 Kristeva, *Powers of Horror*, p. 11.

24 'The abject from which he does not cease separating is for him, in short, a land of oblivion that is constantly remembered. Once upon blotted-out time, the abject must have been a magnetized pole of covetousness' (Kristeva, *Powers of Horror*, p. 8).

25 Galle's engraving (*c.* 1600) is taken from a drawing by Jan van der Straet (*c.* 1575) and reproduced above, p. 169.

26 Frank Kermode, ed., *The Tempest, The Arden Shakespeare* (London, 1962), p. xxxiii. Kermode quotes the relevant passage from *Purchas His Pilgrimage* (1613): 'One among them, the eldest as he is iudged, riseth right up, the others sitting still: and looking about, suddenly cries with a loud voice, *Baugh, Waugh* . . . the man altogether answering the same, fall a stamping round about the fire . . . with sundrie outcries.'

27 For a useful account of New World masques in England, see Virginia Mason Vaughan, '"Salvages and Men of Ind": English Theatrical Representations of American Indians, 1590–1690', in R. Doggett, ed., *New World of Wonders: European Images of the Americas, 1492–1700* (Washington, D.C., 1992), pp. 114–23.

28 See my 'Shakespeare's Virginian Masque', *ELH*, 53 (1986), pp. 673–707.

29 For an illuminating account of Natural Law in the period, see R. S. White, *Natural Law in English Renaissance Literature* (Cambridge, 1996).

30 Patriarchal symbolism is very important to the Virginia discourse. Crashaw and others imagine the 'planting' of a godly commonwealth in the wilderness as equivalent to the feats of the Biblical patriarchs. An image of bearded and robed patriarchs tending plants adorns the title page of *A True Declaration of the Estate of the Colonie in Virginia* (London, 1610), a direct source of the play. Prospero's harshness in some way suggests Sir Thomas Dale's regime of 'laws moral and martiall' in Virginia.

31 An important source of Natural Law thinking in the period, Aristotle also provided the principal authorization for slavery in the New World. See Lewis Hanke, *All Mankind Is One: A Study of the Disputation between Bartolomé de las Casas and Juan Ginés de Sepúlveda in 1550 on the Intellectual and Religious Capacity of the American Indians* (DeKalb, IN, 1974).

32 In Robert Johnson's *The New Life of Virginea* (1612), the project of civilizing the

Indians is conceived in terms of returning them to an aboriginal state of virtue from which they have degenerated since the dispersal of peoples after Babel. The combination of history and nature puts the Indians on a par with the primitive Britons.

33 R. S. White makes the point that the traditional Thomist idea of natural law (that human beings were naturally virtuous) and the Puritan assumption that natural virtue was radically accessible (in spite of the Fall) were made obsolete by Hobbes, who saw no reason for believing that virtue was innate to human nature (White, *Natural Law*, 'Epilogue', pp. 243–51).

34 'Hariot's Brief and True Report of the New Found Land of Virginia', in A. L. Rowse, ed., *Voyages To The Virginia Colonies by Richard Hakluyt* (London, 1986), pp. 107–36.

35 Richard Eden, *A Vyage rounde about the worlde* (1526), in Edward Arber, ed., *The First Three English Books on America* (New York, 1971), p. 252.

36 *Elizabethan and Other Essays by Sir Sidney Lee*, ed. Frederick S. Boas (Freeport, NY, 1968), p. 297.

37 *Ibid.*, p. 298.

38 *Ibid.*, p. 299.

39 Michel de Certeau, 'Psychoanalysis and Its History', in his *Heterologies: Discourse on the Other* (Manchester, 1986), pp. 3–16.

40 De Certeau, 'Psychoanalysis and Its History', p. 3.

41 See de Certeau's suggestive essay 'Montaigne's "Of Cannibals": The Savage "I"', in *Heterologies*, pp. 67–79. On the absence of objective reportage, Grafton observes that whereas 'from the standpoint of the modern historian the Great Encounter . . . pure accounts – straight transcripts of Columbian logs and Indian speeches – would be far more valuable than the mediated knowledge their texts offer . . . no such texts could in fact have been produced in the early modern world (if indeed they could be produced now)' (*New Worlds, Ancient Texts*, p. 147).

42 For complex and nuanced accounts of 'forgetting' in *The Tempest*, see Jonathan Baldo, 'Exporting Oblivion in *The Tempest*', *Modern Language Quarterly*, 56/2 (June 1995), pp. 111–44; Mary Fuller, 'Forgetting the *Aeneid*', *American Literary History*, 4 (1992), pp. 517–37.

43 Peter Hulme, *Colonial Encounters: Europe and the Native Caribbean, 1492–1797* (London, 1986), p. 118.

44 *Le Nouveau Petit Robert* (Paris, 1993) loosely defines *remords* as 'anguish accompanied by shame caused by consciousness of wrongdoing'. This is shown as having derived in 1170 from *re* + *mordre*. *Remordre* is defined as (1) 'to inflict suffering by means of remorse' (2) *mordre de nouveau* or 'bite once more'.

14 PATRICIA SEED: 'THIS ISLAND'S MINE': CALIBAN AND NATIVE SOVEREIGNTY

1 See my 'Taking Possession and Reading Texts: Establishing the Authority of Overseas Empires', *William and Mary Quarterly*, 49 (1992), pp. 183–209, and *Ceremonies of Possession in Europe's Conquest of the New World* (Cambridge, 1995). 'Even the modern legal systems based on Roman Law are not based directly on the legal system of Rome. Rather, they are derived from the European Ius Commune, which is – essentially – Roman Law as it was interpreted and reshaped by medieval jurists . . . in the process of adoption/reception many Roman rules were amalgamated with, or amended to suit, the legal norms of the various European

nations' (http://www.jura.unisb.de/Rechtsgeschichte/Ius.Romanum/english.html).

2   The two major exceptions to this rule are Ernest Nys, *Etudes de droit international et de droit politique*, 2 vols (Brussels, 1896–1901), and James Brown Scott, *The Spanish Origin of International Law* (Oxford, 1934). More typical are Spanish perspectives such as Camilo Barcia Trelles, *Francisco de Vitoria, fundador del derecho internacional moderno* (Valladolid, 1928), and Ramon Hernández, *Francisco de Vitoria: vida y pensamiento internacionalista* (Madrid, 1995). Such perspectives contrast sharply with those of Henry Wheaton, *History of The Law of Nations In Europe And America: From The Earliest Times to The Treaty of Washington* [1842] (New York, 1845), frequently cited by the nineteenth-century US Supreme Court. Popular modern English-language histories, such as Arthur Nussbaum, *A Concise History of the Law of Nations*, revd edn (New York, 1962), and the textbooks of international law in American law schools usually begin with Grotius. Starting historical narration in this way requires displacing the beginning of international law from the sixteenth to the seventeenth century. See Karl Mommsen, *Auf dem Wege zur Staatssouveranitat: Staatliche Grundbegriffe in Basler juristischen Doktordisputationen des 17. und 18. Jahrhunderts* (Bern, 1970). A typical Dutch title is Dirk Graaf van Hogendorp, *Commentatio de juris gentium studio in patria nostra, post Hugonem Grotium* (Amsterdam, 1856). Part of the motive behind the claiming of Grotius rather than Vitoria as the founder of international law is the desire for a Protestant rather than a Catholic genealogy. One of the unusual compromises in this context has involved Alberico Gentili, the Italian-born Protestant who fled to England and who therefore can be claimed by both sides as the founder of international law. However, this trend remains relatively undeveloped. See Aurelio Saffi, *Di Alberigo Gentili e del diritto delle genti* (Bologna, 1878); Gesina Hermina Johanna van der Molen, *Alberico Gentili and the Development of International Law: His Life, Work And Times* (Amsterdam, 1937). While non-Spanish speakers often claim that the Spanish origin of international law is no longer credible, recent Spanish textbooks such as Juan Antonio Carrillo Salcedo, *El derecho internacional en perspectiva historica* (Madrid, 1991) offer a very different outlook.

3   Seed, *Ceremonies of Possession*.

4   Peter Hulme, *Colonial Encounters: Europe and The Native Caribbean, 1492–1797* (London, 1986), pp. 154–5, 163–4.

5   Further details of this analysis are in my forthcoming *American Pentimento*, chap. 1.

6   Bernard Bailyn, *The Peopling of British North America* (London, 1987); Carl Bridenbaugh, *No Peace Beyond The Line: The English In The Caribbean, 1624–1690* (New York, 1972).

7   Allowing or encouraging policies of 'peopling' occurred in connection with the development of commercial export agriculture in the ABC countries (Argentina, Brazil, Chile).

8   Popular support for enduring native ownership remains weaker in Argentina and Chile, where battles of a century or longer were fought prior to establishing such guarantees.

9   Details on this come from chaps 1 and 2 of my *American Pentimento*. See also J. C. Smith, 'The Concept of Native Title', *University of Toronto Law Journal*, 1 (1974), p. 24; Brian Slattery, *Ancestral Lands, Alien Laws: Judicial Perspectives on Aboriginal Title* (Saskatoon, 1983).

10 The US Supreme Court together with the Congress established the doctrine of native title between 1810 and 1835. In Australia and New Zealand, judicial independence of the Privy Council occurred only in the twentieth century.

11 The details in this and the preceding paragraph come from chap. 3 of my *American Pentimento*.

12 See Thomas Southey, *Chronological History of the West Indies* (London, 1827); Nellis M. Crouse, *The French Struggle for the West Indies, 1665–1713* (New York, 1943); Carl Sauer, *The Early Spanish Main* (Berkeley, 1966); Mendel Peterson, *The Funnel of Gold* (Boston, 1975); Paul E. Hoffman, *The Spanish Crown and the Defense of the Caribbean, 1535–1585* (Baton Rouge, 1980).

13 See Armand Nicolas, *Histoire de la Martinique*, 2 vols (Paris, 1996), I, pp. 46–7; Pierre Pluchon, ed., *Histoire des Antilles et de la Guyane* (Toulouse, 1982) (which underplays the rôle of the buccaneers); Edward Long, *The History of Jamaica*, 3 vols (London, 1774); Wim Klooster, *Illicit Riches: Dutch Trade in the Caribbean, 1648–1795* (Leiden, 1998).

14 Diane Purkiss is highly critical of Shakespeare's use of witchcraft. She says he 'buries popular culture under a thick topdressing of exploitative sensationalism, unblushingly strip-mining both popular culture and every learned text he can lay his hands on for the sake of creating an arresting stage event' (*The Witch in History: Early Modern and Twentieth-Century Representations*, London, 1996, p. 207). Both she and Robin Briggs (*Witches and Neighbours: The Social and Cultural Context of European Witchcraft*, London, 1996, p. 275) emphasize the bilateral inheritance pattern of communities of witches in England against the more popular (but incorrect) assumption that they were matrilineal.

15 See John Gillies's essay in this volume.

15 GORDON BROTHERSTON: *ARIELISMO* AND ANTHROPOPHAGY: *THE TEMPEST* IN LATIN AMERICA

1 See the acute commentary by Stephen Orgel in the 'Introduction' to his edition of *The Tempest* (Oxford, 1987), pp. 31–6.

2 Originally published in the major Buenos Aires newspaper *La Nación*, where 'El triunfo de Calibán' had also appeared, on 25 May 1898: see Darío's *Obras completas* (Madrid, 1955), IV, pp. 569–76; and Carlos Jáuretegui, 'Calibán, ícono del 98. A propósito de un artículo de Rubén Darío, *Revista Iberoamericana*, LXIV, 184–5 (1998), pp. 441–9. I am grateful to Luis Rebaza-Soraluz for the references to *De Sobremesa* and Poe's short story.

3 *Ariel*'s debt to the French is usefully summarized by Gerard Aching, *The Politics of Spanish American Modernismo: By Exquisite Design* (Cambridge, 1997), p. 157ff., although in this study there is nothing about how Fouillée's prior rejection of the apparent Old World cynicism of Renan's *Caliban* inspired Rodó's rejection, along with his desire to 're-attach' Ariel to life and society (see the 'Introduction' to my edition of *Ariel*, Cambridge, 1967, pp. 2–6). In just this regard, the characters of *The Tempest* play major rôles in 'Ariel o la agonía de una obstinada ilusión', the third part of *Humanismo burgués y humanismo proletario* (1938), by the Argentinian Aníbal Ponce, who examines the growth of revolutionary philosophy in the West 'from Erasmus to Romain Rolland', without however so much as mentioning Rodó or other fellow Latin Americans (*Obras completas*, ed. H. P. Acosti, Buenos Aires, 1974).

4 'El cruzará la historia humana, entonando, como en el drama de Shakespeare, su canción melodiosa, para animar a los que trabajan y a los que luchan, hasta que el cumplimiento del plan ignorado a que obedece le permita – cual se liberta, en el drama, del servicio de Próspero, – romper sus lazos materiales y volver para siempre

al centro de su lumbre divina' (José Enrique Rodó, *Obras completas*, ed. Emir Rodríguez Monegal, Madrid, 1957, p. 242). All translations into English are my own.

5 'El nombre de Ariel significa, en la evolución de las ideas que han preparado la actual orientación del pensamiento hispanoamericano, la afirmación del sentido idealista de la vida contra las limitaciones del positivismo utilitario; el espíritu de calidad y selección, opuesto a la igualdad de la falsa democracia y la reivindi- cación del sentimiento de la raza, del abolengo histórico latino, como energía necesaria para salvar y mantener la personalidad de estos pueblos, frente a la expansión triunfal de otros . . . Tuvieron aquellas páginas la virtud de la oportu- nidad, que explica su difusión extraordinaria y la repercusión de simpatía que las ha multiplicado en mil ecos ('El nuevo Ariel', in *Obras completas*, pp. 1136–7).

6 See, for example, Gonzalo Zaldumbide, *José Enrique Rodó* (Madrid, 1919); Alberto Lasplaces, *Opiniones literarias* (Montevideo, 1919). Then, in 1927, Héctor González Areosa (in no. 37 of another Montevidean journal entitled, yet again and ironically enough, *Ariel*), announced that for the new generation of Uruguayans Rodó was no longer an active intellectual presence. Yet half a century on, Carlos Maggi still found it necessary to repeat the message (*El Uruguay y su gente*, Montevideo, 1965, p. 20). At conferences and other events organized to mark the upcoming cente- nary, leading Uruguayan intellectuals (e.g. Mabel Moraña and Fernando Ainsa) continue to explore the issues raised by *Ariel*.

7 Bell Gale Chevigny and Gary Laguardia, eds, *Reinventing the Americas* (Cambridge, 1986), p. 23. Juan Antonio Mella and Carlos L. Rodríguez were among the Communist *arielistas* of Cuba. Useful details of the promotion of *arielismo* throughout America are given by Martin S. Stabb, *In Quest of Identity: Patterns in the Spanish American Essay of Ideas, 1890–1960* (Chapel Hill, NC, 1967); Guido Rodríguez Alcalá, *En torno al Ariel de Rodó* (Asunción, 1990), pp. 95–110; Aching, *The Politics of Spanish American Modernismo*, pp. 95–104. See also Henríquez Ureña's own classic work, *Las corrientes literarias de Hispanoamérica* (Buenos Aires, 1964).

8 Roberto Fernández Retamar, *Caliban; apuntes sobre la cultura en Nuestra América* (Mexico City, 1971). On Rodó and Sánchez, see my 'The Literary World of José Enrique Rodó', in R. G. Mead, *Homenaje a Luis Alberto Sánchez* (Madrid, 1983), pp. 95–104.

9 In the 'Introduction' to his edition of *The Tempest* (pp. 5, 20), Orgel notes that Setebos, the god worshipped by Caliban's mother, is probably Patagonian. A useful survey of *The Tempest*'s wider impact on the Americas and Africa is given by Wolfgang Bader in 'Von der Allegorie zum Kolonialstück: Zur produktiven Rezeption von Shakespeares *The Tempest* in Europa, Amerika und Afrika', *Poetica*, 15/3–4 (1983), pp. 247–88.

10 'A few months ago José Enrique Rodó died in Palermo on his way from South America to France. This statement probably conveys no meaning, and it may be that it is made here for the first time in England . . . Our ignorance may seem the more ungracious if we learn that Rodó's most remarkable essay is called *Ariel*. This sensitive and exalted thinker, familiar with the finest culture of Europe, found the symbol of his aspirations for the world in the English poet's *Tempest*' (Havelock Ellis, 'Rodó', in his *The Philosophy of Conflict, and Other Essays in Wartime* [Boston, 1919], p. 5). See also *Ariel*, trans. F. J. Stimson (Boston, 1922); *The Motives of Proteus*, trans. Angel Flores (London, 1929), which includes Ellis's essay as a pref- ace.

11 'Reading Rodo today, it is windy stuff: very over-written (at least in translation), impossibly idealistic and reeking of cultural snobbery. It illuminates something important about Bevan that he should have taken him as his personal prophet'

(*Nye Bevan*, London, 1987, p. 67). Before Michael Foot published his two-volume work (*Aneurin Bevan*, London, 1962, 1973), Vincent Brome also noted Rodó's importance in his *Aneurin Bevan: A Biography* (London, 1953).

16 PETER HULME: READING ·FROM ELSEWHERE: GEORGE LAMMING AND THE PARADOX OF EXILE

1 George Lamming, *The Pleasures of Exile* (London, 1984); Aimé Césaire, *Une tempête* (Paris, 1969); Roberto Fernández Retamar, 'Caliban: Notes Toward a Discussion of Culture in Our America', in his *Caliban and Other Essays*, trans. Edward Baker et al. (Minneapolis, 1989), pp. 3–45; Octave Mannoni, *Prospero and Caliban: The Psychology of Colonization*, trans. Pamela Powesland (Ann Arbor, 1990).

2 Aimé Césaire, *Discourse on Colonialism*, trans. Joan Pinkham (New York, 1972), pp. 39–42; Frantz Fanon, *Black Skin, White Masks*, trans. Charles Lam Markmann (New York, 1967), pp. 83–108. Doubt has recently been cast on whether Césaire actually taught Fanon; see Richard Price, *The Convict and the Colonel* (Boston, 1998), p. 244, n. 23.

3 Fernández Retamar, *Caliban and Other Essays*, p. 8.

4 See his 'Caliban Revisited', also in *Caliban and Other Essays*, pp. 46–55, and the three further essays included in his *Todo Calibán* (*Milenio*, 3, 1995); cf. Goffredo Diana and John Beverley, 'These Are the Times We Have to Live In: An Interview with Roberto Fernández Retamar', *Critical Inquiry*, 21 (1995), pp. 411–33.

5 Fernández Retamar, 'Caliban', pp. 21–6. The reference is to Domingo Faustino Sarmiento's *Facundo* (1845), a key text for the study of Latin American culture.

6 An important essay that makes imaginative use of Retamar's work is Richard Halpern, '"The picture of Nobody": White Cannibalism in *The Tempest*', in David Lee Miller et al., eds, *The Production of English Renaissance Culture* (Ithaca, NY, 1994), pp. 262–92.

7 *Psychologie de la colonisation* was relatively little known in the English-speaking world even after its translation in 1956.

8 Joan Dayan, 'Playing Caliban: Césaire's *Tempest*', *Arizona Quarterly*, 48/4 (1992), pp. 125–45 at 141.

9 The essay in this volume by Marina Warner discusses Prospero's description of Sycorax (whom he never saw) as 'blue-eyed hag'.

10 Michael Dobson, '"Remember / First to Possess His Books": The Appropriation of *The Tempest*, 1700–1800', *Shakespeare Survey*, 43 (1991), pp. 99–107.

11 Edward Said, *Culture and Imperialism* (London, 1993), p. 295.

12 Lamming, *The Pleasures of Exile*, p. 6.

13 Peter Hulme, 'George Lamming and the Postcolonial Novel', in Jonathan White, ed., *Recasting the World: Writing after Colonialism* (Baltimore, 1993), pp. 120–36.

14 Lamming, *The Pleasures of Exile*, p. 13.

15 Bill Ashcroft, Gareth Griffiths and Helen Tiffin, eds, *The Post-Colonial Studies Reader* (London, 1995), pp. 12–17.

16 *The Pleasures of Exile*, p. 9. Prospero is presumably the Law, preventing Caliban from worshipping his gods.

17 *The Pleasures of Exile*, p. 11.

18 *Ibid.*, p. 12.

19 *Ibid.* Later he speaks of the book as being addressed to West Indians, but he clearly has other readers in mind here.

20 *The Pleasures of Exile*, p. 12.

21 *Ibid.*, p. 13. For historical contextualization, see Kenneth R. Andrews, *Trade, Plunder and Settlement: Maritime Genesis of the British Empire, 1480–1630* (Cambridge, 1984), pp. 116–34. Lamming runs together Hawkins's first two voyages of 1562–3 and 1564–5, the first English slaving voyages, although the transatlantic trade in slaves was by then well established. His quotations are taken from Richard Hakluyt, *The Principal Navigations, Voiages, Traffiques and Discoveries of the English Nation*, 12 vols (Glasgow, 1903–5), X, pp. 7–8, 24–5. Lamming's novel, *Natives of My Person* (1972), draws in a very general way on Hakluyt's account of these early voyages. Hawkins's crucial contacts with Pedro de Ponte, in the Canary Islands, are fictionalized in Antonio Benítez-Rojo's novel *Sea of Lentils*, trans. James Maraniss (Amherst, 1991).

22 *The Pleasures of Exile*, p. 13.

23 *Ibid.*, p. 15.

24 Janheinz Jahn, *A History of Neo-African Literature: Writing in Two Continents*, trans. Oliver Coburn and Ursula Lehrburger (London, 1966); Rob Nixon, 'Caribbean and African Appropriations of *The Tempest*', *Critical Inquiry*, 13 (1987), pp. 557–78. Jonathan Bate, author of several influential books on Shakespeare, recently admitted – and lamented – his ignorance of Lamming's work until the early 1990s ('Caliban and Ariel Write Back', *Shakespeare Survey*, 48, 1995, pp. 155–62).

25 *The Pleasures of Exile*, p. 85.

26 Frantz Fanon, *The Wretched of the Earth*, trans. Constance Farrington (Harmondsworth, 1967), p. 27. Oddly, it was Fanon's use of the term, rather than Lamming's, that entered Caribbean cultural criticism through Kenneth Ramchand's adoption of the phrase 'terrified consciousness' to discuss the work of white West Indian writers: see his *The West Indian Novel and Its Background*, 2nd edn (London, 1983), pp. 223–36.

27 *The Pleasures of Exile*, p. 229. Caliban, though undoubtedly present in the formulation 'slave', is not actually named in this paragraph, since in one sense – as 'canybal' – he is not 'separated from his original ground' in the same way, although dispossession is perhaps a form of exile too.

28 Georges Bandelier, 'La situation coloniale: Approche théorique', *Cahiers internationaux de sociologie*, 6/11 (1951), pp. 44–79. For an interesting reassessment of this tradition, see Emily Apter, *Continental Drift: From National Characters to Virtual Subjects* (Chicago, 1999), pp. 77–95.

29 On the 'sixth act', see Supriya Nair, *Caliban's Curse: George Lamming and the Revisioning of History* (Ann Arbor, 1996), pp. 56–7.

30 *The Pleasures of Exile*, p. 15. This last form of exile is, perhaps, a suggestion that Césaire adopted in having Caliban demand to be called 'X'.

31 *The Pleasures of Exile*, p. 15.

32 *Ibid.*, p. 107.

33 *Ibid.*, p. 110.

34 *Ibid.*, p. 109.

35 *Ibid.*

36 *Ibid.*, p. 27.

37 *Ibid.*, pp. 97–8, 98–9, 101–2, 111.

38 *Ibid.*, p. 99.

39 *Ibid.*, pp. 112, 113, 115, 116.

40 First published in 1933, but reprinted as late as 1970 as an aspect of *Modern Shakespearean Criticism: Essays on Style, Dramaturgy, and the Major Plays*, ed. Alvin B. Kernan (New York, 1970), pp. 45–76.

41 *The Pleasures of Exile*, p. 104.

42 *Ibid.*, p. 104, 115, quoting I.ii.56–7.

43 *Ibid.*, p. 111–12.

44 *Ibid.*, p. 102.

45 *Ibid.*, p. 111.

46 In Lamming's first novel, *In the Castle of My Skin* (1953), three young boys are accused of attempted rape after being caught looking through the window of the white landlord's estate house. In *Water with Berries* (1971), Myra, daughter of the plantation owner, gives a horrifically graphic account of her rape by disaffected servants and dogs.

47 Supriya Nair, *Caliban's Curse*, struggles with considerable success to offer a positive assessment of Lamming's work despite her evident distaste for its sexual politics (pp. 66–8). Lamming's last novel to date, *Native of My Person*, ends with the chief female character saying to her female companions about their men: 'They are a future we must learn.'

48 Cf. 'We are sexual creatures by instinct; we have to be taught that sex is related to reproduction. If Prospero taught Caliban everything he knows, that is how Caliban learned of the demographic advantages of sex with the only woman on the island' (Orgel, 'Introduction' to *The Tempest*, p. 55). And cf. Patricia Seed on 'peopling' the island, in this volume).

49 *The Pleasures of Exile*, p. 15.

50 For example, David Sundelson, 'So Rare a Wondered Father: Prospero's *Tempest*', and Coppélia Kahn, 'The Providential Tempest and the Shakespearean Family', in Murray M. Schwartz and Coppélia Kahn, eds, *Representing Shakespeare: New Psychoanalytic Essays* (Baltimore, 1980), pp. 33–53, 217–43. This approach was opened up in earlier work by Norman Holland, esp. 'Caliban's Dream', *Psychoanalytical Quarterly*, 37 (1968), pp. 114–25.

51 Marina Warner, *Indigo, or Mapping the Waters* (London, 1992), p. 400.

52 See the thoughtful essay by Barbara E. Bowen, 'Writing Caliban: Anticolonial Appropriations of *The Tempest*', *Current Writing*, 5/2 (1993), pp. 80–99, which argues that at least since 1970 Third World readings of *The Tempest* have been above all engagements with other Third World writers rather than primarily engagements with Shakespeare's text. This may well be true, and it certainly opens up interesting pedagogical possibilities, which Bowen goes on to explore. *The Pleasures of Exile* is earlier (1960), but even if it were to fall within Bowen's periodization, I would want to keep open the possibility of different levels of engagement.

53 However much weight is given to editorial, historical or philosophical arguments that serve to undermine the solidity of what has come down to us as the Shakespearean text of *The Tempest*, the degree of actual scholarly consensus about what is being discussed when someone writes 'Shakespeare's play, *The Tempest*' emboldens me to put philosophical worries about the nature of 'the real text' on hold.

54 Stephen Greenblatt, *Learning to Curse: Essays in Modern Culture* (New York, 1990), p. 25.

17 LUCY RIX: MAINTAINING THE STATE OF EMERGENCE/Y: AIMÉ CÉSAIRE'S *UNE TEMPÊTE*

1 Aimé Césaire, quoted in Richard D. E. Burton, *Assimilation or Independence? Prospects for Martinique* (Montreal, 1978), p. 1.

2 Homi Bhabha, 'Remembering Fanon', in Frantz Fanon, *Black Skin, White Masks*, trans. Charles Lam Markmann (London, 1986), p. xi.

3 Noted in Robert Eric Livingston, 'Decolonising the Theatre: Césaire, Serreau and the Drama of Négritude', in J. Ellen Gainor, ed., *Imperialism and Theatre: Essays on World Theatre, Drama and Performance* (London, 1995), pp. 182–98.

4 Quoted in Livingston, 'Decolonising the Theatre', p. 192.

5 Lilyan Kesteloot, *Black Writers in French*, trans. Ellen Conroy Kennedy (Philadelphia, 1974), p. 242 (my italics).

6 Carl Degler, *Neither Black nor White* (Wisconsin, 1971), esp. pp. 205–64.

7 Edouard Glissant, *Caribbean Discourse: Selected Essays*, trans. J. Michael Dash (Charlottesville, 1989), p. xix.

8 Michel Giraud, 'Dialectics of Descent and Phenotypes in Racial Classification in Martinique', in Richard D. E. Burton and Fred Reno, eds, *French and West Indian: Martinique, Guadaloupe and French Guiana Today* (London, 1995), pp. 75–85.

9 From *Légitime défense*, quoted in Kesteloot, *Black Writers in French*, p. 19.

10 René Maran and Gilbert Gratiant, quoted in Kesteloot, *Black Writers in French*, pp. 31 and 33–4:

Ah! toute la douceaur de ma petite enfance
Ces languissantes nuits du port de Fort-de-France
Paradis végétaux
Enchantez-moi longtemps du jeu de vos prestiges.
. . .
Coffre à baisers
Colibri du tourisme
Bijou géographique

Cher jardin des petits cadeaux
Sol pour les démarches souples
Et l'ample enjambée des femmes de couleur
Petit cirque des corridors du coeur
Familière boîte à surprise.

11 Suzanne Césaire, 'Misère d'une poésie: John-Antoine Nau', *Tropiques*, no. 4 (1941).

12 R. M. Albères, *L'Aventure intellectuelle de XXe siècle* (Paris, 1959), quoted in Kesteloot, *Black Writers in French*, pp. 38–9; cf. Michael Richardson, ed., *Refusal of the Shadow: Surrealism and the Caribbean* (London, 1996).

13 Sartre, quoted in Kesteloot, *Black Writers in French*, p. 45.

14 Richard D. E. Burton, 'The French West Indies à l'heure de l'Europe: An Overview', in *French and West Indian*, pp. 1–19.

15 Susan Frutkin, *Black Between Worlds: Aimé Césaire* (Miami, 1973), p. 9.

16 Césaire, quoted in Frutkin, *Black Between Worlds*, p. 47.

17 Livingston, 'Decolonising the Theatre', p. 184.

18 All quotations from *Une tempête* are taken from Philip Crispin's forthcoming translation, published by Oberon Books.

19 Livingston, 'Decolonising the Theatre', p. 193.

20 Glissant, quoted in Benita Parry, 'Resistance Theory / Theorising Resistance, or Two Cheers for Nativism', in Francis Barker et al., eds, *Colonial Discourse/ Postcolonial Theory* (Manchester, 1994), pp. 172–96.

21 Helen Gilbert and Joanne Tompkins, *Postcolonial Drama: Theory, Practice, Politics* (London, 1996), p. 8.

22 Césaire, quoted in A. James Arnold, *Modernism and Négritude: The Poetry and Poetics of Aimé Césaire* (Cambridge, MA, 1981), p. 44.

23 Parry, 'Resistance Theory / Theorising Resistance', pp. 179–80.

24 Bhabha, 'Remembering Fanon', p. xiii.
25 Parry, 'Resistance Theory / Theorising Resistance', p. 182.
26 Fanon, *Black Skin, White Masks*, p. 135.
27 Sartre, *Black Orpheus*, quoted in Fanon, *Black Skin, White Masks*, p. 133.
28 Fanon, *Black Skin, White Masks*, p. 134.
29 Sartre, *Black Orpheus*, quoted in Fanon, *Black Skin, White Masks*, p. 133.
30 Peter Hulme, *Colonial Encounters: Europe and the Native Caribbean, 1492–1797* (London, 1986), p. 121.
31 Joan Dayan, 'Playing Caliban: Césaire's *Tempest*', *Arizona Quarterly*, 48/4 (1992), pp. 125–45.
32 Fanon, *Black Skin, White Masks*, p. 60.
33 Dayan, 'Playing Caliban', p. 138.

18 MARTHA NELL SMITH: H.D.'S 'THE TEMPEST'

1 H.D., *By Avon River* (New York, 1949), dust jacket. Page references in the text are to this edition.
2 Quoted by Susan Stanford Friedman, 'Remembering Shakespeare Differently: H.D.'s *By Avon River*', in Marianne Novy, ed., *Women's Revisions of Shakespeare: On the Responses of Dickinson, Woolf, Rich, H.D., George Eliot, and Others* (Urbana, 1990), pp. 143–64.
3 H.D., 'The Guest', *By Avon River*, p. 3.
4 Alicia Ostriker, *Stealing the Language: The Emergence of Women's Poetry in America* (Boston, 1986), pp. 211–13.
5 H.D., *Paint It Today*, ed. and intro. by Cassandra Laity (New York, 1992), p. 63.

19 DAVID DABYDEEN: HOGARTH AND THE CANECUTTER

1 Dated *c.*1735, oil on canvas; Nostell Priory, Wakefield.
2 Mary Webster, *Hogarth* (London, 1978), p. 12.
3 Lawrence Gowing, *Hogarth* (London, 1971), p. 40.
4 Ronald Paulson, *The Art of Hogarth* (London, 1995), p. 120.
5 *Ibid.*, p. 120.
6 Benita Parry, 'Between Creole and Cambridge English: The Poetry of David Dabydeen', in Kevin Grant, ed., *The Art of David Dabydeen* (Leeds, 1997), pp. 47–66.
7 David Dabydeen, 'The Canecutters' Song', in his *Slave Song* (Mundelstrup, 1984), p. 25.

MERLE COLLINS: ENVOY

1 Interview with George Kent, Professor of English, University of Chicago, 1973, first published in the March 1973 issue of *Black World*, later in Richard Drayton and Andaiye, eds, *Conversations: George Lamming Essays, Addresses and Interviews, 1953–1990* (London, 1992).
2 Drayton and Andaiye, *Conversations*, p. 92.
3 William Wordsworth, *Poetical Works*, ed. Thomas Hutchinson, revd Ernest de Selincourt (Oxford, 1969), p. 66.

Further Reading

This bibliographical essay is designed to survey the state of (the) play, and to help readers follow up each of the sections in 'The Tempest' and Its Travels. Our emphasis is on work published in the last decade: the references contained in this volume and in the items listed below will point to earlier materials.

GENERAL

As with any text by Shakespeare, there are many good editions of The Tempest. Stephen Orgel's Oxford edition, published in 1987 and reprinted in the World's Classics series in 1994, has been our reference point for this volume. Frank Kermode's Arden edition, originally published in 1954, is still valuable; a New Arden edition has been prepared by Alden T. Vaughan and Virginia Mason Vaughan (London, 1999). Barbara A. Mowat and Paul Werstine's New Folger Library edition (New York, 1994) is also worth consulting.

Some of the most influential essays on The Tempest, old and new, have been gathered in casebooks and other collections: see D. J. Palmer, ed., Shakespeare: The Tempest (Basingstoke, 1991); Virginia Mason Vaughan and Alden T. Vaughan, eds, Critical Essays on Shakespeare's 'The Tempest' (New York, 1997); R.S. White, ed., The Tempest: Contemporary Critical Essays (London, 1999); Nigel Wood, ed., The Tempest (Buckingham, 1995); Gerald Graff and James Phelan, eds, The Tempest: A Case Study in Critical Controversy (New York, 2000); Harold Bloom, ed., Caliban (New York, 1992); and Shakespeare Survey, 43 (1991), a special issue on 'The Tempest and After'.

Essential guides for the Shakespearean traveller include Thomas Cartelli, Repositioning Shakespeare: National Formations, Postcolonial Appropriations (London, 1999); Kate Chedgzoy, Shakespeare's Queer Children: Sexual Politics and Contemporary Culture (Manchester, 1995); John Gillies, Shakespeare and the Geography of Difference (Cambridge, 1994); John Gillies and Virginia Mason Vaughan, eds, Playing the Globe: Genre and Geography in English Renaissance Drama (Madison, 1998); Andrew Hadfield, Literature, Travel, and Colonial Writing in the English Renaissance, 1545–1625 (Oxford, 1998); Kim F. Hall, Things of Darkness: Economies of Race and Gender in Early Modern England (Ithaca, NY, 1995); Terence Hawkes, ed., Alternative Shakespeares Volume 2 (London, 1996); Margo Hendricks and Patricia Parker, eds, Women, 'Race', and Writing in the Early Modern Period (London, 1994); Peter Holland, English Shakespeares: Shakespeare on the English Stage in the 1990s (Cambridge, 1997); Lemuel A. Johnson, Shakespeare in Africa (and Other Venues): Import and the Appropriation of Culture (Trenton, NJ, 1998); Jeffrey Knapp, An Empire Nowhere: England, America, and Literature from 'Utopia' to 'The Tempest' (Berkeley, 1992); Joan Pong Linton, The Romance of the New World: Gender and the Literary Formations of English Colonialism

(Cambridge, 1998); Ania Loomba and Martin Orkin, eds, *Postcolonial Shakespeares* (London, 1998); Jean-Pierre Maquerlot and Michèle Willems, eds, *Travel and Drama in Shakespeare's Time* (Cambridge, 1996); and Valerie Traub, M. Lindsey Kaplan, and Dympna Callaghan, eds, *Feminist Readings of Early Modern Culture: Emerging Subjects* (Cambridge, 1996).

I LOCAL KNOWLEDGE

After a period in which critics' sights tended to be set on *The Tempest*'s global contexts, many recent essays have called for a return to the local. For some critics this has meant returning to the text itself for traditional close reading: see Russ McDonald, 'Reading *The Tempest*', *Shakespeare Survey*, 43 (1991), pp. 15–28, and John S. Hunt, 'Prospero's Empty Grasp', *Shakespeare Studies*, 22 (1994), pp. 277–313. For others it has meant attending to the state of Shakespeare's text and conditions of production and performance: see Douglas Bruster, 'Local *Tempest*: Shakespeare and the Work of the Early Modern Playhouse', *Journal of Medieval and Renaissance Studies*, 25 (1995), pp. 33–53; John G. Demaray, *Shakespeare and the Spectacles of Strangeness: 'The Tempest' and the Transformation of Renaissance Theatrical Forms* (Pittsburgh, 1998); and Michael Dobson, *The Making of the National Poet: Shakespeare, Adaptation, and Authorship, 1660–1769* (Oxford, 1992) and '"Remember / First to possess his books": The Appropriation of *The Tempest*, 1700–1800', *Shakespeare Survey*, 43 (1991), pp. 99–107.

Other critics have returned to Elizabethan and Jacobean culture and recovered discursive contexts that shed light on the play: these include David Baker, 'Where is Ireland in *The Tempest*', in *Shakespeare and Ireland*, ed. Mark Thornton Burnett and Ramona Wray (New York, 1997), pp. 68–88; Jonathan Bate, *Shakespeare and Ovid* (Oxford, 1993); Curt Breight, '"Treason doth never prosper": *The Tempest* and the Discourse of Treason', *Shakespeare Quarterly*, 41 (1990), pp. 1–28; Mark Thornton Burnett, '"Strange and woonderfull syghts": *The Tempest* and the Discourses of Monstrosity', *Shakespeare Survey*, 50 (1997), pp. 187–99; Frances E. Dolan, 'The Subordinate('s) Plot: Petty Treason and the Forms of Domestic Rebellion', *Shakespeare Quarterly*, 43 (1992), pp. 317–40; Graham Holderness, '*The Tempest*: Spectacles of Disenchantment', in Graham Holderness, Nick Potter and John Turner, *Shakespeare: Out of Court* (London, 1990), pp. 136–94; David Scott Kastan, '"The Duke of Milan/And His Brave Son": Dynastic Politics in *The Tempest*', in *Critical Essays on Shakespeare's 'The Tempest'*, ed. Virginia Mason Vaughan and Alden T. Vaughan (New York, 1998), pp. 91–103; Leah Marcus, 'Levelling Shakespeare: Local Customs and Local Texts', *Shakespeare Quarterly*, 42 (1991), pp. 168–78; David Norbrook, '"What cares these roarers for the name of king?": Language and Utopia in *The Tempest*', in Gordon McMullan and Jonathan Hope, eds, *The Politics of Tragicomedy* (London, 1992), pp. 21–54; and Julie Robin Solomon, 'Going Places: Absolutism and Movement in Shakespeare's *The Tempest*', *Renaissance Drama*, n.s. 22 (1991), pp. 3–45.

II EUROPEAN AND MEDITERRANEAN CROSSROADS

The Mediterranean world connected Europe and North Africa, invoked the Classical world of Greek and Latin culture, and provided a set of imperial pretexts and intertexts. The presence of Virgil in Shakespeare's play, and his rôle as a mediating figure between the Classical and the Renaissance worlds, has been extensively discussed. But there have been suggestive new forays, including Mary Fuller, 'Forgetting the *Aeneid*',

American Literary History, 4 (1992), pp. 517–38; Donna B. Hamilton, Virgil and 'The Tempest': The Politics of Imitation (Columbus, 1990); Heather James, "'How came that widow in?": Allusion, Politics, and the Theater in The Tempest', in her Shakespeare's Troy: Drama, Politics, and the Translation of Empire (Cambridge, 1997), chap. 6; and Margaret Tudeau-Clayton, 'Shaking Neptune's 'dread trident': The Tempest and figures of Virgil', in her Jonson, Shakespeare and Early Modern Virgil (Cambridge, 1998), chap. 6.

For readings that resituate the play in its Mediterranean contexts see Jerry Brotton, "'This Tunis, sir, was Carthage": Contesting Colonialism', in Ania Loomba and Martin Orkin, eds, Post-Colonial Shakespeares (London, 1998), pp. 23–42; Barbara Fuchs, 'Conquering Islands: Contextualizing The Tempest', Shakespeare Quarterly, 48 (1997), pp. 45–62; Marjorie Raley, 'Claribel's Husband', in Joyce Green MacDonald, ed., Race, Ethnicity, and Power in the Renaissance (Cranbury, 1997), pp. 95-119; and Richard Wilson, 'Voyage to Tunis: New History and the Old World of The Tempest', ELH, 64 (1997), pp. 333–57.

III TRANSATLANTIC ROUTES

On the 'transatlantic' dimensions of The Tempest, see Jonathan Baldo, 'Exporting Oblivion in The Tempest', Modern Language Quarterly, 56 (1995), pp. 111–44; James Black, 'The Latter End of Prospero's Commonwealth', Shakespeare Survey, 43 (1991), pp. 29–41; Richard Halpern, "'The picture of Nobody": White Cannibalism in The Tempest', in The Production of English Renaissance Culture, ed. David Lee Miller et. al. (Ithaca, NY, 1994), pp. 262–92; William M. Hamlin, 'Men of Inde: Renaissance Ethnography and The Tempest', Shakespeare Studies, 22 (1994), pp. 15–44; Gesa Mackenthun, 'A Monstruous Race for Possession: Discourses of Monstrosity in The Tempest and Early British America', in Tim Youngs, ed., Writing and Race (London, 1997), pp. 52–79; B.J. Sokol and Mary Sokol, 'The Tempest and Legal Justification of Plantation in Virginia', Shakespeare Yearbook, IV (1997), pp. 353–80; and Mark Taylor, 'Prospero's Books and Stephano's Bottle: Colonial Experience in The Tempest', Clio, 22/2 (1993), pp. 101–13.

Two essential resources for anyone interested in tracking Caliban through the play and through history are: Alden T. Vaughan and Virginia Mason Vaughan, Shakespeare's Caliban: A Cultural History (Cambridge, 1991), and Nadia Lie and Theo D'haen, eds, Constellation Caliban: Figurations of a Character (Amsterdam, 1997). Among the writers and artists who have made use of the figure of Caliban in their creative work are Kamau Brathwaite, 'Letter Sycorax', in his Middle Passages (Newcastle upon Tyne, 1992), pp. 75–88; Michelle Cliff, 'Caliban's Daughter: The Tempest and the Teapot', Frontiers, 12/2 (1991), pp. 36–51; Jimmie Durham, 'Caliban Codex' (cf. Jimmie Durham, London, c.1995, pp. 76–89); Lemuel Johnson, Highlife for Caliban (Trenton, NJ, 1995); and Suniti Namjoshi, 'Snapshots of Caliban' in her Because of India (London, 1989), pp. 85–102.

Women writers – especially those from the Caribbean and North America – have increasingly identified with Miranda: see Coco Fusco, 'El Diario de Miranda / Miranda's Diary' in her English is Broken Here: Notes on Cultural Fusion in the Americas (New York, 1995), chap. 1; Elaine Showalter, 'Miranda's Story', in her Sister's Choice: Tradition and Change in American Women's Writing (Oxford, 1991), pp. 22–41; and the essays in Marianne Novy, ed., Women's Re-Visions of Shakespeare: On the Responses of Dickinson, Woolf, Rich, H.D., George Eliot, and Others (Urbana, 1990), Novy, ed., Cross-Cultural Performances: Differences in Women's Re-Visions of Shakespeare (Urbana, 1993), and Novy, ed., Tranforming Shakespeare: Contemporary Women's Re-Visions in Literature and Performance (New York, 1999).

Aside from the Latin American texts discussed in Gordon Brotherston's essay, the most famous appropriation of Ariel has been Sylvia Plath's Ariel (London, 1965); cf. Ted

Hughes's response (to both *The Tempest* and Plath's identification with Ariel) in *Birthday Letters* (London, 1998). Ariel has also made a come-back as a Caribbean writer: see Michael Dash, 'Ariel's Discourse: French Caribbean Writing After the Storm', *Journal of West Indian Literature*, 1 (1986), pp. 49–58.

For the various locations of Sycorax see Abena P. A. Busia, 'Silencing Sycorax: On African Colonial Discourse and the Unvoiced Female', *Cultural Critique*, 14 (1989–90), pp. 81–104; Lemuel A. Johnson, 'Whatever Happened to Caliban's Mother? Or, The Problem With Othello's', in *Shakespeare in Africa (and Other Venues): Import and the Appropriation of Culture* (Trenton, NJ, 1998), pp. 17–179; Diane Purkiss, 'The Witch on the Margins of "Race": Sycorax and Others', in her *The Witch in History: Early Modern and Twentieth-Century Representations* (London, 1996), pp. 251–75; and Elaine Savory, 'Returning to Sycorax/ Prospero's Response', in *The Art of Kamau Brathwaite*, ed. Stewart Brown (Bridgend, 1995), pp. 208–230.

Two good introductions to H.D.'s *By Avon River* are Susan Stanford Friedman, 'Remembering Shakespeare Differently: H.D.'s *By Avon River*', in Novy, *Women's Revisions of Shakespeare*, pp. 143–64; and Diana Collecott, '"Re-membering Shakes-pear": Negotiations with Tradition', in her *H.D. and Sapphic Modernism* (Cambridge, 1999), pp. 221–57.

Among the many other works that have recently been found (in Lemuel Johnson's words) 'prowling the fringes / of the tempest' are Russell Hoban's 'Some Episodes in the History of Miranda and Caliban' (in *The Moment Under the Moment*, London, 1992), David Malouf's *Blood Relations* (Sydney, 1988), Philip Osment's *This Island's Mine* (in *Gay Sweatshop: Four Plays and a Company*, ed. Philip Osment, London, 1989), Gloria Naylor's *Mama Day* (New York, 1988), Dev Virahsawmy's *Toufann* (Port Louis, 1991), Marina Warner's *Indigo, or Mapping the Waters* (London, 1992) and John Edgar Wideman's *Philadelphia Fire* (New York, 1990).

Acknowledgements

We are grateful to the University of Maryland, first for bringing the editors together during 1993–94 (when Peter Hulme was a Rockefeller Foundation Resident Fellow in the Humanities) and then for sponsoring a conference on 'The Tempest in the Old World and the New', which brought together many of the contributors to 'The Tempest' and Its Travels. We would also like to acknowledge the input of Eric Cheyfitz, Joan Dayan, Virginia Vaughan and Virginia Bell, who participated in the conference and the early conversations that helped to shape this book. We owe particular thanks to the Department of Literature at the University of Essex, for financial support via its Research Endowment Fund; to Philip Crispin, Rachel Clare and Ric Allsopp for their generosity with the materials featured in 'On the World Stage'; to Brandi Adams, for assistance with research; and (above all) to Susan Forsyth and Claire MacDonald for helping to keep things on an even keel.

As a transatlantic venture in its own right, finally, this book would not have been possible without the assistance of the many people who carried its contents across the ocean via airmail and e-mail.

Photographic Acknowledgements

The editors and publisher wish to express their thanks to the following sources of illustrative material and/or permission to reproduce it:

Beinecke Rare Book and Manuscript Library, Yale University, New Haven, CT: pp. 43, 45; by permission of the British Library, London: pp. 6 (51.c.3) and 9 (Harl 6855 f 27); by permission of the Trustees of the British Museum, London: p. 52; by permission of the Syndics of Cambridge University Library: pp. 87, 109, 110, 111; Richard Caspole: p. 68; Rachel Clare: pp. 159, 161; courtesy of Jimmie Durham: p. 179; by permission of Edinburgh University Library (shelfmark La.III.283, fol. 254^v): p. 56; by permission of the Folger Shakespeare Library, Washington, DC: pp. 1, 29, 71, 107, 112, 201; by kind permission of the Masters of the Bench of the Honourable Society of the Middle Temple, London: p. 12; National Library of Australia, Canberra, ACT: pp. 186–7; National Trust Yorkshire Photographic Library/John Hammond, reproduced by permission of the Winn family and the National Trust (Nostell Priory): p. 259; Patrimonio Nacional, Madrid: p. 135; Pau Ros: pp. 151, 154; Jan Rüsz: pp. 163, 165; the Vicar and Parochial Church of St John the Baptist Church, Burford, Oxon: p. 48.

Index